BOLIVAR
AND THE POLITICAL THOUGHT
OF THE
SPANISH AMERICAN REVOLUTION

THE ALBERT SHAW LECTURES ON DIPLOMATIC HISTORY, 1930
THE WALTER HINES PAGE SCHOOL OF INTERNATIONAL RELATIONS

BOLIVAR
AND THE POLITICAL THOUGHT
OF THE
SPANISH AMERICAN REVOLUTION

BY
VÍCTOR ANDRÉS BELAUNDE

OCTAGON BOOKS

A DIVISION OF FARRAR, STRAUS AND GIROUX

New York   1978

Copyright 1938 by The Johns Hopkins Press

Reprinted 1967
by special arrangement with The Johns Hopkins Press

Second Octagon printing 1978

OCTAGON BOOKS
A DIVISION OF FARRAR, STRAUS & GIROUX, INC.
19 Union Square West
New York, N.Y. 10003

LIBRARY OF CONGRESS CATALOG CARD NUMBER: 67-18750
ISBN 0-374-90532-0

Manufactured by Braun-Brumfield, Inc.
Ann Arbor, Michigan
Printed in the United States of America

PREFACE

The contents of the present volume consist essentially of lectures on Bolivar given at the Sorbonne in the year 1927 under the auspices of the *Groupement des Ecoles,* material used in the course on the Hispanic-American Revolution at the University of Miami in 1928 and 1929, and the lectures delivered at the Johns Hopkins University in the Albert Shaw series in 1930 to honor the centenary of the Liberator's death.

The manuscript of this book was in course of preparation for the printer when, in August 1930, the dictatorship which had caused my exile was overthrown. This change in the situation in Peru interrupted my historical studies, and since then political and diplomatic labors have absorbed my entire time. Only within the last year have I been able to give the final touches to this work which appears under the imprint of the Johns Hopkins University.

The present volume constitutes a synthesis of the general ideological panorama of the revolution and a detailed analysis of Bolivarian thought. Any work of synthesis is an adventure and great is the risk that some important fact will escape in the effort to present a view of the whole; while on the other hand in too minute an analysis the living unity of the thought or the spirit might be lost. I have tried to the limit of my ability to avoid these two shoals. I have ventured herein to recreate the ideological currents of the Eighteenth Century and their repercussions in America, because this provides the necessary frame for a picture of the Liberator. Bolivar does not imitate or follow the current blindly; he always presents an idea of unquestionable originality and power. Others will follow the main currents: jacobinism, federalism, monarchic traditionalism, imperialism or dictatorship. Departing from American ideologues, Bolivar embodies the program of organic, hierarchical and technical democracy in contrast to the currents of individualistic democracy or monarchical reaction.

In describing the spiritual development of Bolivar in an essay published, in 1930, in the Bulletin of the Pan American Union commemorating the centenary of the Liberator's death, I said:

". . . unquestionably, one must clearly differentiate the following stages of Bolivar's political philosophy: first, that of the radical or demagogic propagandist whose program was the destruction of the old régime and a definite break with Spain; second, that of the revolutionary leader who advocated a strong and stable unitarian government to win the military conflict; third, that of the statesman who applied the same principles of unity, stability, and efficiency to the definitive political organization of a conservative republic, administered by an intellectual and moral élite; fourth, that of the victor in the struggle for independence, desirous of forming a vaster national entity from the different nations he had liberated, a government based on a semifederal and semidemocratic imperialism, showing unquestionable Napoleonic influence; fifth, that of the statesman who, facing the complexities of the political problem and of the continued existence of Greater Colombia, hesitated between a conservative centralized republic under a vigorous executive, and the formation of separate governments in the respective historic national nuclei, which together would form a simple federation; sixth, that of the dictator who attempted to preserve national unity, and who, convinced of the transitoriness of this form of government, placed upon the will of the people the responsibility for deciding its destinies.

Enlightened and impartial analysis will reveal the fact that five of these six stages have several characteristics in common, with differences of emphasis and circumstance: nationalism, republicanism, respect for the will of the people, unitarianism, a professional and independent congress, administrative discipline, efficiency, and order, independence of the judicial power, importance of cultural, ethical, and religious factors, stability of institutions, and continental solidarity. Such is the essence of Bolivar's thought."

The characteristics of Bolivar as thinker and doer in the political realm stand out with greater clarity in the first three stages which constitute the ascending steps in his career. From the year 1810 until the year 1825, Bolivar's line of thought, paralleling his conduct as a soldier and military leader, never wavers. But from the fourth stage on, that is, after the independence of America has been achieved, variations begin to appear; nationalism and amphictyonic organization are replaced by a supernationalistic or imperialistic plan: the Federation of the Andes; centralized and technical democracy gives way to the semi-federalism of the electoral colleges; and the professional Senate, which was the soul of the Republic, gives way to the life-term presidency, now considered the center of the political structure.

Many have sought to find in this supernationalistic *democratic Caesarism* the true law of Bolivarian thought. Partisans of personal government in America have claimed to find support and precedent in Bolivar. It is only fair to say that there exist abysmal differences between the various forms of personal government. If at certain times Bolivar believed that dictatorship or a régime of personal influence was necessary, he never believed that such a régime, in any case transitory, should be lacking in ethical standards or technical form.

In America there have been many personal governments, some having a certain nationalistic flavor, others aimed at economic prosperity, still others simply arbitrary and brutally despotic. None of these types of government can claim parentage in Bolivar's concept.

The true disciples and followers of Bolivar in America are those who like him have sought to perform that always most difficult, often impossible task of adapting the essence of republican institutions to the needs of stable, strong and efficient government; the statesmen who drafted the Chilean Constitution of 1833 and assured its successful functioning; Alberdi, who inspired the Argentine Constitution of 1853 and those who consolidated that charter; Bartolomé Herrera in Peru and those who supported the Constitution of 1860; and finally Rafael Nuñez and Miguel Antonio Caro in Colombia, who restored Colombian unity.

Whenever I have attempted to show the complexity of Bolivar's thought, indicating frankly the changes and even the contradictions therein, it has always been considered a threat to the glory of the Liberator. A distinguished Cuban writer once said *à propos* a lecture of mine in Havana that my thesis presented Bolivar in the guise of Hamlet, a Bolivar who formed the ideal of Andean empire only to abandon it regretfully; a vacillating and uncertain Bolivar, anxious for the continued existence of Greater Colombia but who did not know whether to adopt the principle of a unitarian republic or to accept the existing nationalisms and join them in a simple federative union; a Bolivar who notwithstanding that he was convinced of the need for a personal government resting on the plebiscite,

resorted for his reforms to assemblies in which he had no
confidence and ended by resigning before them the dictatorship in which he had not been able to succeed.

The historian must seek the truth and not draw an
idealized picture. Nor should we reproach that very legitimate viewpoint which may be called the cult of the glory
of the Liberator.

Historical truth does not diminish his stature; the vacillations, the emendations, the variations, not only in direction but in his spiritual stage when facing the tremendous
reality of America, indicate his essential humanness, and
this is the very foundation of his incomparable greatness.
A Bolivar who was infallible, faultless, an inflexible Bolivar,
unresponsive to the influences of his environment, to the
ideas of his friends; a Bolivar who was not influenced
on the one hand by the ideal of building up great units,
and on the other by the realistic teachings of small nationalisms; a Bolivar who was not swayed between the dictates
of revolutionary ethics, which called for institutions, and
the demands of governmental necessity, which called for
personal action, would be an unreal, dehumanized Bolivar.

The contrasts which appear in Bolivar's thought merely
reflect the contrasts which actually existed in the American
scene. The spiritual and political panorama of Hispanic-
America presents these conflicts: the conflict of our tradition of absolutism with the democratic ideal of the
revolution; the conflict of continental solidarity based on
language and culture with nationalism deeply rooted in
geographic, subethnic and psychic phenomena; the conflict
between democratic changes which were in the atmosphere
at that period and the need for a stable and strong government; the conflict between the need for an independent

middle class of small landowners and the fact of the *latifundium* and the intellectual and bureaucratic proletariat; the conflict between political equality and the racial and social differences within each nation; the international conflict of our cultural ties with the Latin nations in full reaction in favor of monarchy, and of our economic and political ties with nations of such different religion and culture.

No solution to these conflicts could be found in the revolution or in the immediate post-revolutionary period. To find the solution was not Bolivar's mission. His merit, great and unique in the history of political thought, is that he described and reflected these conflicts with the pen of a master. Bolivar's life and thought are the land and the soul of America incarnate.

There is another quality of effective greatness in Bolivar which explains his internal struggles, his vacillations and changes. Bolivar is not only a *vital hero* like Napoleon or a political animal like Mirabeau, in the sense in which Ortega y Gasset describes him. The *vital hero* never vacillates, he proceeds straight to his objective without doubts and without deviating. Imperturbable, he follows where his dreams and his instincts lead. But Bolivar united to the great qualities of *vital hero,* which were necessary to his military success, the illumination of an ethical conscience. That ethical element, not always to be conciliated with the unhappy state of affairs in America and the practice of government, is what in Bolivar leads to doubts, emendations and variations. If sometimes he yields to vital aspirations or illusions he always returns to his standards, and this is not an indication of weakness but of true greatness. Napoleon felt no regrets nor did he feel that things

might have been other than what they were until at
St. Helena he was visited by the Spirit; in Bolivar the
Spirit was always present, and there is in him, as in no
other hero, the eternal struggle between Spirit and Life.

Bolivar himself has described this spiritual state with
these words: " To save the country I have had to be a
Brutus, and to repress civil war I should have to be a
Sulla. Such a character does not become me; I would
sooner lose all, even life itself."

To appreciate the unique value of Bolivar's thought in
American history we need only turn our attention to the
formula of Angostura. Bolivar takes from democracy the
concept of national sovereignty and individual rights; but
he desires to liberate the political structure from the domination of the will of individuals and the empirical and
immediate (presentist) exigencies of universal suffrage.
He sees that *democratism* (as Maritan has said) makes
all work of continuity impossible. In thinking of this
continuity and of the intellectual and moral elements of
government, Bolivar had an intuition of the real evil in
pure democracy, that is, the placing of society, which is
not only an organism but a psychic entity, in the present
time, which is mechanical time, and not in human time,
which is the integration of the past with the present and
the future; an integration produced by the synthesis of
historical experience with the needs of the moment and
the influence of the ideal. In this sense Bolivar resembled
the great French master Hauriou who confers only powers
of control on the majority (*Pouvoir majoritaire*) and leaves
the business of government to a minority (*Pouvoir minori-
taire*) constituted by authority based on natural qualities
of competence, honor and will to command.

The constructive work in America was shattered against obstacles superior to all capacity and all effort. To his friend Sir Robert Wilson, Bolivar said: "No one in Europe knows what it costs me to maintain equilibrium in some of these regions. It will sound like a myth to describe my services, which are like those of a man condemned to carry an enormous weight to the summit only to turn around and carry it down again to the abyss. I find myself fighting against the combined efforts of a world; for my part I am alone and the fight, therefore, is very unequal and so I ought to be defeated. History itself cannot furnish me an example to encourage me, not even mythology can show us a like miracle. What we read of Bacchus and Hercules is in reality less than what is demanded of me. Shall one man alone be found to build up half a world? And such a man as I!"

Bolivar was convinced that his ideal of organic and technical democracy represented the constructive reaction after the destructive work of the Revolution. Bolivar compared his work to that of Napoleon after the anarchy of the French revolution; but later he sees that the parallel is not true because America is not France, nor is he Napoleon.

In the history of the revolution in America there is a double conflict; one external, the fight against exterior elements; the other intimate, in the soul of the hero, between political and international ideals and the realistic vision of the facts; between the abstract principles of revolutionary ethics and the immediate experience of the revolution which leads Bolivar to declare, for instance, that "the only means of governing America is by an able despotism."

Bolivar, disillusioned by the Congress of Panama, formed the ideal of the Federation of the Andes. When this failed he embraced the idea of the continued existence of Greater Colombia, which derived from the early successes of the revolution. An understanding of reality told him that the continuance of this political unit was impossible; nevertheless he strove to maintain it. It would be absurd to attribute this obstinacy to a secondary purpose; it was an irresistible attraction to the work itself. The following words, taken from a letter to Briceño Méndez, throbbing with sincerity, come from the depths of Bolivar's soul: "No passion blinds me here, and if passion served some purpose, in decisions of this kind, it would be to give incontrovertible proof of purity and disinterestedness. My only love has always been that of the fatherland; my sole ambition, its liberty. Those who attribute to me anything else do not know me and have never known me. I am so tormented by the base accusations that I have personal ambitions that I am resolved, nay driven, to go away and prove to them the contrary, and I would do more were it necessary."

One who penetrates into the psychology of Bolivar will discover that the Liberator loved glory more than power and would a thousand times rather have sacrificed the latter to the former had he not believed that an imperative superior to his true mission was forcing him to continue an impossible struggle.

The constitutional discussions in the United States, the arguments between Hamilton and Jefferson, had a happy outcome and the federal formula represented an equilibrium sustained by decisive objective factors: geographical conti-

nuity, racial homogeneity, economic orientation, a long
tradition of self-government.

The history of American thought is a tragedy which
develops in five acts. In the first, the elements of the
conflict are presented, the Spanish tradition, the religious
sentiment, the spirit of reform, the new economic necessities, the revolutionary example, the international situation.
In the second act, the struggle begins to create a new
political life, and this struggle leads to anarchy and disaster.
The forces of reaction predominate. In the third act, the
heroes, taught by past experience, attain military success,
win independence and attempt to build, perhaps too fast,
the edifice of new institutions. But in the fourth act, the
forces of disintegration reassert themselves, more powerful
than ever: geographical distances, racial incoherence, in-
curable poverty, lack of culture in the masses, individualistic
wills, ideological anarchy, semibarbaric *caudillos*; all these
elements in the end destroy the work achieved at such
great cost in the final years of the revolution. In the
fifth act, there appear only ruins. It is a somber picture
that Bolivar paints for us in his well-known *Mirada a la
América española.* Over that picture of ruins come death,
assassination, the exile of the heroes.

Bolivar was mistaken in the ideal of the Federation of
the Andes, and more especially in the means he adopted
for its realization—armies of occupation and plebiscites
which only serve to disturb the political problem in
America. San Martín also was mistaken when he chose
to dedicate himself to organizing Peru, which had not yet
been liberated, rather than continue the campaign against
the Spanish in the Peruvian Sierra. These are human
errors, inevitable shadows on the picture in which all

cannot be light and clarity. But these errors cannot be
attributed to ulterior purposes. Later developments suffice
to efface this groundless suspicion from the heroic figures
of America. San Martín eliminates himself to assure the
independence of Peru by facilitating the arrival of Bolivar,
under whose command he offered to serve. He believes
that his separation from the people he liberated will
eliminate one factor which might injure the organization
of the nation, and he condemned himself to a long exile.
Bolivar believes that the anarchy and ingratitude of Colombia open to him the doors of an exile which would
mean freedom for him, and nevertheless, he is impelled to
the hopeless struggle. The withdrawal of San Martín and
the continuance of Bolivar have the same characteristics
of abnegation and sacrifice. San Martín dies after an exile
made bitter by the anarchy and the long tyranny his country
suffered; and Bolivar, after the long death struggle of
Greater Colombia, which coincided with his own, dies as
he is about to enter on his exile. Boulogne-sur-Mer and
San Pedro Alejandrino are linked in the annals of America
across a distance of twenty years. And the tragedy of the
revolution closes with the death of the heroes, framed
between sea and sky, under the same star of suffering and
glory.

December, 1937.   V. A. B.

CONTENTS

ACKNOWLEDGMENTS

I wish to express my thanks to the Johns Hopkins University, under whose auspices this book is published, paying homage at the same time to the memory of Dean John H. Latané who displayed such cordial interest in my lectures in 1930; to the University of Miami and in particular to its President, Bowman Ashe, who furnished me with facilities of every kind for my course and studies on Bolivar; to Professor W. Stull Holt of the Johns Hopkins University who has given me his intelligent assistance; to Professor Martinenche, of the University of Paris, who put at my disposal every facility for consulting the library of the *Groupement des Ecoles* and who introduced my lectures with encouraging phrases; to Dr. M. L. Radoff who has displayed patience and scholarship in the revision of the manuscript and in the proof-reading; to M. Lescar, editor of *Revue de L'Amérique Latine*, who published some of these chapters. I remember with gratitude the cooperation of the late Marius André who translated them into French. I am indebted also to Mr. Robert McNicoll who translated the greater part of the work with the great competency he has acquired in Hispanic-American matters; to Miss Alberta Losh, my secretary in the years 1929 and 1930, who gave her intelligent cooperation in the preparation of the early chapters; to Mr. Carlos Ortiz de Zevallos who with great devotion has aided me in verifying the quotations and has collaborated efficiently in preparing the bibliography; to the Director of the Pan American Union, Dr. L. S. Rowe, who has encouraged my work by affording me the use of the important library of that institution, the staff of which aided me with great good will; to the Director of the Library of Congress for the facilities he afforded me for consulting Hispanic-American sources; to the Director of the Yale Library who gave me access to the Bingham Collection, and particularly to Mr. Hiram Bingham who permitted me to see the Sucre Archives.

V. A. B.

CHAPTER I

THE SPANISH BACKGROUND

Political thought in the United States is largely determined by traditional liberal British institutions and the influence of the philosophy of enlightenment. Spanish-American political thought is the result of more complicated
factors. When Hispanic-American independence was proclaimed, the philosophy of enlightenment had achieved its
most radical results in the French Revolution; and the
United States had created a new political formula, the
federal form of government. During the process of the
Hispanic-American Revolution a compromise was found between monarchy and democracy in the so-called constitutional monarchy, presenting another possible model; and
Great Britain continued her steady political evolution with
her peculiarly realistic methods. In Spanish-American political thought we should consider not only the Spanish tradition and the philosophy of enlightenment but American
federalism, French jacobinism, British realism, and constitutional monarchism. All of these currents, converging in
South America, inspired so many diverse projects and political institutions that our continent was converted into the
most extensive political laboratory the world has ever
known.

Some of our historians and sociologists make the mistake of considering only the influence of these foreign
models, neglecting entirely the Spanish background. There
is a reaction now against this attitude. These imported
principles and institutions were certain to undergo some

modification by environment and by historical forces. And further, some ethical and juridical traditions in colonial society were not so radically different from the new importations. Life is a continuous process. The Spanish-American Revolution was neither a creation *ex nihilo* nor the absolute imposition of a foreign ideal.

The political structure established by Spain in her colonies had a well-developed institutional and legalistic character. The Spanish system, although absolutistic, was chiefly a system of institutions and laws. Some of the principles inspiring them might have been wrong, but the formal value of these institutions and laws was without doubt a great base for political life.

THE CABILDOS

When America was discovered, the medieval democratic institutions of Spain, such as the *cabildos* and the *cortes,* were declining. The king affirmed his influence through the *corregidores;* and the Council of Castille, a technical and aristocratic body, was taking the place of the Parliament or *cortes* constituted by the representatives of the towns.[1] Nevertheless, the *cabildos* were established in America in the way and the form in which they were practiced in Spain before the introduction of the *corregidores.* They had, at the beginning, great powers, electing, in some cases, the governors, or assuming, in others, such as that of Venezuela, in the sixteenth century, the government of

[1] "A fines del siglo XIII los reyes se reservan derecho de nombrar Alcaldes y Jurados municipales. En toda la península a partir de la segunda mitad del siglo XIII los consejos pierden con los usos y ordenanzas del Cabildo, su autonomía política." (Oliveira Martins, *Civilización Ibérica,* 203-204.)

the provinces in the absence or death of the Governor-General.[2]

The *cabildos* in America were of a peculiar character. In Europe the town councils were the organs of the bourgeoisie, destined to counteract the influence of the feudal lords. In America the town councils were composed chiefly of *encomenderos,* who were wealthy Spanish settlers, having rights in certain respects similar to the feudal lords. Thus feudalism and municipalism, which were opposites in Europe, appear together in South America. From the beginning, the town councils, or *cabildos,* had an oligarchic character, but it is necessary to say that this oligarchy was the only representative element of the newly-established social groups, and the only organ relatively independent of the general political machine of the Empire. It represented in a limited aspect the ideal of self-government because of the right to elect the *alcaldes,* with judicial functions, and to renew themselves, until it became customary to sell the offices of *regidores.* They administered their own estates and revenues, issued some ordinances in local affairs, and appointed attorneys and other functionaries.

The establishment of the *corregidores* in the constructive period after the conquest came to check the influence of the *cabildos* in judicial and administrative affairs. In certain cases the *corregidor* replaced the *alcalde.* The Crown appointed *corregidores* not only to preside over the Spanish towns but also for the Indian districts for which municipal institutions were created. The *corregidor* became the pre-

[2] Decree of December 8, 1560. Quoted by Vallenilla Lanz, *Críticas de Sinceridad y Exactitud,* 27.

siding official of the *cabildo ayuntamiento,* sharing with it
the authority to issue ordinances.[3]

The idea that the *cabildos* were democratic or semi-
democratic bodies was general after an essayist in the
Edinburgh Review (January 1809) emphasized the importance of these institutions in Spain and in the new continent, saying that in contrast with their powers in Europe
the American *cabildos* spread their influence beyond the
limits of the town to which they nominally belonged. The
English philosopher affirmed that the people chose the
regidores, and these the *alcaldes,* and quoted Depons to the
effect that the powers of the *cabildos* in America were
greater than those in Spain.

Writers of the nineteenth century in America, such as Alberdi, and Sarmiento, praised the *cabildos* as the elected representatives of the people.[4] There was one dissonant voice
in this chorus of praise. Lastarria despised the *cabildos* because they were the instruments of the will of the king
and of his interests. In recent years the romantic and democratic conception of the *cabildos* has been submitted to severe
criticism, chiefly on the part of Argentine writers. Agustín
García, accepting that theoretically the *cabildos* appointed
their judge, administered their estates and exercised modest
municipal functions, says that the situation was in practice
adulterated by the authorities in charge of the enforcement
of the law. He does not give any value to the elections, since

[3] For the relations between the *corregidores* and the *cabildos,* see
the interesting essay of C. E. Castañeda, *The Corregidor in Spanish
Colonial Administration.*

[4] Ramos Mejía considered the *cabildos* to be " an active and
providential institution which warmly defended popular rights."
(*Historia de la Evolución Argentina,* 353.)

they were annulled by the right of confirmation.[5] The influence of the *cabildo* was in inverse proportion to the importance of the towns. Their rôle depended upon the power and importance of the functionaries appointed by the king. Finally, García said that the death blow to the *cabildos* was struck by the *Ordenanza de Intendentes*, which gave to the royal functionaries the right to supervise the collection and investment of the revenues of the *cabildo*. Ayarragaray states categorically that the *cabildos* were simply bureaucratic dependencies without political functions and without real activity; it was the revolutionary movement that gave them transitory and irregular functions. Del Valle denies the popular origin of the *cabildos*, reminding us that the *regidores* were at first appointed by the *adelantado*, afterwards by the election of the old members; and finally the offices were sold.[6]

Montes de Oca, in his famous monograph, *Los Cabildos*, differing from this extreme point of view, takes a moderate position. He says that monarchic absolutism did not succeed in converting the *cabildos* into blind instruments of oppression; that they were, by virtue of their adaptation to the environment, the genuine representatives of the bourgeoisie, that they moderated the rigor of the law or petitioned its modification, and that although the " *Ordenanza de Intendentes* " gave to these officials some municipal functions, they left untouched in the hands of the *cabildos* some political ones, such as oath, examination of title, and control. He summarizes his position in this way: " In colonial times the *cabildos* were the advance guard of the

---

[5] Agustín García, *La Ciudad Indiana*, 164.

[6] A. del Valle, *Derecho Constitucional*, 20 ff.

local interest, and, during the revolution, the cradle and the *point d'appui* of self-government." [7]

This discussion is not closed, and cannot be, until thorough research shall have been made in the archives of the various *cabildos*, and chiefly in the Spanish Archives, regarding the correspondence between the *cabildos* and the King of Spain. In spite of this difference of opinion, one thing is clearly established, that the *cabildo*, feudal in its origin, oligarchic in its evolution, a self-perpetuating body during one epoch, and composed, in its last days, of officials who bought their positions, had an entirely different origin and represented an interest different from the general political hierarchy established by the monarchy. The *cabildos* also took care of local interests with differences in functions and influence depending on opportunities, circumstances, and places; elected judges and attorneys, and exercised the right of petition. It is possible to affirm, putting aside the discussion as to whether it was democratic or nondemocratic in character, that the *cabildo* was the real foundation of colonial society, the living cells of the different kingdoms of the Spanish Empire.

This explains the rôle that they played in the movement toward independence, leading or reflecting the popular feeling.

The *cabildos* tended to represent more and more the Creole element. Even in Buenos Aires, where the Spanish oligarchy was so powerful, Moreno obtained equal rights of representation for the Creoles so that the *cabildo* consisted of five Spanish *corregidores* and five Creoles.[8]

[7] P. 45.
[8] Del Valle, 33.

The *cabildos*, through an ancient customary institution called *cabildo abierto* (open council) were able to take the advice or reflect the opinions of the towns, or at least of their best elements. There is also discussion about the importance of the *cabildo abierto*. According to Groussac, there was no reference to it in the works of Solórzano, the greatest political writer of Spanish America in colonial times, and a law of King John II expressly prohibited their meetings.

The historian, Levene, observes correctly that not all the institutions in Spain and Spanish America had legal character, some of them being only customary. Regarding Spanish-American legislation, the great Code of 1680 does not include any provisions for the *cabildos abiertos*, but it does not ignore them, for it prohibits the election of attorneys in such meetings. It is not possible to deny the functioning of this institution in colonial times, although it was not very frequent. The other question refers to the character of the meeting. The *ayuntamiento* did not invite every inhabitant to this *cabildo abierto*, but only persons of a certain importance from whom they might get advice, so that the institution was not an open meeting but rather an enlarged council, its proper name being *consejo abierto*. On the eve of independence the number of persons invited was greater, representing a considerable part of the population.

THE AUDIENCIAS

The affirmation of the royal prerogative took place in America with the establishment of the *audiencias*, presided over by viceroys, or captains-general. The absolute rule of the military leaders, the conquerors, and the exceptional functions of the *cabildos* were to disappear. The régime of charters, contracts between the crown and the *adelantados*, explicable in the period of the conquest, was replaced by the régime of laws. We approach the constructive period, in which the *audiencia* will play a decisive rôle. In Spain, this institution was chiefly judicial; in America, it had political functions.

Representing the king with full authority, using his seal, the *audiencias* came not only for the administration of justice as supreme tribunals in the larger districts or kingdoms, but also as advisory bodies to the viceroys and governors with the mission of reporting directly to the Crown and judging and enforcing the responsibility of all officials. Thus through the establishment of the *audiencias* two fundamental principles of government were introduced into America: balance of power and responsibility. And, further, from the sociological point of view, a permanent link was established between the units, or the social cells, the towns, giving cohesion to the small districts and territories in the form of larger aggregates, which were practically national nuclei. The individualistic character of the conquerors and the early governors vanished before the authority of these institutions. Ruiz Guinazu says in his important work, *La Magistratura Indiana* that the *audiencias* represented a tendency toward jurisdictional autonomy in spite of royal decrees and the ill-controlled jealousy of the viceroys and governors.[9]

The construction of the *audiencias* was not arbitrary. Inspired generally by geographic, racial, and historical considerations, it closely followed the nationalistic demarcations

[9] P. 38.

of the pre-Colombian times. In the middle of the seventeenth century there were already in America thirteen *audiencias*, corresponding to well-defined geographical divisions. They were not all of the same rank nor did they have the same functions. Those established in the capitals of the viceroyalties and captaincies-general were the prætoria of these officials. The first extended their influence to the districts of the so-called *audiencias subordinadas*, presided over only by a regent, and whose functions were chiefly judicial. But even these subordinate *audiencias* exercised, exceptionally, political functions, and performed administrative duties, as is proved by the history of the *audiencia* of Charcas.

THE INTENDENCIAS

The great political reform at the end of the colonial epoch was the extension to the colonies of the institution of the *intendencias*, introduced by the Bourbons in Spain, in imitation of the French model. As in the case of the *cabildos*, there is a great discussion regarding the real character of the régime of the *intendencias*. To some authors, among them Ingenieros, the *Ordenanza de Intendentes* of 1782 decentralized the viceroyal administration, giving the new officials well-defined autonomic powers, reinforced by the fact that they were appointed directly by the king.[10] Another Argentinian writer, González Calderón, goes so far as to say that the decentralization produced by the ordinance was federalistic in its formations and projections. We do not share this opinion. It is not possible to affirm that the spirit of the ordinance was decentralizing. On the contrary, the

[10] *La Evolución de las Ideas Argentinas*, 195.

traditional spirit of the institution was to make royal action more effective. At the beginning the viceroys were deprived by the ordinance of financial functions, which were charged to an official called *super-intendente*. But this division was by no means a decentralization, since the *intendentes* were entirely subordinate to the new officials. Moreover, this régime was abolished, and financial functions were restored to the viceroys.

Previous to the establishment of the *intendencias*, a gap existed between the *corregidores* and the viceroys; between the local districts, in many cases composed only of Indians, and the larger groupings with certain nationalistic character. The *intendencias* came to fill this gap, creating an intermediate officer whose counterpart already existed in the ecclesiastical hierarchy, *i. e.,* in the diocese presided over by a bishop whose authority lay between the parish priests and the archbishop. This intermediate official, from the political point of view, made possible a more effective central action. The argument that he was appointed by the king and not by the viceroy, and therefore had a tendency to be independent of the viceroy, has no value, because the old *corregidores* were also appointed by the king. It is possible to say that the *intendentes* were *corregidores* with larger districts and wider authority. Some of them were opposed to the autonomous activities of the *cabildos*. The régime of *intendentes* was directly opposed to the idea of division of powers, since the *intendentes* had functions that were judicial and municipal, as well as political and military. In spite of the nature and the spirit of the new institution, it had the indirect effect of strengthening the social groups represented by the old Spanish towns, generally capitals of the new *intendencias*. Thus, before the War of Independence, the new grouping was the base of a sectionalistic tendency. In the period of revolutionary anarchy and confusion, these new political units became oligarchic centers with federalistic proclivities.

Summarizing what has been said, we may conclude that we owe to the Spanish political structure, (1) the base for local government, in the *cabildo;* (2) the general line of nationalistic differentiation in the viceroyalties, captaincies-general with their *audiencias;* (3) the basis of territorial demarcation in the intermediate groupings, or *intendencias.* Municipal life, national demarcation, and administrative hierarchy, no matter how imperfect, were transmitted to us by our colonial society.

THE BASIS OF NATIONAL DIFFERENTIATION

I should like to stress chiefly the second point, since it was generally assumed that liberal and democratic principles, because of their wide acceptance in Spanish America, created different national consciousnesses. The truth is quite the reverse. The national consciousness, created by geographic and social factors, crystallized in the principal colonial institutions, had, at the proper historical moment, its expression in liberal and democratic institutions.

It would be a fascinating study to trace the germs of nationalistic feeling since the conquest, and to find their manifestations in the works of our early historians, chroniclers, and poets. The conquest was not the extension of Spanish territory, but the creation of new societies. It was a double process; biological because of the mixture of races, and political because of the adaptation of Spanish institutions. The territories were not only considered provinces within the framework of a symmetrical and administrative organization, but kingdoms (*reyno*), and they were so called. Kingdom was the word used, not only by the historians and geographers in official documents, but by the king himself. The word *reyno* was used in the title of the royal decree for the creation of the supreme council of the Indies.

These kingdoms were not annexed to Spain or attached to the Spanish bodies but were incorporated in the Spanish Crown, according to Solórzano, as feudatory kingdoms, or as the *municipia* of the Romans, without losing any of their rights, forms, or privileges. This idea, existing from the beginning, explains the Council of the Indies, entirely independent and with the same rank as the Council of Castille, the number, importance, and exceptional powers of the *audiencias pretoriales* and the special legislation for America, completed and codified in the momentous *Recopilación de Leyes de Indias*. The Peruvian, Álvarez, was right when he said: "The Crown of Spain united to the Empire of the Incas did not cause the latter to lose its rights of empire." [11]

The nationalistic differentiation which had its expression in the *audiencias pretoriales* acquired in the most important sections of Hispanic America a decisive confirmation when the viceroyalties of Santa Fe (1739) and Buenos Aires (1776) were established.

Regarding the viceroyalty of Buenos Aires, Matienzo made this observation: "La vice-royauté dura 34 ans (1776-1810) et cet espace de temps, bien que relativement court, fut cependant suffisant pour faire naître chez les peuples le

11 *Preferencia de los Americanos en los Empleos*, 1820.

désir, sinon l'habitude, de former un seul groupement; ce désir uni aux interêts qui étaient apparus autour de l'organisation vice-royale constitua une véritable force de cohésion plus ou moins puissante." [12]

The Spanish monarchy was not one nation but really a confederation of nations; the Independence may be explained as the disintegration of this enormous political unit.

Early in the nineteenth century Walton repeated this remark of Humboldt, " According to the old Spanish laws, each viceroyalty is not governed as a dominion of the Crown; but as an insulated province separated from the mother country. All the institutions that together form a European government are to be found in the Spanish colonies which we might compare to a system of confederated states were the colonists not deprived of several important rights in their commercial relations with the old world." [13]

In the eighteenth century the most enlightened Spanish leaders were well aware of this nationalistic complexity of the Empire and of the necessity of establishing new institutions in agreement with this character. The project attributed to the Count of Aranda, of establishing three independent kingdoms in Spanish America: Mexico, Tierra Firme, and Peru, has attracted the attention of scholars, but it was not the first one. A similar plan was suggested by the famous minister to Ferdinand VI, Carvajal y Lancaster, thirty years before the independence of the United States, the event which gave Aranda or his French advisers motive to think of the establishment of semi-independent kingdoms. In the early nineteenth century, Godoy revived Aranda's project

[12] *Le Gouvernement représentatif fédéral,* 53.
[13] *An Expose of the Dissentions of Spanish America,* 1814. P. 25.

with certain important modifications, protesting that his thought was entirely Spanish and that nothing was going to be lost by the Crown of Castille. This new project consisted in sending, instead of viceroys, infantes with the title of Prince Regent, in order to conciliate the pride of the Creoles. The other reforms were: the establishment of a senate composed half of Spanish and half of Americans, reformation of the laws according to the exigencies of the time, and giving the tribunals and regencies the final authority on every matter except those in which the interest of the mother country was concerned, or in those relating to the general interest of all the colonies. The Godoy idea recognized four national groups because there were at this time four viceroyalties. The plan is very similar to the policy followed by England in the nineteenth century with her dominions.

The economic changes introduced in the time of the Bourbons were aiding the establishment of nationalism. In the time of the Fleet system there were only two economic or commercial units in Spanish America, one for Mexico and the other for the southern continent. With the reforms that culminated in the so-called *Reglamiento de Comercic Libre,* in 1778, the different kingdoms acquired the right to trade directly with Spain, thereby confirming their economic autonomy.

Briefly, political changes, economic reforms, and progress in culture were accentuating, in the eighteenth century, the process of nationalistic evolution in all the colonies. Paul Groussac has expressed much the same idea. He feels that after the middle of the eighteenth century, the colony began to be obscurely conscious of its destiny. It felt vaguely the antagonism created between its own development and the visible decadence of the metropolis. Even the progressive and liberal effort of Charles III, while it was short-lived and lacking in originality perfected the instrument of the future emancipation.

The eminent Mexican historian, Sierra, said very truly that the Spanish evolution, of which the last expression was the Spanish-American nationalities, did not have as its object the creation of national personalities, but, on the contrary, tried to prevent this. But the vigor of the Spanish race was such that this phenomenon took place in spite of everything. In treating the Revolution of New Granada, Groot expresses the same idea.

THE IDEOLOGICAL CONTRAST

If it is true that we may find continuity between colonial life and our present condition from the point of view of the nationalistic spirit and the main lines of our social structure, a great contrast exists between the leading principles of colonial society and the ideas proclaimed by the Independence. Let us remember the main features of colonial political life: divine character of the sovereignty of the king, disregard for individual rights, race and class differences, complicated social and political hierarchy, confusion of powers.[14]

[14] The King was called, " Sacra Cesarea Real Majestad ", and even the ecclesiastic authors used the expression, " Ambas Majestades ", putting on the same level the Divine and the human. The political and social organization was doubled to a certain extent depending on the racial differences. It will be easy to indicate the law of the Indies allowing slavery, establishing compulsory work, the guilds or corporations, and obligatory evangelization. (We have a list of these laws opposed to the new ideas in the essay written by the Licenciado Demetrio Sodi, *Revista Jurídica de la Escuela Libre de Derecho* No. 14, December 1916.)

The Chilean historian, Amunátegui, reminds us also of the royal decrees regarding visits to libraries and book-shops and forbidding the preachers to treat political matters in the pulpit. Lastly, as we have observed, judicial, political, and economic functions were confused in the *Ordenanza de Intendentes*.

Through foreign influences a complete change was consummated, if not in reality, at least in the intellectual sphere, and new principles were proclaimed: national sovereignty, political and civil equality, and division of power. Were these ideas entirely unknown or completely denied in colonial society? Doubtless the legal and social structures and the general trend of events were opposed to them, but beneath these factors there were some ethical and juridical traditions which approached the humanitarian ideals of the Revolution.

Not all of the scholars in colonial society shared the conception of the divine and absolute rights of the king. The philosophy of St. Thomas and of his disciples, Suárez, Victoria, and Soto, was favorable to the sovereignty of the people and the limitation of the rights of the Crown. As René Moreno, the Bolivian historian, rightly said, " The doctors of Chuquisaca studied the *Summa* of St. Thomas—that there was a right to resist a tyrannical power, and a certain theory, according to which, in the definite absence of the King, the sovereignty reverts to its origin, *i. e.,* the people." [15]

THE UNDERLYING FACTORS

The contrast between reality and religious and philosophical conceptions in colonial society is even more striking

[15] *Últimos Días Coloniales, Narración,* 53, 261, 379.

as regards the principle of equality of the races. This idea was emphasized at the time of the conquest. Missionaries or apostles, such as Montesinos and Las Casas in America; scholars such as Victoria and De Soto in Spain, maintained the Indian's right to be treated as a free vassal of the Crown. Under the influence of this great ethical and juridical movement, the new ordinances were promulgated, creating a conflict between the feudal interests of the settlers and the ethical conception held by the Crown and the Church. It is true that the conflict, ended by a compromise at the beginning, was steadily followed up by the consolidation of *encomiendas,* so that the idealistic movement failed. But the principles remained as an effective influence creating an intellectual tradition. This is proved by the writings of Father Miguel de Agia and the Peruvian, Diego de Avendaño, whose work, *Thesaurus Indicus,* deals with the obligation of the Crown towards the Indians. He combats slavery, affirming that liberty comes to man by natural law. Father Avendaño does not differentiate between the Indian and the negro, stating categorically that the sale of slaves is a violation of justice and right. The great jurist, Solórzano Perreyra, was influenced by this movement, which fact explains the great place given in his works to the Indian questions. This ethical tradition had its highest expression in the incorporation in the *Recopilación* of 1680 of all the laws and decrees issued in behalf of the Indians. To defend the natives it was not necessary to invoke the humanitarian philosophy of the eighteenth century; it was enough to revive the ideas and doctrines of the theologians of the conquest and their followers in the subsequent periods. It is true that in many cases the writers of the eighteenth and nineteenth centuries in Spanish America did not make special reference to the scholars, such as Suárez and Victoria, regarding the principle of sovereignty, or to Las Casas, Montesinos, Agia, and Avendaño, regarding human rights and equality of the races. They preferred to quote Puffendorf and Grotius, Montesquieu and Rousseau. But undoubtedly they knew and studied the old treatise writers such as Suárez, Mariana and Saavedra Fajardo, setting forth the principles of sovereignty and criticizing the absolute powers of the king, and chiefly the jurists who wrote especially for the Indians such as Solórzano, Pinelo, and others, who, as Professor Levene said, influenced the revolutionary generation because of their learning and their ideal of a juridical and technical government.[16]

These intellectual and religious conceptions were also making themselves felt in regard to the *mestizos* or mixed races. Although placed above the Indians in the colonial structure, their social and political standing was not the same as that of the whites, either Spanish or Creole. They were excluded by certain laws from higher education in the colleges and universities, and, of course from the practice of the liberal professions. However, it must be noted that these laws were not always strictly applied. In reality, persons of mixed race could attain to a high education, and certain professional positions were open to them. The work of the Church, essentially democratic, succeeded in lessening the strict social hierarchy of the State. We have a very interesting and direct proof of this fact. The following is taken from a pamphlet containing the address delivered at the Cortes of Cadiz by the American representatives and published by the *mestizos* of Lima: " There is no class of

[16] *La Revolución de Mayo y Mariano Moreno*, I, 35.

Latin and Rhetoric in which one cannot find distinctly plebeian elements including Indian and mixed people. There are also many colleges and universities belonging to the religious orders in which philosophy and theology are taught to young people of all kinds of color and birth . . . the religious orders of the town of Lima have preserved us from the ignorance to which we were condemned by the false policy of the century." In agreement with this, the constitutional historian of Chile, Luis Galdames, said: " The *mestizos* did not know any other culture than that spread among them by the Church. Without this unselfish and persevering help, the *mestizo* would never have escaped the servitude to which he was condemned by the covetousness of his dominators." [17]

As for the Creole element, whites born in America, the situation is precisely the opposite. We have seen that legal conditions were unfavorable to the *mestizos,* but that they were modified in reality by religious institutions. In the case of the Creoles the strictly legal situation was favorable. Early laws ordered that governmental positions should be filled preferably by the descendants of the conquerors, discoverers, and settlers. This law was never abrogated and was incorporated in the great code of 1680. In spite of this, the practical policy of Spain was precisely the contrary. The Creoles were seldom appointed to high positions such as viceroy, captain-general, or judge, notwithstanding the opinion of Solórzano and the prudent advice of the ministers, Campillo and Macanaz, in the eighteenth century.

The most famous Spanish authors regretted the monopoly of all governmental posts by Spaniards. Amunátegui re-

[17] *Evolución constitucional de Chile,* I, 19.

ferred to Acosta, León Pinelo, Pedro Ortega Sotomayor, Nuñez de Pineda y Bascuñán.[18]

The legal principle, establishing not only equality between Creoles and Spaniards but even preference for the former, remained one of the bases of remonstrance of the Creoles, a factor in the Revolution. We have eloquent testimony of this in the speech prepared by Mariano Alejo Álvarez in 1811 and printed in Lima nine years later. Álvarez quotes Ley 14, Titulo II, Libro 3, " That the sons and natives of the provinces should be given positions and rewarded where their forefathers served us; those to be rewarded first who were married." After referring to the philosophical arguments of Plato and Aristotle, and to the Roman and Canon Law, and even to the Spanish law in the *Novissima Recopilación* ", the eloquent pleader said: " Shall our town be governed by those who did not found it, our temples ruled by those who did not rear them? " [19]

Álvarez was educated in Charcas where these ideas were general among the lawyers and scholars of the famous university of San Javier, as in the other universities of America. The rights of the Creoles and the national personality of the colonies, two decisive factors in the Revolution, were drawn from the legal and juridical foundations laid by Spain herself.

The influence of the Spanish tradition was even greater in the fundamental question regarding the relations of the church and the state. The King of Spain, because of the right of *patronato*, controlled the church in America, as was recognized even by the ecclesiastical authors. The su-

[18] *Precursores de la Independencia,* III, 63.
[19] *Preferencia de los Americanos en los Empleos,* Lima, 1820.

premacy of the civil over the ecclesiastical power, so zeal-
ously maintained by republican governments, has its roots
in the well-established colonial tradition.[20]

[20] The useful book, *Gobierno de los Regulares* by Padre Parras,
contains these significant quotations from Father Silva: "En
aquellos estados de las Indias, además de ser Rey en lo temporal
en el modo común de Monarquía, es V. M. Procurador, Patrono,
y como Legado de lo espiritual que fué el fin que llamó a los Reyes
Católicos a conquistas tan extrañas y peregrinas, para las quales
los sumos Pontífices los hicieron como Vicarios suyos, y lo mismo
a los demás Reyes de España, que les sucediesen . . . de lo qual
resulta, que los dichos Reyes son inmediatos administradores de la
predicación y conversión de aquellos naturales, porque para este
fin fué elegida la industria Real, su especial providencia, solitud
y cuidado, a fin de que con todo ello acudan a este negocio de tan
grave importancia." (I, 12).

CHAPTER II

INFLUENCES FROM OUTSIDE

Spanish-American thought among the cultured ruling class was decidedly influenced by the philosophy of the eighteenth century. This influence, as in Spain, came largely through the group of writers who wrote the *Encyclopédie*. De Pradt sums it up by saying, in regard to Spain, " The *Encyclopédie* was not written there, but it had penetrated thoroughly. Spain participated in the cultural advancement of the time with less furor but with an efficacy equal to that of any other country." [1]

This same penetration of ideas took place in Spanish America, although there it had more obstacles to overcome. All the intellectuals, to a certain degree, were tinged with the ideas of the *Encyclopédie*. Some through the influence of Spanish teachers, such as Campillo Aranda, Campomanes, and Jovellanos. Others through the direct reading of the more famous books of the French.

The most interesting and typical example of the smuggling in of these books is the case of the friar, Diego Cisneros, in Peru. Taking advantage of the privileges that were his by virtue of his authorized trade in missals, breviaries, and other devotional works, he introduced a vast library of liberal books into Lima. This library was used by his friends and protégés, the editors of the *Mercurio Peruano*.[2]

[1] De Pradt, *La Europa y La América en 1821*, I, 338.
[2] Jorge Guillermo Leguía, *El Precursor*, Lima, 1922.

The man who introduced the writings of the encyclopedists in Chile was Antonio José Rojas, who, according to
the historian Galdames, served Robertson as a correspondent
and authority on the Spanish-American colonies during his
long stay in Spain.[3]

In the La Plata provinces, works of Voltaire, Rousseau,
Bayle, and Filangieri were found in the libraries of prominent members of the clergy, such as Bishop Azamor.[4] In
Charcas the library of Canon Terrazas, according to René
Moreno, contained, besides works of religion, science, and
literature, not a few of philosophy and politics, for which
the Inquisition was searching with inexorable zeal.[5] In New
Granada surely the famous library of Nariño contained
philosophical books, although they did not appear in the
judicial inventory that was made at the trial to which
he was submitted after the publication of *Derechos del
Hombre*.[6] The *Manual del Colombiano* published in 1825
and made, according to the editor, from excerpts of Volney,
Holbach, and Helvetius, reveals how great was the influence of these authors. In Venezuela, according to Count
Ségur, works of Rousseau and Raynal were hidden in the
hollowed beams of the roofs. "The Count of Ségur mentions a physician, whom he visited in Venezuela, who
showed him the works of Rousseau and Raynal, which were
usually hidden in a hollow beam, out of the reach of
official inquirers."[7]

[3] Luis Galdames, *Evolución Constitucional de Chile.* Santiago,
1926. P. 67.

[4] José P. Otero, *La Révolution Argentine,* 130.

[5] René Moreno, *Últimos Días Coloniales, Narración,* 61.

[6] See the inventory in "El Precursor" *Biblioteca de Historia
Nacional.* Bogota, 1903. Pp. 164-178.

[7] Bernard Moses, *The Intellectual Background of the Revolution
in South America,* New York, 1926. P. 35.

The Peruvian, Vidaurre, is a typical follower of the encyclopedists. We have in his books valuable data which enables us to know what forces influenced the mental life of the Creole at the end of the eighteenth century. " Since academy days ", he said, " I had read Bocaria, *The Spirit of the Laws,* and the first four volumes of *Legislation* by Filangieri; my delight in natural law had caused me to take instruction in Grotius, Puffendorf, and Heinecio." [8] " Montesquieu, tolerant; Filangieri, opposed to the Inquisition; Bentham, a materialist; Rousseau, irreligious—these are the penates of his library." [9]

The philosophy of the eighteenth century did not imply the direct acceptance of revolutionary ideas. Most of the encyclopedists were advocates of an absolute monarchy directed by the philosophers or of a so-called enlightened despotism. But the ideas of the *Encyclopédie,* combating, as they did, tradition and authority, opened the way to revolution in France and the United States, and by reflection, in Spain and Spanish America.

In respect to Rousseau, it is evident that no other author, with the exception of Raynal, was so widely read in Spanish America. We find quotations of Rousseau not only in the revolutionary, but also in the reform period, even in the moderate writers, as Baquíjano. Rousseau was the intellectual idol of Rodríguez, the teacher of Bolivar; and the pedagogical ideas of Espejo, the great reformist of Quito, were based on the *Émile.* Some of the leading ideas of Bolivar in his period of agitator and demagogue are entirely Rousseauistic, as is, in certain moments, his style, especially

[8] *Plan del Perú,* 122.
[9] *Cartas Americanas,* Philadelphia.

in his more literary works. According to the Chilean historian, Vicuña MacKenna, Father Henríquez, the Chilean journalist, imitated by preference the style of Rousseau. His influence was absolute in the Peruvian Vidaurre, although this author discusses and even denies the influence of the *Social Contract* in the Revolution, reminding us that Rousseau felt that the worst tyranny ought to be suffered before the banner of revolution should be raised. Monteagudo, the great revolutionary writer of the South, agreed to a certain extent with this view of Rousseau, when he confessed that after having read the *Social Contract* it appeared to him favorable to despotism. And the Colombian, Rocafuerte, reproached Rousseau for his theory that a republic can exist only in a small territory; he cited the example of the United States to refute this statement. In spite of this, the *Social Contract* was the basic theory of the Revolution, inspiring the writers and the leaders of the movement. The culminating manifestation of this influence is seen in the translation of Rousseau's famous book into Spanish and in the prologue written for it by Mariano Moreno, the soul of the revolutionary movement in Argentina.

Montesquieu was not so widely read because of his depth and his realistic point of view. He was frequently mentioned, but quotations were probably from second-hand sources. Of course, some of the writers of the reform period knew him directly, as is proved by the quotations found in Baquíjano in the *Elogio de Jáuregui* and in Abad y Queipo in *Informe del obispo y del Cabildo de Michoacán, al rey sobre jurisdicción y inmunidades del clero americano*. Montesquieu was also thoroughly known by Bolivar. The main principles of the Liberator in his speech of Angostura are taken from the *Esprit des Lois*, but it is not possible to say the same thing about the other political leaders of South America. Groussac is inclined to believe that Moreno knew Montesquieu only through Filangieri; and Monteagudo, according to Costi, quoted Montesquieu only twice.[10]

The influence of Raynal was far greater. His favorable concepts regarding the Creoles naturally received the most sympathetic acceptance in America. The Chilean, Rojas, called him a " divine genius." The pages of *The Philosophical History of European Establishments in the Indies* fell as a sudden burst of light on the spirit of Moreno and inspired in him admiration for the English people and language.[11] This famous book was also the favorite reading of Monteagudo, according to the Argentine writer Señor Otero.

The famous letter of Raynal to the deputies, May 31, 1791, in which he advocated an active and vigorous government to counteract the general tendency to augment the power of the people was the bulwark of the moderate reaction in the process of the Revolution. It was quoted by President Lardizábal, of the Cortes of Cadiz, and commented upon in the pamphlets of the time. It is undeniable that the ideas of Raynal about the executive power had a great influence on Bolivar, although the Liberator did not quote the French writer on this subject. Raynal brought forward every argument to prove the injustice of the colonial policy of Spain and of her treatment of the Creoles, so that his book was " the true sum of the Revolution ".[12]

[10] Levene, *La Revolución de Mayo y Mariano Moreno*, I, 31.

[11] René Moreno, *Últimos Días Coloniales, Narración*, 62.

[12] Emilo Viasse, quoted by Galdames, *op. cit.*, 65. It is necessary to remember that Raynal's book had many contributors and is now

Let us now turn to the North American Revolution and the political ideas of the United States. Although an understanding of English was not so general among the Creoles as the knowledge of French, and the viceroy, O'Higgins prohibited the importation of foreign papers, yet the more important facts of the North American Revolution were generally known. Already the dictionary of Alcedo had given a significant account of American independence. This revolutionary example is praised in the famous letter of Father Viscardo y Guzmán. The statement of the historian, Melchor Martínez, concerning the Chilean Revolution is classic. He accuses the "Boston Republic" of utilizing the clandestine commerce with the Spanish colonies to proclaim the injustice and tyranny of the overlordship of Europe, and to offer to help them to throw off the yoke of the mother country.

We have proof that this propaganda was effective in the decree of 1791, which ordered great vigilance in excluding from the country all medals or other articles which referred to the liberty of the Anglo-American colonies.

Professor Robertson devotes a whole chapter in his *Hispanic-American Relations* to the political influence of the United States. He makes especial reference to García de Sena, author of *La Independencia de Costa Firme Justificada por Thomas Paine treinta años ha* (1810), containing the translations of the Constitution of the United States and of the Declaration of Independence. Similar translations were made by Miguel de Pombo in New Granada in 1811. Professor Robertson reminds us also that Belgrano trans-

---

considered to be superficial. The famous letter, considered as ill-timed even by the conservatives, is now attributed to Count Guibert.

lated the Farewell Address of Washington, and Moreno quoted Jefferson's notes on Virginia.[13]

In the year 1812 Father Camilo Henríquez translated the speeches of Madison, the inaugural speech of Jefferson, and a speech on treason and rebellion taken from the Baltimore *Register*.

In the same year, there was published in Philadelphia a pamphlet entitled *Manual de un Republicano para el uso de un Pueblo Libre*. It contains a dialogue between a teacher and a pupil and presents a defence of the North American government in the form of an exposition of the ideas of Rousseau. The translator, who appears to have been a Venezuelan, adds some notes in which he defines " equality before the Law ", defends the bicameral system and the presidential veto, as well as the election of senators by the state legislatures; and maintains that the judicial power is not only a sub-agent of the government, but a power as independent as the others. This pamphlet, of course, was destined to spread political ideas of the United States throughout South America.

[13] The following quotation regarding a pamphlet published about an address of the Archbishop of Charcas refers to the fact that the ideas and work of Franklin were well known in this remote Spanish region.

" Carta apologética de la breve Arenga. El objeto de la Arenga citando a tan inmortal personaje (Franklin), ha sido mostrar que con la llegada del señor Arzobispo a Charcas, la Universidad auxiliada con sus luzes presentará modelos tan completos en la cultura de las ciencias, como ha presentado la Pensilvania en el héroe Franklin. Juicio crítico sobre las impugnaciones hechas a la Arenga." (René Moreno, 28.)

We owe to Chandler's book, *Inter-American Acquaintances*, interesting data regarding the commercial relations established between the United States and South America during the early years of the nineteenth century.

Regarding the influence of the American constitution, we shall simply recall that the Acts of Federation of 1776 served as a basis for the federal acts of New Granada; that the American constitution of 1787 was practically copied, as Gil Fortoul says, by the Venezuelan constitutional assembly of 1811. In the La Plata region, the Uruguayan *caudillo*, Artigas, in his famous instructions of the year 1813, tried to find a middle ground between the two great North American constitutional documents.

Robertson has said that Austin translated the American constitution and gave it to the President of Mexico, Ramos Arispe.[14] It is not necessary to mention the fact that the Mexican constitution of 1824 and the Central American constitution of 1825 were inspired by the constitution of the United States.

The influence of the United States ought to be studied chiefly in the process of the South American Revolution through the writers who, having lived in the United States, became admirers of its institutions. Some examples are Rocafuerte, Vidaurre, and Dorrego. The first, born in Guayaquil, educated in Europe, arrived in the United States in 1820, and soon became thoroughly acquainted with the government and institutions of that country. He decided to spread the knowledge of American ideals and institutions in the southern continent, and for this purpose published, in 1821, the pamphlet entitled *Ideas Necesarias para todo Pueblo Independiente que Quiera Ser Libre,* with translations of Paine's *Common Sense* and of John Quincy Adams' speech made on the anniversary of the Declaration of Independence.

[14] *Op. cit.,* 64.

Two years afterwards, he published, in New York, his most important work, *El Sistema Colombiano*, including some chapters of Paine's *Common Sense*. Rocafuerte criticized the liking shown by South American intellectuals for Machiavelli, Rousseau, Montesquieu, Mably, Benjamin Constant, and de Pradt, and states categorically, that the true creed to follow ought to be found in the works of Paine, in Jefferson's *Inaugural Address*, the *Farewell* of Washington, and the speech of Bolivar on taking oath under the constitution of 1821. Rocafuerte defends the manner in which the Senate is chosen in the United States and says that it fulfills its purpose better than the House of Lords in England. He sustains in a general way the efficacy of the American system as opposed to that of Great Britain.

The Peruvian, Vidaurre, friend and companion of Rocafuerte, became as enthusiastic as the latter in his admiration for, and approval of, American institutions. In his *Cartas Americanas,* published also in the United States, he criticized the English government. In his speeches in Trujillo, in 1824, he repeated the comparison of the English and American governments, conceding the superiority of the American on account of the organization of the executive and judicial powers. The evolution of Vidaurre from constitutional monarchism to republicanism was due to his stay in the United States during the years 1822 and 1823.

The Argentine, Dorrego, and his companions of the federal and democratic party were exiled to the United States by the government of Buenos Aires in 1815, and they reaffirmed their political creed in that country. The example of the United States was invoked by Dorrego in the discussions on the constitution of 1826. The orator and leader of the Argentine federal party followed, as did Rocafuerte and Vidaurre, the North American conception rather than the centralistic tendency of Rivadavia.

The outbreak of the French Revolution aroused tremendous enthusiasm among the cultivated Creoles of Spanish America. Belgrano tells us, in his autobiography, that after this change the people considered as tyrants those who opposed the enjoyment of the rights that God and nature have conceded to men. Vidaurre wrote in 1828: " The dawn of the Republic in France dazzled my first youth. My imagination magnified its glories."

Mancini describes the enthusiasm of Nariño and the group of friends gathered at his home when they read, in the work of Salart de Montjoy, the history of the Revolution and the National Assembly, and the Declaration of the Rights of Man. Nariño decided to translate and publish the Declaration.

The *Audiencia* of Caracas cited as one of the causes of the rebellion of Gual and España in Venezuela " The sending to La Guayra of 800 French prisoners taken in Santo Domingo who contaminated the people of the colony with the revolutionary maxim, and the admission of the French immigrants who abandoned Trinidad when this island passed under English control ". The program of Gual and España was saturated with the ideas of the French Revolution.[15]

José Antonio Torres, author of the *Memorias Sobre las Revoluciones,* maintains that the spirit which animated the rebels was the same spirit as that of the French Revolution and not an imitation of that of the North American Republic.

[15] Gil Fortoul, *op. cit.,* I, 95f.

When the South American Revolution started, in 1810, the jacobin policy of governing the Assembly through clubs and setting up executive power vested in committees named by the legislative body was imitated in nearly all South American countries. The patriotic societies of Venezuela and Argentina had the character of jacobin clubs. Everywhere the executive power was collective and entirely submissive to the Legislature. Jacobin exaltation was apparent in leaders and orators like Coto Paul in Venezuela. Robespierre counted a good number of admirers; his name often appeared as a pseudonym in articles and letters and even as a title for newspapers. Nevertheless, it is not possible to say that this enthusiasm was shared by all classes including the popular group. The historian, Duarte Level, says that the influence of the French Revolution in Venezuela was largely secondary: "Its ideas did not find acceptance because they ran counter to religious beliefs. Thus it was that after the 29th of April, 1810, the publication, in the *Gazette* of Caracas, of articles on religious toleration produced such a disagreeable impression that there was not a Venezuelan who would defend them." [16] This fact is confirmed also by Gil Fortoul.

The excesses of the Revolution were condemned by the more sober-minded writers. Our Creoles were not disposed to look upon the Revolution as a bloc, after the idea of Clemenceau. Even the revolutionary leaders who were considered very advanced took this eclectic point of view.

Luna Pizarro in Peru, defending the appointment by the congress of a committee in which executive power was vested, rejected the analogy between this measure and the

[16] *Historia Militar y Civil de Venezuela*, 244-263.

"horrible example of France, in which the 'tribunal of blood' established by the convention was superior to it".[17] Still more representative is the opinion which we find in the periodical called the *Abeja Argentina*,[18] which attributed the American Revolution to the philosophical development of the half century previous, and considered that France, because of the change achieved between these two events, was "a theater of passions, in place of a conflict of ideas". It continues: "If the French Revolution, with all the genius and civilization of its people, deceived all those who had had faith in it, and a ferocious soldier came to occupy the throne of the kind, but arbitrary, Louis, that example helps the present generation to avoid following its steps." [19]

Regarding the English influence, we may say that although it was not so general as the French and American, it was at least equally intense and efficacious. We find quotations of Hume and Malthus in the reformers. The principles of political economy of Adam Smith were known through the French translations and résumés of Condorcet, translated in turn into Spanish by Belgrano. The history of America, by Robertson, was widely read, competing in influence with the works of Raynal. According to the historian Levene, Moreno took inspiration from Robertson.

The Peruvian Vidaurre, the most interesting case of versatile mentality in Spanish America, and perhaps the best

[17] M. F. Paz Soldán, *Historia del Perú Independiente*, 2° periodo, 5. *La Revolución francesa y la América del Sur* by Luis Alberto Herrera, has interesting considerations on this subject but it contains no historical data.
[18] No. 6.
[19] *Ibid.*

read man of his time in the field of political thought, paid
tribute to the English writers. He tells us that Locke's small
book was his teacher after he left Heinecio: " I have not
scorned Rousseau, but in the English orators I always found
more luminous principles . . . Pitt, Fox, and Sheridan I
have studied continually." His *Discursos* in Trujillo have
references to Sheridan and to Burke. It is not possible, however, to base a general judgment upon a case of erudition,
manifestly unusual, such as we find in Vidaurre.

The most important instance of British influence, of
course, was that of Bolivar. The English constitution inspired the political conceptions of the Liberator, chiefly in
the project of Angostura. Bolivar represents a point of
view precisely opposite to that of Rocafuerte. He constantly
repeats: " Liberty is English." The letters of the last part
of his life reveal that he was faithful to this admiration for
British institutions.

Bentham, the great English jurist, was perhaps, after
Rousseau and Raynal, the best known author in South America. His book, *Principles of Morals and Legislation,* was
used as a text in Colombia until the conservative reaction of
1928.[20]

The paper, *El Español Constitucional,* edited in London,
became the organ of British influence for Spain and South
America.

The books of Paley on natural philosophy and theology
were also read in South America. In the debates of the
Constitutional Assembly of Mexico, Becerra, one of the

[20] According to *Larrázabal* 40,000 copies of the works of Bentham
translated into French were sold in South America before the death
of Bolivar.

enemies of the federal form of government, upheld Bentham, Paley, and Blanco White against Rousseau.[21]

As London was the center of the agitators and diplomats of South America, it is quite understandable that many of them were influenced by British culture. This is manifest, chiefly, in Bello and other political writers such as García del Río.

To complete this sketch it is necessary to refer to the special influence of two personalities in South American political evolution. These are Baron Alexander von Humboldt and the Abbé de Pradt. Humboldt has contributed more than any other author to the national consciousness of America through the knowledge of geographical factors. The essays on the government of New Spain and the *Travels* revealed to the Creoles not only the beauty of American nature and the value of its resources, but also the increasing numerical importance of its population. Humboldt was the first to observe that the Spanish possessions were different kingdoms and the bases of different nationalities. The great naturalist contributed not only by his book but also by his presence and conversations during his travels to awaken nationalistic feeling among the Creoles who came in contact with him. Mancini does not hesitate to attribute to the influence of Humboldt on Bolivar the conception of the grandeur and sublimity of the nature and destiny of South America: The historian Pereyra said that " Humboldt was the chivalrous lover of America, the romantic admirer of its landscapes, the geographer and the naturalist, and the true founder of the social philosophy of the American countries." [22]

[21] L. Montiel Duarte, *Derecho Público Mexicano,* II, 13.
[22] *Humboldt en América,* 8.

The work of de Pradt is far less important and of different character. He was the great advocate of American Independence and its warm and enthusiastic defender during the long process of realization. His theory of the three ages of the colonies convinced the South Americans of the inevitableness of emancipation. He saw, as did Humboldt, the nationalistic differentiation in the old Spanish Empire. Bolivar quoted him on this subject in his famous letter of Jamaica.

De Pradt followed the progress of the Revolution through all its aspects and changes, agreeing at times with the formula of a traditional monarchy, but realizing later that this was impossible. His spiritual solidarity with the South American Revolution is revealed in his unconditional admiration for Bolivar and the defence of his dictatorship against the attacks of Benjamin Constant. Partisan of one-man rule, de Pradt should be considered as the precursor of the advocates of democratic Cæsarism.

The facts which we have presented should not lead us to the conclusion that influences from abroad were major factors in the revolution. With them, or without them, the revolution had to come. We repeat that the philosophic influences and the liberal revolutionary influences, are found only among the élite as we see when we study the ideas of the precursors. This élite was not opposed, at first, to tradition and to Spain, but gradually adopted a liberal viewpoint. It is this upper class which finally harmonized the exterior influences with the interior factors of the revolution which we examined in the first chapter.

The effect of the thought of the upper classes was to direct and orient the efforts of the masses, but they did not initiate these popular movements towards liberty. The middle classes of Creoles and *mestizos* formed the basis of the general movement. Neither the economic nor the political factors involve the intellectual influences, although they are at times tangential or mere contributing factors. The political factors, affirmation of nationality, the will for power, are instinctive and natural forces.

The masses had this instinct towards nationalism. The intellectuals, the liberal leaders, gave the basis for the technical mental development of the revolution. This development was unfortunately of a very radical character, and this fact explains many of the failures of the first period of the revolution. This early period was marked by the greatest influence of the propaganda of the radicals.

Independence had to overcome sectionalist instincts and the radical ideas of the intellectuals and find its personification in the famous *caudillos* of the second period. By them and through them independence was achieved. In them ideas were not importations or imitations: the full vision of independence came to them in the midst of and during the experience of the years of struggle.

CHAPTER III

THE IDEOLOGY OF THE REFORMISTS

THE GROWTH OF NATIONALISM

In all America, during the last years of the eighteenth century, there was an intense intellectual nationalistic movement. The ruling class dedicated itself to the study of the various regional problems, principally with emphasis on economic and pedagogical questions. This intellectual nationalism had an ancient and well-established background in Spanish America. It began with the first geographic accounts and continued in the early histories and chronicles. It was accentuated in the outstanding Jesuit works and was evident in the leading personalities of the Colonial period, such as Sigüenza y Góngora in Mexico, Peralta and Llanos Zapata in Peru, in whom world-wide humanistic culture was matched by their interest in the affairs of their own countries. The expatriated Jesuits showed this intellectual nationalism strongly, for in their case it was increased by home-sickness. Father Clavigero writes the history of Mexico while Father Molina does the same for Chile, and Father Velasco for Quito.

The reformist spirit and economic nationalism which we have found in America is the reflection of the transformation which took place in Spain after the establishment of the Bourbon dynasty and chiefly in the time of Charles III. The Bourbons brought to Spain a more accentuated conception of the absolute power of the king, and a certain spirit of reform. During the reign of Philip V, academies and seminaries were founded and the literary movement encouraged. Ferdinand VI " created the merchant marine, fostered industry, and favored internal commerce." [1]

Renewing a tradition that came down from writers such as Vives, Father Mariana, and Martínez Marina, a new school of economic writers appeared, such as Santacruz, Ustariz, and Bernardo Ulloa. After visiting many countries of Europe, Bernard Ward, an Irishman, presented, under the auspices of Ferdinand, his famous *Proyecto Económico*. Special mention should be made of the illustrious minister of Philip V, José de Campillo y Cossio, who wrote, in 1743, the *Nuevo Sistema de Gobierno Económico para la América*. He proposes an imitation of the English colonial system; describes the defects of the religious organization, such as the excessive number of clergymen, and the accumulation of wealth in the hands of the church; and he advises marriage between Peninsulars and Creoles. Campillo devotes a special chapter to the Indians, saying that they are " the richest mine in the World which should be exploited with the most scrupulous economy ". [2]

He advised the sending of general overseers to the Indians and proposed the creation of *intendentes* to carry out a new policy of distribution of land and building up of agriculture and trade. He insists upon the obligation on the part of the State to distribute the uncultivated land of America among the natives. He is in this the precursor of the reformists, San Miguel and Abad y Queipo, whose ideas we shall study later.

---

[1] Jovellanos, *Obras*, I, 313.

[2] E. del Valle Iberlucea, *Los Diputados de Buenos Aires en las Cortes de Cádiz*, 154.

During the reign of Charles III the reformist spirit reached its climax with the progressive ministers, Campomanes, Arranda and Florida Blanca. Spain fully entered into the intellectual currents of the Encyclopedia and the political system which was called " Enlightened Despotism ".

Nobody better embodied this spirit of reform, which was both in agreement with the monarchic principle and with Catholicism than the noble personality of Gaspar Melchor de Jovellanos, the author of the *Informe sobre la ley agraria, Elogio de Carlos III* and *Memoria sobre la educación Pública.* Jovellanos was the master, the true model of the American reformists, who followed his ideas and tried to imitate his style.

Intellectual nationalism manifested itself in two ways both in Spain and America: the educational reform, facilitated by the suppression of the Jesuits, and the rise of economic studies directed by the patriotic societies founded in the various Kingdoms.

THE PEDAGOGICAL REFORM

Since 1756, the illustrious Peruvian physicist, Llanos Zapata, had advocated the banishment from the colony of all the useless ideas, sophistries, and irrelevancies which had been spawned by the cult of Aristotle.

The reform in the universities and colleges began in Spain, in 1769, with a plan presented by a Peruvian, Olavide, in which a change in instruction was advocated for the University of Seville. This plan was applied to the University of Salamanca in 1770. A year later, the reform of the University of Lima was considered by a committee called *Junta de Temporalidades.*

In the proposed regulations of April 30, 1771, there were established, in the faculty of Jurisprudence, classes in natural law and in international law, which were to be taught according to the principles of Heinecio. The study of Spanish Law, divided into public and private, was also added. The stated purpose was to " impart some idea of the Indian laws and the criminal procedure regulated by the provisions of our law ".[3]

In 1772 the Canon Maciel of Buenos Aires presented a petition, asking that teachers be given the right to teach according to the facts arrived at by experiment in the modern academies, rather than by a previously established authority.[4]

Liberal and nationalistic reform had to contend with almost insuperable obstacles in the tradition-bound universities and colleges. (The opposition shown in the University of Lima to the report presented by the *Junta de Temporalidades* is a well-known fact.) But the reform was carried to its logical conclusion in new schools founded at this time. These were known as " Carolinian Colleges " (*Colegios* or *Convictorios Carolinos*), in honor of the King in whose reign they were established. The new spirit was evident also in the schools of mining and the natural sciences. But the new institutions would not have sufficed for reform; men of new energy were also needed. These were forthcoming in such men as Rodríguez de Mendoza, Chávez de la Rosa in Peru, Canon Maciel in Buenos Aires, the Fathers Goicochea and Delgado in Central America, Caballero and Varela in Cuba, Salas in Chile, Espejo in Quito,

---

[3] *Junta de Applicaciones de los Bienes de Jesuitas,* Lima, 1772.
[4] Rafael Altamira, *Historia de la civilización Española,* IV, 342.

and José Mutis and Archbishop Caballero y Góngora in New Granada.

Maciel, as rector of the Carolinian college established in Buenos Aires, in 1783, brought a vigorous spirit to his work, as is clearly shown in the petition we have mentioned. As for Father Goicochea, we ought to refer to his criticism of Aristotle and his studies of the problem of beggary, showing that he had studied the manner in which the problem was outlined in France by the Society of Soissons, in 1779.[5] Bishop Chávez de la Rosa converted the seminary of San Jerónimo into a center of new studies, changing its plans, methods, and personnel.[6] The intellectual leadership of Lima passed from the old university and the seminary to the new College of San Carlos, after the application of the new plan prepared by the Rector Rodríguez de Mendoza and his co-workers, Ribero and Moreno. The new features were the teaching of ethic and logical philosophy, national and international law, according to Heinecio, and the physics of Father Isidoro Celis, a follower of Newton. The national law, freed from the Roman elements, and constitutional law, were taught under the name of " moral philosophy ".[7]

The report of Rodríguez de Mendoza, made on October 29, 1791, concerning a new plan of examination, reflects the new spirit. The Peruvian teacher criticizes the time-worn examinations which were based on the most obscure writings of Aristotle, and proposed the setting-up of a sys-

[5] *Repertorio Americano*, 1929, Nos. 21, 22, and 23. Rodríguez Beteta.

[6] *Boletín del Museo Bolivariano*, No. 15 (containing a biography and eulogy of the famous Bishop).

[7] Jorge Guillermo Leguía. *El Precursor*, 41.

tem based on more practical questions and giving the student liberty to choose his own opinion; meanwhile he advocated the completion of the use of the syllogism by a dialogue of free, but concise, questioning.[8]

In Chile, there was established a Carolinian college, yet there it is not in the Carolinian college but in the Academy of San Luis founded by Manuel Salas, that we find the experimental tendencies of the time. The object of the academy was to apply education to industry with the study of arithmetic, geometry, physics, and drawing.[9]

The Cuban reformer, José Agustín Caballero, like his contemporary, Rodríguez de Mendoza, explained the doctrines of Newton, Bacon, Locke, and Condillac in the Havana Seminary. " He was the first to speak of experimental physics."

Like Maciel he asked that teachers be permitted to arrive at their beliefs " freely and without exact submission to the doctrine of the school ". [10]

The intellectual movement in New Granada went far beyond the limits of a mere institutional reform. It was incarnated in the person of Mutis, the initiator of the work of the Botanical Expedition and a professor of mathematics and Newtonian philosophy in the College of Rosario. Around him there grew up a whole generation of naturalists such as Lozano, Caldas, and the later famous Francisco Zea. The one who took the greatest part in the plans of Mutis was the Archbishop Virrey Caballero y Góngora.

[8] *Mercurio Peruano* III, No. 91.
[9] M. L. Amunátegui, *Precursores de la Independencia Chilena,* III, 343.
[10] Max Enríquez Urena, " Literatura Cubana ", *Archipiélago.* Sept., 1928.

The progressive Prelate was trying to found a new university as a substitute for the old Thomistic colleges. His intellectual orientation is expressed in these words: " The whole object of the plan is to substitute the applied sciences for the merely speculative studies, in which, until now, there has been a sad loss of time; because a kingdom full of products to be utilized, of land to be cleared, roads to be opened, swamps and mines to be drained, water to be controlled, and metals to be refined certainly has greater need of citizens who will know how to serve nature and to calculate and to manage the compass and rule than of those who will understand the abstractions of reason, first matter, and substantial forms." Identical ideas were expressed some years later by Caldas, a disciple of Mutis.[11]

In Venezuela, the school officially called the Rosario College adhered closely to the principles of scholasticism, although there were isolated individuals like Colonel Castro and the Capuchin, Andujar, who followed mathematical studies.[12]

In the region of Quito, the new ideas had their center in the patriotic society, " Escuela de la Concordia ", founded by the Marquis of Silva Alegre and Francisco Xavier Espejo, the latter a personality whom we cannot omit in a study of American thought. The son of an Indian of Cajamarca, he removed to Quito where he graduated with the medical degree. He was in Bogota for a time and became acquainted with the men who represented the new tendencies there. In Quito he published the periodical entitled *First Fruits*

[11] Groot, *Historia Eclesiástica y Civil de Nueva Granada* II, 37, 122.
[12] Letter of Andres Bello to Pedro Gual, *Archipiélago*. Sept., 1929.

of the Culture of Quito. His idea was to defend the new methods of instruction, under the influence, probably, of Rousseau's *Émile*. With very effective eloquence, he criticised the ancient pedagogic method, proposing in its place the Socratic method, in order to arouse the students' curiosity. He placed all his hope in youth, in which he saw learning reborn, and in " that fire of patriotic love which constitutes the moral essence of the body politic ".

Espejo was not merely a factor in reform or intellectual nationalism. According to his biographer, the eminent historian González Suárez, Espejo had in mind a plan of definite independence for the colonies. A plan which would set up in each colony a separate republic, governed only by the natives. This was in 1795. The plan was discovered and Espejo was put in jail, where he died.[13]

In the region of Charcas, in upper Peru, there was also a Carolinian Academy composed of young jurists. This institution, half representative, and half deliberative, was something like a superior course of the University of San Javier, so famous in colonial history for its law classes. The Carolinian Academy was something like a club or a debating society prepared to adopt revolutionary ideas.[14] It may be said in summary that the intellectual agitation consisted mainly in the new liberty and the new philosophical influences, the development of mathematics and the natural sciences and the teaching of American Law.

[13] Gonzalo Bulnes, *Nacimiento de las Repúblicas Hispano-Americanas,* I, 69ff.

[14] René Moreno, *Últimos Días Coloniales, Narración,* 175.

THE ECONOMIC SOCIETIES

The economic societies were founded in imitation of their Spanish prototypes which, in turn, were based on the model established by the Basque society inaugurated in 1764. These institutions were also called patriotic societies, and took other names in the different kingdoms of America. Father Goicochea was the protector of the patriotic society of Guatemala. In Peru the Philharmonic Academy founded by Rossi, Unánue, and Egaña was converted into a patriotic society whose organ was the famous *Mercurio Peruano*. Governor Las Casas, in 1793, founded the economic society of Cuba. During the enlightened government of Espeleta in New Granada, a society of lovers of letters met on certain days of the week to discuss scientific, literary and artistic matters. This society was called " Tertulia Entropélica ".

Besides Rodríguez de Mendoza, the prominent figures of the group in Peru were Unánue and Baquíjano. Unánue reformed medical studies, inaugurated the Amphitheatre of Anatomy and by his study on the climate of Lima, in which he points out the social influences of climate, deserves to be considered one of the founders of American sociology.[15] Baquíjano published in the *Mercurio* his historio-political dissertation upon the commerce of Peru. There is in this work a clear understanding of the relative poverty of the Peruvian territory; and the obstacles to the development of industry and agriculture are clearly shown. It is possibly because of these difficulties that he was led to exaggerate the importance of mining.

[15] Luis Alayza P. S. *Unánue, Bolívar y San Martín.*

The censorship and total suppression of the latter part of this essay, relative to the reform of customs charges and the free traffic in quicksilver, reveals that Baquíjano took, in this part, a rather radical view of his subject.

As far as political ideas are concerned, Baquíjano at the very beginning reveals himself as being faithful to the idea of an enlightened despotism, refuting the idea of division of powers as in the English system. He evolved, however, with the times, and adopted regional liberalism. The great number of friends and disciples of Baquíjano represent the penetration of the ideas of the year 1812 into Peru. This fact and the protection he gave to the papers founded in Lima, after the establishment of the constitution of 1812, prove his new viewpoint. His work, like that of the *Mercurio* in general, is united with the simple growth of nationalism, which was the basis for the Revolution.[16]

Very similar to the tendencies of Baquíjano were those of the Cuban, Arango y Parreño, the Chilean, Salas and of the Argentinian Belgrano, later famous in the struggle for independence. Whereas mining was considered as the first industry of Peru by Baquíjano, Arango gave the first place to agriculture in Cuba. His discourse on the subject marks the beginning of economic studies in Cuba. As agriculture is closely related to commerce, Arango, as secretary of the consulate, presented a report upon the development of both.[17]

Manuel Salas, in 1796, wrote an account of the condition of agriculture, industry, and commerce in Chile. In it he

[16] *Boletín del museo Bolivariano,* No. 12. Here may be found not only Baquíjano's master work, his eulogy of Jáuregui, but also the excellent biography of the Peruvian precursor written by Don José de la Riva Agüero.

[17] Max Enríquez Ureña, *Literatura Cubana.*

pictures the paradoxical economic condition that was general in Andean America. That condition was as follows: there was an immense potential wealth and a small population; yet, on account of the slight exploitation of the first, there was an over-abundance of laborers. Thus stated, the problem of development of the natural resources and the problem of poverty are evident.[18] Belgrano, a friend and correspondent of Salas, represents the new economic ideas; a student of Campomanes and translator of the principles of political economy, he is also a figure in this growth of nationalistic feeling.

Interested in the study of the great problems of agriculture, commerce, and industry, he planned a vast program of popular education. To him alone is due the founding of the School of Navigation and of the Academy of Drawing in the Consulate. There have been few more serious studies of the Spanish commercial system of that time than Belgrano's. The science of this system consisted in " buying at one price and selling at another, four times as great ".

Belgrano presented reports in his official capacity of Secretary to the Consul of Buenos Aires, spreading the ideas of free trade and defending the introduction of foreign products and the interchange of these products with those of the colonies. He founded also the *Seminario de Agricultura* which was the first representative of the liberal and progressive press in Buenos Aires.[19]

The economic and literary societies founded in America did not confine their activities to the study and discussion

[18] Galdames, *Evolución Constitucional de Chile*, I, 29.
[19] Varela, *Historia Constitucional de la República Argentina*, I, 404.

of cultural and nationalistic subjects. They published or supported periodicals to spread and popularize their ideas, marking the inauguration of the press in South America. We have referred to the *Mercurio Peruano* and we ought to mention the *Papel Periódico* of Cuba and the *Redactor Americano* of Bogota.

THE LAND PROBLEM

The most serious question in Mexico and in Peru was not the development of commerce, mining and industry, but the problem of the natives, in its double aspect: land, and labor. Such a grave question could not be overlooked, and, it was studied thoroughly in this period of intellectual nationalism. It was stated in Mexico and warmly discussed in upper Peru. The Bishop of Michoacan, Antonio de San Miguel, in his famous *Informe sobre Inmunidades del Clero,* to which we have referred in the preceding chapter, pointed out the principal aspects of the native problem. He showed what a wide gulf separated the Spanish minority (both Peninsular and Creole) which was only a tenth part of the population, from the mass of Indians and *Mestizos.* The Spanish element owned nearly all the wealth and property, while the rest of the people lived only by manual labor. This contrast was more terrible in America than elsewhere since there was no middle class. The Bishop paints the miserable condition of the natives inside the narrow limits of the villages, where they lived only on the communal estates which were not to be divided. He describes the inconvenient features of the so-called communal treasuries, which took the major part of the Indians' products, yet by the vicious system through which it was administered it did not furnish timely support to the Indians in their periods of need. The Indians were governed by the officials of these same communities, who lived in idleness and were interested only in maintaining the ignorance of the rest of the population. The measures which were designed to protect the Indians had produced, on the contrary, bad effects, and were conducive to the Indians' remaining in a state of indifference or apathy. The half-castes, branded by their payment of tribute, lived in a constant state of irritation toward the whites.

The report refers to the old system of *repartimientos* which had caused the revolution of Tupac Amaru; the evil had increased with the sub-delegates, created by the newer plan. The sub-delegates, being paid only on a fee basis, sought to increase their incomes by illicit means. The Bishop, with prophetic vision, announced that the influence of the clergy would not be sufficient to keep the Indians loyal to ties that offered them no advantages. He bravely asked that the tribute be abolished, that the laws be amended so that they would not weigh heavily on those who should be admitted to all civil rights, and that there be passed for Mexico an agrarian law similar to those of Asturias and Galicia, so that the small farmers might till the ground which the great proprietors had left uncultivated. The report maintains that, if the Indians and the half-castes should be given full rights, the income of the Royal Estate would increase. Humboldt, without guaranteeing the calculations of the report, supported the idea, saying that if the different classes were made equal, the income would increase with the better state of the Indians and the abolition of the head tax would not cause a deficit.[20]

[20] Alexandre de Humboldt, *Essai Politique sur le royame de la Nouvelle Espagne*, Paris, 1811. I, 433.

The importance of the document we have reviewed authorizes us to give further particulars. Its real author was the Vicar of the Diocese of Michoacan, Manuel Abad y Queipo. In a note of the *Informe* he said: "In the presentation of proofs of the main subject, I find reasons to propose to the government for the first time, progressive and beneficent ideas in behalf of the Americas and their inhabitants, especially those who have no property, and in behalf of the Indians and half-castes. Therefore, I propose eight most interesting laws. They are as follows: the abolition of general tribute of Indian and half-caste; the abolition of the condition of inferiority and dishonor in which the half-castes are placed; the gratuitous division of all the lands of the Crown among the Indians and the half-castes; the division of the lands of the village communities among the Indians of every village, giving them full property rights; an agrarian law that will confer upon the people a right, equivalent to ownership, upon the uncultivated land of the great proprietors, by means of leases of twenty or thirty years, free from title, transfer tax or any other tax; free permission for the Indians to settle in the villages and to build there, paying only a just rent; sufficient salaries to the territorial judges; and absolute freedom for the establishment of cotton and wool mills." [21]

Is it not true that the entire social program of the Revolution is found in these reports and proposals? The leaders of the movement of 1810 and the Cortes of Cadiz did not do more. The tribute levied on Indians and half-castes was abolished, and communal property was divided (a measure that proved to be inconvenient later). But in one essential

[21] *Obras de García Icazbalceta,* IX, 284.

point the Revolution stopped short of the ideas of Antonio de San Miguel and Abad y Queipo—the distribution to the Indians of the uncultivated lands of the large landlords.

NATIVE LABOR, THE MITA

Victoriano Villava, six years earlier, had studied the other aspect of the American native problem—compulsory labor in the mines, that is, the *mita*. Named attorney of the *audiencia* of Charcas and " Natural Protector of the Indians ", he assumed these duties with vision, and with extraordinary energy and zeal. His speech concerning the *mita* in Potosi is a representative document. The Argentinian historian Levene, to whom we owe the initiative in establishing for Villava the fame of having been a true precursor of American independence, outlines the central ideas of this study in this manner:

" First, the work in the Mines of Potosi is not a public work.
Second, even if it were public, this fact would not give the right to force the Indians to perform it.
Third, the Indian is not so indolent as is supposed.
Fourth, even if he were indolent in the highest degree, that fact would not authorize anyone to use violence in obliging him to work." [22]

In the development of his ideas Villava utilizes not only generous humanitarian sentiments but also sound economic principles when he affirms that " the growth of mining in disproportion to industry and agriculture would come to be a real detriment which would disturb the equilibrium of the currency ". His thesis brought forth a reply from the

[22] Ricardo Levene, *La Revolución de Mayo y Mariano Moreno*, I, ch. III.

governor of Potosi, Paulo Sanz, who maintained that the character of the work was public, and that the compulsory labor was to the interest of the State and of the native himself. There began, thus, a very interesting debate on this important problem. In his rebuttal Villava confesses that the Indians had not been bettered by the establishment of *intendencias*, and reaffirms his opinion that the gradual exhaustion of the mines would call for greater and greater numbers of slaves to work them. He points out, as did San Miguel, the possibility of a native uprising. This debate had practical effect as well as academic interest. Villava obtained the suspension of the tax on certain Indians and the cessation of the *mita* in respect to others.

The vigorous spirit of Villava did not limit itself to mere opposition to the *mita*; he also planned a reform of the entire Empire in which we find several points worthy of our attention. Villava was not a revolutionist, but a reformer. He thought that the monarchy was necessary on account of geographic and historic forces, but he desired a monarchy in which the succession could be collateral, in order to avoid rule by children or women. He also criticised the pomp of the Spanish Court. His ideal monarchy would be under the moderating control of a national council, composed of persons chosen by lot from the candidates presented by the local districts. This council would enact the laws and levy the taxes, " criticise the delays of the courts and remain as a body for the suppression of special privileges ". He censures the system of education by which only the philosophy of Aristotle was taught, the Roman laws, the Canon law, the theology of scholasticism and peripatetic medicine.

Referring to the relations between Spain and America he did not ignore the fact that reforms might lead to independence, but he thought that the preservation for Spain of American commerce was more valuable than political domination. He proposed that the system of viceroys be done away with, and that the *audiencias* be composed of Spaniards and Americans in equal proportions. He would replace the sub-delegates by *alcaldes* chosen from the three American candidates named by the *audiencia*.[23]

The plan of Villava preserved what we may call imperial unity. There was not a council for each district, but the American districts were represented in the National Council just as were the peninsular provinces. The plan reveals the influence, not only of the Encyclopedists, but also of the Girondin ideas of the Revolution. Villava is the real originator of the ideology of the year 1812.

For us, he presents another interest; in him we see many of the new ideas combined with the principles of colonial tradition. This is shown in his references, above all to those of his master, the great Solórzano Pereyra.

COMMERCE IN LA PLATA

If the principal problem in Peru and Mexico was that of the aboriginal race, in its double aspect of land and labor, the great problem in the La Plata district was the question of free commerce. Not only the progress, but the very existence of that district, depended upon commercial activities. The Viceroyalty of Buenos Aires was founded with the right to have direct intercourse with the different ports

[23] "Apuntes para una reforma de España, sin trastorno del gobierno monárquico y de la Religión por el Señor Doctor Victoriano Villaba del Cuerpo de S. M. y fiscal de la Real Audiencia y Cancillería de la Plata." René Moreno, *Últimos Días Coloniales, Narración,* 41.

of Spain, thus breaking the Peruvian monopoly. But this limited concession did not satisfy the inhabitants long, because Spain could not absorb all their products nor give them in return the things they needed. The last decade of the eighteenth century was marked by a series of petitions for free commerce. The first was presented in 1793. In 1794, the proprietors of Montevideo, and Buenos Aires asked that they be permitted to export beef; in 1798, they renewed their petition of 1793. Distinguished personages, such as Marco del Pon, Encalada, and Belgrano had supported the rights of the producers. The debate was renewed, in a manner especially interesting to us, at the eve of the Revolution. The English merchants had presented a petition to the Viceroy Cisneros, on August 6, 1809, requesting that, with all precautions, they be authorized to dispose of the articles on their boats.

When this petition passed to the consulate and to the municipal council, these bodies gave a favorable answer. But the consul of Cadiz was naturally opposed, for he must defend the Spanish monopoly. He even suggested the reestablishment of taxes to compensate for the customs duties. They also professed religious motives, in opposing this trade, enlarging upon the danger of contact with a Protestant country like England.

This argument of the monopolists had a definite reply in the petition that Mariano Moreno drafted in defence of free trade. This document expressed the internal economic factor in the Revolution of the southern continent. Moreno maintains that the true wealth of the region consists of its agricultural products, that the interests of the agriculturists are the interests of the country itself. He refutes, point by point, the allegation of the Cadiz merchants, and even the

provisions and restrictions suggested by the consulate of
Buenos Aires. He states that it is necessary to give the merchants liberty to look out for their own interest, " because
they know how to regulate the traffic better than all regulations ". Inspired by economic liberalism, the statement of
the planters, if it is the last of the attacks against the
monopoly in point of time, occupies the first place for its
clear vision and dialectic force.[24]

THE PLAN OF VIDAURRE FOR PERU

A year afterwards, 1810, and during the time when the
great uprising was beginning, another eminent Spanish-
American lawyer, the Peruvian, Vidaurre hurriedly wrote
(in eleven days he tells us) a critical description of the
colonial system. Vidaurre in this period still " Spanish as
few, and convinced of the union of the kingdoms, where
our fathers were born and where we now live ", reflects
the last manifestation of reformist thought within loyalty
to the imperial unity. His plan for Peru is, therefore, a
dividing point of the two periods. In it he paints, from
a direct personal viewpoint, the very grave defects of the
colonial organization and points out a plan of reform without leaving the strictly monarchic structure.

The Plan of Peru contains, as we have said, a criticism
and a project of reform. Vidaurre presents to us a dark
picture of colonial administration. No doubt exaggerating
the state of affairs somewhat, he pictures to us " viceroys
surrounded by sycophants in their palaces, resting in luxury
and hearing nothing but what was told them by a venal as-

[24] See the exhaustive study on *La Revolución de Mayo y Moreno*
by Prof. Ricardo Levene.

sistant, a corrupt secretary, and three or four vile parasites, tools of their pleasures; the police abandoned, the militia forgotten, and the tribunals of justice unvisited ".

As for the *audiencias,* the judicial negligence that he relates seems in part that of the present: " They assembled an hour after the stated time, commenced three or four cases, and all remained pending." The criticism is especially directed at the subdelegations of the *intendencias.* These offices were sold at four, eight, or nine thousand pesos. The subdelegates engaged in trade, in the traffic in mules, and obliged the Indians to labor without rest. The position of collector of the tribute was sold for one, two or three hundred pesos, and they granted the lands of the *repartimientos* to those who made the greatest gifts to them. He alludes to the great incomes of the bishoprics. Extending his criticism beyond political institutions, he speaks of the municipal councils; and he outlines a dark picture of the social state of Peru: " The great preoccupation of Peru, and above all, of Lima, is wishing that children apply themselves to nothing but the clergy or to the lawyer's profession, causing an abundance of young men without future."

Let us look now at Vidaurre's constructive plan. With respect to the *audiencias,* he proposes the palliative remedy of a visit and the abolition of commercial and profit-seeking undertakings. He is more radical and more fortunate in his treatment of the *intendencias* and the subdelegates, the principal cogs in the colonial machinery. Following the division of principal powers, he proposes that the intendants and subdelegates shall have no part in any case in the courts, confining their activities entirely to the sphere of political government and military affairs. Advancing the ideas of the La Plata revolution, he advocates the appointment of

members of the town councils and of men who had held
public office to these positions. The intendants were to hold
office six years, could not have Indians in their service, and
were to be judged by the *audiencia*. Those who had factories
or commercial establishments could never be subdelegates.

In the economic order, Vidaurre proposed the creation of
a bank for habilitation with capital provided by war funds,
by the income from land grants, from the inquisition, from
the deposits of the consulate, and from religious guilds. In
respect to commerce, Vidaurre opposes the monopolies but
is a protectionist in regard to tariffs.

With his reformist urge, Vidaurre even wished to regulate and improve the Church, although he affirms that toleration is destructive of the state. He proposed the exemption
of the poor from payment of ecclesiastic fees and the dedica-
tion of two-thirds of the ecclesiastic income to charity.

As for the foreigners in Peru, he decided to give them
the privileges of plebeians; and to those who married Peruvians and had resided four years in the country, the rights
of patricians were given.

All of this reform plan culminates in the creation of a
new institution, " Protector of the Kingdom ". "After most
weighty consideration, I imagined a certain power which
would be similar to the dictators, censors, ephors, high
counselors or chief justice of Aragon, subject to the monarch but inspired by solid principles of justice and security." Each city was to select four *vocales* (representatives), two patricians and two plebeians who, assembled in
the capital of the viceroyalty, were to elect the " Protector ".
This officer was to oversee the work of the viceroy, declare
whether or not the cases were administrative or judicial,
bring suit against the viceroy in cases of mal-government,

before a tribunal composed of the Archbishop and two
fiscals, assume the general governing power, control the
tribunals, supervise the colleges and appoint lieutenants.

In short the " Protector " was to be an attorney-general
or a permanent inspector with great powers, not appointed
by the King but elected by the cities.[25]

The reformist ideas of Vidaurre did not presuppose the
creation of a new government, it simply involved altera-
tions in the old colonial machinery. The distinction between plebeian and patrician was maintained. The social
cell was the city or the oligarchy of the Creole landowners.
Legislative power was to remain absolutely with the King.
The town councils only gained the nomination of intendants,
and subdelegates, and the election of the *vocales,* who chose
the Protector. The social structure of the colony was kept
untouched. The nationalism of Vidaurre came to reveal
itself in the institutions of control but not in legislative or
executive functions. Vidaurre is still a man of the *ancien
régime.*

A superficial study of the facts that we have considered in
the two preceding chapters would lead to the conclusion
that the pioneers of American culture proposed a radical
ideological change and an absolute abandonment of the
ethico-religious basis of colonial society. Nothing, however, could be more contrary to the truth. Our forerunners
adopted the *Tecnos* and the *Logos* of the 18th century;
but with admirable instinct they kept the traditional *Ethos.*
At the same time that they tried to spread experimental
methods and applied sciences to industry, and accepted the
psychological doctrines of the school of Descartes and Locke,

[25] *Plan del Perú.*

the economic principles of Adam Smith, and the political ideas of Montesquieu and Rousseau, they continued faithful to traditional ethics and to their religious faith. This attitude has appeared to some to be paradoxical and insincere. But we observe that this is not the first instance in history in which scientific and even philosophical currents have developed within loyalty to the morals and dogma of religion. The study of the Renaissance in Europe teaches a definite lesson in this regard. In the majority of its leaders the new scientific methods and the love of nature went side by side with religious feeling, which was the legacy of the middle ages. It is not possible to doubt the sincerity of the religious feeling of men like Cusa, Copernicus, Kepler, and Galileo. Religious indifference or skepticism appeared among the humanists who represented a literary rather than a scientific inspiration. Regarding philosophy, it continues permeated with the idea of God until the 18th century, and Cartesian Philosophy, which dominated European thought until English sensualism and Kantian criticism, was adopted by the great figures of the church, such as Malebranche, Fénelon, and Bossuet; but this process of adaptation that took place in France in the sixteenth and seventeenth centuries did not extend to Spain until the eighteenth century. Precisely in this century the equilibria between science and faith, philosophy and religion, were broken by the Encyclopedia. The development of mathematics was followed by that of the natural and social sciences. Spain, which had a brief awakening in the sixteenth century, appeared to have a reawakening during the reign of Charles III, and her vast colonial empire shared this rebirth.

Although behind the model that she was going to imitate there were anti-religious feeling and absolute breach of the

medieval ethical traditions in Spain, the process of conciliation and the movement toward equilibrium which took
place in France in the sixteenth and seventeenth centuries
were repeated. The great personalities in Spain and America belonged to two worlds. They were medieval because
of their morals and faith, and modern because of their love
for the natural and social sciences. In this dualism lies
their greatness. They kept the strong sap, the marvelous
discipline, the supreme dignity of life, the strong sense of
absolute values that only catholicism has been able to in-
spire, and at the same time, open-mindedness, enthusiasm,
and dynamic energy before the new ideas and methods concerning nature and society. The majority of the reformers
were ecclesiastics, Goicochea, Rodríguez de Mendoza, Maciel, Caballero, Cisneros, and Varela. To the hierarchy belonged San Miguel, the Archbishop Caballero y Góngora,
the Bishops Chávez de la Rosa and Espada y Landa. The
adaptation of the traditional ethico-religious ideas to the
new scientific and social orientation was not merely instinctive in these men. Nor was it merely the contradictory super-
imposition of one state of mind upon another. It was the
result of a conscious and deeply thought out process. We
have many proofs of this. Rodríguez de Mendoza, the
Peruvian reformer, said that the new ideas were opposed
neither to the old nor to better ideas.

Father Caballero called his philosophy eclectic. In his
disciple, Varela, as has been observed by Henríquez Ureña,
his great endeavor was to find the necessary equilibrium between the firm sincerity of his religious feeling and the
innovations in the science and in the philosophy of his time.
"Espejo," said González Suárez, "knows how to differentiate between the novelties in public law and the novelties

in religion ". He was a sincere Catholic who, even in advancing toward the dangerous field of clerical and monastic questions, advocated submitting all things to the absolute decision of the Pope, only arbiter of the church.

These conciliatory tendencies between the traditional faith and the new philosophy were so true and deep that they were preserved in the following generation. We have no special reason to suspect the sincerity of Moreno when, in his preface to the translation of the *Social Contract,* of Rousseau, he formulated some reservations regarding the thought of this writer and declared himself faithful to the Catholic Church. The opinion that political reforms ought not to endanger the religious basis of society was widespread. Camilo Enríquez agreed with Moreno when he affirmed that, " it is necessary to establish a moral basis upon religious principles. Wide experience has proved in all parts of the world that the speculations of the materialistic philosopher, substituting new principles of morality, have resulted in a tremendous corruption of custom. The maxims of philosophy are generally weak and they abandon a man put in a difficult situation ".

Nothing could be more arbitrary than to give a like and anti-religious character to the Spanish and the American revolutions. Certainly there was an extreme jacobin party attempting to carry out an ecclesiastical reform in the French way, but such a tendency was not found in the other elements of the emancipation movement.

Certain writers, accustomed to affirming, by routine or prejudice, a parallelism between the French and the Hispano-American revolutions, established a permanent bond between religious and political currents. The Argentine historian, Otero, invokes the testimony of de Tocqueville regarding the indissoluble union of political and religious orientation. But he overlooked the fact that the phenomenon described by de Tocqueville in France did not take place in Spanish America. France passed from the period of conciliation of the seventeenth century to a mere deism or to the materialism of the eighteenth century. In Spain and America the situation was different, as we have shown. In America we shall see that nationalism and democracy were working together with religious feeling.

The Spanish-American reformers followed the example of their brothers and masters in Spain. Regarding the famous members of the Basque Economic Society, the historian, Melchor Fernández Almagro said, " Even though Peñaflorida, Narros, and Altuna breathed the spirit of the century, they did not fail to be Catholics. It is clear that this catholicism, generous and intelligent, was by no means a hindrance to their scientific curiosity and to their attractive reformist longings ". He referred to the relations between Altuna and Rousseau again, saying, " The first one died in the bosom of the Church, master of faith and tolerance ", and he added, " these old Christians knew how to be new intellectuals and how to make Azcóitia [his home] a stronghold of catholicism with an open field for culture and free discussion ".[26]

[26] *Orígenes del régimen Constitucional en España*, 35.

Chapter IV

THE NATIONALISTIC SPIRIT OF THE REVOLTS OF THE XVIII CENTURY

In a previous chapter dealing with the internal and external factors in the Hispanic-American Revolution we have pointed out the importance of the sentiment of Nationality (conscious in the leading classes, instinct in the popular masses) in the various kingdoms or regions of the Spanish Empire in America. The rebellions of the eighteenth century: that of Tupac Amaru in Peru and of Socorro in New Granada are the early and bloody manifestations of this sentiment. We are going to face now great movements of the masses of the population. Each of these insurrections had economic or financial cause: the *repartimientos* (compulsory distribution of merchandise among the Indians), in Peru, and the *alcabala* (transfer tax), in New Granada; but in both revolutions the program was not limited to the cessation of the abuses of the *corregidores* and the abolition of taxes but involved other projects of governmental reforms of nationalistic character. It is not necessary to insist upon the fact that none of these movements tended to establish absolute independence. The breach with Spain and the idea of complete sovereignty appear only after the revolutions of 1809 and 1810, following a process that varies in the different regions. There is a period of nationalistic gestation followed by another of struggle for independence. From this correct point of view the revolutions of Tupac Amaru and of Socorro constitute significant stages of the first period.

In spite of the popular—we may say, multitudinous—character of this movement, the two revolutions differ because of the varied composition of the popular classes in the regions in which they broke out. In the heart of New Granada, in the region of Socorro and the neighboring zones, the popular element was predominantly of the mixed class. As is well known, the pure Indian element tended to be absorbed by the white element in New Granada. In the Southern Peruvian region—Cuzco and the Collao plateau—the masses were chiefly aborigines. We may say that the revolution of Tupac Amaru was indigenous and that the revolution of Socorro was *mestiza,* or mixed, and not proletarian, as the historian Bulnes has described both..

The indigenous element in the Peruvian revolution has led some to consider it a racial and not a nationalistic revolution, a retrospective case of racism, last manifestation of a disappearing people; not a futile attempt to affirm a nascent nationalism but the last effort of one about to die. The truth is that the revolution has this double character. Evidently it has as a decisive factor the racial consciousness that was awakened and vibrant from Cuzco to Charcas. The authority of the leader was based upon his royal blood—he pretended to be the heir of the Incas. The revolution in its development revealed the hatred against the whites and *mestizos* and the ferocious, destructive instinct of the primitive people. The racial aspect of the revolution of Tupac Amaru was marked by Humboldt with his customary penetrative insight. The great naturalist said: "At the beginning of his campaigns, Tupac Amaru protected the ecclesiastics and the Americans of all colors. Revolting only against the Europeans, he made partisans among the mixed and Creole people; but the Indians, distrusting the sincerity

of their new allies, soon began a war of extermination on all
who were not of their own race." Humboldt alludes also to
the title assumed by Tupac Amaru and the respect " which
he inspired in the Indians, who, in spite of their fear of
the Spaniard, and although they were surrounded by the
victorious army, prostrated themselves at the side of the
last ' Son of the Sun ' when he crossed the street of Cuzco
on the way to his execution ".[1] Nevertheless, it is necessary to point out some facts that attenuate the preceding
judgments. Not all the Indian chiefs, *caciques,* joined the
movement of Tupac Amaru. Of sixteen *curacas* (chiefs),
three were against the Indian revolt: El Inca Saguarada,
Diego Chuquihuanca, and Mateo García Pumacagua.[2]

The historian Riva Agüero said rightly that while many
Indians remained indifferent to the rebellion, some *mestizos*
not only made common cause with the Indians but were
using them as tools.[3]

We have no special reason to think that Tupac Amaru
personally, and at least at the beginning of the revolution,
was not sincere in his protestation of loyalty to the King
of Spain and to the Catholic religion, and in his invitations
to the Creoles and the *mestizos* to fight together against the
Europeans. Loyalty to the King was a feeling corresponding
to the widespread myth of a paternal and just monarch, a
kind legislator entirely different from the cruel agents who
were disobeying his mandates. The order imparted by Tupac
Amaru to suppress the *corregidores* was issued in the name
of the King. In his ultimatum to the *Cabildo* of Cuzco, he
spoke of leaving to the King of Spain the direct dominion

---

[1] Humboldt, I, 450.

[2] Philip A. Means, *La Rebellión de Tupac Amaru,* 17.

[3] José Baquíjano, *Boletín del Museo Bolivariano.*

that he had, without diminishing the obedience that was due him.[4] Such protestations of loyalty are repeated even more emphatically in his letters to the Spanish chief, Areche: " His writings are full of loyalty to the Spanish monarch, and there is neither a fact nor a document that would stand against this except an apocryphal decree, product, as Mendiburu believed, of the flattery of the colonial authorities." [5]

We have even greater reason to believe in the sincerity of his religious feeling. He said in his inaugural proclamation: " The priests will have the esteem and respect due to their estate and equally so the religious orders and the monasteries." The conduct of Tupac Amaru in the revolution is a proof that he tried to abide by this declaration. Not only among the Indians and the cultivated mixed class to which he belonged, but in the masses, the Christian religion and the Catholic liturgy had penetrated deeply. The revolution, in its progress, might have substituted an Inca for the King, but it was not possible to think of the restoration of the cult of the Sun.

His intentions regarding the Creoles and the *mestizos* appear not only in the inaugural proclamation but in other documents such as that which was addressed to the province of Chichas. He said: "All measures have been taken for the preservation and protection of the Spanish and Creoles, *Zambos* and *Indios,* and for their tranquillity, because they are our countrymen and compatriots, born in our land and of the same origin as the natives, having suffered equally the oppression and tyranny of the Europeans."

[4] Bulnes, *Nacimiento de las Repúblicas Americanas,* I, 46.
[5] Emilio del Solar, *La Revolución de Tupac Amaru,* 140.

The wording of this proclamation deserves to be considered thoroughly, because it defines the new national feeling. Its essential elements are mentioned in their proper importance: birth in the same land, the same origin and the same blood for the Indians and partially so for the *mestizos*, and solidarity in interest. Doubtless the hatred of the Indians for the Creoles and the *mestizos* was general, but we ought to remember that the rebellion was caused chiefly by the abuses of the *corregidores*, who were Spaniards in great majority. The anonymous author of *Relación Histórica de la Revolución de Tupac Amaru* attributes the policy of the Inca leader regarding the Creoles and the *mestizos* " to a provisional and shrewd strategy while he was looking for a way of getting rid of all that might embarrass him ". Considered only as strategical and provisional, the program of Tupac Amaru contains already the main basis of a new national solidarity, impossible perhaps of crystallization under Indian leadership, but certain and sure under Creole and *mestizo* direction in the outbreak of twenty years later.

In accordance with this moderate and limited program, the Indian leader demanded not only the cessation of the evil, the abuses of the *corregidores*, but the abolition of the *mita* and, what was more important, the substitution for the *corregidores*, of *alcaldes* of the same Indian nation without more power than that of the administration of justice, and, finally, a Christian policy toward the Indians and others as well. He demanded also the erection of a royal tribunal, *audiencia*, in Cuzco, where a viceroy would also reside, in order that the Indians might have the recourse of appeal nearer to them. The case of Tupac Amaru is truly tragic. His moderate program did not attract the Creole element and the majority of the mixed people, and he lost control of the rebellion, which lacked discipline, organization, and definite orientation. In spite of everything, the revolution showed a spirit of protest and displayed a just program of nationalistic character, being at the same time an ending and a beginning, and as Riva Agüero said, " The last manifestation of a nationality and the first cry of a new one ".

The revolution of Socorro had as a consequence the new policy of the overseer, Piñeres, who doubled the *alcabala* and the tax for the defence of the Barlovento Islands. He also doubled the price of monopoly articles, tobacco and brandy. Such measures produced the desperation of the people, who revolted at the cry " Long live the King and down with bad government ". In spite of the lack of true leaders and efficient direction, the insurrection spread, forcing some town councils to suppress the new taxes. The rebels, numbering thirty or forty thousand, approached Bogota. A committee called " La Junta de Tribunales ", composed of representatives of the different institutions, and in charge of the government, decided to send delegates with broad authority to treat with the rebels who offered peace under these conditions: first, abolish the Barlovento tax, second, suppress the monopoly of tobacco, third, exempt the Indians from payment of parochial fees, fourth, do away with the transfer tax on fruits and comestibles and reduce to only two per cent the payment of tax on all other taxed articles, and fifth, recognize the prior right of natives or nationals to government positions of first, second, and third class. This peace offer alludes also to the antipathy for the natives shown by the European element and asks that

European employees who showed signs of desiring self aggrandizement be banished from the colonies.[6]

It is worth while to call attention to the proposals which are political in character. The positions of first, second, and third rank ought to be given to the natives or *nacionales*. This demand practically meant that they not only claimed the lower and intermediate functions but the highest ones as well, a position that was entirely in agreement with the laws of the kingdom to which we have referred in the first chapter. The rebels asked something more: the suppression of the Spaniards' attempts to violate the principle of equality. All the nationalistic spirit of the insurrection is embodied in this petition.

The uprising was pacified by the acceptance of these conditions, but very soon the Spanish authorities decided to disregard this agreement. The viceroy and the Spanish functionaries started the absurd policy of retaliation and chastisement, in flagrant violation of the pact. One of the delegates protested against this attitude, and for this reason the *audiencia* ordered his execution, according to him the same fate as that of the leaders of the revolution. The rebellion of Socorro failed because it was an inorganic reaction of the popular masses and lacked the orientation which the leadership of the upper classes gave to the movement of thirty years later. At any rate its program formulated one of the bases of the revolution: the right of the Creoles to governmental positions. An important lesson about the strength

[6] " Capitulaciones Exigidas por los Comuneros de la Nueva Granada al Gobierno Español el 7 de Junio de 1781." Restrepo, *Historia de Colombia, Documentos.* (Paris, 1827) VIII, 40. See also *Biblioteca de Historia Colombiana*, IV.

and the suddenness of a popular movement was taught by this otherwise abortive rising.[7]

We ought to mention also another movement of popular character that took place among the negroes and mixed people of the province of Coro in Venezuela. In this movement the influence of the French Revolution seems as important as racial and economic factors. The rebels proclaimed the " law of the Frenchman ", the republic, the abolition of slavery, and the suppression of taxes. The Venezuelan sociologist, Pedro Arcaya, said that it was easy to understand that in this revolution there was no coherent plan nor did the rebels know the meaning of the words, " law of the French " and " Republic ". However true this may be, it is, nevertheless, quite obvious that this insurrection indicates the possibility of an awakening of racial consciousness among the lower elements of colonial society.[8]

[7] Samper, *Derecho Público Interno de Colombia*, I, 13.

[8] *Estudios de Sociología Venezolana*, " Una Insurrección de Negros en 1795."

CHAPTER V

THE IDEAS OF THE PRECURSORS

The title of precursor has been applied by antonomasia to Nariño in Colombia and to Miranda in Venezuela. This is due not only to their influence in the growth of a nationalistic spirit, but to the fact that they were the first to have the idea of absolute independence; and they began the propaganda and the struggle for it. Their efforts and sacrifices fill the first chapters of the struggle for freedom. Men of thought as well as of action, their plans cannot be omitted in a history of political ideas.

In another chapter there is recorded the fact that we owe to Nariño the publication of *The Rights of Man*. As his friend, Espejo had done in Quito, he founded a literary club in Bogota. The trial in court, which followed his famous publication of *Derechos del hombre,* gave him an opportunity, in his defence, to explain his political ideas under the signature of his lawyer. His plea is, therefore, a fundamental document in the history of American thought. With great ability, he maintains that the rights of Man, as set forth in the publication which was the cause of the suit, were upheld and had been approved by eminent writers of Madrid whose works circulated freely in spite of the censorship of the tribunal of the inquisition. He ties up the new doctrines with the philosophy of Seneca, the legal tradition of Spain, the Christian philosophy of St. Thomas, the theories of Heinecio and of Capmany, and the prevailing ideas in Spain at that time, as expressed in widely circulated books, such as, *Espíritu de los mejores diarios* and the *Enciclopedia metódica*.

This argument was more than the ingenious stratagem of a lawyer, it was the expression of a great truth. The new doctrines, inasmuch as they pertained to the rights of individuals, had a very ancient origin in Stoic philosophy, and principally in the Christian philosophy of the middle ages. Therefore we cannot be surprised that Nariño makes interesting quotations from St. Thomas of Aquinas, but it is noteworthy that he does not refer to the disciples of St. Thomas, Victoria and Suárez, the real founders of modern Public Law.

The references made, in the plea, to Spanish works of the period reveal the close connection between reformist thought in Spain and in America. The plea also favors religious toleration and the principle of equality between the mother country and the colonies; it combats the commercial system, and concludes with the statement that the subordination of the colony to the mother country depends upon the granting of guarantees and the equality which should be established with respect to the Spanish, and that "the opposite system and the example and proximity of the new republics would stimulate them to plan another government, which would be more suitable for them ".[1]

Until this moment Nariño apparently belongs to the party in favor of national autonomy, but very soon, without faith that Spain would carry out the policy of reforms, he decides for absolute independence and consecrates his life to the revolution. Sent to the Peninsula, he makes a jest of Spanish justice and travels through France and England. In England

[1] E. Posada, *Nariño*, 82. *Biblioteca de Historia Nacional*, II.

he makes suggestions to Pitt but rejects the idea of annexa-
tion to the British Empire, " because this would be selling
his country to another nation ". He returns to his country
to spread the revolutionary ideas in a series of romantic
journeys. Surprised by the Spanish authorities, he is obliged
to enter into an agreement with them to forego his seditious
enterprises. We will see him again at the outbreak of the
revolution in 1810.[2]

The figure of Miranda stands out in bold relief in the
history of the independence. He is an international per-
sonage. World history records few cases in which an ideal
is so persistently followed. Did the ideal of complete independence surge up in the heart of the great " Precursor ":
at the beginning of his career, when, as lieutenant-colonel
of the Spanish forces, he fought against the English in
Florida, did he have this plan? Was it formulated when he
fought at the side of the North American rebels—in the
same years in which the rebellions of Tupac Amaru and
Socorro took place? From this early date, without declining
any test or weakening before any obstacle, he worked for
independence. He succeeded at last, in 1805, in organizing
an expedition; and he returned to Venezuela to assume the
direction of the nascent republic.

The political ideas of Miranda evidently did not have
the same value as his adventures and his persistent effort in
favor of the American independence, but they should be
considered in a study of American political thought, not
only as a reflection of the thought of the period, but because
some of his ideas had influence on later plans and projects.
The fact that Miranda, from his early youth, had a political

[2] Bulnes, I, 103ff.

turn of mind is revealed by the diary of his journey to the
United States in 1783-84, which has recently been published.[3] To Miranda, the happy condition which the new
states enjoyed was the result of the fact that they practiced
what he called the " British Constitution ". Regarding the
constitution of Massachusetts, he formulates an interesting
observation which discloses that he was a reader of Montesquieu and a close observer of the economic basis of the
United States: " Here I have had the pleasure of communicating with the famous republican, powerful agent in
the past revolution, Mr. Samuel Adams. He is a gentleman
of talent and understanding, especially in the field of legislation. We had a very extended conference upon the matter,
and he finally agreed with me after he had fully considered
these points. The first was: how, in a democracy whose
basis is Virtue, there is no place designated to it? that, on
the contrary, all the dignity and powers are given to Property, which is justly the blight of such a democracy. The
other was: the contradiction I observed between admitting,
as one of the rights of humanity, the right to worship a
Supreme Being in the manner and form in which it pleased
one, yet afterwards excluding one from all legislative or
executive office if he did not swear that he was of the Christian religion . . . grave solecisms, without doubt. . . . He
also told me many interesting things about the origin, principles, and occurrences of the late revolution, according to
me most affectionate treatment." [4]

The idea of establishing a social order upon the basis of

[3] *The Diary of Francisco Miranda, Tour of the United States,
1783-84,* Hispanic-American Society, 1928.
  [4] *Ibid.,* 118.

Virtue, which inspired Miranda in 1783, also appeared in the *Areopagus* of Bolivar of 1818.

The trips that Miranda made through England and the European continent in the ninth decade of the eighteenth century did not take from him his early admiration for England, since we see in the plan of government that he presented to Pitt in 1790 that he incorporates some of the institutions of the British Monarchy. The executive power is exercised by an Inca or Emperor, which is an hereditary office. There is a higher chamber or senate composed of *caciques* who hold office for life, and a lower house composed of representatives elected every five years. The judicial power is in the hands of officials appointed to office for life by the monarch. Besides these institutions, Miranda renews others of classical antiquity: *censors,* chosen by the senate and confirmed by the Inca, to watch over the customs of the senators (with the power to expel them from the senate merely by writing their names on the tablets of their office) and over those of youth, in particular as regards institutions of learning and their teachers; *ediles,* named by the senate with the approval of the Inca, who were to care for the roads, ports, and monuments of the Empire; and lastly, *quaestors,* chosen by the lower house to look out for "the public interest in all things relative to finance". In accordance with the idea which later was to prevail in the United States, the project of Miranda set forth that if the laws were found to be in opposition to the constitution of the State, they should be considered null by all the tribunals.

Concerning the amendment of the constitution, the project of Miranda, besides demanding as in American fundamental law, a vote of two-thirds in the chambers, also demanded a vote of three-fourths of the judges. In the case in which the initiative came from the Inca and the judicial power, the proportion of the votes was to be exactly the reverse.[5]

The military activities of Miranda in the armies of the French Revolution, in which he attained the rank of general, did not take from him his fondness for political ideology. He published, in July 1795, a pamphlet in which he expressed his ideas for the saving of France from the difficult situation in which she then found herself.[6]

Miranda remains faithful to the main principles of Montesquieu, attributing all the evils of the French situation to the confusion of powers: He criticises the Convention for having transferred the whole power to the committee of public welfare and for having absorbed the judicial power. He advocates equality among the three powers, maintaining that the executive has the right to supervise the manner in which the legislative body exercises its mandate and to denounce to the people any attempts of the legislative body to hinder the executive functions and endanger the public liberty. Referring to France, he said that it was necessary to give her the most vigorous and firm government. Regarding the judicial power, Miranda favors appointment for life by the sovereign with a stipend sufficient to obviate bribery. Miranda was at this time a partisan of woman suffrage, at least in matters that concerned women, such as marriage, divorce, and education. He continued to

---

[5] Gil Fortoul, *Historia Constitucional de Venezuela*, I, 97.

[6] *Opinion du Général Miranda sur la situation actuelle de France et sur les rémèdes convenables à ses maux.* Cited by C. Parra-Pérez, *Miranda et La Révolution Française*, 307.

adhere to the bicameral system. From the Utopians of the Girondin party he accepted only the censorship of the state for the preservation of good customs and the safe-guarding of Virtue. Concerning religion, Miranda favors the established church and the nationalization of the Catholicism prevailing in Latin countries. Briefly, it is possible to say that the thought of Miranda departs entirely from jacobin doctrines, leaning rather toward the old English conception of moderate and organic liberalism.

In 1797 Miranda resumed his activities in behalf of South American independence. According to an agreement signed in Paris with some citizens of the United States, he took it upon himself to try to prepare an army in England with which to invade South America. He tried also to get the help of the United States, believing that an alliance between the Spanish and Anglo-Saxon peoples was the only hope that remained to liberty, which had been so audaciously outraged by the abominable maxims of the French Revolution, and the only means of forming a balance of power capable of stopping the destructive and devastating ambitions of the French system.[7]

In a letter to Caro, a Cuban whom he had sent to the United States to further this project, Miranda reiterates his anti-jacobin creed, recommending to Caro that he make clear to the conspirators of New Granada the necessity of avoiding by all means the jacobin system, a system that would make liberty a tomb rather than a cradle, as had been demonstrated by the whole history of the French Revolution.[8] Similar thoughts are found in the correspondence of Miranda with Adams and Hamilton.

[7] *Ibid.*, 382.
[8] *Ibid.*, 385.

At this point it is proper to present the leading ideas concerning a revolutionary movement toward absolute independence, taking into consideration the relation that existed between its leaders and the *Precursor*. We refer to the conspiracy of Manuel Gual and José España, discovered by the Spanish authorities in Caracas in 1797. The so-called " ordinances " found among the papers of the conspirators were inspired by the idea of one country for all the Americans. (Article 5 and Article 25 speak about the *Pueblo Americano* and say that the decrees of the commanders will be issued in the name of the *Pueblo Americano*.) These ordinances embodied the program of the conspiracy. Among the outstanding articles are found those relative to the provisional committees; respect for ecclesiastical organization and wealth; abolition of taxes on food-stuffs and the land transfer tax; equality of the whites, *mestizos,* Indians, and Negroes, the only distinction to be based upon merit and virtue; opening of all ports to the countries of the old world; abolition of the tribute and of slavery; universal military service for all men between the ages of 17 and 45. According to the historian, Gil Fortoul, the program of 1797 contains the germ of the plan carried out by the patriots of 1810 and 1811.

In 1801, Miranda redoubled his efforts before the English government to get its help in the enterprise of freeing Hispanic America, and in the year 1790 he drafted new constitutional projects which have been revealed recently by Professor Robertson, discoverer of the archives of Miranda. In his new edition of *The Life of Miranda,* he says: " The plans sketched in 1801 . . . provided for a more centralized and monarchial type of government than did the projects of 1790." Dealing with the idea of establishing a dictator, he adds: " In this respect Miranda's project resembles the plan of Iguala by which Agustín Iturbide became Emperor of Mexico. . . . In truth Miranda's national plan of 1801 derives significance from the fact that it was a unique proposal to superimpose a representative government of monarchic type upon modified Spanish institutions. The Sieyès, of Spanish America, must have been influenced by the political ideas of Pitt, Turnbull, and Vansittart." [9]

Only five years later, Miranda succeeded in carrying out his plan of invading the continent. With the economic support of England and with the aid of his friends in the United States he started his expedition toward the coast of Venezuela. The economic ties that he had with England did not impose upon him any obligation except that commercial franchises were to be accorded to the British nation. Miranda never thought to replace Spanish rule with British rule in South America. His " Declaration " and other documents are overwhelming proofs of the high ideals of the man. It is not our task to record the history of the failure of this expedition, but we should refer to the proclamation that Miranda addressed to the inhabitants of Venezuela. He said in it that the object of the expedition was independence under the auspices and protection of the British navy. He made an eloquent appeal to the Indians and the *mestizos* whom he called " Citizens " affirming that rewards and distinctions would be accorded only to virtue. He points to Holland, Portugal, Switzerland, and the United States as examples in the struggles for freedom.

The regulations of the new Government, included in ten

[9] I, 231.

articles remind us of the ordinances of the conspiracy of Gual and España. The *cabildos* would exercise all the civil, administrative, and military functions and would send to the general headquarters one or two deputies who would meet in general assembly to form the provisional government.

The failure of the Miranda expedition was due to the fact that public opinion was not prepared for such a sudden change in government.

The people were suspicious of British help. The Indians and the *mestizos* were loyal to the Spanish Monarchy. The only element that would have been able to participate in the revolt was the Creole aristocracy, and Miranda, as the historian Gil Fortoul rightly observed, neglected to win this element for his cause.

Three years later, when Spain was being invaded by Napoleon, the Creole aristocracy, under the guise of loyalty to the absent and deposed King, found an opportunity of replacing the Spanish authorities. Miranda followed very closely the political events of Europe and their consequences in America, and he saw also that the invasion of Spain by Napoleon presented an opportunity to carry out his old plans. Then he decided to send to the Marquis del Toro, leader of the Venezuelan aristocracy, two projects, one of provisional and another of federal government for the colonies. These projects were intercepted by the governor of Curaçao and returned to London. According to the project of provisional government, the Spanish authorities were to be displaced by the municipal councils of the cities, to whose membership was to be added a third of Indians and negroes. These appointments were to be confirmed by the *commissions* formed of natives who had an annual income of fifty dollars and who were not servants. The town councils were to name one or more representatives to be members of the provincial assembly which was to be in charge of the government until the federal government should be established. The tribute was to be abolished as well as the Tribunal of the Inquisition. Import duties were to be reduced by 15 to 20 per cent.

In the definite project of government on a federal basis, the creation of these three institutions was called for: municipal councils or *cabildos*; provincial assemblies, on the basis of land ownership and a certain income; and, crowning this structure, there was set up a new legislative body called the Colombian Council. Miranda adopted the French unicameral idea, but he accepted the American principle as regards the veto of the executive power which could be overruled only by a two-thirds majority in the council. Miranda also copies the American principle as to the modification of the constitution, calling for a two-thirds vote of the council, and also of three-fourths of the provincial assemblies.

Miranda abandons the English idea of the executive power, unipersonal and hereditary, proposing instead two Incas, holding office for ten years, one of whom was to remain near the legislative body while the other was to travel through the colonies of the Empire. As for the executives of the provinces, there were to be two *curacas* elected by the provincial assembly for five-year terms. He repeated the idea of the *quaestors,* or administrators of the public treasury; the *ediles,* in charge of the highways; and the *censors,* six in number, who were to watch over public instruction and customs. In the judicial department, the judges were to be elected for life by the provincial commissions. The tribunals were to be constituted in imitation of those of the United States and England. The executive power was to appoint a high national court, composed of a chairman and judges chosen from among the national judges.

The church government was to be regulated by a provincial council, which revealed Miranda's nationalistic and regalistic tendency. The plan which established the Roman Catholic as the national religion, at the same time proclaimed the most complete religious toleration.

Both the first and second plans of Miranda separated by eighteen years, repeat the same error in believing that national unity was possible for the whole Spanish Empire. Both pay verbal homage to the autochthonous tradition and decorate themselves with institutions patterned after the Roman style. But it is necessary to confess that the last plan appears to be inferior, since it accepts the jacobin institution of the single chamber, the impossible duality of the executive power, and the popular origin of judicial power.[10]

Closely related to the work of Miranda, there is another celebrated document which constitutes the first political proclamation of independence, the first call to freedom. It is the famous letter to the Spanish Americans from the Peruvian Jesuit, Juan Viscardo y Guzmán. Its author merits consideration, not only as one of the forerunners of nationalistic growth, but of absolute independence, at the side of Miranda and Nariño. He was born in the town of Pampacolpa in 1747, in the intendency of Arequipa. He entered the Company of Jesus as a novice in Cuzco where the decree of suppression overtook him. In consequence, he was taken to Italy, remaining in Masacarrara for several years. From

[10] Gil Fortoul, *op. cit.*, I, appendix no. 2, 512.

there he went to France and later to England, where he put himself in the service of Pitt, who had received from Miranda the idea of utilizing the expatriated Jesuits. In spite of the fact that they lived in London at the same time, it seems that Viscardo and Miranda did not visit each other. Viscardo died in 1798, discontented with the attitude of the English Government. He willed his papers to Rufus King, who later gave them to Miranda.[11]

The letter of Father Viscardo is a vehement and eloquent plea for independence. It contains in brief form a very severe criticism of the colonial government and of the state of affairs which " obliges us to buy the things we need at the highest prices and to sell our products at the lowest prices. They have closed to us as in a besieged city all the roads through which other nations could give us, at moderate prices and by fair exchange, the things we need ". He explains the absolutism of the Spanish Monarchy by the wealth of the Indies. " The royal authority is similar to the sea as it comes out of its bounds and inundates all the monarchy, and the will of the King and his ministers becomes the universal law." He presents as an example of this arbitrary rule, the deportation of the five thousand Jesuits, under the pretext of security of the monarchy. " The government ", he says, " has converted into an instrument of oppression and ruin the methods which have been entrusted to it for the protection and safeguard of individuals ". He ridicules the project of union and equality between the Americans and Spaniards in Europe, which desire was expressed by the government in a royal decree, considering

11 Regarding the life of Father Juan Pablo Viscardo y Guzmán, and the text of his famous letter, see *Boletín del Museo Bolivariano*, December, 1928. See also *Edinburgh Review*, Jan. 1809.

that equality was impossible between " masters and slaves ".
He believes that the right of Spain to exact fidelity has
ceased: " since the rights and obligations of ruler and ruled
are reciprocal, Spain has broken the ties which have united
us to her and endeared her to us ".

He adds to this legal argument the geographical argument: " The distance between the places, which of itself
proclaims our natural independence, is yet less important
than our interests. We need, primarily, a government which
is in our midst, to distribute those benefits which constitute
the purpose of our social union." He invokes the gratitude
due the pioneers " who expended for us their perspiration
and their blood, that the theatre of their glory and labor
should not be converted into the scene of our miserable
slavery ". He states also the obligation of preserving " those
natural rights received from our Creator, the precious rights
which we may not alienate. The free enjoyment of these
rights is the inestimable heritage which we should leave to
posterity ". He refers to the liberty of Portugal and of the
United Provinces. " The valor with which the English
colonists of America have fought for the liberty which
they now so gloriously enjoy covers our indolence with
shame." He affirms that the wise and virtuous Spaniard
who silently mourns the oppression of his native land will
applaud our enterprise in his heart. He concludes with a
vision of the future in America, " peopled by men of all
nations, and forming a single great family of brothers ".[12]

[12] The letter of Father Viscardo has in it the reference to Montesquieu previously mentioned: " The Indies and Spain are two
powers under a single master, but the Indies form the principal
part, and Spain the accessory." He also transcribes as a note the
writings of Montesquieu concerning the works of the Jesuits in
Paraguay.

MIRANDA AND JUDICIAL REVIEW OF LEGISLATION

In tracing the possible influences which led to Miranda's insertion in his project of a constitution (1790) for the proposed South American Empire of the clause that laws in conflict with the constitution must be considered null and void, it is necessary to consider what had been the development of this question in the United States.

Although the doctrine was not positively promulgated by the Supreme Court until February 1803, the arguments which finally secured its acceptance were circulated and discussed as early as 1787 and 1788. Miranda, during his first visit to the United States in 1783-84, made contacts with important sources of American political thought, notably with Madison, Jefferson, Rufus King, Smith, and Hamilton. It is possible that in remaining in touch with his friends in the United States in the years 1784 to 1805, when he returned to solicit government aid, he became informed of their attitude toward the problem of judicial review, and perhaps even received the account of the debates in the Constitutional Convention. The extreme admirers of Miranda would not think it necessary to establish so direct a link. They might say that he, too, familiar as he was with the Constitution of the United States, was able to derive the principle " with inexorable logic from the nature of the instrument itself ".

CHAPTER VI

THE REVOLUTION IN SPAIN AND ITS REPERCUSSION IN AMERICA

The activity of Napoleon in the Iberian Peninsula, invading Portugal and dethroning the Bourbon dynasty in Spain, produced two effects: the removal of the reigning house of Portugal to Brazil and the outbreak of the national revolution in Spain. The independence of Brazil was a consequence of the first, the Hispano-American revolution of the second. This explains the diverse character of Brazilian and Hispano-American independence. The first is the importation of a dynasty; the second is the extension to the new world of a national and democratic revolution.

The Spanish revolution, in addition to this double character, showed a spirit of religious affirmation. It was inspired by the sentiment of national independence. It was nourished by the most genuine popular feeling, and it strengthened itself by its defense of Catholicism in the struggle with French jacobinism. On the patriotic and religious instinct of the masses there was superimposed—at times artificially, in the opinion of Fernández Almagro—the advanced ideology of the intellectual leaders. Popular at its base, the movement became liberal because of the intellectual direction of these leaders. Its national character corresponds to Spanish nationalism, a nationalism which is neither centralist nor unitarian but regionalist or federalist, a nationalism of the union of communes. The movement began about the town councils of the ancient capitals of the kingdom—true regions—there the revolutionary *juntas* were formed, many of which assumed full power.

When the throne had disappeared, local autonomy, regional sovereignty, took on new life. National life maintained itself dispersed in various centers. The attitude of the country is not determined by an initiative or direction which comes from above; it is the result of the convergence of various elements which stimulate together the heart of a common sentiment. It is necessary that the action impose itself united by the formation of a superior organism.

It was in this fashion that the central *junta* of Aranjuez was constituted. Conscious of its rôle, it said concerning the other *juntas*, in its manifesto of October 26, 1808, " The only means that remains to them for the preservation of their independence is a general federation ". Central power is created by the representation of the local centers. " The various *juntas* named deputies and convened to form this center of authority." The Supreme *junta* of Seville, which took the place of that of Aranjuez, says in its manifesto that the passing of federalism was a necessary result of the creation of a central power. The same manifesto invokes unity as the essential principle of monarchy. This joint action, entirely in accord with the ideas of its leaders, proved the liberal character of the revolution. The manifesto of the same supreme *junta* of Seville said: " We cannot take a step toward independence without taking one also toward liberty."

Because it is nationalist, the Spanish revolution is monarchist. The *junta* of Aranjuez had said in its manifesto: " The Spanish revolution has, because of this, characteristics which are entirely different from those which were present in the French revolution: the latter had as many opinions about forms of government as there were factions: in ours there is no more than one opinion, a universal wish: heredi-

tary monarchy and King Ferdinand VII." This monarchism
is not incompatible with liberal ideas, at least in the thought
of the revolutionary leaders. Speaking of the fruits of victory, the manifesto united the consecration of liberty with
the restoration of the throne: " your monarch restored to
his throne or avenged, consecrated in a constant and solemn
manner to civil liberty; the relations with our colonies tight-
ened more fraternally and, consequently, more usefully ".

These last phrases reveal in the leaders of the revolution
the conviction that a change had to be made in the relations
between Spain and America. Already the *junta* of Seville,
June 17, 1808, referring to the loyalty of the Americas,
affirmed that they would join with Spain because the same
perils menaced them. The solidarity and fraternity toward
the Americas which appeared everywhere in the manifestoes
of the leading revolutionary *juntas* ought to have resolved
itself into an effective means of giving the colonies representation in the central *junta*. The royal order of January 22,
1809, was issued with that objective in view. " Considering
that the vast and precious dominions which Spain possesses
in the Indies are not in reality colonies like those of other
nations or mere *entrepôts*, but an essential and integral part
of the Spanish monarchy, and wishing to tighten in an indissoluble manner the sacred bonds which unite both dominions . . . His Majesty has been pleased to declare that ' the
kingdoms, provinces and islands which form the said dominions ought to have representation close to his royal person
and by means of suitable deputations to become part of the
Central Governing *Junta* of the kingdom '." Unfortunately
the dispositive part of this decree did not correspond with
the principles of fraternity and equality which it proclaimed.
The various kingdoms of America were put in the same

category as the town councils and the little regions of Spain. We shall see shortly how the idea of representation will appear when the Cortes were convoked and how at that time the same error was made of not giving the Americas proportionate representation.

What was the spontaneous reaction of the American people to the French invasion and the enthronement of Joseph Bonaparte? The evidence is unanimous in indicating loyalty to the Spanish monarchy and fervent adherence to Ferdinand VII, leader and symbol in Spain and in America. Furthermore, for some time in the colonies, the rivalry between Creoles and Spaniards had become more marked. The native aristocracy was acquiring what we would call today " class consciousness ". Over and above this rivalry there existed the sentiments of religious unity and monarchic loyalty. The Napoleonic invasion and the position of the king, which was considered legitimate and which was hallowed by popular imagination, awakened everywhere a patriotic feeling for the defense of religious unity and of the unity and integrity of the monarchy. The French, according to the understanding of the Creoles, were going to destroy the first and replace the second. Yet the resurgence of racial and political patriotism could not presuppose the unconditional adherence to the authorities existing in America, nor obedience to the weak and changing revolutionary officials raised to power in the Peninsula.

The acephalism of the throne, like the popular revolution and the formation of independent *juntas* in Spain, confronted the colonies with the problem of political government. A century earlier, during the war of succession (1700-13), the colonies had maintained peaceful obedience to the existing authorities in the hope of a solution to the dynastic problem in Europe. The same policy was urged by the Viceroy Liniers in Buenos Aires; but the circumstances were not the same. The philosophy of the eighteenth century had created a different political *ambience* in the world. In the war of succession, two dynasties and two pretenders confronted each other; and the Spanish people were divided or indifferent. In the war of independence of 1808, the entire nation took arms against the foreign invader, assuming through its *juntas* the government of the state. This semi-democratic government, representative of the Peninsular population, pretended to govern all the Spanish empire with the authority of the king, limiting itself to granting minor participation to the American dominions. However the *juntas* recognized that the colonies were an integral part of the monarchy, which meant that they should enjoy the same rights. The logical consequence of the formation of *juntas* in Spain was the formation of like *juntas* in America and the federation of all of them. But the Spanish revolutionary government did not understand it that way; it continued the subordination of the American people to pre-existing Spanish authorities. The colonies could not accept such a policy. Their loyalty was directed toward the throne and the person of the captive king, but it did not extend to the people of the Peninsula, only a part, like themselves, of the monarchic unity. This principle, felt and spoken everywhere, is the ideologic factor in a series of movements or manifestations which we shall observe in the new world and which will lead to the declaration of independence.

The first effect, in the colonies, of the revolution in Spain was the weakening of the authority of the Peninsular governors and functionaries or the accentuation of the rivalries between the various organs of the administrative structure created by Spain. The *cabildos* felt that their voice must be heard. The *audiencias* affirmed their superiority and their representation of Peninsular interests; and in some cases, subordinate governments denied obedience to superior governments, as in the case of Montevideo. We are in the presence of a real disintegration of the Spanish Empire, and at times, Professor Levene is correct when he explains the independence by this process of disintegration. Naturally, the *cabildo*, the powerful agency of national landed property and the governmental arm enjoying greatest popular prestige, imposed its authority. In Mexico, it is the *cabildo* which affirms loyalty to the king, refusing to recognize any Spanish *junta* and accepting the viceroy only as an interim officer. The Licenciado Verdal said that sovereignty had returned to the people, and as the viceroy inclined to support himself on the neighboring country and on the Creole *cabildo*, the *audiencia* which represented the Peninsular spirit brought on the revolution and deprived him of office (September 15). For the moment the Spanish party triumphed, but the revolutionary seed had been sown. In Venezuela, we observe the same phenomenon of affirmation of the monarchy coinciding with the proposal to form *juntas* like those established in Spain. The *cabildo* frightened the captain-general and the group of Spanish judges, forcing them to surrender all communications received from the French and forcing also a declaration of loyalty to Ferdinand.

In Montevideo the ambition of the Governor, Elio, his enmity for Liniers, and the old rivalry with Buenos Aires developed into an open rebellion against the viceroy on the part of Elio. The *cabildo* of Montevideo, the majority of whose members were Spaniards, declared for Elio, and this triumph of the Spanish element indicated, as in Mexico, governmental disintegration, and opened the field to the Creole party.

Another symptom of this same disintegration is the revolutionary attempt of the Spanish element in Buenos Aires against the viceroy Liniers, whom they considered to be in sympathy with the French cause.

Two things stand out clearly in this historic moment: the unanimous rejection by Peninsular and Creole opinion of the Napoleonic proposals, as revealed in the hostile reception of the special envoys of Napoleon in Mexico, Venezuela and Buenos Aires, and the tendency of the Creole element to make its voice heard and to disavow the constituted authorities on the Peninsula.[1]

American opinion was not seduced by the more or less liberal bases of the project for a constitution, approved at Bayonne, and which included:

(a) Equality of rights with the mother country.
(b) Unrestricted agriculture.
(c) Freedom of commerce for the colonies among themselves and with the mother country.
(d) Suppression of special privileges.
(e) Permanent representation in Madrid and American representatives in the Indies Council.

Certainly, we cannot fail to consider, in the history of American thought the project of Bayonne, because it was to influence the liberal orientation of the Spanish revolution and to further indirectly in the American people the consciousness of their rights.[2]

---

[1] Mitre, *Historia de Belgrano*, 4ª edición, I, 230.
[2] See the *Manifiesto de la Junta de Sevilla*, Cadiz, June 17, 1808; *La Suprema Junta Gubernativa a la Nación Española*, Aranjuez, October 26, 1808.

Chapter VII

THE INSURRECTION OF THE *CABILDOS*

One of the most striking features in the history of Spanish-American Independence is the fact that the revolutionary outbreaks in the different provinces took place nearly simultaneously. If we ignore a few isolated early uprisings, we may say that the years 1809-10 mark the effective beginning of the Revolution. In 1809, outbreaks occurred in Andean America, in territories which had belonged to the old Incan Empire and which later had formed part of the Viceroyalty of Peru. Revolts took place in the *audiencias* of Quito and La Plata, which had only been annexed to the Viceroyalties of Santa Fe and Buenos Aires in the middle of the eighteenth century. Chuquisaca issued a revolutionary pronouncement on May 25th; La Paz took a similar step July 16th, and Quito, also, on August 10th. Unfortunately, these moves came to nothing.

The movement of Chuquisaca merits special mention as representative of the new American attitude toward the Spanish revolution. The factors which determined it were the rivalry between the president and the *audiencia* and the popular suspicion that the authorities were going to hand over the country to the Princess Carlota Joaquina, who as sister of Ferdinand VII, wished to assume the regency of the Spanish Empire during the captivity of the kings. The Princess succeeded in forming a supporting party, more or less appreciable, among the liberals of Buenos Aires. What interests us in the movement of Chuquisaca is its essentially juridical appearance and its philosophical proclamations.

94

This movement was essentially intellectual, a doctoral rebellion. There took part in it the *audiencia* and the university, the toga and the cloister. This party refused to recognize the *junta* of Seville at the time when the power of that body seemed to be consolidated and when other colonies were inclined to recognize it. René Moreno, who has left us an exhaustive history of this movement, characterizes it in the form of a syllogism:

The syllogism with which the doctors made the Upper-Peruvian revolution—and that peripatetic force caused all the brave and not a few of the incautious timid to rush into the public arena—was the following: Major premiss: Colonial vasselage is a tribute due not to Spain but to the person of the legitimate Bourbon King of Spain; Minor premiss: Our legitimately sworn king and natural lord Don Fernando VII abdicated along with all the Bourbon family of Spain, and now he will not return. Conclusion: since the monarchy is legally and definitely without a head because of the vacancy of the throne, the Bonaparte king or any other king which the Spaniards might wish to choose must be disobeyed, the present delegates and mandatories of the extinct sovereign authority should cease to exercise their functions, and this being the case, the high provinces should provide for their own government which should have *interim* status as long as there is no confirmation of the death of our beloved King, Don Fernando VII, and until a legitimate successor to the sovereignty of America presents himself.[1]

The *audiencia* assumes the government in the name of King Ferdinand. The university, the *cabildo* and the populace are carried away by the movement. Intimately related with the movement of Chuquisaca was that of La Paz, on July 16, which was directed against the *intendente* and the bishop. This movement is of exceptional interest. It is

[1] *Últimos días coloniales, Narración*, 385.

peculiar because of the popular and religious character which was given it by the participation of the lower clergy. In the movement of La Paz the logical consequences of the revolutionary principle were carried to extremes. The *mestizo* element predominated in La Paz, and the revolutionary party was almost entirely composed of this element. La Paz advocated a complete rupture with Spain from the beginning. The Charcas party was moderate; that of La Paz was radical. The proclamation to the people of La Paz, July 16, 1809, was the first which declared without quibbling for war with Spain.

One month later there was to break out a similar revolution in another Andean center, led by the Creole aristocracy and the professional men who predominated in the *cabildo*. The ideas which inspired them were defense of the purity of religion and the rights of the king and of the fatherland. In the manifesto of the *junta* of Quito, August 10, 1809, it is stated: " That the same right which Seville has to form an *interim junta* to be supreme in the government of Spain is shared by all of the kingdoms of America. . . . And since the governors were no longer approved, they had, without any doubt, ceased to exercise their functions, and sovereignty had of necessity reverted to the people."

During the same year, in Bogota, the situation did not result in a revolutionary crisis, but the *cabildo* of Santa Fe in protesting against the diminished participation in the government granted to the colonies by the supreme *junta* of Seville, believed it pertinent to affirm certain principles of equality and sovereignty of much consequence in the revolutionary ideology. The *memoria* written by Don Camilo Torres, after affirming that " the inhabitants of America are as much Spaniards as the sons of Don Pelayo, and as much deserving, for this reason, of the dignities, privileges and prerogatives of the rest of the nation as those who, having descended from the mountains, expelled the Moors and then populated the Peninsula ", then affirms the necessity of a meeting of the provincial *juntas* so that the voice of America may be heard in Spain. " If you do not listen then to the Americas, if they do not manifest their desires by means of a competent and worthily authorized representation, the law is not made by them, for it does not have their sanction." The *memoria* concludes by pointing out the perils of a policy which would aim at anything other than eternal separation from Spain.

In the following year, however, the insurrection broke out with renewed force in the capitals of the Viceroyalties and Captaincies-General: Caracas on April 19, Buenos Aires, May 25, Santa Fe, July 20, and Santiago de Chile on September 18.

In all parts, this movement was headed by the *cabildo,* that is, by the Creole aristocracy which wished to supplant the Spanish authorities by *juntas* like those set up in Spain after the fall of Ferdinand VII. In its manner of starting and in its orientation, the Revolution of 1809-10 resembled closely the political movement in Spain. " The Revolution in America ", says Alberdi, " was only another phase of the Spanish Revolution." As far as this period is concerned, the celebrated publicist is right. Mariano Moreno, the soul of the Argentinian Revolution, justified this imitation of Spain by saying, " It may be recalled that all the Spanish provinces were set up together, and that the people of America have equal rights with those in Europe." [2]

2 *La Doctrina Democrática, Biblioteca Argentina,* 204.

The political theory which gave a legitimate aspect to this movement was that sovereignty reverts to the people in the absence of the king. The discussions taking place in the " open *cabildo* " held in Buenos Aires, May 22, clearly stated the application of this theory which, although it was, as Mitre said, perfectly in accord with the monarchic form of government, yet was essentially revolutionary in the conclusions that could logically be drawn from it.[3]

The Bishop of Buenos Aires advanced the idea that America was a dependency of Spain and of the Spanish. The jurist Castelli opposed this view, referring to the oath of loyalty to Ferdinand VII and the text of the Laws of the Indies, which set forth the absolute personal power of the monarch. He affirmed that, in his opinion, it was the people who conferred authority on rulers. The attorney of the *audiencia,* Dr. Villota, although recognizing the principle that the people had the right to look to their own preservation, in the absence of the king, objected to the move taken by Buenos Aires in setting up a new government without the sanction of the other provinces. In answer to this, the other Creole jurist, Juan José Paso, said that the urgency of the circumstances explained and justified the attitude of Buenos Aires. It, as the part of the Spanish Empire advancing into the face of the common danger, had the right to take the initiative in the matter without the delay involved in submitting it to the congress of the other provinces, which would have to be called at once.[4]

Moreno states the theory of popular sovereignty in the following manner: " In this reversion of powers (caused

[3] González Calderón, I, 13.
[4] *Ibid.,* 16.

by the absence of the king) not only does each people re-
assume the authority that all of them, acting together, had
given to the king, but every citizen should be considered
to be in the same state as that existing before the social
contract was entered into. Only from this social pact proceed the mutual obligations that bind vassals to king." [5]
From this idea he proceeds to state the right of the people
" to choose a head, in order to rule themselves according to
whatever political formula the body politic may set up ".
Referring especially to the *juntas,* he says that they themselves might assume the representative sovereignty which,
in the absence of the king, had vanished. In the North,
Camilo Torres expressed a similar thought. Torres was the
guiding spirit of the Revolution in New Granada just as
Moreno was in the Argentinian movement. He said: " With
the monarchy dissolved and Spain lost, are we not in the
condition of sons who become of age at the death of the
father of the family? Each one enters into the enjoyment
of his individual rights and sets up his own hearth and
governs himself." [6]

The very same concept is found in the act passed by the
municipal government of Caracas, which reads: " In such
a case, natural law and all other laws dictate the necessity
of providing means of self-preservation and defense and
of setting up inside of these nations themselves a system of
government which will take care of the needs we have
mentioned and exercise the sovereignty, which by the same
token has reverted to the people, in agreement with the
wise provisions of the early Spanish Constitution and the
maxims which have been set forth in innumerable papers

[5] *Doctrina Democrática,* 252ff.
[6] Mancini, *Bolívar,* 71.

by the former supreme *junta.*" [7] The same idea appeared in the Chilean revolution.

The anonymous author of the *Catecismo Político Cristiano,* said:

" The Americans were able and were forced to form provincial *juntas* like those which the provinces of Spain formed dependent on the central *junta* in which they were represented. The governors of America like the governors of Spain lost their authority and jurisdiction as soon as the prince who delegated them disappeared. In this case the authority to nominate them or to form the provincial government which might be best adapted for the common wellbeing had devolved on the inhabitants and provinces of America as well as on those of Spain."

[7] Gil Fortoul, *op. cit.,* I, 118.

CHAPTER VIII

THE CORTES OF CADIZ AND THE PROBLEMS OF
AMERICA

The insurrection of the *cabildos* in Spain and in America necessarily tended to a superior integration, that is to say to the realization of national unity or of national unities, given the system of national differentiation which was followed in the Spanish Colonial Empire. Popular sovereignty did not exhaust itself in its local organism; nor was the formation of local executive *juntas* sufficient. It was necessary to create, with the representation of all the people, a body which might represent national sovereignty. In Spain such a movement was not an innovation but a restoration, for it presupposed the return to the purest and most glorious national tradition: the convocation of the Cortes of the Kingdom (Cortes del Reino).[1]

In America the movement for integration by the convocation of Assemblies appeared, and it followed the great national groups of Viceroyalties and Captaincies-General. With revealing uniformity the initial centers of the revolution did not attempt to form a federal congress of all America nor to submit themselves simply and completely to the Cortes or the Parliament which might be convoked in Spain. The assemblies which were called, or the mere projects of assemblies, attached themselves to the Kingdoms: La Plata, Chile, New Granada, Venezuela and Mexico. Nothing reveals more clearly that at the moment

[1] E. Gómez Baquero, *Nacionalismo e Hispanismo,* 237.

of the breaking out of the revolution in America there did not exist a continental consciousness but diverse national consciousnesses.

Naturally, the Spanish *junta,* and soon the Council of the Regency, were not able to conceive of the Spanish Monarchy as an aggregation of autonomous peoples. For the leaders of the Spanish revolution the Kingdoms of America, although they were not mere *entrepôts* or colonies and formed an integral part of the Spanish Monarchy, according to the declaration which we have cited, were not, nevertheless, diverse entities which might be united only by the "golden link" [2] of the King's person. The American Kingdoms were elements of the Spanish nation and not just constituent parts of the monarchy. There were not various nations within one monarchy but a single nation, formed of the Peninsula and the Dominions across the waters, under a single monarch.

Misunderstanding was, therefore, inevitable between Spain and America, in spite of their being united at that moment for both the principle of liberty and the sovereignty of, and the fidelity to, Ferdinand VII. The conflict which was waged between Spain and America from 1809 to 1813 was not a conflict of old with new ideas. Within the new *régime* of liberty and of popular sovereignty which Spain and America proclaimed, the conflict came to center on the concept of the nation and on the constitution of the Spanish Monarchy. If the Spanish politicians of the Cortes of Cadiz had, like the author of the project which was attributed to the Count of Aranda, or like Godoy himself, sought an alliance or a new union with the national organisms

[2] English in text. (Translator's note.)

whose outlines were just appearing in America, they might have preserved the Spanish Empire in the form of a federation of peoples under the direction and safeguard of the Monarchic principle.[3]

Neither the Spanish liberals of the English school like Jovellanos, nor those of the French school like Quintana and Arguelles examined the problem with this criterion. They were at bottom hegemonists, imperialists and unitarians. The only idea which appealed to them was to form a single representative body in which Spain and America would be joined in an indivisible sovereignty. Naturally, within this plan American representation would be given only to those countries in which revolutionary *juntas* had not been proclaimed, that is to say to those which had continued to submit to the ancient Peninsular authorities.

There was assigned to America only one deputy for each of its Kingdoms and Captaincies-General. The *cabildo* of Bogota proposed that six be allowed for each viceroyalty and four for each Captaincy-General; and, each city which was the capital of a province or the seat of a bishopric, should have one deputy in addition.

This last criterion predominated in the Regency, without doubt in the effort to conciliate American public opinion. The Regency decree said: " There will come to take part in the national representation of the extraordinary Cortes of the Kingdom deputies from the provinces of New Granada, Peru, Santa Fe, Buenos Aires; and from the Captaincies-General of Puerto Rico, Cuba, Santo Domingo, Guatemala, Provinces of the Interior, Venezuela, Chile and the Philip-

[3] See Alvaro Flórez Estrada, *Examen Imparcial de las Diferencias de la América con la España,* 16, 23, 36.

pines. . . . These deputies will be one for the chief city
of each district. . . . The election will be by vote of the
Ayuntamiento of each capital which will name three native
born individuals of the province gifted with probity, talent
and education and exempt from all reproach, and he who
is drawn first shall be the deputy to the Cortes." [4]

In spite of this important modification relative to the
representation of the American Kingdoms in the central
organism, it was not possible to prevent the conflict caused
by the pre-existence of revolutionary *juntas,* which substituting themselves for the Spanish authorities, had assumed
the government in Mexico, in Rio de La Plata, in New
Granada, and in Venezuela. The Peninsula leaders did not
wish to negotiate with these *juntas* nor would the *juntas*
accept representation except on the basis of the recognition
of the legitimacy of their authority.

Faced with the impossibility of obtaining representation
from the provinces in which revolutionary *juntas* had been
formed and given the need for immediate action, they proceeded to name deputies chosen by the Hispano-American
residents in Europe. The American deputies numbered
thirty, thus in practice the representation of the ancient colonies was reduced.

The first act of the Cortes had to be the legalization or
proclamation of the mother principle of the popular rising, that is to say national sovereignty, and this sovereignty

---

[4] The Historian Groot makes these comments: " We see here
two things: One, that the number of American representatives was
considerable, not being one for each province but one for each chief
city of a district of each province which is divided into districts;
and, two, that the election of deputies conducted by the *cabildos*
was not subject to the approval of the authorities." *Historia
Eclesiástica y Civil de la Nueva Granada,* II, 166f.

was assumed in its fullness by the Cortes. Muñoz Torrero was the Corypheus of this declaration to which the Americans contributed with their votes and discourses.

Concerning the relations between Spain and her former dominions, the Decree of October 15, 1810 took its inspiration from an absolutely unitarian criterion with every idea discarded which would involve the acceptance of the federation of nuclei or their uniting by means of the bond of monarchy. Here are the words of the Decree:

> The General and Extraordinary *Cortes* confirm the incontestable concept that the Spanish dominions of both hemispheres form one *single and identical Monarchy, one single and identical Nation and one single family* and that by the same token the inhabitants of these European dominions and of those beyond the sea have the same rights as the inhabitants of the Peninsula.

In a word the equality of individuals was proclaimed without regard for the collective differences created by the groups which had tended to develop their own national character through a period of evolution of three centuries. The Spanish Monarchy and the Spanish Nation, integrated by its dominions, thus appeared to be an indivisible unity. This was the unanimous opinion of the liberals of the year twelve (*doceañistas*).

Having defined the concept of sovereignty, the Cortes continued its declarations and pronouncements within the liberal program. By a decree of February 11, there was established equality of representation for Spaniards and Americans, freedom of agriculture and equal opportunity for public office. By decree of November 10, freedom of the press was established; by decree of December 9, the Inquisition was abolished.

In regard to the form of government the liberalism of 1812 took its inspiration from the French constitution of 1791; in endeavoring to conciliate popular sovereignty with hereditary monarchy it is beyond question that the minds of the year 1812 were influenced by the famous letter of the Abbé Raynal who argued for the existence of an executive power which would not be a simple designation of the legislative assembly.

Jovellanos, a great admirer of English institutions, recommended setting up a Parliament with two chambers, an upper chamber in which the nobility and the clergy would be represented and a lower house elected by popular vote; as a matter of fact the division of representation corresponded to the tradition of the ancient Spanish Cortes.[5] But the wise opinion of Jovellanos was not followed, and the *junta* decided, contrary to the recommendation of the commission of the Cortes, for the popular principle of the single chamber without representation of the estates, explaining that there existed insuperable difficulties in the application of the other practice in the present state of the Nation and above all in the extension of it to the American provinces. In America, Arguelles said, there are no noblemen; it was not possible in America in that period to elevate a class by conferring titles or knighthood in order that it might assume the powers of the metropolitan nobility. This state of affairs would automatically eliminate the upper chamber if it was to be limited to this category. To omit this estate from the representation allowed the provinces beyond the seas was equivalent to declaring the colonies inferior to the mother

[5] E. del Valle, *Los diputados de Buenos Aires en las Cortes de Cádiz*, 18.

country, humiliating them and depriving them of the kind of prestige of which men of all countries and of all times have not permitted themselves to be deprived.[6]

The opportunist argument of Arguelles coincided with the fundamental orientation of the liberalism of 1812 for which a second chamber of noble or religious character had an anti-democratic character. The uni-cameral principle favored by the Cortes of Cadiz will influence American constitutional law as is proved by the similar uni-cameral clauses of the Constitution of Apatzingan and of the Peruvian Constitution of 1823.

We must pause for a moment to consider the important matter of the equality between Spaniards and Americans which was championed brilliantly by the deputies of the Kingdom of Peru, Ramón Feliú and Vicente Morales Duárez. Feliú applied the theory of the sovereignty of the provinces and of individual sovereignty: American representation was to be proportional to the sum of the sovereignties of the American provinces and proportional to the sum of its individuals. The pacification of America, said Feliú, is quite proDable and even certain if we grant this request and others; but if we deny it the situation is desperate. Morales Duárez established equality, invoking in addition to political reasons, arguments of juridical character. He invoked the decree of September 1529, included in the first law of the first chapter of the third book, which said that the Americas are incorporated in and united to the Crown of Castille; they had been neither the slaves nor the vassals of the Crown of Spain.[7]

[6] *Ibid.*, 20.
[7] *Discursos de los Diputados de América*, Lima, 1812.

Concerning the vote of the colored peoples, or the half-castes, Uria, the deputy for Guadalajara, proposed only the requirements of property and profession. The deputy for Costa-Rica, Castillo, alluded to the difficulty of taking a census and praised the half-castes of America in these terms: " The half-castes are the people in America who, almost exclusively, farm, work the mines and bear arms." The deputy Arispe repeats figures which demonstrate that the half-castes form the largest part of the population as well as the most laborious and that they are remarkable for their peacefulness. Salazar, the deputy for Lima, attacked the article which limited the vote of the half-castes as vague and as fraught with dangerous consequences, and he affirmed that the principal part of the armed forces was always composed of this class. Feliú, deputy for Lima, denied the supposed difference of opinion among the Americans on this point and noted the injustice of a requirement for them which did not extend to foreigners.

We must refer also with special emphasis to the resolutions adopted by the Cortes of Cadiz in respect to the native population. The rights of the Indians were eloquently defended by the Peruvian deputy, Vicente Morales Duárez, member of the constitutional committee who became the presiding officer of the Cortes.[8] But we find the true inspiration for the policy of the Cortes of Cadiz in this matter in the writings of Abad y Queipo, author of the famous report subscribed to by Bishop Antonio de San Miguel and praised by Humboldt to which we have referred so many times. The Cortes abolished the forced service of the Indians (*mita*) and the tribute, and declared the Indian

[8] *Colección de discursos de los Diputados de América,* Lima, 1812.

proprietor of the land. They stopped only at the question of the division of great rural estates (*latifundios*), very advanced points in the agrarian program of Abad y Queipo; but although they did not adopt these radical proposals, they charged the provincial *diputaciones* created by the constitution with the accomplishment of a series of measures tending to make effective the division of community land, equipping them for cultivation and providing funds for the community banks. In short, there was proposed a practical program designed to bring about the development of agriculture among the aborigines and to give them the means of consolidating the community lands which had been divided.[9]

The work of the Cortes of Cadiz in respect to the American aborigines coincides with or was inspired by the measures taken by the revolutionary movement of Mexico and of South America and resulted in extending the emancipation movement; and we have already seen the influence which they had on some of the measures taken by San Martín and on the famous decrees concerned with the indigenous class signed by Bolivar during his stay at Cuzco. Moreover, when the absolute monarchy was reestablished by the decree of December 15, 1814, which dissolved the democratic town councils (*ayuntamientos*) and reestablished the society and the ancient privileges of the Indians, that is to say their communities, it did not reestablish the tribute.

A detailed study of the Constitution of Cadiz is not within the scope of this book, but we must examine those institutions which passed from Spain to America like the provincial *diputación*, which with the object of administra-

[9] *La constitución de 1812 en Nueva España.*

tive decentralization was incorporated in the constitution both for Spain and for America. These provincial *diputaciones* differed from the *cabildos* in that they were of popular origin, being elected like the deputies to the Cortes, while the *cabildos* were of an aristocratic and oligarchic nature.

Besides this democratic character the provincial *diputación*, as it functioned in America, tended to consolidate the administrative unities formed by the old cities, the seats of bishoprics, the capital of the *intendencia* or the ancient *partidos*. The Constitution of Cadiz changed the character of the *cabildo* which had been an oligarchic institution and provided for its election by popular suffrage.

The Constitution of Cadiz had only an indirect ideological influence on those territories which were touched by the revolutionary wave like Venezuela, New Granada, Chile and La Plata. The return to the absolute régime and the abolition of the Constitution coincided with the reestablishment of the Spanish rule in Chile, in Quito, in Venezuela and New Granada and the near extinction of the revolutionary movement in Mexico.

In Peru the ideologic movement of the Cortes of Cadiz had an enormous repercussion. José I. Moreno, one of the most distinguished professors of San Carlos, prepared a commentary of this political charter and considered it to be the type of mixed government recommended by Montesquieu. And the young liberals, like Sánchez Carrión and José María Corbacho who were later to become fanatic republicans and partisans of absolute independence, praised it without stint. The liberal mentality of Peru was *reformista* as Riva Agüero proved in his essay on Baquíjano, and as Vidaurre affirmed in his *American Letters*.[10]

[10] *Cartas Americanas*, II, 66.

The university and the *cabildo* applauded the measures taken by the Cortes of Cadiz in respect to the Inquisition.

Freedom of the press appeared as a reality in Peru in the publication of the periodicals *El Peruano, El Investigador* and *El Argos Constitucional*.[11]

In Mexico, according to Justo Sierra, the provisions of the Constitution of Cadiz were reflected in the institutional movement, principally in the work of the provincial deputations which represented an effort at decentralization.[12]

NOTE

Here are the words of the historian Priestley summing up the treatment of American problems by the Cortes of Cadiz: " The American delegates to the Cortes on December 16 presented to it for consideration the aspirations of the people of Spanish America, as they understood them. Their demands were made under eleven points. (1) They demanded equality with Spain in representation in the Cortes for the American realms, on a population basis. This the Cortes rejected, alleging fear of the Indian populations. (2) Their demand that agriculture, manufacturing, and the mechanical trades should be freed from all restrictions, was accepted without debate. But their proposals (3) that commerce should be absolutely free, whether carried in Spanish or foreign bottoms, (4) that free trade should be granted between America and Asia as well, and (5) that all restrictions of this kind should be immediately abolished, all brought forth the warmest discussion, as a result of which it was decided to take no action until the advice of the American commercial and governmental bodies could be ascertained. The pretension (6) that all government monopolies should be abolished, with compensation in special duties on all monopolized articles freed, was also postponed, the only lucrative monopoly then being

---

[11] A collection of these periodicals is to be found in the Bingham Collection in the Yale University library.

[12] *Colección leyes y decretos, México, 1829. Constitución de 1812 en la Nueva España.* I. Montiel y Duarte, *Derecho público mexicano.* Introduction, p. 5.

that of tobacco. The suggestion, (7) that the working of American quicksilver mines should be made free was adopted without debate, as was the proposal (8) that all Americans, whether Indian or white, were to be given the same political rights as Spaniards. But when it came to granting (9) that at least half the offices in the several kingdoms should be given to natives, postponement was again taken. The same action was taken upon the proposal (10) to create a nominating board to control the equitable distribution of political offices. The eleventh point, which called for the re-establishment of the Jesuit order, was almost unanimously rejected; many of the American delegates themselves opposed it, though a generation earlier the Marquis of Croix had said of the Jesuits, when they were expelled from all Spanish America, that they absolutely controlled the minds and hearts of the Mexican people. *The Mexican Nation*, 227-228.

CHAPTER IX

FROM SOVEREIGNTY TO ABSOLUTE INDEPENDENCE

In spite of the vigorous doctrine implied in the insurrection of the *cabildos*; the affirmation of the principle of popular sovereignty which carried with it the logical conclusion of absolute independence, the *juntas* in America limited themselves to saying that they assumed the government only to preserve the rights of the sovereign. In all these manifestoes there was an unmistakable tone of more or less strict loyalty to the King.[1] It has been believed that this tone was a clever recourse of the directing minds, who did not wish to alarm the masses among whom the monarchic and religious sentiment was still very strong—or perhaps it was an effort to avoid international complications, chiefly with England who was then allied with the Spanish Monarch.

Samper, who has written very interestingly in reviewing the revolutionary movement, establishes a difference existing between the philosophic or directive element, which did not favor loyalty to the king, and the popular element which was ingenuously sincere in its protestations of allegiance. In reality the problem is even more complicated. When Monteagudo said that the Revolution commenced without plan and continued without method, he was at least partially correct. The important consideration in the be-

[1] The *junta* of La Paz, although repeating the formula of the preservation of the King's rights, put the rights of man first.

ginning was simply the establishment of a separate government and framing of a constitution for each province.

The question as to what relation these governments should bear to the Crown of Spain was of secondary importance. The matter remained pending with all possibilities open to consideration in its settlement. In no one better than in Moreno can we see this state of mind which existed in the early period of the Revolution. For this point of view, his *Miras del Congreso* is a representative document. He saw with all clarity that the logical consequence of the principle of popular sovereignty was the declaration of absolute independence. But at the same time, he points out all the dangers involved in this far-reaching step. He warns that such a declaration of itself would not produce the radical transformation of ideas and customs that such a government called for. It may be said that he looked forward to the establishment of a new authority and the framing of a constitution as valuable training in self-government, but on the other hand, he did not desire to place himself in open opposition to the sentiment of loyalty to the captive king. He saw, however, that the constitution that was to be voted on would ultimately bring with it opposition to this feeling. Thus being confined to loyalty to the monarchic principle he contemplates all possible solutions, such as the naming of a regent from the royal family or the election of a central *junta* like that in Spain. He later discusses the relations among the various local governments in America, that is, the idea of an American congress. He points out the inconvenience and impossibility of maintaining such an organization.

Outside of these points, Moreno presents no concrete or constructive solution. It is the embryonic period of the revolution; questions and possibilities were the order of the day. In pointing out this fact, we do not wish to criticise the great Argentinian. Ricardo Rojas points out that Moreno did not clearly outline the constitutional problems that caused bloody conflict shortly after his death. His work, certainly enormously important, consisted in propaganda for, and the application of, the principle of popular sovereignty within an opportunist program.[2]

The same limited plan is found in all the other revolutionary centers. The instructions given to the Venezuelan commissioners sent to England reveal the same limited purpose: to safeguard political liberty, to defend the country, reduce duties, simplify the administration of justice, develop commerce—all without giving up loyalty to Ferdinand VII, alliance with the Spanish patriots or sympathy with American interests.[3]

The revolution carried hidden in itself the process which was to cause a definite break with Spain, that is, absolute independence. But before it could proceed to this second stage, it had first to pass through a period of preparation, varying in the different countries on account of the greater or lesser clarity of vision of the directing forces as well as because of more objective factors. The Colombian Revolution reached this stage before the revolutions in either

[2] It is only fair to state that the *Miras del Congreso* was of the year 1810 and that Moreno died the following year. Every consideration leads one to the conclusion that if he had lived, he would have been a partisan of absolute independence, like Nariño, Bolivar and Monteagudo.

[3] Mancini, *Bolivar,* 312. Bolivar, then a delegate of the Venezuelan *junta* in London, neglecting his instructions, sought the help of England for independence.

Argentina or Mexico. In La Plata, the fervent propaganda of Monteagudo directed towards Independence, and Artigas strove for it in his celebrated instructions of 1813; but, on the other hand, others, such as Gorriti thought it the most dangerous step which could be taken and one which would retard the progress of the cause, partly because of the internal situation, but largely on account of international difficulties.[4] This opinion was the prevailing one in the Assembly of 1813, which nevertheless, did away with the oath of allegiance to Ferdinand. Only in 1816 was the independence of La Plata definitely declared by the Congress of Tucuman. In Mexico, the Congress of Chilpansingo declared independence in 1813 largely because of the influence of Morelos.

The first declaration of absolute independence was made by Venezuela where Bolivar was the decisive factor. The Congress of Caracas, like all assemblies of its type, was slow and hesitating in taking such a decisive step.

In contrast with the Congress of Caracas, was the Patriotic Society, a truly jacobin club, founded by Miranda and Bolivar. Bolivar very eloquently expressed the fundamental ideas of the revolution in speaking before this club. If the same ideas were being expressed by Nariño, in New Granada, and Monteagudo, in La Plata, none could state these arguments more clearly or in bolder relief than did Bolivar in his famous speech. These are his words: " In the National Congress they are discussing what course should be taken. And what do they say? That we should commence with a confederation—as if we all are not confederated against foreign tyranny! That we should consider the re-

4 *Reflecciones*, 342. Instructions of Jujuy to his deputy.

sults of Spanish policy—What does it matter to us whether Spain sells her slaves to Bonaparte or keeps them herself, if we are resolved to be free? These doubts are the sad effect of our ancient chains. That we should prepare for great projects with calm—Are not three hundred years of calm sufficient? The patriotic committee respects the National Congress, as it should, but the Congress should hear the Committee, the center of enlightenment and of all the revolutionary interests. Without fear let us lay the cornerstone of South American Independence. To hesitate is to be lost." [5]

Under the pressure of the Patriotic Society and convinced by the eloquent words of Bolivar, the Assembly proclaimed the independence, which was then promulgated under the date of July 14, 1811. The example of Caracas was followed later by New Granada. The act of federation of the united provinces proclaimed absolute independence on November 27, 1811.

Thus in the first moment of the South-American Revolution, Bolivar was already present with the decisive thought and influence that could not successfully be opposed

[5] Gil Fortoul, I, 145.

Chapter X

BOLIVAR AND THE REVOLUTION

The sentiment of the colonies had crystallized into an intense feeling of local nationalism which was co-existent with the old loyalty to the Spanish Crown. This being the case, the projects for complete independence, supported only by foreign forces, could not gain ground. Nor could the attempt to change the sovereignty in favor of a third power succeed, although such a change would favor local interests. This colonial nationalism, as we have defined and presented it, was to give a truly American character to the Revolution later. To be successful, the Revolution had to develop from purely local origins.

History confirms what we have just said. The first attempts of Miranda to liberate America, based as they were on external support, failed miserably; not only through errors and adverse circumstances, but also because they did not conform to the principle of national spontaneity.[1] The people were not moved to action by a stimulus that came from outside; they were probably afraid that success would mean only a change of masters. Additional confirmation is seen in the failure of the English expedition to La Plata, the so-called Reconquest. Neglecting the economic advantages at stake, the Creoles of Buenos Aires, moved by a vigorous national feeling, reconquered the capital of the La Plata viceroyalty, repulsing subsequent English expeditions. This triumph was the culmination of the patriotic spirit.

[1] This is also the opinion of Gil Fortoul, *op. cit.*, I, 113.

In spite of obvious differences, Miranda's expedition and the British invasion of Buenos Aires, were both parts of the same English policy. Their failure is explained by the existence of a national spirit in Venezuela and in Argentina. In the first instance, this spirit did not come to the support of Miranda's noble but premature attempt, and in the second it sounded the call to arms against a confident and arrogant invader.

Regarding the attitude of the Creoles of Buenos Aires against the English invasion Varela says:

" The political consequences of the reconquest of Buenos Aires were highly important. The colonist had disappeared, and he had been replaced by the citizen conscious of the rights which permitted him to enjoy an independent fatherland and the freedom which it offered him; he was conscious also of his duties, which obliged him to defend with his blood and with his life this fatherland, to which he owed all, and his own hearth established in it." [2]

In short, it is obviously necessary to rectify the viewpoint that has dominated many historians in regard to the origins of the South American Revolution. Instead of giving greater emphasis to external causes, we must consider more closely the inherent or internal cause, namely conscious nationalism. We must discard the mistaken tendency to explain the extremely complex progress of the revolution solely by economic causes, the desire for free trade, the political ambitions of the Creoles, favorable international circumstances, such as the invasion of Spain, or by the effect of French Revolutionary principles, or by imitation of the American Revolution.

To all of these causes, we must add the existence of a national spirit and the ripening of a feeling of patriotism.

[2] *Historia Constitucional de la República Argentina,* I, 33.

Lastly, to make the story complete, we must now emphasize a decisive element, which positivist sociology has never been able to explain, the mysterious rebirth of the energy and of the heroic will of the race, which after centuries of somnolence, miraculously surged forth again in the performance of great exploits such as the conquest—great on account of the difficult nature and extent of its theatre, but even greater in its moral significance. I have had the opportunity, in a paper on the *Centennial of Independence*,[3] of developing more fully this explanation of the Independence—the explanation we call the *voluntaristic*, in contrast to the *economic* explanation of Ingenieros the *intellectualistic* of the majority of writers, and the *international* theory of Lord Bryce.

The move for independence became evident simultaneously in all the expanse of the colonial Empire. It may be said, however, that there were three principal foci, one in Mexico and two in South America: the Colombian movement headed by Bolivar, and the Argentine. These foci correspond to the great political entities of the colonial organization: the Viceroyalties of Mexico, Santa Fe, and Buenos Aires. The other unit, the Viceroyalty of Peru, at this period, represents the Spanish resistance. But it is unjust to censure Peru for the part it played, because it was determined beforehand by historic forces. Peru was the nucleus of the Spanish military and political power, just as it had been the great aboriginal empire before. In the first period of the struggle, the directing Spanish element could effectively control the revolution within that immediate area by drawing on the inexhaustible hordes of natives.

[3] Rice Institute Pamphlet. Houston, Texas, October, 1923.

Powerful forces, in Peru, as well as in the other Spanish territories, were in operation, tending to develop the national feeling towards a desire for simple autonomy. In spite of the serious difficulties placed in its way by the immense Spanish power and the intellectual orientation we have indicated, the spirit of insurrection in Peru gave signs of being as noble and as strong as in the other regions.

It was in Peruvian territory that the native uprising led by Tupac Amaru took place. This event is the oldest antecedent of the Revolution. From 1805 to 1819, conspiracy followed conspiracy, some of them as important as that of Pumacahua which, according to the historian Riva Agüero, corresponds in temper to the Mexican one of Hidalgo and of Morelos.[4]

Neither should it be forgotten that the assistance of Peru decided the battle of Pichincha, which completed the liberating movement in the North, nor that by their tenacity and heroism, the Upper Peruvian guerillas, contributed to the consolidation of liberty in the South. Finally, Peruvian troops and leaders were of paramount importance in the battles of Junin and Ayacucho. Peru was not the passive field in which converged the Colombian and Argentine movements, but the favorable theatre in which these forces merged with those formed from its own people.

The movement in Mexico was principally a popular insurrection, or, better, an uprising in the rural communities. Although the spirit of independence, as well as mere autonomy, was very strong in the Creole aristocracy of the

---

[4] *La historia en el Perú,* 465. See also García's " Sentido simpático de nuestra historia" (*Mercurio Peruano,* Nos. 56, 57) for an exposition of this historic rôle of Peru.

cities, the action began in the country and under the direction of the clergy.

The popular uprising had been defeated before the Creole forces, converted to the idea of Independence, made an agreement with the Spanish element on the basis of the monarchic system. Thus, the Mexican movement is characterized by two features: the popular and democratic impulse of the rural uprising, and the conservative and monarchical direction which established the independence.

The eminent Mexican historian, Justo Sierra, makes evident the popular character of the movements headed by Hidalgo and Morelos and of the armies they raised. The patriotic party, according to Sierra, was made up of part of the higher clergy, all the lower clergy, the Mexican personnel of the administration, a majority of the Creoles, an immense majority of the *mestizos,* and the mass of the natives.[5]

The failure of the popular uprising and the monarchic form under which Mexican independence materialized, took away from the Mexican situation the rich and varied elements which are so evident in South America.

In La Plata, the center of the movement was the viceregal capital. There the Creole aristocracy and the popular element of the cities were the joint defenders and advancers of the revolutionary ideology. Revolt also appeared in the rural sections. This movement was to produce the leaders who later rose in the North and in the *Banda Oriental.* The revolution became stronger day by day, developing an effective military organization. The tendency to spread all over the country became more and more evi-

[5] *Évolution Mexicaine,* I, 68.

dent. The centripetal force was to give it a truly American character, consolidating the movement and engendering a constructive political program on the part of the directors.

Let us note that these factors came at different times and in different places. The ideology of, and the propaganda for, the revolution are represented by Moreno and Monteagudo. The rural insurrection is represented in Artigas and Guemes, the former opposing the rule of Buenos Aires. The national military organization is typified by Belgrano; the spread of the movement and the development of the American army, by San Martín; the constructive thought, by the work of Rivadavia, which found its highest expression in the Constitution of 1826.

The Revolution in Colombia has all the richness of various factors and elements which we have observed in the case of La Plata: intellectual leadership for the Revolution in the cities; popular uprisings in the country which at first were loyal to the King, but later joined the Revolution; national military organization; American influences, and lastly, constructive political thought. But these elements, far from becoming more separated all the time, became concentrated and exalted in a single man, in a prodigious personality, a synthesis which was to give them a supreme and compelling unity. This man is Bolivar. His speeches and proclamations are those of Moreno and Monteagudo intensified; he organized armies like those Belgrano commanded, and with the marvelous versatility which Rodó so masterfully described, headed the mass of plainsmen which submitted with Páez, thus embodying the characters of both San Martín and Artigas. From the very beginning, his work appears to be of American character. He liberates Venezuela from New Granada, then again, New Granada from Venezuela. He invades Quito and triumphs in Peru. In the very beginning, also, he has a clear vision of the American world and of the lines of thought which ultimately were expressed at Angostura. These various diverse elements, by being concentrated in him, did not become weaker, but were intensified. Independence reached in him its highest expression, when, as a culmination to the local plans, he added a plan for international organization, a program for American union and solidarity.

The La Plata revolution was broad in its scope and American in character. With Monteagudo it followed the idea of continental organization. Later it followed a nationalistic current under Rivadavia. Meanwhile in Bolivar the idea of a permanent American union had been constantly kept in the foreground.

Having studied the background of the period and the questions involved, we can make a more detailed study of Bolivar's ideas for national and international organization. In making such an investigation, we must lay aside predetermined conceptions of right and left. A kind of political mysticism, a belief in the miraculous virtue of certain institutions, has perturbed and colored the criticisms of many who deal with Bolivar. There is also another error to avoid, that of setting forth Bolivar's thought as absolutely unified and consistent in development. Bolivar's thought covered a trajectory of twenty years, it forms a true parabola, in which we have to observe the ascension, the zenith, and the inevitable fall. In this course, objective and subjective influences determine notable variations.

At the close of the eighteenth century, the first manifestations of a political philosophy appeared in Spanish America Two well-defined trends were evident, one progressive or reforming and the other revolutionary. The reforming trend presupposed the continuance of Hispanic unity by a monarchy or a federation of monarchies, and was closely linked with the intellectual movement of the time of Carlos III, as personified in Aranda, Campomanes and, above all, Jovellanos. Their disciples were such American reformists as Baquíjano, Villava, San Miguel, Abad y Queipo, Salas, Arango, Belgrano, and Vidaurre. Revolutionary ideas, on the other hand, found their inspiration primarily in the independence of the United States and, later, in the French Revolution; this school of thought was, therefore, more directly connected with the political principles of the latter countries. Viscardo y Guzmán, Espejo, Nariño, and, especially, Miranda, represented the radical or revolutionary movement, or the desire for absolute independence. Their program was to break with Spain; its logical conclusion, to establish the republican form of government in separate nations. Miranda, however, proposed a monarchy including all Spanish America. As for Bolivar, conditions in Venezuela, on the one hand, and circumstances of his life and education, on the other, placed him from an early age in direct contact with revolutionary or radical influences.

In a letter addressed to Santander in May 1825, Bolivar refutes the statements of Mollien in regard to his education. After allusions to Rodríguez, Bello, and Padre Andújar, his first teachers, and to his studies in the Academia de San Fernando in Madrid, he says: " Certainly I am learned neither in the philosophy of Aristotle nor in the criminal code, but it may well be that M. Mollien has not studied so closely as I, Locke, Condillac, Buffon, D'Alembert, Helvetius, Montesquieu, Mably, Filangieri, Lalande,

Rousseau, Voltaire, Rollin, Berthot. . . ." [6] These words show that, in contradistinction to those who incorporated new ideas into traditional philosophy or harmonized the two, Bolivar, from early youth, was dominated by eighteenth century thought, assimilated from original sources, and uncolored by the adaptations of Spanish reformists. Education and environment and, let us add, temperament were all contributing factors in Bolivar's radical and revolutionary attitude. His deep affection for his native land, with the tremendous influence of Humboldt and the feats and warlike program of Miranda, completed the work. All this explains the unique position of Bolivar from the time of the first insurrections, as compared with that of other American leaders who long had felt the weight of reforming or evolutionary theories. Little by little, at a rate which varied in the different countries, the reformists became radicals or revolutionists; in Bolivar the revolutionist was apparent from the first.

Within the bounds of a general orientation, the thought of Bolivar displays moments of hesitation and even contradiction, due to the fundamental feature of his mental make-up, a duality caused by two elements which compose his character. He is a dreamer and a realist, a poet and a man of action. Bolivar being thus constituted, his thought will not have absolute logic or harmony, but it will not be less great on this account. On the contrary, this conflict in his make-up will emphasize the human element and lend us the key to the tragedy of his life. This duality and this conflict in Bolivar's ideology make it more representative of the land and of American history.

[6] V. Lecuna, *Cartas del Libertador*, IV, 337.

This feature is the fundamental characteristic of his mentality. Unamuno observes that Bolivar's cult of glory makes him similar to Don Quixote. His heroic energy and his indomitable will, his qualities as a doer, are explained by his Spanish ancestry. He is one of the *conquistadores* of the sixteenth century reincarnate and imbued with the new humanistic ideal. His education added elements of intellectualism and rationalism, and there was still the exaltation and lyricism of Rousseau in his make-up. Bolivar is, because of this, the first of our romantic writers. Humboldt brought to him the feeling of admiration for the magnificent natural environment of America, while Napoleon gave him the fascinating example of the military hero and political creator.

Rousseauism was added to Quixotism, accentuating his tendency to identify his person with his mission. Besides these dreams, besides the romantic rapture which was reflected in his exploits and in his style, there is, in wondrous contrast, a profoundly realistic vision of circumstances, of facts, and of men. His inspired perception penetrated into the most hidden things, he saw the most obscure detail of the confused situation.

No one else in all America saw so clearly; no other could paint its life so vigorously or in such bold relief. This clear vision inspired all his political ideas and explains his originality and the manner in which his plans conformed with the needs of the moment and with the historic method. Again we point out that this realism was his birthright as a Spaniard, it is the essential attribute of the race, it is the realism of Cervantes, the realism of the picaresque novel, of the pictures of Velásquez, of the tapestries of Goya; it is above all, the realism of the great men of action which

Spain has produced: like Cortez in military emprise, like the mystics Ignatius Loyola or Teresa of Avila.

Rousseau added to Don Quixote and pure realism gives us two Bolivars, not only separate but at times opposed. Art has known how to present the two phases of Bolivar with an intuition which has been lacking, perhaps, in biographers and historians. The Bolivar of the statue of Caracas and of that of Lima, triumphant on his horse, which rears arrogantly, is the exalted Bolivar, he of the dreams of greatness, the Bolivar of the delirium of Chimborazo, of the sublime rapture of Potosi. The Bolivar of Bogota, sculptured by Tenerani and described in the immortal ode of Miguel Antonio Caro; defeated, sad, anxiety in his appearance, hands in repose, the sword inert, is the Bolivar who bore in his eyes the weary vision of the sad reality of America, and in the droop of his lips, the bitterness of all disappointments, the Bolivar of the tardy repentance, of the prophetic thunder, and of the pessimistic predictions. Nevertheless, in both aspects he reflects all that is deepest in our lives. It could be said that he, with his double nature, the eponymous hero, like a god of mythology, embraces all the mystery of our destiny. America, by inexorable law, is called to realize his brightest dreams or to fulfill his darkest visions.

Chapter XI

BOLIVAR FACED BY JACOBIN ANARCHY

It has been maintained, and with good reason, that the war of independence was a civil war. Vallenilla Lanz has given us the proofs of this thesis. We are able to go even farther and say that there was a double civil war in the struggle for independence: war between the partisans of independence and the loyalists, and war between the bands which the partisans of independence formed immediately and which represented the diverse interests of the different cities of one province or kingdom.

Immediately after the outbreak of the revolutionary movement there was manifested in every section a tendency toward a superior organization for each large province, viceroyalty or captaincy-general. The revolution broke out in the smaller units, the *cabildos* and the old cities, but the process of concentration began immediately in the four great nuclei of South America, the viceroyalties of Santa Fe and Buenos Aires and the captaincies of Venezuela and Chile. The *juntas* established by the *cabildos* of the capitals invited the *cabildos* of the other cities or of the lesser provinces to elect a sovereign body to decide the destiny of the country.

The composition of these assemblies and their relations with the provisionally constituted governments gave rise to very grave conflicts. In none of the viceroyalties, however, did these conflicts become as serious as in that of Santa Fe. The invitation of this city encountered the objections of Cartagena. Cartagena proclaimed the principle of the absolute sovereignty of the small provinces. During the first part of 1811, says José de la Vega, there existed no definite political organization.[1] Cartagena, Antioquia, Citara, Popayan, Cali Neiva, Mariquita, Pamplona, Casanare, and Tunja formed other small states each of which was ruled by an independent *junta*.

In Venezuela the provinces heard the appeal of Caracas and formed an assembly. But this assembly did not escape the rivalry between Caracas and Valencia and the pretensions of the other cities or provinces which opposed the formation of an effective central régime. Mérida, Trujillo and Pamplona anticipated the federal constitution with constitutions of their own.[2] " Each province," said Bolivar, " governed itself independently, and following the example of the provinces, each city pretended to the same prerogatives, citing the example of the provinces and the theory that all men and all peoples enjoy the right of instituting at their own pleasure the government which seems more suitable to them." This movement tended to give itself expression by displaying the popular banner of the federative formula. It would be a mistake to suppose that its appearance all over America, and with so much strength, was due solely to the imitation and the imperfect adaptation of an imported ideology. A phenomenon as serious as this one must surely have had deeper causes.

This provincial sovereignty has been attributed to the survival in America of the regional and autonomic sentiment of the Spanish provinces and to the similar organization of the colonies which conferred certain functions on

[1] *Federación en Colombia*, 29.
[2] Gil Fortoul, I, 157.

the *ayuntamientos* or *cabildos*. Others have contended that the colonial organization had, in a general way, a centralized character. The *corregidores* of the cities depended in judicial matters on the *audiencia* and in political matters on the viceroy or the captain-general. The small provinces or *corregimientos* thus found themselves centralized from this dual point of view. The introduction of the régime of the *intendencia* in America did not lessen but accentuated this centralizing tendency. The *corregidores* became subdelegates of the *intendentes* and the latter were, like the old *corregidores,* subordinate to the viceroy and to the *audiencia.* The introduction of this new hierarchy, as we have proved, accentuated this centralization.[3]

The decentralization established by the administrative councils of the Constitution of Cadiz is not to be found in Buenos Aires, Caracas and Santa Fe for this provision of the constitution did not apply to them. Perhaps, as Justo Sierra believes, it had some influence in Mexico, in the formation of small local oligarchies, bases of the future federalist party. One of the causes for this widespread provincial movement may be found, as José de la Vega has indicated, in the reaction against the centralism of the colony; but in my opinion the decisive factor lies in the very nature of the revolution and in the interests which it created. When the central authorities had been swept aside and the authority of the mother country no longer recognized, the government fell necessarily into the hands of local oligarchies or of the *caudillos* who took the lead in the popular insurrection. So much for the fact. As for the doctrine, what we have is the logical result of the

[3] *Ibid.,* I, 158.

application of the principle of communal sovereignty when the Peninsular authorities had disappeared. This doctrine was exaggerated by jacobin and federalist imitation.

This is the true origin of American federalism. Let us then invert the terms in which the problem has been stated. In a general way, it is not badly applied ideology which created the movement or the tendency but the tendency supported by determined interests which encountered its ideology. Naturally, the effect reacts on the cause. That explains what we may term the double political base—psychological and economic—of federalism in America.

Even in the cases in which the small provinces succeeded in grouping themselves, forming either general *juntas* or constituent assemblies, there appeared another tendency fatal to the conduct of the war and to the formation of a solid government. These assemblies or legislative bodies labored under the double jacobin delusion of believing society might be saved by the drawing up of a constitution or by the theoretical proclamation of principles and by assuming that the executive power would submit completely to them as the depository of sovereignty.

Naturally, the real men of thought and action in the independence movement combated this tendency vigorously. Nariño, in *La Bagatela* ridiculed the federalist proposals, considering it an absurdity to apply servilely the forms of government of other nations dictated by an entirely different set of circumstances. The New Granadian provinces, in his opinion, provided for men, for revenue, for everything with the exception of the will to be sovereign, so that if they were erected into independent states they would find themselves, like many doctors, with a title but no science.[4] The

---

[4] Vega, *op. cit.*, 33.

same precursor exclaimed, in the journal which has already been mentioned, in words of moving eloquence:

" Enough of vain discourses, enough of chimerical hopes, fruit of carelessness and of indolence and of that gift of ridiculous illusion which will submerge us anew in servitude. . . . The moment has come to conquer or to die, to replace arguments with bullets." [5] Ignacio Herrera, one of the deputies, presented the decisive argument against federation. The revolution of North America found its thirteen provinces divided among themselves, independent and subject to their respective chiefs while the entire new kingdom of Granada obeyed one viceroy and had only two tribunals of justice. In North America each province retained the fundamentals of its inheritance, while the new kingdom of Granada concentrated the interests of all its territory.[6]

In spite of this mystic federalism and constitutional fervor, in the same New Granada, before the consequences of the civil war, there was felt the need of constituting a general government, strong and energetic, which might be capable of saving it from political crisis. Venezuela, induced by tragic circumstances, faced with the triumphant Spanish reaction, saw that the dictatorship of Miranda was impotent to prevent the collapse of the first Venezuelan republic. The experience of this tremendous collapse and the lessons learned from the internal struggles of New Granada were destined to prepare in the figure who dominated the American revolution the most vital and eloquent production of the true political thought and orientation which was to be achieved.

[5] Mancini, 437.
[6] Vega, 37.

As in the declaration of independence, the opportune and decisive words were pronounced by Bolivar; in this critical moment of the struggle and of political organization, the ideas of Bolivar appeared to give the exact nature of the problems and to indicate the certain course to follow. We have seen that here and there isolated voices have been heard which suggest the true principles and which contain parts of the true program of action. All of those hesitant truths, intuitions and observations are concentrated magnificently in Bolivar and appear in the manifesto directed to New Granada from Cartagena, without doubt the first great political document of the revolution. In it there already stands out the profoundly realistic vision of measure and of men which is to be the essential note of the thought of Bolivar. In it appear truly dynamic ideas, true active principles. As Mancini has said, " It is satisfying to the spirit, in an epoch of tentatives, of imprecision and of disorders that a clear voice, eloquent and sonorous, speak the language of reality." [7] Bolivar attacks the political utopias of the revolution with more efficacious irony even than Nariño: " In such a manner ", he says, " that we have philosophers for leaders, philanthropy for legislation, dialectic for tactics, and sophists for soldiers." He condemns the criminal clemency which provides that each conspiracy be followed by a pardon and each pardon by a conspiracy. He points out the error of not having a permanent army which would have been capable of overcoming the first misfortunes of the campaign. He paints, as it might be done today by the pen of a Maurras, the financial slovenliness into which the nascent democracy was being drawn,

[7] P. 447.

dissipating the public revenue in frivolous and prejudicial
projects and particularly in salaries of office holders, magistrates, legislators and local officers. He paints the jacobin
anarchy with extraordinary relief; and yet it is true that
he does not bring against federation the definitive argument that appears in Herrera and Monteagudo; on the contrary, he says that it is the most perfect system and the one
most capable of providing human happiness, but he declares
that we are lacking in the virtues and the preparation which
that government demands. Then he enunciates a principle
of political relativism, of universal worth, when he affirms
that the government should mold itself to the character of
present circumstances, of the times, and of the men who
live in it. With two strokes he pictures to us the fundamental vice of popular elections: they become mechanical
because of ignorance in the country and domination by the
factions in the cities. With the dolorous and palpitating
example of Caracas before him, he recalls the importance of
an authority which functions with rapidity and with vigor
and of a simple government instead of a languid and indifferent confederation. Refraining diplomatically from referring to the acts of New Granada while considering those
of Caracas, it is obvious that the first are to be associated
with the second and that his political advice is based on a
double experiment. The saving ideas of unity, concentration, solidity, energy are then praised in his incomparable
manner.

There are still other principles in the manifesto of
Cartagena. The struggle requires not only unity and energy
in action, but union and solidarity between the former colonies. Immediately after the revolution, the proposal was
made to unite all the countries in the common fight; this

was the meaning of the circular letter sent by the *juntas* of Caracas to all the *ayuntamientos* of America and of the project of Martínez Rosas in Chile. This idea of solidarity appears in a concrete and tangible form in the manifesto of Cartagena. New Granada will not be free unless Venezuela is free. The Spanish resistance at Coro initiated the fall of Caracas, and Coro is to Caracas what Caracas is to all of America. Not only for the sake of this solaridity, but also because of the advantages of offensive warfare, he outlines a new, liberating expedition to Venezuela, like the one that he was to conduct in the prodigious campaign of 1813. That principle of solidarity in the struggle for independence and the principle of offensive warfare at all costs, proclaimed since 1812 by Bolivar, were to form the two firm bases of the revolution. San Martín in the south will realize this program; La Plata will not be free if Chile is not free, and the liberty of Chile will be ephemeral unless it is followed by that of Peru. Bolivar was to fulfill his program exactly; the revolution synthesized itself in two words: attack and unite.

The manifesto of Cartagena took on, therefore, the double character of a revolutionary program and a supreme political lesson. Marius André was correct in saying that if on the day following the manifesto a premature death should have put an end to his career, Bolivar would none the less have been the most clairvoyant genius of the dawn of the South American republics. He passes beyond his epoch and gives lessons to future democracies.[8]

In face of the spontaneous disunity, incoherence and inertia in the revolution, Bolivar rose up representing unity, cohesion and the dynamic and creative impulse.

[8] *Bolivar et la Démocratie*, 77.

The picture which we have here sketched of jacobin anarchy in the first period of the American revolution would not be complete if we did not refer to the course which this revolution followed in Rio de la Plata.

The anarchy of the provinces of the north of South America manifested itself in governmental incoherence disguised under the cloak of federalist ideology. This same anarchy in the region of La Plata, at least for the years 1810 to 1813, had a central character and manifested itself in a perpetual crisis of the executive power, to which it gave, unfortunately, a collegial or collective character from the very beginning. The political problem in the Rio de la Plata establishes itself then in an entirely different fashion: there are no aspirations for "self government" at the beginning in the provinces as there were in Venezuela and in New Granada. With exception made of Uruguay and the ancient government of Paraguay, which took on exceptional importance during the earliest days of the colony, and which set up a government that recognized the Spanish Regency, and the provinces of Upper Peru which were quickly recovered by Spanish reaction, the provinces accepted in one form or another the direction of Buenos Aires and the principle of national unity which the *juntas* and triumvirates there supported. The policy of Moreno parallels that of Bolivar in the matter of the efficacy of action. If the famous plan of operations is his own, the politics of Moreno drew its inspiration from strictly jacobin models. But Moreno was only the secretary of a *junta* which assumed power. This *junta* expanded later by the incorporation of the provincial deputies and created in this way a monstrous power formed of a numerous group which exercised both legislative and executive powers. The *junta*

saw itself obliged to set up a triumvirate whose secretary was
Rivadavia, who occupied in this *junta* the position of
Moreno. The executive power continued in a state of
crisis. Neither the great influence of the secretaryship, nor
the vigorous personality of those who held it, Moreno and
Rivadavia, succeeded in achieving efficiency and stability
in the executive power. The only one who saw clearly in
this crisis was Monteagudo, who proclaimed, following the
example of Venezuela, the need of dictatorship. The first
triumvirate entered into conflict with the *junta* which had
created it, succeeded in suppressing it and in assuming,
by the decree of October 22, 1811, the legislative powers
which the *junta* had exercised. Political law in La Plata was
a kind of parricide. The *cabildo* of Buenos Aires created
the first *junta*, the *junta* dissolved the *cabildo;* the *junta*
then chose the first triumvirate and was in turn dissolved
by it. In spite of the intelligence and the activity of Rivadavia, the first triumvirate was not able to consolidate its
position. A movement of the *cabildo* of Buenos Aires, inspired by the *Lautaro* Lodge, in which Alvear and Monteagudo were all-influential, overthrew the first triumvirate,
and substituted for it a second triumvirate instead of organizing frankly a uni-personal executive power. In accord
with the jacobin obsession of the times and in contrast with
the ideas which Bolivar had proclaimed in the manifesto of
Cartagena, the second triumvirate found no better solution
for political anarchy than the convocation of the constitutional assembly of 1813, thus reopening the period of discussion when the period of action had hardly begun. The
unrealistic measures born of the most generous liberalism
of the assembly of 1813 did not create the organisms or the
spiritual *milieu* that the revolution required. The election

of that assembly set a new course for the political problem,
originating this time the question of federalism. The
provinces of the eastern bank (*banda oriental*) of the La
Plata river at the beginning in the power of the Spaniards,
formed the center of a *caudillista* movement which was
personified in the disputed figure of Artigas.

And then there appeared in Rio de la Plata, beside the
struggle with Spain, the civil war between the patriotic
elements. The reinforcements sent to Montevideo by Spain
and the disasters suffered by the army of the North in
Vilcapuquio and Ayoayo finally convinced the triumvirate of
the necessity for unifying the executive power. Here are
the words of the message sent to the assembly: " The experience of ruling, the understanding of our compromises
have taught this government that in order to furnish the
impulse which our enterprises demand, the concentration
of power in one hand is indispensable." The assembly accepted this principle of unity, and the head of the executive
power received the title of Supreme Director of the United
Provinces. He was to hold office for two years and to be
aided by a Council of State composed of nine members.
The measure adopted by the assembly was late in coming.
Revolutionary anarchy was spreading at the same time that
Spanish reaction was gaining strength.

If we now look at the complete picture of the revolutionary process in La Plata, we shall see in it the contrast
which I have pointed out. In it there is nowhere to be found
the disintegration which appears in the north of South
America; the errors of the government derive from defects
of orientation and from anarchic tendencies in the capital
itself. Only one constant note is perceived in the movements
of the epoch; gravitation toward revolution and principal-

istic illusion. Instinctively, Moreno, Rivadavia, Monteagudo incline to follow a policy of unity, concentration and efficiency. But, unfortunately, Moreno passes rapidly from the scene; Rivadavia inspires the complicated mechanism of the provisional Statute which will bring about even greater complications; and Monteagudo, in spite of having had the vision of the necessity of dictatorship since 1812, assists in the formation of a second triumvirate and in the creation of an assembly. In addition to this disorientation, there stands out in the revolution of La Plata the factor of more accentuated personalism. Every current is personified in a *caudillo*. The revolution is a series of *pronunciamientos* from soldiers and from demagogues authorized by the *cabildo* of Buenos Aires. The anarchy in the Rio de la Plata did not go from the periphery to the center, but from the center to the periphery, and only in the year 1813 does there appear, with Artigas, the autonomist and secessionist feeling of the provinces and then only after three years in which *juntas*, triumvirates and assemblies alternated in complete anarchy. The revolution, as the historian Varela confessed, sailed along without a compass insofar as plans for the definitive organization of the country were concerned.

We shall conclude by recalling that when the federalist idea appeared in La Plata, it was combated by thoughtful men, as it was in New Granada and in Venezuela. Monteagudo expressed himself in this fashion in 1815:

" The federation was formed for the purpose of creating a body able to combat external dangers, and it was formed by peoples who were previously united by no bonds. Since their individual forces were not sufficient to drive out the tyrant, they gave up their independence in order to combine with other provinces and in this fashion to ward off the torment which menaced them.

" In all of this one observes the eagerness of the peoples to augment their vigor and their union. But when they are united by bonds even closer than those demanded by the Confederation itself, when various peoples by the force of circumstances find it necessary to tighten the bonds which unite them, it is clear that to adopt a form of administration which, far from consolidating these same bonds, relaxes them relatively, then one is running head on to the precipice which one is seeking to avoid." [9]

The same argument appears in Gorriti: "A federation presupposes states already organized and constituted, while in the congress there were represented only inform provinces, without any interior organization sufficient for their own needs, and consequently, destitute for the most part of means of supporting the trials of a federation." [10]

Rivadavia believed, like Moreno, says Andres Lamas, that the action of the executive in struggling against armed reaction should be free and absolute in every sphere during the period in which it holds power.

The superior men of La Plata saw, then, with realistic criteria, the perils of federalism. Their arguments are those which Juan Bautista Alberdi was to repeat with fine clarity and brilliance a half century later.

Note: See the text of the famous Manifesto or *Memoria* of Bolivar addressed to the citizens of Nueva Granada, Cartagena de Indias, December 15, 1812, in *Documentos para la Historia de la Vida Pública del Libertador de Colombia, Perú y Bolivia,* José Felix Blanco. Caracas, 1876, IV, 119. For the revolution in the La Plata provinces, see *Varela, Historia Constitucional de la República Argentina* and González Calderón, *Derecho Constitucional Argentino.*

---

[9] Monteagudo, *Obras Políticas,* 351.
[10] *Reflecciones,* 367.

Chapter XII

FORMATION OF NATIONALITIES IN AMERICA

The American Revolution has as its moving principle the sovereignty which reverts to the people, a concept which ties the revolutionary ideology to the same principles of Spanish legislation.

Unfortunately, in the first revolutionary moment, which is the moment of destruction and inspiration, the only thing which sovereignty attempts to secure is free relations between province and province, internal democratic organization by frequent elections, the greater influence of the assemblies and the collective and temporary character of the executive power. All these evils have been described in the preceding chapter from the point of view of the necessity of a continued and concentrated union, which the triumph of the revolution demands. But besides this unfavorable and dark aspect, there is another, luminous and fecund, the awakening of sovereignty in America and its enthusiastic realization of the formation of nationalities by the free will of the people.

In general, these nationalities followed the lines of geographical unities and even respected certain bases of ethnological differentiation in so far as the aborigines were concerned. The national constitution called for the prior consecration of the will or rather of the desire of the inhabitants after the separation from Spain. All the ideologues of the revolution said, from the Licenciado Verdal in Mexico to Martínez Rosas in Chile, from Camilo Torres in New

Granada to Moreno in Buenos Aires that the provinces had recovered the full right of deciding their destiny and, for the same reason their nationality.

The nations of America will have, from the physical point of view, a base of geography, and they will feel in a general fashion the historic influence of antecedents of colonial structure, but their definitive constitutions will appear as the culminations of spontaneous movements, consciously directed toward superior integration. These movements are reflected in the invitation sent from an ancient capital, the directing nucleus, for the purpose of accomplishing this integration, to the *cabildos* which are the elements of the social organization, and the answer of these *cabildos* of the provinces. In some instances the integration is produced in a unitarian form of government, as was the case, at first, in Buenos Aires and in Chile, and in others, under the federal form, in its two degrees: simple federation in New Granada and a true federal state in Venezuela. Whatever may have been the process which this organization underwent, the defects which it had and the breakdowns which afflicted it, from the point of view of military and political efficiency, the historian must see in it not only the origin from the chronological point of view of the American nationalities but the juridical foundation of nationalistic differentiation in America. We should, therefore, although it be only hurriedly, refer to this movement.

The movement for American independence originated in the *cabildos* which were the living cells of the colonial organism. Each province, through its *cabildo,* assumed the sovereignty which reverted to the people on account of the absence and imprisonment of the Sovereign. This is the fundamental idea which appeared in all the independence moves: in Chuquisaca, in Quito itself, in Caracas, in Cartagena, in Santa Fe, in Chile, in Buenos Aires, in Asuncion and in Montevideo. The *cabildos*, as the highest authorities within the provinces, assumed the sovereignty. The *cabildos*, freely combining with one another, following the lines of colonial affinity or of geographic and economic ties, came to establish the various nations. The colonial boundaries indicated, in a general way, the lines along which such combination took place. But this was no imperative rule. National unities depended only on the free will of the provinces in which sovereignty was temporarily vested.

In this way we see that the *cabildo* of Caracas called together the other *cabildos* of the Captaincy-General of Venezuela. An entity was formed called the United Provinces of Venezuela, which became a nation when these provinces signed a compact and by their joint volition declared their independence. The Caracas Declaration of Independence says:

" We, the representatives of the United Provinces . . . solemnly declare to the world that these United Provinces are, and shall be from this day, in fact and in justice, free States, sovereign and independent. . . . In order that this our solemn declaration shall be valid, firm and lasting we give and pledge, one province to another, our lives, our fortune and the sanctity of our national honor." [1]

The identical phenomenon took place in New Granada: on July 20, 1810, the independence movement broke out and a *junta* was set up. Nine days later, the *junta* sent a circular to the provincial *cabildos*, calling a Congress and saying:

---

[1] J. F. Blanco, *Documentos para la historia de la vida pública del libertador,* III, 112.

" For the time being the government established shall be provisional, until the same body of representatives shall call a General Assembly of all the *cabildos.*" [2]

When this congress convened, a year later, and approved the Federal Act, it affirmed in it the free determination of the constituent elements. The second article says:

" There shall be admitted to this Confederation all provinces which were considered as such on July 20, 1810, and which in virtue of that right continued and reassumed their internal administration and governance since that time."

The third article, setting aside the boundaries of the old *audiencias,* respected the free adhesions produced by self-determination on these terms:

" There shall also belong [to the Confederation] those provinces or municipalities which did not belong to New Granada in the said period, but still were connected to it by ties based on geographical position, commercial relations or similar reasons, and now wish to join the Confederation, or to become part of one of its component provinces." [3]

In Chile, at the invitation of the *cabildo* of Santiago, a Congress convened which contained representatives of the other *cabildos* of Chile.

The resolution of the *cabildo* of Buenos Aires assuming the government was immediately followed by an invitation to the provinces to send their representatives to a *junta* set up by the Buenos Aires *cabildo.*

The invitation sent by the above *junta* was not accepted by Paraguay, in spite of the fact that its government had been part of the Viceroyalty of Buenos Aires. Instead a *junta* was formed in Asuncion which assumed the sovereignty of the province. Once its attempt to subject Para-

[2] *Ibid.,* II, 570.
[3] *Ibid.,* III, 345.

guay was defeated, the *junta* of government at Buenos
Aires bowed before the principle of free determination.
On August 28, 1811, the governments of Buenos Aires and
Paraguay became reconciled and, on October 12 of the same
year, an agreement of Friendship and Alliance was signed
between the two *juntas*.[4]

Years later a conflict arose between the Buenos Aires
government and General Artigas. The principle of free
determination of nationality was affirmed, both by the great
number who followed the " Jefe de los orientales ", and by
the representatives of the *junta* which was formed in that
province in 1813. In this way the bases of the Uruguayan
nation were established, disregarding the districts of former
audiencias and viceroyalties.

The first period of the revolution in America, from 1809
to 1815, concluded with the triumph of Spanish reaction in
almost all of America except in La Plata, La Guiana and
some parts of Mexico. Compensating for the obvious governmental anarchy, the lack of political preparation, the
jacobin exaltation and federalistic excess, we can see the un-
disturbed legacy which the great chiefs of these great movements left to the heroic period: the translation into a living
and constructive reality of the principle of sovereignty in
the formation of nationalities. And thus, the rubric of " insurrection of the *cabildos* " should be completed by another
" formation of nationalities ", and the qualification of " revolutionary federalism and jacobin anarchy ", by that of " bases
of the national constitution ".

These bases are so firm that they are transmitted to
the second period (1815-1824) and reflect, not only, as
before, the idealistic declaration of the old city councils

[4] *Ibid.*, III, 316.

but the pragmatic and fecund direction of the leaders of the revolution. When San Martín crossed the Cordillera and freed Chile, the government which was set up in that country was molded within the organization and in the framework which were given it by the ancient assembly convoked by the *cabildo* of Santiago and constituted by the free adherence of the *cabildos* of that kingdom.

San Martín advanced as far as Peru. His whole revolutionary plan consisted in seeking the adherence of the inhabitants, and the favorable declaration of the *cabildos*. Trujillo adhered to the independence movement. The independence of Peru was consecrated and was planned before the *cabildo* of Lima, and as the adherence of the other provinces was desired, a congress was convoked in which they were represented.

Bolivar followed an identical program. He dreamed from the Jamaica period, perhaps even from the time of the manifesto of Cartagena, to unite Colombia and Venezuela. This ideal was proclaimed in Angostura, but its realization did not come about until the Congress of Cucuta, where the representatives of New Granada were convoked with those of Venezuela. And when the liberating armies advanced toward the region of Quito, Bolivar sought in the plebiscite of the *ayuntamientos* the constitution of Great Colombia. Quito rose, and oaths to uphold the Colombian constitution were sworn in Riobamba and in Cuenca.

The great leaders of the revolution were able to rectify the ideology and the methods of the epoch of the insurrection of the *cabildos,* but they respected and proclaimed the principle of sovereignty in the great national integrations which they did not wish to found by the process of military conquest but by the free adherence of the liberated peoples.

CHAPTER XIII

CONSTITUTIONAL IDEAS, 1811-1815

The Venezuelan Constitution, approved in the year 1811, was modelled on the North American Constitution of 1787 and the French declaration of the Rights of Man. The political organization followed, step by step, that established in the United States in the matter of division of powers, provincial sovereignty, and bicameral system. The lower house was chosen by the people and the upper house by the provinces. It also gave the central government authority over the army, the marine, the coinage, foreign commerce and relations. The difference appears in the executive power which, in place of being uni-personal, is held by three individuals. The term of office in both the executive and legislative departments is the same in the two constitutions. The laws passed by the provincial legislative assemblies are submitted to the judgment of the central congress.

The provincial constitutions also established a collective executive power and provided for the broadest municipal autonomy. The people of each province have the right of recalling their appointees to the legislative assemblies. According to Gil Fortoul, the deputies of the year 1811 " always had in sight the Constitution of the United States and they often copied it, but they did not imitate its conciseness and reserve, but on the other hand drew up a treatise on political law with profuse definitions of the theory of the institutions and frequent digressions into moral philosophy ".[1]

[1] I, 168.

148

In La Plata they did not at once proceed, as was done in Venezuela, to a declaration of independence and to the setting up of a constitution; but they did have to issue various decrees in order to organize the administration. The most important one was issued February 10, 1811; it related to the establishment of the provincial committees. In the capital of each province there was established a committee which had charge of all the matters which by old laws and ancient ordinances were in the jurisdiction of the president or governor (*intendente*). All of these committees were in complete subordination to the superior committee, that of Buenos Aires. The presidents of these committees were named by the central government and the other four members were chosen by the people. This organization replaced the colonial system, consisting of unipersonal authorities and appointments, by a system of collective authorities largely of popular origin. The subordination of the provincial committees to the central committee showed full acceptance of the principle of national unity. This decree presupposed a principle of decentralization, but not of federalism, as some have believed.

On October 22 of the same year, the same Government issued an order which, together with the above decree, could be said to constitute the first draft of Argentinian fundamental law. According to it, the supreme *junta* of Buenos Aires would assume the functions of a legislative department, besides its selection of the executive power, vested in a triumvirate and three secretaries, whose duty it was to make administrative appointments and to defend the State. This regulation did not go into effect, as the triumvirate then in power dissolved the *junta* or committee. Under the influence of Rivadavia, who desired a more efficient execu-

tive authority, they exacted a provisional statute whose bases
were: 1. Renewal alternately every six months of the
members of the Government and the implied indefinite
duration in office of the three secretaries, who thus came
to represent the continuity of the Executive authority.
2. Concession to the Executive authority of some judicial
functions and the right of adopting whatever measures
might be necessary for the defense and safety of the country. 3. The calling together of a representative assembly,
in which Buenos Aires was to have a dominant position, of
all the provinces. This statute also remained without effect
after the fall of Rivadavia and the rise to power of a new
triumvirate which was to convoke the first Argentine assembly in the year 1813. We should observe that until
this moment the frankly federal idea had not been advanced
in La Plata; the preponderant influence is the jacobin with
its program of the absolute sovereignty of the *juntas,* the
collective authorities being concentrated in their hands.
Rivadavia strives for an executive authority with extraordinary powers, but unlike Bolivar, he does not dare to proclaim the clear principle of unity of the executive authority.
Instead he tries to gain stability indirectly through the
secretaries.

In New Granada, various provinces set up constitutions
for themselves. The federalistic idea had even more development and diffusion than in Venezuela. In fact it had
taken root to such an extent, that when an effort was made
to unite the various provinces, the form decided upon was
not a federal state but only a confederation. The one personality which best represented this tendency was the author
of the *Act of the Provinces of New Granada* Camilo Torres.
José de la Vega says that, comparing this act with the Ar-

ticles of Confederation adopted by the United States in 1777, we cannot draw any other conclusion but that our delegates almost literally copied this primitive work of the United States.[2]

A government without a central nucleus and so pliable could not exist. In the Congress itself the centralistic tendency triumphed. Owing to the influence of Fernández Madrid, an act was passed by which the branches of war and state were united.

Let us hear the testimony of Samper on the constitutions of the provinces of New Granada: " The same defects and the same qualities are apparent in all the constitutions of Cundinamarca and Tunja, Casanari and Pamplona, Cartagena and Antioquia, Mariquita and Neiva. As for the defects—products of French inspiration, of Latin impressionability and of the candor of some Creole philosophers—they are: a spirit much more theoretical than practical; an obvious tendency to give excessive authority to the legislative power, estimating it to be supreme and of which the executive power is a mere instrument; a profound confusion between the electoral and the legislative, the judicial and the administrative; and an objective of excessive regulation which shows itself in the mixture in every constitution of measures of civil law and penal, fiscal measures and rules of procedure, regulations for the military and the police, with measures truly essential to the state. In all of these constitutions there is a lack of method, of precision and of conciseness, and frequently the simple maxims of morals and of politics are confused with the imperative precepts pertinent to a fundamental idea." [3]

[2] Vega, *Federación en Colombia*, 37.
[3] *Derecho Público Interno de Colombia*, II, 110.

In this same year, 1812, the Constitution of Cadiz was promulgated, which is an important event in the development of political ideas in America, and which had influence, though slight in the viceroyalties of Mexico and Peru. It represented the adaptation of the principles of the French Revolution to the monarchic form of government. The legislative authority is entrusted to a single assembly, the Cortes, composed of deputies chosen by the provincial electors, who in turn, are named by the district electors, and these last chosen by the electors in the local parishes. In the section relating to the judicial authority, the Constitution of Cadiz emphasizes individual rights. The most interesting part to Americans, is its decrees relating to local government. The ancient *ayuntamientos* had a truly popular origin. In each province there were established the so-called provincial *diputaciones,* whose members were named by the electors of the district on the day following the election of the deputies to the Cortes. These entities had powers in urgent cases and moreover were to be vigilant in preserving the rights guaranteed in the constitution. Although the political chief of each province was named by the King (article 324) it is evident that the establishment of the provincial *diputación* involved a principle of administrative decentralization which assumed considerable importance. The Constitution of Cadiz established a council of state and the Cortes took part in naming this body.

In 1813, the first Argentine assembly convened. Its legislative work, according to Ingenieros, like that of the Cortes of Cadiz " adjusted itself faithfully to its Parisian model, with the exception, naturally, of certain questions of local concern ". The assembly did not take the radical step of declaring independence but affirmed the absolute sovereignty of the United Province by removing the name of Ferdinand from the oath. It firmly established the national unity of Argentina by declaring that the deputies of each province were the deputies of the nation.[4]

In the organization of executive authority, the assembly abandoned the collective form by creating a Director (laws of Jan. 22 and 26, 1814) who was to be guided by a council named by the same assembly and who was to hold office for two years. The three secretaries of the office established previously were to remain as members of the council. Although this executive power was not as effective as the situation demanded, it was still an important step in that it did away with the old triumvirate. This action was due chiefly to the influence of Monteagudo, who praised a strong, and even a dictatorial government. In this point his belief coincides with the thought of Bolivar, who had proclaimed similar ideas in his Cartagena manifesto. The director was given powers regarding the carrying out of the laws, national defense, foreign relations, and the appointment of all functionaries. He also could suspend the provisions relating to individual guarantees in times of special stress, such as foreign invasion or domestic uprisings.

In La Plata, the federal viewpoint appears in the famous instructions given by Artigas to the Uruguayan delegates to the assembly of 1813. Artigas asked for the establishment of a Federation. His thought, according to Hector Miranda, " without exactly following either of the plans alluded to (the American Constitutions of 1777 and 1787), still was profoundly influenced by the Federal Constitution of 1787, and, with the plan of the seceding states of 1861, repre-

[4] González Calderón, *Derecho Constitucional Argentino*, I, 61.

sented a more clearly defined intermediate form of government between those two patterns ".[5]   In reality, the important thing, as far as these instructions were concerned,
was the affirmation of the sovereignty of the small provinces,
the references being vague as far as the supreme government of the nation was concerned (Articles 4, 7, 30). It
cannot be said that the real purpose of the author of these
instructions was to contribute to the formation of a strong
national entity with a truly efficient government.   The
political plan involved was a middle way between the Venezuelan Constitution of 1811 and the New Granada Constitution of 1812.   By the same token, we cannot assign it a
higher value than these documents receive in the judgment
of Gil Fortoul and José de la Vega, if we leave to one side
all feeling of patriotic pride.

The insurrection in Mexico was characterized by certain
peculiar aspects which set it off from those of the other
regions of America.

We have already said that this insurrection had a rural
character and that it was led by ecclesiastics, like Hidalgo
and Morelos.   These priestly leaders were inspired by the
same feeling toward the native race as that of Antonio de
San Miguel and Abad y Queipo.   Hidalgo declared the tribute abolished; Morelos was obsessed by social problems.
The character of his preoccupation is revealed in the famous
reform program which he wrote for the Congress of Chipal-
cingo on the betterment of the condition of the working
classes.

Within this orientation the policy of Morelos was at first
moderate, and he tried to conciliate the Spanish proprie-

[5] *Instrucciones* del año XIII, 263.

tors. He did not wish to harass them simply because they were proprietors, and he limited himself to asking for means to put into the hands of the people the necessities of agriculture in agreement with the same policy which was consecrated in the functions conferred on the provincial *diputaciones* by the Cortes of Cadiz. But the progress of the war convinced Morelos that he could not count on the support of the Spanish proprietors, but rather on their open hostility. Then he adopted a radical policy which aimed at the exploitation of all plantations exceeding two leagues in area and the destruction of the metal works and sugar mills, " instruments with which they make war on us ". [6] The congress which Morelos summoned considered a project of Ignacio Rayon, and it is surprising that it did not include the program of social reform of the revolutionary leader.[7]

In 1814, the first Mexican document was signed in Apatzingan. Following the French model, it invests a congress with sovereignty. This congress is chosen by the provinces in the doubly indirect method we have observed in the Constitution of Cadiz. The congress named the members of the government, the supreme court, and the court of residence, which decides the responsibility of the functionaries. The executive authority is composed of three people who alternate in the post every four months. The supreme court is renewed annually.

Besides the indirect electoral system, the single assembly is another feature that marks the similarity of the Cadiz and Mexican constitutions. Professor Priestly observes that the Mexican constitution is a combination of the French

[6] *Centenario de la Constitución del 24*, 14.
[7] *Ibid.*, 26.

ideals of nationalism and equality and the deficiency of fiscal materials and administrative responsibility found in the Spanish model. Sierra also notes the similarity in the two documents and arrives at the logical conclusion that the Mexican is an adaptation of its Spanish predecessor.

In opposition to the Venezuelan constitution of 1811 and the New Granada Act of 1812, the Apatzingan document does not establish the federal form of government. The first two were derived from American models, the last from a recent Spanish model; but they were in accord in the ultra-democratic character of the government; and there is a particular point of similarity between the act of 1811 and the Mexican document in the feature of collective and renewable government.

The constitutions voted for Venezuela, New Granada, and Mexico were dead letters. They simply remained theoretical declarations in the face of the triumphant Spanish reaction. The only region of America where the application and development of these new systems were possible was La Plata, which maintained its independence. But there the sudden changes in the government prevented the consolidation and normal development of a constitutional system. There was also a widely varying viewpoint among the leading men, as far as constructive work was concerned. It was easy to copy the liberal principles of the legislative assembly, of the French Convention and of the Cortes of Cadiz, but it was difficult to establish or create institutions which, in practice, would make the necessary transition between the colonial and the new régime. It is no exaggeration, but strict justice, to say that jacobinism in La Plata, as in all America, useful for its primary enthusiasm and impetus, was absolutely fruitless as far as its constructive work is concerned. An impartial historian has to differ radically with the opinion of Professor Ingenieros, who is inclined to consider all demagogic agitation and all radical undertakings as good things in themselves.

The jacobin enthusiasm engendered and maintained anarchy, giving place, as a natural result, to the authoritative reaction which operated in such an accentuated form that the restoration of monarchy was not long in coming. The very Assembly which in 1813 and 1814 gave the laws which awoke the admiration of the Argentinian publicists, from López, Mitre and Avellaneda to Rojas, Ingenieros, and González Calderón, in August of the last year cited, gave the executive authority the right to enter into negotiations with the Cortes of Cadiz. To the menace of a new Spanish expedition to La Plata, the insurrection of Artigas, and the anarchy in the littoral territories, the Director could find no answer but the establishment of a monarchy. His commissioners in Europe, Belgrano, Rivadavia and Sarratea, elaborated a constitutional project for " The United Kingdom of La Plata, Peru, and Chile ", the crown of which was to be offered to the Infante Francisco de Paula, son of Charles IV. There was also urged perpetuity and irremovability of the monarch, ministerial responsibility, a higher chamber representing the nobility (dukes, counts, marquis) and a lower house formed by the deputies of the people. This proposal, first made before Charles IV, later repeated before Ferdinand VII, was set aside by the refusal of the latter, an indication of the attitude Spain was to assume years later when confronted by similar proposals made on the basis of Punchauca and the treaty of Cordova.

Director Alvear suffered from a greater disorientation the following year, finding himself unable to dominate the anarchy of the country, he did not hesitate to ask for an English protectorate. Alvear, having fallen as a result of an uprising in the army, which should have been fighting Artigas, and the Assembly having been dissolved, a new government was set up. This consisted of a Director and a Committee for Observation, which issued the Provisional Statute of 1815, by which full sovereignty was temporarily vested in this body. The Statute was to govern Buenos Aires and those provinces which freely accepted it. According to González Calderón " it was of federalistic tendencies, recognizing the provinces, for the first time in the constitutional history of the country, as having the right to choose their own governors ".[8]

[8] *Op. cit.*, 68.

CHAPTER XIV

BOLIVAR'S REPUBLICAN AND NATIONALISTIC
FAITH

Bolivar carried out the Cartagena program in his resplendent campaign of 1813; but the second Republic of Venezuela fell before the onslaught of the hordes of Boves and Morales. The movement for independence still lacked the popular element, the decisive element of the rural masses. In New Granada, civil war flamed out again; rivalry among the provinces and revolt against the government continued. It became the mission of Bolivar himself, on returning to New Granada after the fall of the second Republic, to intervene in these civil wars in behalf of the central government and those principles which he had so eloquently formulated.

In La Plata, the triumvirates were followed by a unipersonal executive power, called the " Director ". But the rivalry between the cities and the capital grew steadily worse, as did the conflict between the central government and the allied local leaders. The royalist reaction held at bay the rebellion of Quito, reconquered upper Peru, and tried to invade the Argentine provinces. It soon controlled the revolutionary movement in Chile, and Spain, free of the French invasion, sent a formidable expedition to South America, which was soon to dominate Venezuela and pacify New Granada, taking Cartagena and controlling Santa Fe. We are now entering the darkest period of the history of the Independence. Bolivar, exiled, was at this

time in Jamaica writing the celebrated letter which constitutes the second great document of the revolutionary
program.

The future of America was until this moment an un-
readable mystery. The revolution had been a contest between powerlessness and anarchy. External factors seemed
to be orienting themselves into an unfavorable combination
—monarchic reaction in Europe, the possibility that Spain
might send reinforcements to America, the attitude of absolute indifference shown by the United States, and English
neutrality. Nevertheless, Bolivar with clear, prophetic vision
was affirming the reality of independence; "The destiny
of America has been settled irrevocably," he said, "the
bond that held it to Spain is sundered; it is less difficult
to unite the two continents than to reconcile the two countries". "Spain is unable to reconquer America; the independence of America is required for the equilibrium of the
world ", he said, in a phrase that Canning was later to use.
The Jamaica letter is not only a document of faith and a
vision of hope in the blackest hours of the revolution, but
it is even greater in its exact analysis of the situation in
each of the American countries, of the state of the revolution and the attitude of Europe and America. Bolivar had,
as no other man of the Revolution, a clear and penetrating
grasp of his problems, his inspired outlook took in all the
vast and complicated panorama of the continent. Again, as
in the manifesto of Cartagena, appears that realistic vision
of our environment which shows his genius: "We are a
separate part of the human race, we possess a world apart,
we are neither Indians nor Europeans, but a species between the legitimate proprietors of the country and the
Spanish usurpers."

Bolivar, at that early date, announced the truth which all later Spanish-American sociologists have repeated, that is the lack of preparation mentally for liberty and independent life. " The position ", he says, " of the residents of the American hemisphere has for centuries been entirely passive, politically they were non-existent. We are still too little elevated from servitude to rise easily to the proper enjoyment of Liberty." He adds, "America was not only deprived of its liberty but even of the advantages of an active and dominating tyranny! "

The modern viewpoint has pointed out the exaggeration of such a portrayal of the ancient colonial régime. It is evident that Bolivar made the picture extreme for propaganda purposes, but no one can doubt that his description was fundamentally correct. The political centralization, as we have said before, was accentuated in the last years of the colonial system. The *cabildos*, earliest germ of American liberty, were secondary institutions in the formidable machinery of the colonial government.

If our colonial past was not such as would fit us for advanced forms of government, the events immediately after the revolution proved our lack of preparation. Bolivar declared emphatically that the incident of Tierra Firme had proved that fully representative institutions were not adapted to our character, customs, or preparation. Speaking particularly of Venezuela, he says: " It has been the clearest example of the ineffectiveness of the federal democratic régime as far as our nascent states are concerned." He foresaw the need for a paternal government which would heal the wounds left by despotism and war, a rule of natural transition from the old Spanish organization to the ideals of the revolution, avoiding " the pitfalls of demagogic anarchy and monocratic tyranny ".

Later, at Angostura, Bolivar is to describe in greater detail the plan of government which is vaguely indicated in the Jamaica letter.

The most interesting feature of the letter is the judgment with which Bolivar takes up the problem of nationalities in America. Two tendencies were then current in America: to consider all the colonial Empire which had revolted, as an indivisible entity destined to be a single state, or to consider each local or provincial sovereignty as an embryo state which would lead to a multiplicity of governments, subdividing the old " kingdoms " or real national nuclei.

Miranda, as we know, was inspired by the idea of the continental unity of Spanish America, although experience had demonstrated its impossibility. In 1816, the legislators of the famous Congress of Tucuman were obsessed with the same idea when they proclaimed the " independence of the United Republics of America ". In imitation of Miranda's first project they decided on a monarchic form of government, reviving the title of " Inca ". Bolivar faced this problem with his habitual realism. " It is a grandiose idea ", he said, " to try to make one nation of all the New World, uniting all its parts by a single bond—but it is not possible, because varied climates, diverse situations, contrary interests, and dissimilar characteristics divide America." "A great monarchy ", he adds, " would be difficult to consolidate, but a great republic is impossible."

The geographic factor, principal basis of nationalistic differentiation, the economic factor, and the psychological factor are all pointed out by Bolivar. Moreno, in his ad-

dresses to the congress, showed that he had the same realistic vision as Bolivar, when he considered the impossibility
of forming an American Congress and referred to the lack
of common economic interests among the various colonial
nuclei. " It is folly to pretend that all the Spanish Americas
form a single state. How are we to reconcile our interests
with those of the Kingdom of Mexico? " Moreno foresaw
the independence of the various provinces or great kingdoms, " Because Nature itself has pointed out this course
in the products and limits of their respective territories." [1]

Beside the economic and geographic factors, there was
the important precedent for the nationalistic division in
the old colonial organization, as we have proven in our
first chapter on the " Spanish Background." The old régime
had pursued a principle of nationalistic division, following
the indications of geographic factors. These separate kingdoms, according to Spanish policy, were united with the
principle nucleus—the crown itself—but there were no
bonds uniting one kingdom to another. It may be said that
the Spanish colonial Empire had a star-like form, and not
the circular form of a chain. That is, each colony was joined
directly to the crown with no connection between colony
and colony. This fact has enormous importance in Spanish-
American history. The Revolution broke the bonds uniting
colony to crown, leaving the several *unities entirely separate
and free.*

Bolivar saw the situation in this light when he said, " I
consider the present state of America to be similar to that
after the fall of the Roman Empire, when each part of
the wreckage formed a political system conforming to its

[1] *Op. cit.,* 274f.

needs, or was led by the ambition of some chief, family, or association ". The paragraph cited points out the factor of personal ambition, the individualism of local leaders, which in the growth of the Spanish-American nations, was to vie with the influences of geographical background and political tradition.

Bolivar was influenced by the Abbé de Pradt when he stated that America would be divided into 15 or 17 states. He criticises the idea of setting up monarchies in each of these states. He holds that the republican form better conforms to this principle of differentiation and will not lead to imperialistic combination. "A state too large in itself or its dependencies ", he says, " finally falls into decadence, loses its free nature and becomes a tyranny, neglecting the principles which could preserve it, and finally relapses into despotism ". In this he follows the idea of Montesquieu. But if he recommends a republican constitution, as we have seen, he rejects the federal form of government for each national nucleus.

The Jamaica letter does not stop at enunciating in a general manner the nationalistic principle. In masterly language Bolivar passes review of all the states, and with prophetic vision indicates the destiny of each one of them. He points out the conflict in Mexico between the popular element and the aristocratic party. He predicts the restoration of monarchy and the life-term presidencies. He states that the countries of the Isthmus will form an association, thus foreseeing the Central American Confederation, which was to continue until 1838. He indicates the union of New Granada and Venezuela, which was to take place the same year, as one of the necessities of the war; but at the same time he accepts the possibility that New Granada would form a single state. He predicts the dominance of the military government in Buenos Aires, and the formation of the Chilean oligarchy, and, finally, he points out the factors that prevented just and liberal rule in Peru, as well as the difficulties in the way of attaining independence.

In such detailed manner, he presents the national development of the different peoples, through an impartial study of the situation and of their characters. But in Bolivar, besides the realistic sociologist, there is also the dreamer, the tenacious idealist. America could not form a single state. But these states could fraternize and form a powerful union similar to the ancient Greek amphictyony. "How beautiful it would be if the Isthmus of Panama should become for us that which the Isthmus of Corinth was for the Greeks. Would that some day we may have the fortune of assembling an august congress of the representatives of the several republics, kingdoms, and empires to meet together and consider the high interests of peace and war." [2]

The Utopia of a gigantic nation is replaced by the idea of an American Federation. After differentiation, imposed by the land and by history, was to come integration of the nations. The ideal of Bolivar, though still far distant, is the end towards which we work, the course towards which we are inevitably drawn, the only saving solution offered by the future.

Upon the same occasion Bolivar grappled with the ethnological problem in America. The war of independence seemed at certain moments a civil war; many *mestizos* loyal to the king fought against the white aristocracy; in Peru,

[2] Lecuna, *Cartas del Libertador*, I, 181.

the indigenous population was turned by the Spanish generals against the Creole aristocracy or mesocracy. But Bolivar was aware that this situation would pass, and that soon, in all the races, the desire for independence and nationality would assert itself. Here are his words: " We have, then, reason to believe that all sons of Spanish America, of whatever color, profess a fraternal affection for each other which no machination can alter. They will tell us that our civil wars prove the contrary. No! Internal conflicts in America have never arisen from differences in caste. They have sprung from divergences of political opinion and from the personal ambition of certain men, like all strife which has afflicted other nations. There is yet to be heard a cry of proscription against any color, estate, or condition, except against European Spaniards." [3]

Years later, in a declaration to San Martín, Bolivar was to see in the fusion of races the formation of a new stock— forecast of the cosmic race of Vasconcelos—the basis of the aggrandizement of the new nations. " Neither we nor the generation following us will see the glory of the republic which we are founding. There will be a new caste composed of an amalgamation of all races, which will produce a homogeneous people." [4]

It would be unjust to omit in this chapter the other American thinkers or leaders who, regardless of the triumph of the Spanish reaction to which we have referred, conserved their faith in the independence of the continent and continued working therefor.

In Rio de la Plata the same persons who had eulogized the policy of conciliation with Spain, on the basis of a monarchy,

[3] Lecuna, *Papeles de Bolivar*, 274.
[4] Parra Pérez, *Bolívar*, 114.

saw that they could not continue in such course and turned to absolute independence, but they kept the monarchical ideal of the restoration of the Inca dynasty as was proposed by Belgrano in the Tucuman Congress.

However, revolutionary faith and the vision of independence will not be reflected merely in declarations and doctrines but in action. In this sense, that faith was best represented by the renowned figure of the other liberator of America, José de San Martín. Bolivar writes, conspires and leads expeditions from Haiti against the coast of Venezuela. San Martín discards any plan to invade Upper Peru, withdraws from the political chaos of Buenos Aires, accepts the modest Government of Cuyo and silently devotes himself to the creation of an army that will liberate Chile and triumphantly reach Peru.

Independence is furthered by Bolivar's exile in Jamaica and San Martín's fruitful confinement at the foot of the Andes.

Faith in the revolution was also conserved in Peru, notwithstanding its being the center of the Spanish reaction. A noble Creole of high intelligence and astounding activity, José de la Riva Agüero, withdraws from the illusion of the *doceañistas,* and with great keenness of vision, with accuracy of analysis and intense patriotic feeling lists the reasons which made independence inevitable. This *Manifestación histórica y política de la Revolución de la América,* written by Riva Agüero in Lima in 1816 and published in Buenos Aires in 1818, is an extremely valuable document for determining the radical revolutionary spirit of that period. He contributed, without doubt, to gaining the opinion in favor of absolute independence of many irresolute parts of the territory which were still occupied by Spanish arms.

The absolutist trend of the monarchical reaction made the Creoles see the lack of foundation of the reformist dream. The absolutism established in Spain spreads to South America, with all its characteristics of violence and blood. Spain will continue the war supported by the Holy Alliance, favored by the neutrality of the United States and, to a certain extent, of England. But America will be free in spite of the will of the Universe, so that Bolivar's prophecy may be realized.

CHAPTER XV

BOLIVAR AND THE CONSERVATIVE REPUBLIC

The situation that Bolivar paints for us in his Jamaica letter became even graver as a result of the Spanish triumphs in New Granada, Chile, and Mexico, and the outbreak of anarchy in La Plata. Nevertheless, it was in this difficult period that the foundations were to be laid for the great movements which were to determine the definite triumph of the revolution.

General San Martín is named Governor of Cuyo in 1814; and it is precisely in the period with which we are dealing that he was completing the last preparations for his inspired plan which was to liberate Chile and Peru. Bolivar, after repeated failures in campaigns with Caracas as their objective, now chose Guiana as the center of his future operations. The foci of the liberating movement are now, not the ancient capitals, but the unimportant and nearly unknown provinces of Cuyo and Guiana. Independence takes on the new and interesting character of individual enterprise rather than an effort of organized governments. The great movement in the South, whose center is in Cuyo, was principally a military enterprise; and San Martín, at least from the political point of view, worked under the orders of the Buenos Aires government. The conditions were different with Bolivar in Guiana. He was, at the same time, chief of the army and the supreme governmental authority; he had to attend to plans for military campaigns and also to the organization of the state. In this exceptional period, this second function was demanded not because of internal need, but for reasons of international cooperation. At all events, it was desired that the insurrection of Orinoco present itself before the world as a state definitely organized. Bolivar decided to call together an assembly, which although incomplete—the larger part of the territory being occupied by Spanish forces—could assume national authority. The assembly met in Angostura and was to make the decisions regarding the grave problem of political organization.

Bolivar in the Cartagena manifesto and the Jamaica letter had used unanswerable arguments in his criticism of the institutions set up by the people of Venezuela and New Granada. Recognizing the ideas of unity, solidity, stability and efficiency in government, he desired that the American people should have, not the theoretically most perfect form of government, but the one most suited to the physical and economic situation as he saw it, and the special conditions set up by the war—in short, the government that would form the best intermediary step between the old Spanish régime and the new régime of liberty.

In his journeys along the Orinoco, and in the midst of that lavish environment provided by the hand of nature, Bolivar occupied himself with his meditations on politics. The circumstances that placed him away from the influence of the political issues that were to arise with the consummation of independence and in the midst of this primitive environment, were effective in giving his thought spontaneity and a sense of reality. Bolivar, at this moment, was simply the searcher who has found the firm basis of his work and who still remembers vividly the lessons taught by an experience composed more of defeats and moments of despair than of hopes and triumphs. Fully conscious of the fact that he is playing a definite rôle, he has to concentrate all the force of his spirit on the discovery of the political and military formulas which can assure the success of his plans. For these reasons the moment that we are now considering marks the zenith of the creative thought of Bolivar. In no other did his fundamental qualities find better expression, his sense of reality and his disinterested and noble idealism. The ideas that we see coming to light in the Jamaica letter and the Cartagena manifesto, receive in the Angostura speech their full development, their true culmination.

Before entering into a detailed study of this thought, it is necessary to record the institutions which had been tried in America up to this time, not because they influenced the thought of Bolivar, but because his ideas were a reaction to them. Such a contrast permits us to appreciate even more fully the marked originality of Bolivar's political ideas.

The aim of giving the La Plata provinces a definite constitution comes up again in the assembly which set up this provisional government and which met in Tucuman in 1816. It took the transcendental step of definitely declaring the independence of the United Provinces. The underlying influences were monarchic tendencies. Belgrano presented his plan of restoring the Inca monarchy. Our purpose does not entail the study of the details of the various plans and suggestions which the Argentinian leaders studied in their search for a monarchic plan. Some historians try to explain these leanings by the fact that Europe at this time was in full reaction against revolutionary ideas—a monarchic reaction which in America was supported by the example of

Brazil. We believe that, besides these opportunist motives, there were others which produced this effect on the men of La Plata. They were of the sincere, though mistaken, belief that a monarchy was not only possible but necessary. They did not see that independence and the republican form of government were united, that autochthonous monarchies were impossible, and that monarchies under the leadership of members of the European ruling houses were subject to the danger that new reactions might again attach them to the older countries, thus destroying the work of the Revolution. They did not see, lastly, that for those thrones there were no candidates who wished to come to America.

The Assembly was moved to Buenos Aires, and after slow preparation, it finally adopted the constitution of 1819 without making any decision as to the form of government, probably with the idea of leaving the door open to any monarchic possibility. The document of 1819 was centralism exaggerated. " In this constitution ", says Avellaneda, " so detailed that it even describes the ceremonial of the sessions, there does not appear one mention of the provinces ". Thus the jacobin tendency was followed by an authoritarian reaction; after the extreme provincial sectionalism, came a strict centralism, thus widening the gap between Buenos Aires and the provinces.

A year before, in 1818, the Director, O'Higgins, with independence proclaimed in Chile, proclaimed the law which organized the executive authority and a senate of five members, and provided for the calling of a congress.

Such, in brief outline, is the picture of the political institutions of Spanish America at the time when Bolivar presented his plan before the Assembly of Angostura. In the North in New Granada and Venezuela the ultra-democratic federal ideas were predominant, the two always united, as Justo Sierra observes. In the South, as a reaction to the anarchy which had endured so long, the centralistic and monarchic idea is strongest.

The first set of ideas has its support in the great North American model; the second in the reaction in Europe. The possibility of conciliating the democratic tendencies and the monarchic plan of government appears in the Spanish attempt at a Constitution in 1812.

Bolivar, as we noted in the beginning of this work, parts from these currents and presents a new formula. His judgment is principally inspired by actual conditions in Spanish America. Citing Montesquieu, he affirms that the laws ought to conform to the topography of the country, the climate, the quality of the ground, to the kind of life led by the people and to their customs. " Behold ", he exclaims, " the code which we should consult, and it is not that of Washington. The excellency of a government does not consist in its theory, its form; not in its mechanism, but in its appropriateness to the nature, the character of the nation for which it is designed."

He emphasizes, as he does in the Jamaica letter, the difference that exists among the peoples of South America, in Venezuela especially. " We realize that our people is not the European people nor yet that of North America, but a compound of Africa and America rather than an emanation of Europe, since even Spain itself is not European, on account of its African blood and its institutions and general character." He then alludes to ethnic inequalities. The greater part of the indigenous race has vanished; the European has mixed with the African and the American, and the former has mixed with the Indian and the European.

In the light of these ideas, Bolivar criticises the Constitution of Venezuela of 1811, insisting that our moral constitution does not yet have the necessary consistency to benefit from a government completely representative. It is noteworthy that Bolivar, on this occasion as on the previous ones, does not advance as a definite argument against the federal form of government, the findings of other thinkers such as Herrera, Mier, Gorriti, and Monteagudo, who all said that federalism was invented in North America with the idea of uniting what was divided, but, on being applied to Spanish America, tended to divide what previously had been united.

Besides the difficulties arising out of following the American model, which was impracticable for its purpose, the Congress of 1811 also made the error of vesting the executive authority in a collective body " consequently subject to the inconveniences caused by the establishment of a periodic government which was suspended and dissolved whenever its members separated ". " Our triumvirate ", adds Bolivar, " lacks unity, continuity, individual responsibility; it is deprived of prompt activity, continuous life, of real uniformity, of immediate responsibility; and a government that does not possess these things which constitute its modality, should be called null."

But if Bolivar, because of real conditions in Venezuela and previous experiences, can criticise the institutions established in 1811: federation, the omnipotent character of the legislative authority and, above all, collective government, he does declare himself a partisan of the republican form of government, of the sovereignty of the people, division of powers, civil liberty, emancipation of the slaves

and abolition of special privileges. "A republican government", he says, "has been, is, and should be, the government of Venezuela". Referring to the first constitution,
he calls it "the immortal document of our rights and of
our laws". He did not hesitate to proclaim political equality,
which is the foundation and basic feature of all democracies.

Marius André, in his book, *Bolivar et la Démocratie,* asks
whether Bolivar was sincere and convinced of what he said.
He attributes these emphatic declarations to tactful policy.
In the opinion of this distinguished writer, Bolivar tried
to camouflage matters to the Angostura Congress so that he
could obtain from it the institutions which were precisely
in opposition to these doctrines.

In our opinion, the problem is even more complex than
Marius André believed it to be. We must not forget that
Bolivar had been nourished on the democratic philosophy
of the eighteenth century and that, besides, he was perfectly well aware of all the implications of the Revolution.
Let us repeat that this democratic philosophy had been the
soul itself of the struggle for Independence.

The experiences of the first years, and later and even more
serious meditations had caused Bolivar to see the fallacy in
the idea that it was enough to proclaim the most advanced
democratic principles and jacobin policies; but, on the other
hand, this evolution in his thought had not caused him to
go to the other extreme. His ideal was to find the formula
which would conciliate fundamental democratic principles
with the necessity for an efficient government. Was this
compromise impossible, as Marius André believes? Without rendering a decision on this question, we believe that
Bolivar was sincere in his search for that formula; in his

Angostura speech it was not his purpose to cover with a mantle of flowers of liberal and democratic rhetoric a plan of authority and reaction. Precisely because he was a realist, he reasoned from the point of view of the geography, ethnology and economics of Venezuela, and he saw that Venezuela required a strong and stable government. The other reality, no less concrete, was the public opinion created by the Independence which would accept only a republican régime with democratic orientation. The jacobins had tried to realize a pure democracy, forgetting the first reality; the deluded reactionaries forgot the second when they tried to set up thrones in America. The merit of Bolivar is evident in having differed from both these extremes. It is not merely a meaningless phrase or a bit of scholasticism when he establishes the difference between what is owing to humanity and what is due to politics, between fundamental rights and liberties and general democratic orientation, and the practical organization of the State. As far as the first is concerned, he considers all the faith and enthusiasm of the revolutionary epoch; towards the second, his policy is relativistic and practical. The distinction made by Bolivar between the democratic ideal and the practical forms of state organization is found expressed clearly in these words of Barthélemy: "The democratic principle appeared only as a rational ideal, towards which the state should tend, always keeping in mind social realities and practical necessities. It does not specify, and it cannot, a precise type of popular government." With the sincerity and valor which are characteristic, he formulates the severest criticisms of pure democracy. "The wisest Greek law-

[1] *Traité élémentaire de droit constitutionel,* 72.

maker did not see his republic ten years, and suffered the humiliation of seeing the insufficiency of absolute democracy in ruling any kind of society, even the most cultured, temperate and limited." Later he proclaims emphatically that indefinite liberty, absolute democracy, are the reefs upon which the republican hopes are to be wrecked. . . . "Angels, not men, are the only individuals who can exist free, tranquil, and happy in the exercise of sovereign power. From absolute liberty there is a descent to absolute power, and the stage between these terms is supreme social liberty. Abstract theories are the things that produce the pernicious idea of unlimited liberty."

And continuing in this tone, he thus condemns the utopians who, aspiring to impossible liberties have tried to dissolve the social body: "The shouts of human kind in the fields of battle and in tumultuous bodies cry out to heaven against the unreflecting and blind legislators who have thought that chimeric institutions could be attempted with impunity."

Knowing history, Bolivar was forced to admit that monarchies and aristocracies had set up strong and enduring régimes. And he is also aware of the weakness, or better, the fragility of the republican régime, especially in countries of complicated structure. "The diversity of origin requires an infinitely steady pulse, an extremely delicate tact, to manage a heterogeneous society whose complicated organism is dislocated, dissolved, or divided by the slightest change."

Having discarded pure democracy, the pragmatic judgment of Bolivar, so far as the organization of the state is concerned, comes to this incontrovertible principle: "The most perfect form of government is that which produces the greatest degree of happiness possible, the greatest degree of social security, the greatest amount of political stability."

Would it be possible to find such a Government inside of the republican-democratic orientation? The sense of reality of Bolivar makes him fix his attention on the most interesting experience of history, the attempt to conciliate the principles of human liberties with governmental efficiency; I refer to the British constitution. The admiration felt for it by Bolivar probably dated from his diplomatic mission to London in 1810, or perhaps from his early journeys to Europe. In the Jamaica letter, that is to say four years previous to the Angostura Speech, in referring to the government which New Granada and Venezuela might adopt, he recommends the British model with great fervor. In political preferences Bolivar parts from nearly all the men of the revolutionary period, who did not cultivate any other than the North American or French models. It was not natural sympathy for the only nation that favored, though indirectly, Spanish-American independence, that led Bolivar to praise the excellence of the British constitution. It was rather because of the manner in which it agreed with the conclusions at which he himself had arrived.

The fundamental idea of Bolivar was to adapt and add to the inevitable and fatal republic, the organization of powers, legislative and executive, of the British system. He praised the division of the legislative power into two chambers: the first of representatives, designated according to the old Venezuelan constitution without any essential reform, and the second, the senate which instead of being

elective was to be composed of the men who had fought
for independence and their descendants. Thus he tried
to perpetuate the *élite* of the men of state and war who
were the true creators of the country. This Senate was,
according to Bolivar's own words, " the basis, tie, and soul
of the republic ".

In continuity of power through the hereditary principle,
Bolivar finds the solidity, cohesion, and the superior culture that he desired as features of his form of government.
For two fundamental reasons, he champions the hereditary
character of the senate: first, because of the independence it
would gain, second, its members might receive the proper
technical education. " This neutral body, in order that it
may remain so, must not owe its origin to the government
or to the people, so that it enjoys a full independence which
neither fears nor expects anything of these two founts of
authority." Bolivar, with admirable intuition, points out
the essential vice of popular elections; the lack of liberty
of the lawmakers from their constituents; the necessity of
catering to their interests, feelings, and preferences. All
the modern conception respecting what we may call electoral
servitude, the *surenchère démagogique* palpitates in the
words of Bolivar.

The future senators, in his opinion, should be educated
in a college especially designed to instruct the future lawmakers of the country. " It is an office for which the candidates should prepare, as it is a position requiring much
knowledge. All should not be left to chance and the outcome of the elections. The people can deceive themselves
more easily than nature perfected by art."

In a letter directed to White, Bolivar had the opportunity
of defining his thought upon the hereditary senate in even

greater detail. His purpose was also to establish a control for the democratic tendency and a principle of governmental stability. Here are his words: "Respecting my senate, I must say that it is neither a nobility nor an aristocracy, the first being established upon the right to manage the government, and the second upon offensive privileges. The function of my senate is to temper the absolute democracy, to mix the form of an absolute government with a moderated institution, because of a recognized principle in politics that a completely democratic government is as tyrannical as a despot. Thus, only a tempered government can be free. How could I hope to temper a democracy except with an aristocratic institution? We should not mix the monarchic form with the popular one we have adopted, but we should, at least, see to it that there is in the Republic an unchanging body which will assure stability, since without stability all political principles are corrupted and end by being destroyed."

In order to judge Bolivar's ideas on the senate exactly, it is necessary to distinguish in them what is secondary and accidental from what is essential. The essential characteristics, according to him are technical capacity and independence in the face of election interests. The minor features are the special means by which he proposes to obtain these qualities. The principles he advances are of undisputed worth and of permanent value. The same is not true of the means he suggests, that is the hereditary principle. It is true that independence had developed a select group of soldiers and statesmen of whom it was wise to make use at this time, but their perpetuation through inheritance represented the introduction into America of a principle which was repugnant to the general feelings of all and

which lacked effective means by which it might be established. Among us the elements which made possible a
Roman Senate or a House of Lords were lacking.

For this reason the Congress of Angostura substituted a
life-term senate for this hereditary senate. Although this
alternative was less opposed to democratic and republican
ideas, it offered a constant danger, if it was established, of
creating a class with privileges which might become abuses.
If the senate did not consolidate its power, it would become
a decorative and parasitic addition to a strong-man government. The scientific solution was to organize the senate
on the basis of economic forces and existing cultural institution. But it is necessary to recognize the fact that, although
in the epoch of the Angostura speech a similar idea had
been advanced by Sieyès and Benjamin Constant, only in
very recent times has it been reflected in well-thought out
plans. We must also add that right after the revolution
there were no important and independent social institutions, with the exception of property and the church, and
that the essential organs of the state could not be based only
on these.

Gil Fortoul says, dealing with the Senate of Bolivar:
" We must admire, nevertheless, the spirit which advanced
beyond its times in philosophical speculation, stating at that
time the problems of social selection. Would the hereditary
principle, perhaps, have preserved the caste of virtuous, prudent and energetic men who strove for independence, and
prevented the disorganizing struggle of continuous civil
wars? This is the secret of the past. It is the secret of
the future to find out how to make social and political
selections in modern democracies." [2]

[2] *Op. cit.*, I, 276.

How was this problem decided in the troubled life of the nineteenth century? In the countries where the military spirit predominated selection was made in rude and bloody civil combats in which the most capable or the most fortunate succeeded in gaining the ascendancy. In other countries in which there were stronger economic interests or a class of landholders, selection was made in a different manner, in favor of a proprietary class, which fortunately was frequently part of, or influenced by the intellectual *élite*. In the middle of the nineteenth century, military bureaucracy and territorial oligarchy tended to be displaced by the rule of a government frankly plutocratic. The political parties always represented small minorities, true oligarchies. Some were recruited from the wealthier classes, others were chosen because of their demagogic aptitude. Democracy could not solve this tragic dilemma except by the organization of syndicates or corporations and their just representation in the state.

The problem that Bolivar tried to solve in establishing his hereditary senate is now reaching an acute crisis in our modern democracies. Everyone knows that they are, in one manner or another, in the control of directing minorities. How should these minorities be formed? The two great principles formulated by Bolivar: technical capacity and independence of demagogic interests, are of living actuality and application today. A disciple of Bolivar today would advocate professional representation in place of universal suffrage as the only source of legislative authority.

As far as the executive is concerned, Bolivar again recommended the British model. " Nothing can be found which would not incline one to decide that it is the perfect model for either an aristocracy or a democracy. Apply in Venezuela this executive authority in the person of a president named by the people or by their representatives and we will have taken a great step towards national happiness." Later he says: "Nothing is so dangerous as weakness in the executive, and if a kingdom had judged it necessary to give him too much power, in a republic this is even more necessary. In republics the executive should be stronger, because all conspire against him, whereas in monarchies, the legislative authority should have the most power, because everything conspires in favor of the monarch."

This observation of Bolivar, justly praised by all his commentators, has been realized in the North American Revolution. The congenital weakness of the republican-federal system, has had in the United States a counterpoise in the strength and efficiency of the executive authority. Bolivar continues: "If there is not put in the hands of the executive all the means which a just viewpoint would indicate, the executive will inevitably fall into nullity or into abuse, which means the death of the government, the results of which are anarchy, usurpation, and tyranny. . . . By the same token that no form of government is so weak as the democratic, its structure should be of the greatest solidity and its institutions designed for stability. If it is not thus, we content ourselves with an attempt at government and do not have a permanent system, we content ourselves with a society ungovernable, restless, and anarchic."

The evolution of Spanish America in the nineteenth century has literally confirmed the Bolivarian law. The constitutional weakness of the executive has led to these two extremes: anarchy or absolute power. The exact truth would be to anarchy *and* absolute power, because after the first, the second has come, and *vice versa*.

Besides the hereditary senate and the stable and efficient executive, Bolivar recommended the establishment of an institution to watch over morals and public education. " Morality and culture are the poles of a republic. If we take from Athens its Areopagus and its guardians of the customs and the laws, if we take from Rome its censors and domestic tribunals, if we take from Sparta its austere establishments, and forming from these three springs a fount of Virtue, we will give our republic a fourth power, whose dominion will be infancy and the hearts of men, public spirit, good customs, and republican morality."

Such is the famous moral power with which Bolivar wishes to crown the edifice of his constitution. The Areopagus of Bolivar was " an irreproachable and holy tribunal (Article XII.) which was to prize all acts of virtue and civic spirit and to publish the shame and ignominy of the sinful and every work of corruption and indecency ". It was composed of two houses. The first, called, the moral chamber, was to direct the moral opinion of all the republic, with jurisdiction not only over individuals but also over families, departments, provinces, corporations, tribunals, authorities and the government itself. This body was to publish statistical tables of the virtues and the vices and comparative lists of the men who distinguished themselves in the exercise of public virtues or in the practice of public vices. In short, it was a sort of formidable lay inquisition with very wide jurisdiction in the realm of morals and customs.

The second house, called the chamber of education, was to watch over the physical and moral welfare of children from birth up to twelve years of age. It was to prepare and publish important works, organize and direct the schools, name the instructors, regulate the colleges, and finally to direct public opinion in cultural matters. It had, as part of the last-named duty, the right to examine all books published and to render judgment on them. In a word, the chamber of education came to be a mixture of department of public instruction, academy, and tribunal of censorship.

Even when some of the institutions or projects of Bolivar are impractical, such as the Areopagus, yet, they are always presented as an indication of a necessity which can be called a grave and transcendent problem. When Bolivar, after having shown an inflexible sense of reality in supporting the dismemberment of Spanish America into different nationalities, later spoke of uniting them in a general congress which would look out for their common interests, he outlined a project that was utopian at that time but which involves a problem that is ever becoming more important—that is, the problem of continental solidarity, which if it is ever solved will likely be solved inside the general outlines indicated by him. In a similar manner, the realistic policy which discarded suffrage as the sole source of legislative authority and which called for a stable and strong executive, recognized the fact that however efficient a political formula might be, a certain amount of organic morality, of effective virtue, was necessary. It is clear that he was mistaken in trying to form artificially this ethical body, including it in the body politic; but this error betrays a fundamental truth: that there cannot be political institutions without an ethical base, and that the political problem is indissolubly connected with the moral problem. Such a conception is wholly in conformity with the modern viewpoint which does not believe in the sole efficacy of political formulas and in virtue outside of economic development.

There existed in America, with all the force of tradition and prestige of universality, the true organ of a superior morality, the church. Although its work, representing the truly shining side of Spanish colonization, was different, always superior, and in many cases, opposed to the work of the state, in the moment of the war of independence it appeared in many cases united to the Spanish monarchy. Not only because of jacobin influence but perhaps in part because of the circumstance alluded to, Bolivar's political plan sought its own ethical support, causing the confusion we have condemned. Some years had to pass before Bolivar was to see the problem with more clarity and be convinced that his best solution would be to give the church independence in the spiritual realm, and to protect and support it.

Condensing this explanation, we can say that Bolivar, in his Angostura speech, presents the new political formula in which the republican principle of government is used as the base; a technical senate, a centralized and efficient executive, and a house of representatives democratically elected are its distinctive features. From the democratic orientation of the revolution, he takes the essential bases: the republican form of government and individual guarantees. To a certain point, he is in accord with the conservative and centralistic movement of La Plata, but he parts from it on the question of monarchy. Of the democratic machine, he selects only the popular election of the house of representatives—a reaction against the ideas and institutions of the first revolutionary period. He does not believe in the supreme and infallible character of the general will, and in any case, wishes to avoid its chances and dangers. This popular opinion is simply one device of the mechanism which he sets up at the side of others, the strong and stable executive, and the senate which he wished to be independent and capable; this last, above all, was the essence of his system. Let us not forget his words when he calls it the base, tie, and soul of his plan. It could be said, then, that the Bolivar plan is a conservative republic directed by a really intellectual and moral *élite*. Gil Fortoul says justly that he did not have confidence in absolute democracy, and that by his character and thought he was inclined to a rule of intellectual oligarchy. The same author agrees that such a government as he proposes was the only transition possible between the colony and independence.

Judging Bolivar's thought in its essential points, we see in it a wise middle term with some accidental variants, the principle which should be conducive to all political progress and social stability. As we have said, it was to be realized, in its essential features, in all the American countries; but at the moment it was proposed it had to struggle against jacobin mysticism (still very strong, especially in the countries that were to form Great Colombia). On the other side, those who were freed or reacted against this influence had passed to the other extreme. The leading personages of America, on escaping from the intelligent influence of Bolivar, moved between two utopias: the utopia on the left which was federalism, and the utopia on the right which was monarchy.[3]

[3] For the text of the Angostura speech see *Documentos relativos a la Vida Pública del Libertador,* Caracas, 1826-16, II, 1. The letter to White is found in Lecuna, *Cartas del Libertador,* II, 177.

CHAPTER XVI

POLITICAL IDEOLOGY OF SAN MARTÍN

The political evolution which was proceeding in Colombia, formed by the union of New Granada and Venezuela already free, coincides with the initiation of constitutional effort in Chile and in Peru. This was a consequence of the liberating work of San Martín.

While the study of the constitutional discussion in these countries once their independence has been declared will find its proper place in other chapters, it is necessary here to refer to the ideological orientations of the great leader who shares with Bolivar the glory of having liberated America.

In this study there cannot be omitted the instructions which San Martín received from the government of Buenos Aires during the military operations for the liberation of Chile. These instructions reflect his thought or, at least, the thought conforms to the instructions.

Although these instructions urge San Martín to exercise all his influence in order that Chile, once liberated, send a deputation to the united provinces and that he obtain by all means a constitutional alliance for a joint policy, the seventh instruction indicates absolute respect for the sovereignty and the popular vote of Chile, following the basic doctrine of the constitution of the nationalities of America to which we have already referred in Chapter XII. The text of this instruction is worthy of being quoted: " Seventh: A general should also be named, and a president with like provisional tenure who unites in himself the executive direction of police, justice, finance and war, and help should be asked in order that, without the loss of time, he may proceed to dictate the measures which he deems necessary for the re-establishment of the supreme government of the country along those lines most in harmony with the common desire of the inhabitants, nor should the general or the army take any other part in this activity than the keeping of the peace and the preventing in a prudent manner that the election become the work of the intrigue of any party against the general will and the security of the army." [1]

San Martín obeyed these instructions scrupulously and left the government of Chile in the hands of the Chilean leader, General O'Higgins, who organized his provisional government, as we have seen, with a senate of five members.

Fulfilling his destiny and going counter to the orders of his own government which demanded that he waste his energies in the chaos in which Rio de la Plata was floundering, and which he left in order to consolidate the independence of his own country and that of Peru, San Martín occupied the coast of Peru, the true center of Spanish power in America. San Martín did not believe that he must pursue the same political course which he had followed in Chile, that is to set up a political Peruvian government and to retain for himself only military functions. In a decree of August 3, he declared: "Henceforward there will be united in my person under the title of Protector the supreme military and political authority of the free Departments of Peru." [2]

What reason did San Martín have to abandon the atti-

---

[1] *Documentos del Archivo de San Martín,* III, 412.
[2] *Gaceta de Gobierno de Lima,* 11 Agosto, 1821.

tude he had had in Chile? It is plain that the circumstances were different. Chile had consolidated her independence after the decisive battles of Chacabuco and of Maipu, while in Peru, after the occupation of Lima and of the proclamation of independence, a large part of the Sierra territory remained in the hands of the Spanish.

In the Provisional Ordinance of October 1, 1821, San Martín explains his conduct and points out his motive for assuming dictatorial powers; here are his words: " While enemies exist in the nation and until the people form their first notions of self-government, I shall administer the directive power of the state, whose functions, without being the same, are analogous to those of the executive and judicial powers. But I shall always abstain from the solemn exercise of the judicial functions, for its independence is the unique and true safeguard of the liberty of the people. . . ." [8]

It is interesting to observe that the great importance which San Martín gave to the independence of the judicial power was also part of the creed of Bolivar and that the Liberator expressed the idea in almost identical words five years later in his discourse on the life-tenure constitution.

Let us examine briefly the essential provisions of the Provisional Ordinance. It recognizes the Catholic religion as the state religion, but grants the right of free worship to dissenters.

It establishes the institution of ministers who must legalize the orders of the Protector. It creates a council of state, of advisory character, since it has only the right to give counsel, of twelve individuals who integrate the Ministers, the head of the army and the General Staff, and the Dean

[8] *Estatuto Provisional*, Lima, 1821.

of the ecclesiastical *cabildo*. It confirms individual rights and declares that there are no crimes of opinion. Finally, it extends Peruvian citizenship to all Americans.

In conformity with the Statute, the decree giving freedom of the press was promulgated.

Another decree created the Order of the Sun to which an aristocratic character was attributed.

From the point of view of form of government San Martín, like all the men of the Rio de la Plata, was a partisan of the monarchical form. His councillor and minister, Monteagudo, from the time of his voyage to Europe, had been converted to monarchism, abandoning his early exalted jacobinism. The idea of San Martín was to realize the monarchic plan by means of the sincere reconciliation of Spain and Peru.

The negotiations called " of Punchauca " embodied the monarchic plan of San Martín.

On June 7, 1821, he proposed an armistice to the Viceroy La Serna, which was concluded June 23. There took place an interview between the Viceroy and the liberator chieftain at which San Martín declared: " No matter how long the struggle might continue, there can be no doubt about the result for millions of men determined to be independent. The armies of Spain will be more useful to Spain if instead of ephemeral gains they might offer commercial markets, profitable relations and permanent peace between men of the same race who speak the same language and have the desire to be free." These words of the discourse of San Martín at the famous interview refer to the liberal revolution in Spain of the year 1820 which re-established the authority of the Constitution of Cadiz and created a bond of spiritual affinity between Spain and America, in spite of the war for independence. Without the hopes which this liberal revolution aroused in the South Americans the negotiations of Punchauca would be inexplicable.

The definitive armistice was signed July 10 and it provided for the naming of two delegates, one by the Viceroy and the other by San Martín to negotiate with the King of Spain. Their instructions were: " To negotiate the independence of Chile and of the province of Rio de la Plata and its establishment in Peru is the object of the mission." [4]

García Camba says that the conditions of this parley were the following: " That the independence of Peru is to be declared, that a regency be established for its government presided over by the Viceroy who will govern independently until the coming of a prince of the royal family."

The foundations of the parley collapsed because of new demands on the part of the Spanish Viceroy. At the same time there failed the mission of García del Río and Parroisien which limited itself to present to his Britannic Majesty a " compromise plan which would conciliate the interests of independent Peru with the interests of England and of Spain ".[5] The war continued. But San Martín, following his conciliatory and pacifist intentions, reiterated his proposals of bases for settlement on July 14, 1822. These fundamental requirements were: " the recognition of independence, the restitution of the property confiscated from the Spaniards, a reduction of 3 per cent in the customs duties, the granting of citizenship to the Spaniards, their admission into the army and the recognition of the debt ".[6]

[4] *Manifiesto y Documentos de las Negociaciones de Punchauca,* Lima, 1821.

[5] *Justificación de la conducta pública seguida por J. García del Río y D. Parroisien,* London, 1825.

[6] *Gaceta de Gobierno,* September 11, 1822.

In regard to the federal idea San Martín, agreeing with Bolivar and with the most realistic leaders of the northern movement as well as with the results of the experience in Rio de la Plata in the unhappy period, 1814 to 1820, showed himself the declared enemy of the federal form of government. Here are his words to the provinces of Rio de la Plata, at the time of undertaking the expedition to Peru: " To think of establishing a federal government in a country so sparsely inhabited, full of jealousy and local antipathies, so defective in knowledge and experience of public affairs, lacking in revenue to provide for the expenditures of the general government, not to mention those which the civil list of each state requires—this is a plan whose perils are too obvious to permit self-delusion even when its faults are obscured by the ephemeral pleasure which illusions of novelty offer." [7]

Concerning the principles of sovereignty or of the popular will as a decisive factor in the forming of nationalities, we also know the criterion of San Martín which conforms with the spirit of the instructions which he received from Rio de la Plata and with the unanimously accepted criterion of the creators of the new nationalities. The historian Bulnes, in referring to the expedition which was organized to operate in the sierra of Peru and which in the event of victory was to bring liberty to the people of Upper Peru, says: " Keeping in mind that the expedition would reach the provinces of Upper Peru, that is to the present-day Republic of Bolivia which then nominally formed a part of the United Provinces of Rio de la Plata, San Martín recommended to Alvarado that he maintain this territory ' intact

[7] Neptali Carranza, *Oratoria Argentina,* I, 209.

and unharmed ' and in the event of liberating it completely, that he call a general congress of these provinces, or at the least, a convention preparatory to a congress, and that he put at the disposition of one or the other the army of the Andes in order that it might be able to decide the destiny of this territory with complete independence and liberty. The members of the government *junta* gave him great freedom of action." [8]

We need not study here the work of San Martín and of his minister Monteagudo from the administrative point of view.

Contrary to the conciliatory policy, and, at times, as a consequence of the breakdown of this policy, Monteagudo furthered the most radical measures aimed at the Spaniards going so far as to expropriate all their property. Meanwhile the forces commanded by the Viceroy La Serna, Canterac and Valdez consolidated their positions in the sierra of Peru and organized a resistance which appeared invincible. San Martín realized that the consummation of independence in the region required the cooperation of Colombia and he solicited it; it was given but not to the necessary extent. This new failure determined the decision of San Martín to abandon the field in favor of Bolivar, who must complete the work of liberation. In internal affairs, he believed his withdrawal would permit the new nationality to organize itself with absolute liberty. San Martín renounced his command before the congress which he called together for that purpose and which will, as we shall see, organize the Public Power (Poder Publico) and consider the Peruvian constitution.

[8] *Bolívar en el Perú,* I, 39.

CHAPTER XVII

THE CONSTITUTION OF GREATER
COLOMBIA—1821

The Congress of Angostura replaced the hereditary senate of Bolivar by a life-term senate. The term of office for the President was set at four years. The Congress of Angostura sanctioned the project of forming a single nation of the ancient Viceroyalty of Santa Fe and of the Captaincy-general of Venezuela which would be called Colombia and which would include the departments of Venezuela, Quito and New Granada. Bolivar realized his old ideal which he had favored since his Jamaican letter. The idea of this union corresponded to the opinion held at that time in those provinces; Bolivar said: "Her wish for the reunion of her provinces [he refers to those of New Granada] to the provinces of Venezuela is also unanimous. The inhabitants of New Granada are profoundly convinced of the immense advantage which would accrue to both peoples by the creation of a new Republic composed of these two nations. The union of New Granada and Venezuela has been my sole purpose since I first began the struggle, it is the desire of the citizens of both countries and it is the guarantee of the liberty of South America." [1]

The formation of this great national unity was determined by the necessities of the war and it was going to have the sanction of victory. War imposed the route to unity in New Granada and in Venezuela.

---

[1] Monsalve, *Ideal de Bolívar, 1783-1824*, 260.

The ideas of Bolivar on the constitution of Greater Colombia had to be discussed anew after the triumph of Boyaca
which assured the independence of New Granada, at the
congress in which all the liberated provinces were represented at Rosario de Cucuta in 1821. In respect to the
permanent union of New Granada and Venezuela three
solutions were possible. The first was the fusion of these
two countries into one united and centralized republic, such
was Bolivar's idea. The second was the formation of a
federative state, each of the three states or provinces con-
serving its autonomy and independence. The third, supported by Nariño, was modelled after the second, but with
the difference that six states were to be erected with artificial boundaries in order to give a maritime outlet to each
one. This plan, according to Vega, was the fruit of Nariño's
relationship with distinguished individuals of the old world;
the separation of powers and the guarantees of personal
rights received the support of Benjamin Constant, and Humboldt had outlined the contemplated territorial division.

It is obvious that from the point of view of the immediate necessities of the war, that the best solution was that
of Bolivar. We must recognize the fact, however, that when
these circumstances no longer were present, the federal
form would be preferable in dealing with the large provinces
or territorial unities, as the facts later proved and as Bolivar
himself thought for a moment. The federation which demanded disintegration when it was applied within Venezuela and New Granada, was a principle of integration when
it was employed to form one federal state from the various
provinces. It is therefore understandable that Nariño could
be a federalist in this sense at that moment without being
in contradiction with his former centralist ideas.

The plan of Bolivar received the support of the majority, and the fundamental law which was voted at Angostura on the union of the peoples of Colombia, that is of the Vice-royalty of New Granada and the Captaincy of Venezuela, was solemnly ratified.

But Bolivar won only this point in the discussions of the Assembly of Cucuta. The legislators there gathered differed even more than those of Angostura from the ideas of Bolivar concerning the practical necessities of the government. The constitution of the year 21, like that of Cadiz, established indirect suffrage but only in two categories. It demanded the ownership of property and the exercise of a profession, service or trade. The House of Representatives was composed of the deputies elected in each province in the ratio of one to each thirty thousand inhabitants. The Senate, contrary to the central idea of Bolivar's system, was of popular origin. Each of the seven departments elected four senators. The mandate was for eight years and the upper Assembly renewed itself by halves. The Senate was vested with the power to judge all officials indicted by the House of Representatives; a two-thirds majority was required for conviction. The judicial hierarchy was composed of a High Court, Superior Courts and subordinate tribunals. The judges of the Superior Courts were appointed by the Executive Power. In the matter of local government, the constitution established *intendentes* for each department and Governors for each province to be appointed by the Executive Power. In the cantons there were magistrates (*juez político*) and *alcaldes* appointed by the *cabildo* of the canton.

Special laws were passed for the abolition of slavery and for the division of the land which the Spanish laws had set apart for return to the natives.

The law dealing with the freedom of the press was inspired by an exaggerated liberalism. In imitation of the law passed by the Cortes of Cadiz and sanctioned in the year 11 by Rivadavia, the offences of the press were submitted to a jury of seven persons of whom six were needed to condemn and two to acquit. This practice brought about what amounted to the complete irresponsibility of the press.

The powers of the Executive Power were very limited in this constitution, but they became even more so when the approval of the Senate was required for the appointment of the Governors and the *intendentes*. But Bolivar obtained three decrees which permitted him to exercise the Executive Power with full freedom thereby creating an absolute dictatorship as the necessities of the war required. The first of these decrees allowed every measure necessary for the preservation of order in the revolting cities. The second decree placed in the hands of Bolivar the army and the organization of the territories which he might liberate and permitting him to use the same powers in other parts of the country when he felt that the safety of the state required it. The third decree conferred on him the right to increase the army and authorized him to exact loans. Gil Fortoul says, and rightly, that from 1811 there may be observed the same contradiction between the revolutionary ideology and the necessity of a dictatorship. This contradiction between theory and practice, between the ideal and life was to make the solution of the political problem in America extremely difficult. How much better it would have been instead of adopting an ultra-liberal constitution and accepting at the same time an absolute dictatorship in fact, to have created a government like the one proposed by Bolivar at Angostura and a stable régime which might be established not by an hereditary senate, but by a professional and technical one free from the influence of demagogic agitation.

The soundest criticism of the Constitution of Cucuta was made by Bolivar himself. He was the first to focus attention on the contrast between the excessively liberal character of some of its institutions and the broad extraordinary powers which it found itself obliged to grant.

The exaggerated intervention of the Senate in appointments and the real control of public officials who were responsible to it were bound to create the most serious obstacles to the efficient functioning of administration. In the case of the government of Venezuela, that attribute of the Senate brought on the revolution of Páez.

Not only did Bolivar dissent from the spirit of the Constitution, but he believed with profoundly realistic vision that the members of the professions and the jurists who composed the assemblies not only did not represent the needs of the people but also that they did not respond to their desires or to the real condition of the Colombian people.

Bolivar, in a letter to Santander, paints a vivid picture of the real situation in America, in which by the side of the little intellectual oligarchies imbued with an abstract and romantic philosophy, there was a scattered, enslaved and semi-barbarous population, a contrast between what we would call today *raison raisonnante* and the instinct of primitive peoples, who required a form of government appropriate to their exceptional conditions in which force and religious sentiment were the only elements of cohesion and civilization.

The constitution of 21 did not fall into the federalist error but neither did it create a strong executive power, and it exaggerated legislative interference in administration. In spite of this, constitutionality created a psychological factor in America, and with the instrument of the Constitution of Cucuta, through the political genius of Santander, it was possible to organize the administration in Colombia, that is to say in the liberated regions, while Bolivar maintained a dictatorship in the theatre of operations of the liberating army.

Chapter XVIII

MONARCHY OR REPUBLIC

While the Congress of Cucuta dedicated itself to the adoption of the democratic and liberal constitution which has been described, the new revolution in Mexico, headed by Iturbide and the government of Peru, under the leadership of San Martín, were frankly becoming oriented toward the establishment of monarchy, the rulers to be chosen from the reigning house of Spain. This plan for the creation of autonomous monarchies in Hispano America was to be accomplished not by direct negotiations carried on in Europe, like those of Belgrano and Rivadavia, but by agreements with the Spanish authorities. We have already had occasion to mention the provisions of Punchauca proposed by San Martín to the Viceroy of Peru. By the terms of the Treaty of Cordova, signed by the Viceroy O'Donojú and General Iturbide, the throne was offered to Ferdinand VII or to another member of the Spanish reigning family; and in the event of a blanket refusal, the crown would be given to any person chosen by the Mexican Cortes. Iturbide formed a regency of which he was president and O'Donojú a member. The provisions of Punchauca were repudiated by the Viceroy La Serna, and the Treaty of Cordova was disapproved by the Cortes of Spain, and by the vote of the liberals. It was made plain again that monarchy in America was utopian since it could not count on the collaboration of Spain.

The plans of San Martín and Iturbide were nothing more than adaptations to the situation created by the war of independence of the project attributed to the Count of Aranda to form separate monarchies of the dominions of the Spanish Empire. Such projects were inspired, moreover, by the visible example of Brazil where, due to the installation of the Portuguese dynasty after the conquest of Portugal by Napoleon, the monarchy had been successfully consolidated, and Brazil was preparing to separate from Portugal and to form a new empire.

One recognizes immediately the difference between the situation of Peru and Mexico in 1821. And equally clear is the difference between Peru and Mexico of 1821 and Brazil of the same time.

It is useless to discuss the advantages which a monarchic régime would have had for America. Even accepting that these advantages are undeniable, it is obvious that the establishment of the monarchy demanded conditions very different from those in which San Martín and Iturbide thought to establish it. The essential basis of the monarchic principle is continuity. Monarchy is a true organism, which may be transplanted like a tree, and not a structure which may be raised at will. Monarchy was possible only in the form of the project of the Count of Aranda. The formation of independent principalities in America might have been realized without any period of transition and altogether in conformity with the law of monarchic continuity. The nations of the Hispanic family would thus have formed the vastest empire or confederation of the earth, under the chain of gold of the monarchic régime. The principle of continuity was achieved for exceptional causes in Brazil, causes which determined the consolidation and the erection of the monarchy in that country. The situation in the other provinces of America was in no way similar. Ten years of warfare and the establishment of their own governments had broken the necessary continuity. Moreover, it cannot be denied that the republican and revolutionary ideology, sharpened in the struggle, had widened the abyss between Spain and America and made all reconciliation more difficult. A new spiritual climate existed on the continent. Finally, the monarchic plans ignored Spanish psychology and the inadaptability of the government of that country to reconciliation with America on the realistic basis of recognition of independence or of autonomy. The noisy collapse of the negotiations of Rivadavia and of Belgrano was the augury of the denial of the terms of Punchauca by the Viceroy La Serna and of the abrogation of the Treaty of Cordova. The monarchic plans not only ignored reality in America, but above all else they ignored the sad reality of Spain. The loss of its immense colonial empire on the continent was not enough to teach the Spanish government a lesson and to induce it to follow in respect to Cuba, a policy of liberty and of autonomy. How was Spain to accept the principles of the nineteenth century embodied in the wise program of the Viceroy O'Donojú when the Cortes of Cadiz, as we have seen, conceived of Spain and its colonial empire as an indivisible monarchy? There is something more, in the event of provisional acceptance on the part of the Spanish government, the transition to federalist monarchy still carried with it this danger, that when the circumstances which had determined this policy had disappeared, Spain, on the base of elements still remaining to her in America, might attempt the full restoration of the *ancien régime*.

The republican form of government was the manifest destiny of America, and it is, therefore, idle to believe that if any of these plans were accepted her fortune would have been different.

Justo Sierra says that this violence (he refers to the struggle between Spain and America) which had such great influence on the destiny of the new nations might have been avoided if the profound and far-sighted patriotism of O'Donojú had animated the statesmen of Spain on the day following the French Revolution.[1] But it is well known that far from following this policy, the Spanish liberals refused to accept even mere autonomy, and concurred only late and only in part in the limited program of reforms which the deputies from the Indies presented.

This opportunity having been lost, monarchic projects appear quite utopian in character. We believe that it is vain to think of what might have been the consequences for Peru of the project of Punchauca: reconciliation between patriots and royalists, avoidance of the dictatorship of Bolivar; no separation of upper Peru, and, therefore, the formation of a nationality which would have been the Brazil of the Pacific. All of this was not possible within the conditions which Spain herself had created. The project of Punchauca was destined to collapse. Even assuming that Spain would have accepted it, it would have been impossible to consolidate a monarchy in Peru. The dilemma was fatal: the monarch received his support from foreign sources, and therefore, independence was destroyed; or he sought support in his own army, and in that case he would be the tool or the instrument of his pretorian guard.

[1] *México y su Evolución*, I, 172.

Every political idea or every political plan had to take into consideration this enormous reality: the situation created by the revolution. It had to take into consideration, furthermore, this other truth: true independence demanded autochthonous authorities without connections with European governments.

In opposition to the attitude assumed by San Martín at Punchauca and by Iturbide at Cordova, Bolivar, when he had the opportunity to treat with the Spanish army led by Morillo, after Boyaca, that is to say when Spain still occupied part of Venezuela, decided to include among the instructions given to his commissioners the following: " If it should happen that it enter the Spanish scheme to propose some prince of the House of Bourbon as sovereign of Colombia, you will protest against such a proposal which will not be accepted under any circumstances even though great advantages are offered with it. This protest should be made not only against a Bourbon prince but against a prince of any reigning house of Europe. Colombia will be independent, sovereign and free of all foreign dominion, or she will cease to exist." [2] Concerning the Mexican monarchy, Bolivar understood the perils with which it menaced Colombia and, in a general way, the independence of America: " If a Bourbon is established in Mexico, it will be to his interest to preserve close relations with the prince reigning in Spain and with the other European powers; all of them will feel it necessary for the sake of their own personal interest to aid him and to sustain him, and the throne of Mexico would constantly have pretensions against limitrophe Colombia whose system must alarm it. The govern-

[2] Gil Fortoul, *Historia Constitucional de Venezuela*, I, 295.

ment of Mexico would establish the most rigorous espionage in our country; it would hasten to grasp the first opportunity which might present itself to invade us; it would take every measure possible against us to divide us, to weaken us and even to annihilate us." [8]

In conformity with this orientation, Bolivar sent a special commission to General San Martín to dissuade him from following the plan of Punchauca. In the instructions given to this commission reference is made to the divisions which would be produced in the army by the proclamation of monarchic principles, the encouragement which it would give to the Spaniards to continue the war in all the countries which had revolted, and finally, the danger that Europe would find a pretext to meddle in the discussions of the South American countries with Spain and to persuade her to impose an absolutist régime. As has been pointed out, Bolivar presented objections of unquestioned value to the monarchic plan, one of domestic nature the other international. Bolivar thought that even if the governments of Peru and of Chile were monarchic, the popular mass was republican.

The rebuff to the importation of the monarchy did not bring Bolivar to accept this same monarchy in the person of some Creole chief. This is, as Bolivar judged, the case of Mexico when Iturbide, the Treaty of Cordova having failed, proclaimed himself Emperor: " Iturbide, now you will know that he made himself Emperor by the grace of Pius the first sergeant. . . . I very much fear that the four strips of crimson which are called Throne cost more blood than tears and give more uneasiness than calm. There

[8] R. Blanco Fombona, *Cartas de Bolívar, 1799-1812*, p. 385.

are some who believe that it is quite easy to put a crown on one's self and that everyone will then adore it; I believe that the time of monarchies is over, and that until the corruption of mankind brings it to abandon the love of liberty, thrones will not return to fashion." [4]

In the famous interview of Guayaquil, it was necessary for the two great leaders of the independence to discuss the question of the form of government. San Martín, still undeceived by the collapse of monarchic attempts, insisted that the government of Peru should not be democratic and that a prince should come from Europe to rule that State. Bolívar answered him that the introduction of European princes was not suitable either to Colombia or to America, because these princes would form heterogeneous elements in the American mass, and he referred him to the reasons developed in the discourse of Angostura. Bolívar believed that monarchy was an artificial creation, an importation of extraneous elements. Would Bolívar then have preferred foreign authoritarianism, active and dominating tyranny, exclusively autochthonous of which he had spoken in the Jamaican letter? This authoritarianism was monarchy without the name.

Between the two extremes of monarchy, that involving European dynasty and the imitation of utopian federalism, was there no other possible form of government for America but the autochthonous dictatorship? Certainly not. We have already said that Bolívar discovered at Angostura the formula of the conservative republic in which he synthesized all liberty compatible with a stable and efficient government. Bolívar thought of the possibility of an organic

[4] Letter to Peñalver, Sept. 26, 1822. Lecuna, *Cartas del Libertador*, III, 97.

democracy, with a strong executive power but with certain bounds clearly established.

According to Gil Fortoul, Bolivar was thinking of the life-term presidency at the Conference of Guayaquil. Bolivar believed that it was best to form, immediately, Republics whose life-term presidents would have the prerogatives of an English monarch but who should be American, and whose parliaments would be the image and the organ of the popular mass.[5] In comparing the ideas of San Martín and of Bolivar the same author says: " Concerning political theory, it should be noted that neither the monarchy of the Argentine nor the republic *sui generis* of the Venezuelan could ever have been adapted to the social milieu of Hispano America, at least in the special form in which they were recommended, so that the constitutional error of San Martín is equal to the constitutional error of Bolivar." [6]

We must dissent from the opinion of the learned historian of Venezuela. In the first place, there is no proof that, in 1822, Bolivar believed the life-term presidency to be necessary. Until the year 1819, he wished a stable government constructed on the essential base of the senate, independent of universal suffrage and of technical character. Bolivar preferred the leadership of an intellectual *élite* to that of a monarch. In the second place, the facts proved that the monarchy of San Martín was utopian because of the resistance of Spain.

The monarchic plan, moreover, presented a danger to the consolidation of the independence, while the bolivarian aristarchia effected the autonomy and independence of the new

[5] *Op. cit.*, I, 339.
[6] *Ibid.*, I, 340.

states by the formation of autochthonous governments out
of the situation peculiar to each country.

In reality, beneath the labels of democracy, Spanish
America was governed, with peculiar variations for each
country, by a select group of statesmen, men of culture and
of high idealism under whose influence there was realized
relative stability and political progress which during the
nineteenth century characterized countries of America like
Chile, Argentina, Peru and Colombia itself and suppressed
the inevitable anarchy of the first years of the revolution.

Bolivar could not fail to realize that the republican form
of government and democratic orientation had molded the
Spanish-American revolution. It is of no interest to us to
know whether Bolivar sincerely embraced the cult of these
principles, or if at heart, as Marius André believes, Bolivar
had lost his democratic faith. It is certain that his realistic
vision not only led him to consider geographic, ethnic and
historic factors which demanded a stable and strong government, but also psychic factors, those which we might call
the spiritual *ambience,* the ideas and general aspirations
which originated the revolutionary movement. The jacobin
current, with its principalistic fever, disregarded the objective factors; the monarchic reaction, the psychic and political
factors. Bolivar knew that no government in America was
possible unless it attempted to find a formula which would
conciliate the effective necessities of stability, efficiency and
morality with the spiritual *ambience* created by liberal mysticism in public opinion furthering the respect for individual
liberties, a mysticism which had been the soul of the revolution. Was it possible to find this formula? Certainly not in
pure democracy, in the democracy of Rousseau from which
Bolivar had begun to be estranged at the time of the mani-

festo of Cartagena and with which he appears to have broken definitely in the discourse of Angostura.

Wedded to the idea of a strong government, he wished it to be at the same time liberal, legalized, and democratic. In a letter to O'Higgins he said: " Chile will do well indeed if she builds a government strong in structure and liberal in principles." [7] After three years' trial of the Constitution of Cucuta, under Santander's efficient and able administration, Bolivar said to him significantly:

" The more I consider your government, the more I am confirmed in the idea that you are the hero of American administration. It is a prodigy of achievement that a new government be eminently free and eminently law-abiding and, moreover, eminently strong." [8]

The political ideas which predominated among the members of Bolivar's group at this time may be seen in this letter of Castillo to Santander, dated Aug. 30, 1820:

" My friend, between philosophy and extreme love of perfection—defects which wrecked the republic and its first leaders—and the departure from all rule and order, there is a certain mean for which we should strive. We should aspire to the establishment of a government at once stable, energetic, and untrammeled for warfare. . . . Enlightenment will not impede the progress of war, and should not be suppressed simply because there are abuses; *the abuses of absolute power will always be greater and more irremediable.* . . . Necessary and beneficial assemblies are not to be proscribed." [The italics are the author's.] [9]

---

[7] Lecuna, *Cartas del Libertador*, III, 8.
[8] *Ibid.*, IV, 258.
[9] *Archivo de Santander*, V, 124.

Chapter XIX

CONSTITUTIONAL ORGANIZATION IN PERU, CHILE AND MEXICO

The debate over the form of government took on special importance in Peru. The patriotic society which Monteagudo had founded took up this subject as a means of preparing public opinion for the realization of the monarchic plan which San Martín and his illustrious minister had adopted. Doctor Moreno, one of the figures of the *Convictorio Carolino* who had defended and explained the Constitution of Cadiz, sustained the monarchic thesis animated with an eclectic and realistic spirit. He begins with this general proposition: the diffusion of public power is in direct proportion to the enlightenment and civilization of the people and in inverse ratio to the size of its territory. The logical consequence would be that in a country of much territory and of incipient culture the government must be concentrated in a single hand. Doctor Moreno affirms that monarchy is more in conformity with nature because it is founded on, and modeled after, paternal authority.[1]

Doctor Moreno, furthermore, presents the historical argument: no other form of government but monarchy has ever been known in Peru; the country is habituated to obedience to kings and to the forms and workings of governmental affairs peculiar to monarchic administration. Finally, he alludes to the heterogeneousness of the races and social conditions of Peru. Manuel Pérez Tudela, who

[1] *El Sol del Perú*, no. 3, May 28, 1822.

represented the republican group, opposed him. His arguments moved about these two ideas: there is no limit to
monarchic power, for it is of the nature of this power to
extend itself, and there is no king and no way to create one.
This second idea presented an argument of realistic character which was incontestable.[2]

Sánchez Carrión, who formed a part of the *doceañista*
group headed by Baquíjano, and now converted to the idea
of absolute independence and republicanism, answered the
arguments of Doctor Moreno in the famous letter which he
signed with the pseudonym of the " solitario de Sayan "
which was addressed to the director of the *Correo Mercantil
y Político* and reproduced by the *Abeja Republicana* of
August 15, 1822. This document is important in political
ideology not so much for the force of the arguments, which
in reality is not great, but because it reveals the psychology
of the moment in which this debate took place. Beginning
with the supposition that government is a political creation
and that it is necessary to choose the best form of government, he studies the faults of monarchy. He is inspired by
the same feeling expressed by Pérez Tudela about monarchic
power. Faced by " the lack of energy and zeal for liberty "
of which Peru has suffered: "A throne in Peru would be a
more despotic business than in Asia, and with the achievement of peace, the commanders would dispute the palm
of tyranny." [3]

Sánchez Carrión does not forget that the restoration of
the monarchy in Spain brought about immediately the perse-
cution of the *Padres de la Patria* and the execution of the

[2] Bernard Moses, *The Intellectual Background of the Revolution
in South America,* 117.

[3] Jorge Basadre, *La Iniciación de la República,* I, 25.

valiant men who had torn the throne from the French eagles. He answers ironically the arguments of Moreno on the extension of territory and the population and customs of the country, and he concludes by citing the republican examples of Colombia, Buenos Aires and Chile and North America.

In the *Sociedad patriótica* they discussed other subjects of high political import. It is worth-while to mention the oration pronounced on October 8th by Doctor don Mariano de Arce on sovereignty. Arce said that it could not pass beyond the limits of the eternal laws of justice which all nations had agreed on as the basis of the rights of man. Therefore, he continued, it is worth-while to study with attention the natural law which must regulate all human institutions.

When the *Congreso Constituyente* was convoked by San Martín, this political debate was transferred to it along with the discussions of the basic institutions of the new life of Peru. The withdrawal of San Martín and the transfer of power to the Congress gave it the responsibility for the organization of the executive power and the regulating of this power to conform with the rights and duties of the parliament. The following currents of thought were apparent: one maintained the necessity of the unity of executive power and of its independence of the parliament; another, in accord with the ideology which predominated in the period of the insurrection of the *cabildos* (1810-14) wished to constitute the executive power by means of a commission or triumvirate depending on the parliament. Larrea said: "No one ignores the fact that a power which is vested in various persons is by its nature slow, shackled and faltering, while that power which is put in the hands of one person is, on the contrary, active and capable of the greatest enterprise." He alludes to the case of Colombia, which from 1812 until 1816 passed through the bitter experiment of a collective government before it remedied this fault by unifying executive power and placing it in the hands of the immortal Bolivar.

Pérez de Tudela affirmed that if " seventy citizens have to deliberate correctly and at length, only one should have the power to execute ". Sánchez Carrión, invoking the memory of the Convention, also opposed the assuming of executive power by the assembly, but he supported the triumvirate with these words: " The presence of only one in the seat of power raises the spectre of a king, that word which signifies inheritance of tyranny." Don Javier Luna Pizarro, the deputy from Arequipa, opposed the unity and the independence of executive power with all his talent and all his prestige. He repeated the *leit motif* of the epoch: the gravitation of all power toward absolutism. " Those who command are clothed with authority without limit." Luna Pizarro defended the thesis that the liberty of peoples had wavered when executive power had been put in other hands than those of the assembly, and he concluded by declaring that the case of Danton and of Robespierre would not be repeated in Peru.[4]

---

[4] *Diario de la Asamblea Constituyente de Lima.* 1822. The following persons, among those most detached from the assembly, voted against that part of the thesis of Luna Pizarro which had to do with the independence of the executive *vis à vis* the assembly: Rodríguez de Mendoza, *el Maestro,* Sánchez Carrión, Mariátegui, Tudela, Larrea and Pedemonte. But Luna Pizarro won his point in spite of the invocation of the principle of the division of powers made by the above-mentioned orators. The *Abeja Republicana* opposed the measure adopted by the congress with these words: " The partisans of the division of power may say what they like, but this can be very good in a permanent constitution."

The Congress named a triumvirate responsible to it which was in reality only a commission submissive to its control. There was repeated in Peru the history of Venezuela and of New Granada. In Buenos Aires the problem of the unity of the executive power was already felt because of the demands of circumstances. The army of Peru, after the failure of the expedition in the South presented itself to the assembly and demanded that the executive power be put in the hands of one person and that this one person be José de la Riva Agüero.

There were two of these demands: the first, February 18, 1823, signed by Arenales, and the other, dispatched by Santa Cruz on February 26 of the same year. The second said: " the character of the governing *Junta*, like that of every body of this kind, is delay and irresolution ", and it concludes by saying: " We consider that only the separation of the executive power from the sovereign congress will restore health to the fatherland." [5]

The Assembly had to yield to the demands of the army, and Riva Agüero was elected president.

In the interval of the acts of the assembly which we have just traced, that body entered completely into the project of a constitutional commission. This project adopted as a basis for suffrage not the ancient *intendencias* but the *partidos,* thus ignoring the structure of Peru. It created a senate shorn of legislative powers with the simple functions of *super-vigilancia* and of appointment. Executive power was set up which " avoided the extremes of excessive power and of being a negative factor without strength and elasticity ". The project established ministerial responsibility

[5] *Manifiesto imparcial de los acontecimientos de la Capital del Perú.*

and " made the administration of justice independent and afterwards declared for the irremovability of judges ".

It did not renovate the whole parliamentary membership, because " the spirit of a legislative body is not amenable to absolute change ". The power of initiating legislation was given exclusively to the deputies, and only a suspensive veto was provided for. The Congress elected the executive from among the eligible candidates which the departments presented in order to combine ability with popularity. It continued the protection of the Catholic Church by the state only by means of those instruments which its " Divine Author announced in the Gospels ". It accepted the principle that the nation has not the power to decree laws which limit the rights of individuals, and qualified this principle in the following manner: " It is especially important to protect these rights, for representative governments founded on the legality of their powers may consider themselves absolute if in their origin sovereignty was not restricted." [6]

This plan of a constitution represents a typical case of the contamination of influences. The division of powers in the most extreme fashion is taken from the American constitution, the single chamber and the departmental *Junta* from the Constitution of Cadiz. The election of the executive by the legislative branch came from the early jacobins of the American revolution itself.

Almost at the same time that the Assembly of Peru discussed and sanctioned the first Peruvian constitution, there began, in Chile, the discussion of the second constitution of that country which was promulgated December 29, 1822. In

[6] *Proyecto de Constitución presentado al Congreso Constituyente por su Comisión de Constitución*, Lima, 1823.

spite of the coincidence of their appearance, the constitutions of Chile and of Peru represented opposite orientations. The Peruvian constitution was inspired by a liberal spirit, the Chilean by a conservative one. The first gave supremacy to the chamber of deputies, with the power of electing the president; the second gave primacy to the senate which assumed ordinary legislative functions, for the national or popular chamber was convoked only in case of conflict between the executive and the senate.

The constitution of Peru sanctioned the press law which, in imitation of the law approved by the Congress of Cucuta, established the greatest freedom for the press tending to bring about the effective irresponsibility of a publisher. On the other hand, the constitution of Chile placed restrictions on the press, since nothing could be published without the previous approval of a tribunal of censors. The ideas of Bolivar on moral force influenced the Chilean legislators; the constitution which they adopted created a national moral register in which were inscribed the names of citizens who had performed some distinguished service for their country.

At the fall of O'Higgins, an assembly was called which voted approval of the constitution of 1823. The Chilean historian Galdames characterizes this political charter in these words: "Administrative centralization, predominance of the executive in union with an aristocratic senate; and private morality as a basis of public right." The Supreme Director is elected popularly for four years and is eligible for reëlection for one additional term if he receives a two-thirds majority. The senate keeps a register of civil merit. The *Cámara Nacional* was an extraordinary assembly of consultants chosen by the electoral assemblies of the department.

Its function was to settle the conflicts between the Director and the senate.

There was a complex system of assemblies that had the right to elect and to censure the principal functionaries of the government. Censorship of the press was established. The constitution of 1823, says Galdames, is more a juridical than a political work. It reflects the ideas of Egaña, in whom is mingled the Catholic tradition with the philosophy of the eighteenth century.

The liberal character of the Peruvian constitution appears not only in the principles enunciated in it, but also in other pronouncements like the one which declared that the nation had not the power to enforce laws which infringed on the rights of the individual.

In the matter of local government, the Peruvian constitution of 1823 created departmental *juntas* who were to serve as councils to the prefects and to present the terms for the appointment of the governors of the province. This manner of selecting the members of the local governments, so different from that established in the Argentine by the constitution of 1819 and in Colombia by the constitution of Cucuta where the central government chose all local officials, had had a long history at that time.[7]

The Peruvian constitution betrayed a decentralist tendency, but not a federalist one. Federalism never took root in Peru. Federalist chaos in Colombia had taught some bitter les-

---

[7] In 1811, the instructions of Jujuy to his deputies contained the following: that the executive power should not name governors for the towns of the united provinces without consultation with a representative of the community, a *junta* similar to those which were formed for the selection of deputies, which should previously propose to the government three candidates upon one of whom the choice must fall. Gorriti, *op. cit.,* 341.

sons; and in La Plata there developed an exaggerated centralist reaction in the constitution of 1819.

Provincial separatism in Peru could not develop because of the greater influence of the government of Lima. In Peru, furthermore, there was no rivalry between the cities, like that between Caracas and Valencia in Venezuela, Bogota and Cartagena in New Granada, or Buenos Aires and Montevideo and Buenos Aires and Cordova in La Plata.

Centralization was more practical and more effective in Peru than in the other colonies. But if federalism did not exist, there did appear the decentralizing tendency which we have pointed out.

Where federalism did triumph in this period was in Mexico. The empire of Iturbide lasted only for a short time. The same year, 1823, which saw the adoption of the constitutions of Chile and Peru marked its fall. Immediately after, a congress discussed the bases of the new constitution. The predominating influence in this assembly was the North American. This influence was not just ideologic as it was in the assembly of Caracas in 1811, but real because of the support which the masonic societies, related with those of the United States, gave to the republican movement.

In spite of the opportune and sound objections of Padre Mier, the Mexican congresses sanctioned a federation dividing Mexico into seventeen states and two territories.

The Mexican constitution of 1824 is a copy of the American constitution of 1787, but with this extra drawback: the executive became in a certain measure subservient to the legislative.

Mexico did not fall into the error of Apatzingan of establishing a collective executive; but neither did it establish a strong executive. The consequence of this was that the government had to overstep the law and become a dictatorship, eternal and dismal fault of equation between the idea and life.

Federalism prepared the way for the disintegration of Mexico.

It is interesting to observe that the federalist tendency appeared in Mexico at exactly the same moment that in the rest of Spanish America a tendency for unity and superior integration was becoming widespread as is witnessed by the Chilean and Peruvian constitutions and, two years later, the Bolivian constitution and the Argentinian constitution inspired by Rivadavia.

The Mexico of this period appears, in a certain sense, to be free of the general current which predominates in Spanish America. The historian Justo Sierra has found the origin of this federalism in the provincial *diputaciones* created by the Constitution of Cadiz. One should add to this administrative antecedent, a consideration of some geographic and, on occasions, ethnic factors. But it is certain that in the evolution of Mexico the federalist tendency has not impeded the effective centralization of the dictatorial régimes of the right and of the left which characterized the political evolution of this country in the nineteenth century.

Chapter XX

BOLIVAR AT THE HEIGHT OF HIS CAREER

The Peruvian constitution of 1823 was only a theoretical declaration. The President-elect Riva Agüero came into conflict with the Congress, dissolved it and organized a Senate " which, composed of a few experienced and respectable men, is far removed from the discord and clamor of tumultuous passions ".[1] The Congress, supported by General Sucre, resisted Riva Agüero.[2] Peru entered a period of civil war, while the Spaniards increased their power in the sierras.

A general history of this dramatic period is not within the scope of this work. We are interested only in its constitutional development, and we must omit the purely military and political aspects.

The collapse of the expedition of the *intermedios* during the government of Riva Agüero left the cause of Peruvian independence in desperate straits. Bolivar, who had vacillated, as his letters reveal, between heeding the call of Peru and signing a peace with Spain which would assure the recognition of the independence of Colombia, understood fully the gravity of the disasters suffered for the sake of general independence in the south of Peru.[3] Spain continued to organize a strong army in the Andean

---

[1] Manifesto of the Senate transcribed in the *Exposición* of José de la Riva Agüero, London, 1824, 109-113.

[2] See the note of Sucre published in the *Gaceta de Gobierno*, 1823, No. 46.

[3] Letters to Santander of January 30, July 3; principally the letter of January 30. *Archivo de Santander*, IX, 222; X, 269.

region, profiting by the loyalty of the native elements for the cause of the king. Bolivar never hoped for a policy of peace with Spain in spite of the attitude of the liberal Spanish government, which sent special commissions to Mexico and Buenos Aires. The restoration of Ferdinand VII to absolute power was imminent, and he would disapprove any pact whatsoever which called for the recognition of the independence of America. The government of Buenos Aires did, however, sign a preliminary peace treaty June 4, 1823 and confirmed it on July 21 of the same year. And Riva Agüero himself, March 1823, at the instigation of Bolivar, proposed an armistice to the Spaniards in the effort to gain time.[4] Riva Agüero continued to adhere to this idea of a possible accord with Spain after his rupture with Bolivar as a means of combating Colombian influence in Peru. In pursuit of this plan—and he was now openly hostile to Bolivar—he proposed to the Spaniards a peace with the same bases as those proposed by San Martín at Punchauca, preferring this sort of settlement to the hegemony of Colombia.[5] But it became very clear from the first moment that no other means remained for the consolidation of independence except the continuation of the war with the greatest energy, and this demanded acceptance of the dictatorship of Bolivar. The Peruvian Congress, which had been reorganized after the dissolution, decreed the dictatorship, conferring on Bolivar supreme political and military authority.

[4] *Gaceta de Gobierno,* 1823, No. 11.

[5] Riva Agüero in his *Exposición* refers to the treaty between Rio de la Plata and Spain; he cites some measures of Colombia, p. 181, and he says that the senate decided for peace on condition that the formal independence of Peru be granted. See *Fastos de la Dictadura,* Arequipa, 1826, 150.

The conflict between Bolivar and Riva Agüero was a great misfortune both for Peru and for the independence of America; for the latter, because of his energy and activity, should have been the leader of Peruvian nationalism. He was superior in spirit and in strength of character to La Mar and to Vidaurre and he did not have the disadvantage of the cloth as was the case of the remarkable Luna Pizarro. Bolivar said in his letter of February 3, 1823 to Santander: "Monteagudo, who is a person of much worth, is an enemy of Riva Agüero because Riva Agüero is the cause of his fall, but he says, nevertheless, that Riva Agüero is the man called to command Peru." [6]

In spite of the continuation of the war, Bolivar with his characteristic energy, proceeded to take the necessary measures for the organization of the country; he set up the judicial power, and decreed measures favorable to the natives from the very beginning. The decree of April 1824 provided for the division of community land among the Indians and named surveyors for this purpose. These measures were broadened and emphasized by other decrees of Cuzco, in July 1825. It was then ordered that the ownership of this land by the Indians was to be limited: they could not alienate any of the land until 1850 and it could never be alienated in mortmain. The personal service of the Indians was also abolished, and every citizen was thenceforward required to collaborate in public works. The Minister Sánchez Carrión in his *Memoria,* published on the twenty-fifth, calls this the first tablet of the agrarian law of Peru and the first practical document of the independence of the Indians.[7]

[6] Lecuna, *Cartas del Libertador,* III, 142.
[7] See on this subject the *Gaceta de Gobierno* of 1824, No. 13, the *Colección Oficial de Leyes y Decretos Paz de Ayacucho,* 1834 and the *Memoria* of Sánchez Carrión, Lima, 1825.

The government of Bolivar also encouraged the working of mines and the establishment of schools with regular clergy property.[8] In spite of the enormous topographical difficulties of Peru and the impossibility of receiving help from Buenos Aires and from Chile, Bolivar followed his plan of moving his army to the Peruvian mountains. He won, on August 6, 1824, the victory of Junin which gave him the central part of the Peruvian Andes and prepared the way for the victory of Sucre, December 9, at Ayacucho, which was destined to seal the independence of Peru and of all the continent.

The capitulation of Ayacucho, which granted citizenship to the Spanish leaders and give them the same rank in the Peruvian army which they had enjoyed previously in the Spanish, represented the reconciliation of Spain and America and created a precedent unique in international history. Military history does not record a more generous capitulation. Gonzalo Bulnes says rightly: " This treaty, celebrated monument of political wisdom and of intelligent moderation, is as glorious for Sucre as the victory itself." [9]

Two days before the victory of Ayacucho, Bolivar invited the various countries to send delegates to a congress at

[8] In order to understand the discussion of political ideas in Peru in the years 1823-26, that is during the Bolivarian régime, one should read the discourses which Manuel Lorenzo Vidaurre published in Trujillo; the *Gaceta de Gobierno; El Nuevo Día del Perú,* in which there was published an interesting historical picture of the revolution; and *El Observador. El Nuevo Día del Perú* defended the concept of sovereignty separate from the jacobin doctrine of pure democracy. The idea of professional representation was found in *El Observador.* The extremely rare exemplars of these early publications are to be found in the Bingham Collection, where the author consulted them.

[9] *Bolívar en el Perú,* II, 332.

Panama, for he felt by that time that the independence of the continent was assured. He realized finally the plan which he had sketched in the Jamaican letter and in his notes to the Director Pueyrredón and which he had pursued in his efforts in Peru, Chile and Buenos Aires.

It is now in order to fix with precision the political and international thought of Bolivar at the heights of his political and military career. Bolivar remained faithful to his idea of national governments, unified and efficient, but within perfectly defined institutional bounds. These national governments which followed the great divisions of the colony, ought to constitute organic democracies and should unite to form a great federation, which would insure their independence and make them respectable in the eyes of the world. Within this plan Bolivar assigned himself a rôle representative of the whole of America. It was his desire to care for the interests of the whole federation over and above those of each country. Bolivar favored for each country a nationalistic government of organic democracy, and for the whole, a close federation. National governments for the different states which had been set up in America and a general federation to preserve external and internal peace, such was Bolivar's idea at the moment in which independence was consolidated. We have a documentary exposition of this thought at the moment of its zenith. In a letter to Santander of January 6, 1825, he seems preoccupied by Venezuela and by the fear that anarchy might spread. He sees a remedy in the American federation: " Only hope that the American congress will meet, keeps me in America." [10] Political changes and psychological

[10] *Archivo de Santander,* XII, 196.

modifications, which we shall study presently, will bring him to replace this political ideal by the formation of one national unity with the countries which he had liberated.

The Peruvian congress decided in 1825 to prolong the powers conferred on Bolivar until the meeting of the new congress which was soon to be elected. Larrea said, concerning the national organization: "This great enterprise cannot be accomplished except by the genius who now attracts the admiration of both worlds." The decree of congress was inspired by these sentiments; it declared that Bolivar had exercised dictatorial power in conformity with the laws thus furnishing an unique example in the annals of absolute power.[11]

Bolivar was anxious to survey the territory in the south of Peru and in upper Peru which had been won to the patriotic cause after the surrender of Olañeta. His letters during this journey reveal that he remained faithful to his idea of being only the president or director of the American federation, for his plan was to organize a nationalist government in Peru. In a letter to Santander of June 28, he says: "It is possible that I shall not go to Lima until a constitutional government has been set up." Soon after he said: "I am the person who should be called to be leader of the American federation." [12] For Peru, Bolivar wished a government of nationalist elements similar to that over which Santander presided in Colombia and to that which Sucre was to found in Bolivia.

In another letter to Santander, October 21, Bolivar told him: "You must give stability to Colombia, and Sucre

[11] *Gaceta de Gobierno*, 1825, No. 13.
[12] *Archivo de Santander*, XIII, 64.

must build Bolivia." [13] In this same month he wrote a letter
to Tomás Heres, which we shall quote in the following
chapter, telling him that a government should be set up in
Peru headed by La Mar and in which Luna Pizarro should
be " Ministro de Gobierno." On October 17 he expressed
much the same idea in a letter to La Mar himself: " You
must no longer frustrate my desires and those of Peru." [14]
In November of the same year, he said to Hipólito Unánue:
" The general congress which has already been convoked
can organize itself without my presence, and you and General La Mar may preside." [15] And although in December of
this year he decided to come for the installation of congress,
nothing permits us to suppose a change in his plan to form
a nationalist government in Peru.

In the course of the year 1825, the ambition of Bolivar
begin to extend even beyond the territories which he had liberated. He was intrigued by the idea of intervening in
Chile and of playing the rôle of mediator and of referee in
the affairs of Rio de La Plata. He says, quite ingenuously,
that he must assume the rôle of mediator and of regulator
of South America.[16] On November 11, 1825 he said to
Santander: " So that you may put forth your best efforts to
prevent the glory of Colombia from remaining incomplete

[13] *Ibid.*, 240.

[14] Lecuna, *Papeles de Bolívar*, 86.

[15] *Ibid.*, 90. He wrote in the same spirit to Luna Pizarro in
December 1825, *Ibid.*, 94.

[16] In February 1825 he shows that he had decided to intervene
in the affairs of La Plata (letter to Santander of February 9, *Archivo de Santander*, XII, 243). In September of the same year, he
said to Santander: " The demon of glory will carry us to Tierra del
Fuego." Lecuna, *Cartas del Libertador*, V, 87.

and I may be permitted to be the *regulador* of all of South America." [17]

But precisely what this rôle presupposed was his absolute disinterestedness in, and independence of, the direct government of any single American country. For the very reason that he assigned himself a rôle which was continental and super-national within the American federation, Bolivar could not be opposed to the nationalist character of the government which was to be erected in each country. It is clear that this super-nationalist and interventionist political rôle carried within itself a principle of personal affirmation which, if it were not satisfied along this course, might choose another of authoritarian and imperialist treatment of the individual countries, which is exactly what happened. But from the psychological point of view the dream of Bolivar at this time, to be president of the American federation and *Regulador* or mediator of South America was still compatible with the idea of organizing nationalist governments in each one of the countries which he had liberated.

Santander, Sucre and even Briceño Méndez fought the interventionist proposals of Bolivar in Rio de La Plata and in Brazil, making him see how dangerous it was to enter into a conflict with the Empire which counted on the sympathies of both the Holy Alliance and England.[18]

This counsel which was well founded mortified Bolivar, although he was fully aware of its soundness. So he fol-

[17] *Archivo de Santander,* XIII, 288.

[18] See the letter of Sucre to Santander of October 11, 1825, the article in *El Constitucional* of Bogota which reproduced *El Peruano* No. 2 of May 20, 1826. Bolivar reached the point of saying to Santander: " Do you know that your advice about my conduct with Brazil now disgusts me." (*Archivo de Santander,* XV, 14.)

lowed it and returned to Lima without embarking on the
adventure to which he had been invited by some admirers
in Chile and by the Argentine commission in Potosi.

When he arrived at Lima, Bolivar insisted that La Mar
take the reins of the Peruvian government in a scene whose
drama is described by *La Gaceta* and which other documents
of the epoch confirm.[19] But La Mar declined. In the month
of February of 1826, Bolivar still hoped to install the congress. We have the rough draft of the message which he
was to present to this assembly. In it was only a hint at a
modification of the constitution.[20] But beginning with
1826, Bolivar began seriously to consider remaining in Peru
and applying to that country the constitution which he had
drawn up for Bolivia on the demand of the assembly of that
country. Two influences set him on this course: (1) Páez
sent commissioners to urge him to create a vast empire
from the Orinoco to Potosi, and (2) the counsel and interests of the men about him. In his letter of February 21 to
Santander, Bolivar speaks of the napoleonic plans which he
has received, and he says that he has sent the outline for the
Bolivian constitution to Páez. On March 7 he informs Santander of the possibility of his remaining in Peru. He says:
" General La Mar is going to Guyaquil because of his illness.
This leaves us with no one to govern Peru. I shall not return so soon, as I am afraid that the country may collapse."
In a letter of April 7 he already expresses the ill-will which
the opposition that appeared in the preparatory sessions of
the congress had inspired in him. He speaks of changes in

[19] *Gaceta de Gobierno,* 1826, No. 13. *Narración biográfica del
G. M. J. de la Mar.* Manuel Vicente Villarán. Lima, 1847.
[20] *Papeles de Bolívar* (February 10), 250.

the Council in favor of more energetic men, and he mentions the fact that he has finished the Bolivian constitution and desires to present it personally.[21]

In the following chapters we shall study in detail the aspect and consequences of the profound change which this alteration of opinion works in the mind of the Liberator at the beginning of 1826, when the independence of South America was definitely consolidated and the Congress of Panama was about to meet.

[21] *Archivo de Santander,* XIV, 129.

CHAPTER XXI

THE LIFE-TERM CONSTITUTION

With the independence of Peru a reality after the victories of Junin and Ayacucho, the next problem was the definite organization of the territories liberated by the army of Bolivar. The Peruvian constitution of 1823 was considered inapplicable on account of its extreme liberal character. On the other hand, the resolution of the people of Upper Peru, favoring the formation of a new nation, made new projects possible.

For a long time it was believed that the separation of the provinces of Upper Peru was entirely the work of the Liberator. He, it was said, wished to create two weak nations on the borders of Great Colombia, whose hegemony he desired to preserve at any cost. Recent studies, however, have destroyed this belief.

The provinces of Upper Peru were separated from the viceroyalty of Lima when the viceroyalty of Buenos Aires was established. They returned to the jurisdiction of Lima during the revolution in Buenos Aires which occurred in 1810. If the boundaries of the nations were to be determined by the limits of the old viceroyalties, it is evident that the destiny of the upper Peruvian provinces would involve a conflict of pretensions between Peru and the republic of La Plata.

It may be said that a policy of international equilibrium would help to cause the establishment of a new state in Upper Peru. But, as far as Bolivar is concerned, his letters prove not only that he was not the originator of the plan, but that he even censured Sucre for convoking the assembly. With independence assured Peru, his purpose was to unite both the upper and the lower provinces in the federal form outlined in the plan of 1826.

The assembly of the upper Peruvian provinces gave the new nation the name of Bolivar and invited the Liberator to write the constitution that should govern it. After seven years, and in very different circumstances, Bolivar again assumed the rôle of legislator. The plan of Angostura and the plan of 1826 are grouped together as the work of Bolivar in the history of American public law. The admirers of Bolivar, without recognizing the differences in these two historic documents, praise him for both of them in equal measure. We do not subscribe to this view, and insist that the difference in conditions, to which we have alluded, determined the fundamental difference between these two conceptions of Bolivar. We believe that the plan of Angostura and the plan of 1826 are distinct, not only from the standpoint of principles, but, above all, in their manner of application. The zenith of Bolivar's work as a legislator does not coincide with that of his career as a soldier and statesman. The year 1826 marked the decadence of his political thought. There were potent influences that determined this decline. It is clear that Bolivar retained all the vigor of his intelligence, but the freshness, the spontaneity, and the absolute disinterestedness of his earlier ideas, were lacking.

The Colombian writer, José Ricardo Bejarano, maintains precisely the opposite view, affirming that the plan of 1826 is the faithful expression of the ideals of Bolivar.

Let it be understood that, in 1819, Bolivar was simply a

lonely seeker for truth, his days of glory were yet to come. In 1819 he was without power, without resources, but not without hope. In 1826, he is at the height of his fame; he is the recognized conqueror. In Angostura, according to his own confession, he held scarcely any territory and had but few soldiers. In 1826, he had liberated New Granada, Venezuela, Quito, and Peru. The applause and acclamations of his triumphal march from Lima to Potosi still vibrated in the air. "Never did the Incas make more pompous marches than those of the Colombian hero", says Gil Fortoul. An entire nation took his name, all the liberated peoples endowed him with immortality. What a chasm separates the persistent plainsman who governed Guiana and the actual dictator of the largest and richest part of South America!

The ideological influences were also different. In Angostura, Bolivar closely followed the plan of government of the English constitution, referring to it in the most complimentary terms. His writings show clearly the effect of the ultra-democratic attempts that had been made by that time. In 1826, his mind is no longer occupied with British institutions. The bitter lessons taught by the jacobin and federal experiments have commenced to fade out. Instead, Bolivar will outline plans in line with the demagogic spirit of the later period and conforming to provincial tendencies.

In spite of his emphatic declarations to the contrary, Bolivar falls under the spell of the Napoleonic example. The plan of 1826 cannot be explained without a comparison with the French consular constitution. The atmosphere in which Bolivar then moved was similar to that of Napoleon. As Lafayette justly said: "Naturally it is impossible that Your

Excellency did not see yourself surrounded, like Napoleon, with subservient men, admirers of your glory and your person." But, outside of this circle it was necessary to consider the more important factor, the opinion of other social classes and that of the mass in general. In Angostura this social factor did not exist. Bolivar, as chief of a group of nomadic soldiers, was able to formulate his political creeds with absolute independence and spontaneity.

In 1826, clear manifestations of a desire for strong and permanent dictatorship came from all sides. Bolivar was perfectly aware of this clamor of public opinion. " It is not only Colombia ", he said, " but every republic of South America that every day feels its weakness of structure more keenly." [1]

Without exaggeration, we may say that, in 1826, South America was ready for autocratic rule. Everything had changed since 1819; psychological influences, social factors, intellectual forces, all tended to build up a popular desire for a strong dictatorship. And Bolivar, the conqueror, lacked the spiritual liberty enjoyed by the tribune of Angostura. If in the moral order, truth makes us free, as the gospel tells us, in the political order, it is necessary to enjoy absolute spiritual liberty to be able to find the exact and applicable truth. Bolivar in this later period was the slave of his own triumph. He was chained, not only to very human and natural ambitions, but also to the exigencies of the situation.

Let us enter now into an analysis of the so-called Bolivian Constitution, the embodiment of Bolivar's plan of 1826. It states (Article 8) that the supreme power shall

---

[1] Villanueva, *Imperio de los Andes*, 172.

be divided into four parts: electoral, legislative, executive and judicial. Bolivar adds a fourth term to the classic division of Montesquieu. Benjamin Constant had previously added municipal power. For this, Bolivar substitutes electoral power. At first view, this appears to be a democratic innovation. In reality, this is an imitation of Sieyès, whose ideas Napoleon used to further his own ends.

The electoral power is vested in the citizens. Every ten citizens named an elector who represented them in the electoral body of the province. (Arts. 19, 20.) The only requisites for citizenship were: residence in the nation, ability to read and write, and the possession of a means of livelihood. Bolivar said in explanation: "Every ten citizens name an elector, thereby having the nation represented by a tenth of its citizens. The exercise of public power requires knowledge and honesty—not the possession of money."

The electoral bodies thus formed would act for four years with the following duties: determination of the qualifications of citizens, presentation of lists of names, three for each office, from which the members of the national legislature, prefects, governors, *corregidores*, mayors, justices of the minor courts, priests, vicars, and pastors were selected. Thus most of the officials were directly chosen by a decimal representation of the people. Thus, according to Bolivar, the electoral power had rights not granted in many other governments that were considered very liberal. Notice that he says: "These attributes closely approach those of the federal system. . . . Nothing is more important to the citizens than the election of legislators, judges, and pastors. The electoral college of each province provides for the needs and safeguards the interests of that province." These sentences reveal his purpose of attracting the support of the federalists and ultra-democrats whom he had condemned with such masterful authority in his manifesto of Cartagena and in his speech at Angostura.

It is not difficult to point out the sources which inspired Bolivar in his exposition of the electoral power. They are found in the Napoleonic constitutions of the years VIII and X, the constitution of Cadiz, and in the Peruvian constitution of 1823. With respect to the requirements for citizenship, there is an appreciable difference between the Bolivian constitution and the French consular constitution. Napoleon in the year VIII established universal suffrage, abolishing the requisite of a tax which the constitution of the year III required. The exercise of citizenship, however, was denied to personal or domestic servants. The Colombian constitution of 1821 and the Peruvian of 1823, which were in force when Bolivar originated the constitution which bears his name, had these requirements for suffrage: age; Colombian, 21, Peruvian, 25, ability to read and write, ownership of property or exercise of some trade or profession. Servants and day-laborers were excluded. Bolivar extended suffrage in that he did away with property requirements, but he still excluded laborers and domestic servants.

There is a certain difference, however, between the plan of Bolivar and that of Napoleon, namely, the first required the possession of a trade and the ability to read and write. This would limit the electoral body somewhat in respect to size, but it cannot be said that it would be reduced to a small minority, " a real oligarchy ", as Marius André says. The literacy requirement would exclude the aborigines, who in our social system occupy a lower plane than that of the popular masses in Europe. But the requirements were more lenient than in any previous constitution. They were indeed liberal to a fault, for with public education extended, the electoral colleges must eventually become large and incoherent assemblies, unfitted by their very nature for the complex tasks which the constitution assigned them.

The principle of decimal selection in different levels of society for the election of officers, came from the French constitution of the year VIII. Bolivar applied it on only one level in creating his electoral colleges. In France, the decimal system was modified by the senate decree of the sixteenth of Thermidor of the year X. This decree established assemblies by canton (composed of all the citizenry), district colleges (*arrondissement*, a member for every five citizens), and department colleges (chosen by the canton assemblies from a list of taxpayers). The cantons presented a double list of candidates for the vacant positions of justices of the peace and municipal officials. The district college, in its turn, presented a similar list for positions on the district council and primary lists for members of the tribunal. The department colleges presented another such list for the selection of members of the departmental council and primary lists for the legislative body. Bolivar simplified this system, by establishing only provincial electoral colleges. In place of a double candidature, the Bolivian colleges presented triple lists. In short, the Bolivian electoral bodies were similar to those of the reformed Napoleonic plan of the year X.

Bolivar varied from the Napoleonic plan in the method

of selecting executive officers. In the French plan, the first consul named these officials. Bolivar, however, was more or less influenced by the ideas that had been incorporated in the Peruvian constitution of 1823, which gave the local bodies the right to present triple lists from which these functionaries were selected.

The right of petition and complaint given to the electoral bodies is similar to the rights given the provincial *diputaciones* in the constitution of Cadiz. We note this difference: the provincial *diputaciones* were limited in size and were more efficient organizations than the Bolivian electoral bodies, which were huge, incoherent masses, and politico-federal in nature rather than local administrative units. Although both institutions were called provincial, they did not embrace the same territory. The *diputación* was based on the ancient *intendencia,* corresponding to the old Spanish city, the seat of the ancient town council and head of a bishopric. This was a true unit of social organization. The provincial college of Bolivar's plan corresponded to the old territorial districts of the *partidos* or *subdelegaciones,* secondary units in our social structure. In this way, the projected organization of Bolivar did not conform with the actual state of affairs in America. Instead of basing the organization on primary existing divisions, he tried to give the social structure a simplicity and a symmetry that would, however, involve a falseness and an artificiality. Bolivar, in spite of his usual awareness of existing conditions, did not see that the intermediate organizations, between central government and the mass of the people, were natural and deeply rooted by the effect of past history. Bolivar also failed to copy the provisions for local institutions of a more restricted nature than the electoral colleges set up by this same consular constitution.

The establishment of the electoral colleges provided for much local interference in national political and judicial affairs, which is, no doubt, a federalistic tendency. On the other hand, by a paradox worthy of note, the Bolivian constitution destroyed provincial autonomy in regard to local affairs. The municipal government was abolished and its powers turned over to the district political authority, in imitation of the Napoleonic system by which the prefects were the only officers of local administration.

Without a doubt this was the greatest defect in the Bolivian constitution. The municipal governments had represented, no matter if imperfectly, the democratic life in the colonial period. It is not denied that the governors and *corregidores,* being nominated by the electoral colleges, also represented a certain principle of autonomy. But they were controlled by the executive department, whose orders they were to carry out. (Art. 132.) Moreover, the principal importance of the local power is its financial authority, and this, according to the plan of 1826, falls in the sphere of the central government.

As far as the maintenance of public order is concerned, although each department organized its part of the national militia, the president of the Republic commanded it within the boundaries of the county. (Art. 82, Insert 12.)

It is evident, then, by all we have said, that under a certain appearance of local autonomy, the Bolivian Constitution built up a central power that could be as absolute and rigid as that in the Napoleonic plan. If in the latter, the prefect was named by the first consul or emperor, he was at least counterbalanced in power by the various general and district councils that were lacking in the Bolivian system.

It would be venturesome to say that, in this most important feature of local government, Bolivar was insincere, that under the disguise of a semi-federal plan he was deliberately laying the groundwork of a rigorous centralism. It can be said that the progress of the American peoples did not call for the semi-federal plan, but for a true municipal autonomy in the ancient *intendencias* or cities, each having separate existence and life. The Bolivian constitution was unmindful of this need for a vigorous local organization, deeply-rooted by history and usage, it substituted an artificial French device with the decimal selection of electors.

The legislative branch was composed of three bodies: the tribunes, the senators, and the censors. This same tricameral form appears in the Napoleonic constitutions. Some powers are common to all three, while some are peculiar to each. All have a part in the selection of the president, vice-president, and the members of the legislative bodies, as well as other national officials, from the lists presented by the electoral bodies.

This is what Bolivar says of this tri-partite organization of the legislative power: " The legislative branch has a form that will necessarily cause harmony between its parts. It will not always find itself divided without any arbiter to intervene, as happens where there are but two chambers. With three, any difference between two will be settled by the third. In all differences between two disagreeing parties, a third is named to decide."

In respect to the special functions of the three chambers, let us again read Bolivar's own words: " The first chamber is the house of tribunes, and it has the sole power of initiating laws regarding the declaration of war or the resumption of peace. It has immediate control of those branches of government which the executive power administers with least intervention by the legislative power. The senate enacts the civil code and ecclesiastical regulations and supervises the courts and public worship. It chooses the prefects, the district judges, governors, *corregidores,* and all the subordinates in the department of justice. It proposes to the chamber of censors the primary lists from which the members of the supreme court, archbishops, bishops, dignitaries, and canons are chosen. The field of the senate is all that pertains to religion and the laws.

" The chamber of censors exercises a political and moral power somewhat similar to that of the Areopagus of Athens, or the Roman censors. They are the representatives of the people, whose duty it is to see that the constitution and popular rights are faithfully observed. I have placed under their ægis the national judgment as to whether the executive power is well or poorly conducted."

In short, we may say that the idea of Bolivar, in regard to the chambers, was to give to the chamber of tribunes the traditional functions of the popular branch of the legislative power in financial and political affairs. The senate was to enact civil and ecclesiastical laws and name the high officers. The censors were to supervise public morality and instruction. In respect to the chamber of tribunes and the senate, Bolivar practically followed the division of powers in a bicameral system. The new element that he introduced in the chamber of censors is nothing but the Areopagus of the plan of Angostura embodied in a political constitution and deprived of its inquisitorial powers, but endowed with others, such as its part in appointment and its rôle as a perpetual guard and protector of the constitution and the rights of the people.

The differences between the legislative branch in the plan of Bolivar and that of Napoleon are immediately evident, in spite of the partial similarity in nomenclature. The chamber of tribunes of Bolivar combined powers that the tribunes and legislative body of the Napoleonic plan held in common. It not only comments on laws but helps enact them. The life-term chamber of censors, like the Napoleonic senate, has more legislative powers than the chamber of tribunes, but it does not play so important a part in the government. In the Napoleonic plan the conservative senate is the principal body, holding a definite pre-eminence over the legislative body and the chamber of tribunes. On the other hand, the chamber of censors found itself on a basis of equality with the other bodies in the matter of filling vacancies in the legislative body. There are functions like this which all three perform as a body.

But if the chamber of censors had less importance than the conservative senate, it also enjoyed more autonomy. By 1810, according to the historian Aulard, all senatorial independence had been lost, all vacancies in offices were filled from a list presented by the first consul. The Bolivian censors, on the contrary, were chosen by the three united bodies from lists presented by the electoral colleges. The resemblance between the Napoleonic senate and the censors was principally in their life-term character and in their duties regarding the fulfillment of the constitution and laws.

The plan of Bolivar was to introduce, by means of this

third body, a conservative element similar to the senate of the plan of Angostura. In fact, the censors had the powers of a true senate. The establishment of this third chamber, without avoiding the popular resistance to anything life-time in character, tended to make the electoral and legislative mechanism very complex.

The peculiar duties of each chamber should depend, logically, on a diversity of origin. In the constitution of 1826 all the members of each chamber are chosen by the assembly of the whole from the lists presented by the electoral colleges.

Election at different times (two years for half the tribunes, four years for half the senators) could not produce the same effect as diversity of origin.

This mixed system of popular primary election and selection by the assembly of the whole, applied to the three parts of the legislative power, erased the differences between the bodies and added to the objectionable features of an oligarchy, those of popular election. Bolivar, in the time of which we speak, had discarded the ideas derived from a study of the English government and imitated the absurd plan of Napoleon, designed to hide with the appearance of a democracy, the restoration of a power more absolute than that of the ancient kings.

The executive power is vested in the president and three secretaries of state. (Art. 76.) Bolivar says in his explanation: " The president of the Republic becomes in our constitution the sun, which, firm in the center, gives life to the universe. This supreme authority should be perpetual, because in societies without a hereditary organization, a central point is needed upon which the other officers depend.

The president of Bolivia will have the rights of the North American executive, with certain restrictions favoring the people. His term is that of the president of Haiti." Later he praises this country: "A life-term president with the power of naming his successor is the most sublime addition to the republican system."

Bolivar had spoken of a life-term presidency since the Jamaica letter. Speaking of Colombia, he said: " Its government could imitate the English, with the difference that, in place of a king, there would be an elective power at the very worst of a life-term nature, but not hereditary if we desire a republic." In Angostura he advocated only a long term of office leaving the door open, as it was in the Constitution of the United States, to a life-term presidency in fact by means of unrestricted re-election. In 1826, he decided to import to America the Napoleonic plan of a life-time consul with power to name his successor. He was, however, unwilling to confess his true model.

Bolivar was careful to point out that a life-term presidency would not bring about a monarchical system. In words of great eloquence and indicating a profound understanding of facts, he held that a monarchical restoration was impossible in America: " Legislators, liberty is today a permanent thing in America. Look at the savage nature of this continent, which of itself rejects a monarchical order. The deserts invite independence. Here there are no powerful nobles, no great churchmen. Our riches have been little in the past, and today are practically non-existent. Although the church enjoys some influence, it is far from aspiring to dominance, being satisfied to maintain its present state. Without these supports, tyrants cannot long endure.

If some ambitious souls strive to rear up empires, Dessalines, Cristóbal, and Iturbide can tell them what to expect. There is no power more difficult to maintain than that of a new prince. Bonaparte, conqueror of all armies, could not triumph over this law, more powerful than empires. And if the great Napoleon could not maintain himself against the league of republicans and aristocrats, who, in America will be able to establish monarchies on a soil ablaze with the brilliant flames of Liberty? The very pediments upon which a throne was reared would be devoured by the holy fire that permeates this land. No, legislators! Do not fear the pretenders to crowns. There will be for their heads the sword that was pendant over Dionysius. If the flaming principles of freedom should die down enough to allow thrones to be constructed, they would still rise up tumultuous from the ashes to tell future ages how men preferred their fatuous ambition to Liberty and Glory."

Just what is the difference between the monarchy that Bolivar so vigorously denounced, and the life-term presidency he proposed? Buchet de Martigny, a French representative in Colombia, who has preserved for us many interesting declarations of Bolivar, said that a life-term presidency with the power to name a successor is merely a throne decorated with the livery of a republic. A monarchy differs from a life-term presidency only because of the hereditary principle on which the former is based, the different conception of the relation between the ruler and the nation, and, above all, in the existence of a varied and strong nobility. The life-term presidency insured a sort of benevolent Cæsarism. Although this was not exactly a monarchy that Bolivar wished to establish, yet democratic sentiment opposed to it the same resistance as to a monarchy. The opposition acquired a new weapon, more dangerous and effective than the protest against the hereditary senate. This was to be expected as a result of the sudden change from a short-term presidency. Previous events, as we have said, had cleared the way for a prolonged dictatorship. The people had, in fact, accepted it as, perhaps, necessary. But its solemn proclamation as a permanent rule would be imprudent and ill-advised. Such an announcement would complicate the terms in which the problem of constitutional organization was stated in America. With his clear understanding of human nature. Bolivar later made the comment to General Briceño Méndez that, "All is provisional in a revolution, and for that very reason it is better thus to remove fears and suspicions ". He did not follow this advice when he made public his project of government, preferring with manly, though imprudent, frankness to explain his plan as he conceived it. Very different have been the tactics of his astute but mediocre imitators in establishing an indefinite presidential term, which, if perhaps necessary in the early period, cannot be justified in the twentieth century.

Bolivar believed that the life-term presidency " avoided the changing administrations caused by party government and the excitement that frequent elections produce such as those recently held in Colombia ". Nevertheless, the Bolivian constitution did not avoid these evils, as the identical or similar effects would be produced every four years by the selection of the electoral bodies, to whom were given so many and so important powers.

Bolivar wished to compensate for the suppression of the

presidential election by the curtailment, or at least, the apparent curtailment, of the executive power. He lessened its traditional powers and denied to it the appointment of government officials. He maintained that in this manner the perpetual presidency would not lead to absolutism. His ideal at this time was the stability of the executive power, not its efficiency. " On it [the executive power] is based all of our government, yet it has little power by itself ", he said. " They have cut off its head in order that no one need fear its intentions and have tied its hands so that it can harm no one. . . . The limits of the presidential power, according to the constitution, are the narrowest known. It appoints only the employees of the treasury, and of the military departments; and it commands the army—these are its powers! . . . Customs agents and soldiers, the only members of this department, are not those most likely to attract the popular fancy. . . . The president is deprived of all influence, he does not name the magistrates, nor the local judges, nor the church dignitaries. This curtailment of power has not been endured in any well-established government."

This last sentence comprises the best self-criticism of Bolivar's plan. It is explainable that Bolivar tried to make the judicial power independent of the executive. In this he conformed to the modern tendency. Could the same be said of the political and the administrative functions? Remember what this same Bolivar said in the manifesto of Cartagena, in the Jamaica letter, in the speech at Angostura, about the necessity for unity, efficiency, and cohesion in government. Now, he praises a headless and shackled executive. How was it possible to obtain an efficient and nation-

ally-concentrated government with political authorities selected from lists provided by electoral bodies, with the
senate the main selective agency?

This system presented very serious difficulties. If in
reality, it were to be consolidated, affirming the independence of the electors and the autonomy of the local authorities more strongly, the central government would become
so weak that national unity would be endangered. It could
return to the secessionism and anarchy of the early years of
the Revolution; anarchy which no one has described more
vividly or combated more earnestly than Bolivar. If, on
the contrary, the government maintained an unshakable control of the electoral colleges and the law, which would
definitely enhance the central power, then, the weakening
of other authorities would necessarily follow, and the established government would become a farce, a comedy of
federalism.

Article 132 of the constitution stated that the powers
of the prefects, *corregidores,* and mayors would be determined by the law, so as best to maintain order and public
security. They were to be gradually subordinated to the
central government. The extent and character of this subordination remained to be determined by law. If they were
not so determined, a new note of insincerity would be given
to the inevitable centralism.

To the essential error of this system, it is necessary to
add its extreme complexity. It could be accepted, perhaps,
that local representatives should have a part in the naming
of prefects. But, never could this system be acceptable in
the appointment of secondary authorities, such as governors,
corregidores, and mayors; even less acceptable is the senate's
power in these matters.

The life-term president of the Bolivian system had the right to name his successor, with the approval of the chambers, as did the first consul in the French constitution of the year X. But this successor remained associated with the president, in the rôle of a chief responsible for the administration. He managed the affairs and signed the communications of all the agencies of administration.

According to Bolivar, the naming of a presidential successor "avoids the elections which produce great disturbance in republics. Anarchy, which is the luxury of tyrannies, but the most immediate and terrible menace to popular governments, is thus avoided". He later compares this system with hereditary monarchy: "If hereditary princes were chosen by merit, and not by fate, and, instead of remaining in inactivity and ignorance, they should put themselves at the head of the administration, there would be, without doubt, more noble and brilliant monarchies which would in turn provide greater happiness for the people."

Marius André has noted the similarity in the thought of Bolivar and that of Comte. The founder of the positivist school ascribes, as does Bolivar, the advantages of unity and continuity to the system which he calls *sociocratic succession.*

Nevertheless, important objections to this system of Bolivar are evident. Since the vice-president is associated with the president in the government, the much-desired unity is dependent on a very variable factor, agreement and accord between these officials. The constitution, to insure this accord, gives the president the right to dismiss the vice-president. (Art. 82, Insert III.) But, as the appointment of a new vice-president involved the approval of the legislative chambers, this dismissal would create a serious conflict, in the case of an active and plotting vice-president, between the legislative and executive powers. It is true that the president would retain the right of naming his successor in any case, because if his first appointment should be disapproved, he could name another. If this appointment should also be disapproved, he might present a third name, and the congress must make a choice among the three names. (In the constitution of the year X, the first consul had this same power, but the senate was forced to approve the third nomination.)

Therefore, in spite of the provisions we have enumerated which were intended to make the presidential power supreme, the system did not avoid the possibility of disagreement between president and vice-president, or between either of them and the national legislature.

In a life-term government, such crises could have no other outcome than a *coup d'état*—or the gradual weakening of the legislative influence until it approached complete extinction. This could not occur in a system of presidential elections, which, although in theory, do not realize the stability of a monarchy, yet, in practice, assures at least constitutional continuity, making the people arbiter of possible conflicts between the legislative and the executive. The lifetime plan or the sociocratic succession system can only function well inside a Napoleonic order, in which the legislature is bereft of all independence. Monarchical succession has been compatible with the effective influence of parliaments. The sociocratic succession of Napoleon, Bolivar, and Comte presupposes the establishment of a completely centralized and dictatorial government.

In respect to the judicial power, Bolivar no longer follows his French model, which gave the first consul the right of naming all the magistrates and judges, except justices of the peace and justices in charge of marriage. The ideals of Bolivar called for a judicial power independent of the executive. But, in following this idea, he does not return to the purely democratic system of election of judges as established in the first French constitutions. Under the influence that inspired all the plan of 1826, he proposes a system by which the electoral college prepares triple lists of names from which the judges are chosen by the senate. The members of the supreme court are chosen by the chamber of censors from a similar list prepared by the senate.

Popular intervention in judicial selections is inconvenient, as the experience of the United States has proven. The ordinary voter is not well prepared to judge of the competence and integrity of magistrates. Let us not forget, on the other hand, that the proposed electoral colleges were political bodies. The system of Bolivar involved the danger of entangling the two branches that he wished to separate. Professional bodies or even municipalities are better qualified than electoral bodies to nominate judges. But, although we do not agree with Bolivar's plan and hold that it is defective, how true and convincing are his words of explanation in 1826, when he states his theory of the rightful rôle of the judiciary in the state! They show Bolivar in his most inspired moments and involve principles of deep political understanding. No one in our political literature has exalted in such terms of vigorous eloquence, the responsibility of the judicial power in the protection of liberty and civil rights.

" The judicial power that I propose, enjoys absolute independence: in no other plan of government is so much given it. The people present the candidates and the legislature picks the individuals who will compose the tribunals. If the judicial power did not emanate from this origin, it would be impossible for it to be, in its fullest sense, the safeguard of individual rights. These rights, legislators, are the ones that insure liberty, equality, and security—all the guarantees of the social order. The real foundation of liberty is in the civil and criminal codes. The most terrible tyranny may be exercised by the courts, through the powerful instrument of the laws. Ordinarily the executive is no more than the custodian of public affairs; the courts are the arbiters of personal affairs, the rights of individuals. The judicial power is the measure of the welfare of the citizens; if there is liberty, if there is justice, they are made effective by this power. At times, the political organization has little importance, provided that the civil organization is perfect, if the laws are rigidly enforced and considered as inexorable as destiny."

Following these same ideas, he repeats in another place: " Civil liberty is the true liberty. Others are nominal or of little influence in respect to the citizens." These declarations reveal the profound understanding of Bolivar. From the very beginning of the Revolution, he gave more attention to civil liberty than to popular participation in the organization of the state, which constitutes their political liberty. The sentences cited, however, do not harmonize with the general tone of the plan of 1826. In general, there is a noticeable effort to make the powers given to the citizens seem very ample, another proof of Bolivar's use of the principle of popular intervention as a cloak for his plan of perpetual centralized control.

He concludes his explanation of the plan of 1826 by stating the responsibilities of public employees and by condemning slavery in as eloquent terms as he defends religious liberty.

Let us note, in respect to the last, that there was a certain contradiction between his ideas as publicly proclaimed and those embodied in the plan of 1826. Religious liberty would logically suppose the separation of church and state—or at least no governmental intervention in church appointments. The constitution of 1826, without saying anything relative to the establishment of a national religion, yet states that bishops, as well as priests and vicars, should be selected by the senate from the primary lists submitted by the electoral bodies. At heart, Bolivar was a regalist and would never have consented to deprive himself of a certain influence in church affairs. But it is necessary to recognize that such influence could only be logically based on the establishment of a national religion.

The constitution of 1826, following the consular plans, places the guarantees of individual rights at the end, although giving to them greater development than do the French constitutions of the years VIII and X. Besides these similarities in order, and the other likenesses we have mentioned, there is another interesting and revealing point of coincidence. Bolivar's plan was approved by the assembly of the upper Peruvian provinces, but on being referred to Lower Peru, it was submitted to the electoral colleges, all of which, with the exception of that of Tarapaca, ratified it.

The plan of Bolivar, like that of Napoleon, employed the popular plebescite. This was also a feature of the method of amending the constitution. Article 140 ordered that, once passed by the chambers of the national legislature, the amendment was to be submitted to the electoral bodies, which, on approving, would grant special powers to the legislature to facilitate the reform. Bolivar thus introduced into America the Napoleonic plan of popular plebescite.

To make a general comparison between the consular system and Bolivar's, it can be said that both are, in different degree, the expression of the same system of democratic Cæsarism. This difference in degree is true because the elements of democracy and those of autocracy were present in different proportions.

In the first consular constitution, the legislative power had a certain independence. There was also a principle of equality and autonomy among its sections. But the senate soon acquired a decisive leadership over the other chambers; the chamber of tribunes was later discontinued: and, lastly, the senate was subordinated to the executive power. Before the establishment of the Empire, the Napoleonic plan gradually developed into an absolute centralism. The only democratic features left were the approval of the constitution by plebiscite and the presentation of some candidates by the electoral bodies. The autocratic authority absorbed the democratic element in reality and in law, thus forming an absolute, congruous and extreme system.

The plan of Bolivar tried, in theory at least, to establish an equilibrium between the autocratic element and democratic features. Bolivar said to Buchet de Martigny: " Perhaps you have seen my project of a constitution for Bolivia,

in which I introduced the best principles of monarchical
government and combined them with the most democratic
principles, thus trying to avoid the evils of both systems." [2]
Did Bolivar really have confidence in this combination?
To Martigny he also made the following statement: " The
only method of governing America is by personal influence.
Laws mean nothing to our people, who cannot understand
them." Is it possible that by this method Bolivar desired
to gain personal power under the appearance of an advanced
democracy? Can we consider as sincere that combination
of democratic and monarchical powers of which he spoke?
When his interlocutor said, with a certain irony, " If
such a system is possible, you are to be congratulated ", he
replied, " It is simply an experiment; experience will let
us judge its merit." This experiment did not take place;
the life-term constitution did not go into effect in Peru and
lasted only two years in Bolivia, so that today we do not
have the criterion of experience by which to judge the plan.
We are unable to say whether it was practicable or whether
Bolivar had hidden in it a plan of Napoleonic absolutism
with the aggravation of incoherence and insincerity.

For Gil Fortoul, the project of Bolivar " was in evident
contradiction with the primitive social conditions of peoples who would at once entrust their fate to the personal
prestige of political adventurers and to the hazards of
civil wars ".[3]

Possible or impossible, sincere or insincere, the project
of Bolivar from the political point of view, presented a
tentative compromise, an incongruent system of mixed

---

[2] Villanueva, *Imperio de los Andes*, 281.
[3] I, 349.

origin. It must be said that Bolivar on joining the extreme principles of autocracy (perpetuity) and the ideals of democracy (popular voice in nominations), gave birth to a defective monstrosity and not an efficient new plan of government.

With his own words we can prove that his purpose was to unite radically opposed principles. Recommending his plan to Páez, he said, " In it are found combined the guarantees of permanence and of liberty, of equality and order ". Later he makes even more significant statements: " The Bolivian Constitution unites all the extremes and all the advantages, since even the federalists find in it most of their desires." [4]

A true intermediate form of government would have consisted in an approximation of the two elements; authority and minority power, and democracy and majority power, building up a coherent and logical organization. But Bolivar, instead of doing as he did in Angostura, searching for such a plan, contented himself, as he said, in combining extremes.

From monarchy, he took the principle of stability; from democracy, electoral power; from the unitary system, the absolute centralization of financial matters; from the federal system, the popular voice in nominations; from the oligarchic system, the life-time character of the censors; and from the system of plebescites, the right of petition and the referendum on constitutional amendments. A true intermediate form of government would not call for this duality of extremes, but for a unity on a middle ground.

Such was the method Bolivar followed in Angostura.

[4] Villanueva, *Imperio de los Andes,* 68.

Between the extremes of an executive power permanent and
hereditary, and one transitory and collective, he there evolved
the unipersonal presidency, elective and for a long term.
Between pure oligarchy and the jacobin régime with its
single assembly, he established the middle course of the
sage bicameral system, with an elective house and a senate,
membership in which would be a profession. He wished
membership in the senate to be hereditary, but the congress
of that time made it of life tenure; the senate might have
evolved into a body based on the representation of corporations or guilds. As a mean between the absolute centralism
of the Napoleonic régime and the chaotic federalism of the
first years of the revolution, he proposed a system of efficient
political unity with respect for municipal autonomy. Accordingly, in the political constitution proposed at Angostura
there were balanced against each other the minority and the
majority, political power and public opinion, stability and
provision for change, because no one element was carried to
an extreme.

Such a combination was impossible in the constitution
of 1826, which emphasized both the principle of authority
and that of popular intervention. The constitution of Angostura created a stable executive and a restricted suffrage;
the Bolivian constitution, on the other hand, made the
presidency of life duration, while amplifying the basis of
suffrage. The heart of the constitution of Angostura was
the senate; that is, a permanent collective institution; the
heart of the life-term constitution was the presidency, or
one person. The first was conducive to stable equilibrium;
the second, to a hazardous situation, vacillating between
despotism and chaos. There was, then, a radical difference
between the two constitutions, the difference which lies be-

tween a conservative republic and a régime tending toward democratic imperialism. For this reason it is hard to conceive how so talented a commentator as Gil Fortoul can say that the Bolivian constitution was based on that of Angostura.[5]

The best criticism which can be made of the former was written by Bolivar himself in an attempt to justify it:

In no covenant of any representative government do I see so much popular liberty, so much direct participation on the part of the citizens in the exercise of sovereignty, and so much strength in the executive power, as in this project. Herein are united all the attractions of federation, all the solidity of central government, all the stability of monarchical governments. All interests are interwoven and all guaranties established.[6]

Bolivar wished to accomplish the miracle of uniting the advantages of all systems, and what he did in reality was to unite all their defects: the absolutism of life tenure, the demagogic agitation of electoral assemblies, the drawbacks of both centralism and federation.[7]

[5] *Historia Constitucional de Venezuela*, Vol. I, p. 456.

[6] *Circular a los Departamentos del Norte*. Villanueva: *Imperio de los Andes*, 173.

[7] See the text of the message of Bolivar and the project of the Constitution in *Documentos relativos a la vida pública del Libertador*, VI, 197-207.

Chapter XXII

THE INTERNATIONAL POLITICS OF BOLIVAR AND THE CONGRESS OF PANAMA

All testimony agrees concerning the thought of Bolivar on the congress of Panama. From the American point of view this congress was expected to form an amphictyonic body which would settle the discord existing between the various component nations and avoid war; from the world point of view, the congress meant a union to counteract the influence of the Holy Alliance and to defend the independence of America. In the mind of Bolivar, at this historic moment, there were both a practical objective and a sensational one to be gained. The project of a military alliance corresponded to the first, and the spectacular gathering of the representatives of all of South America, with England present as well, corresponded to the second.

On May 30, 1825 Bolivar said to Santander: "Were this congress no more than staff headquarters of the Holy League, its utility and its importance would be immense." The *Gaceta de Gobierno*, organ of the Bolivarian régime, on publishing the invitation circulars to the congress and some replies, refers to the necessity of counteracting Spain and the Holy Alliance: "A great assembly of representatives of all the nations is going to deliver this hemisphere from the infantile state in which it finds itself." [1]

[1] See the *Archivo de Santander*, XII, 381 and the *Gaceta de Gobierno*, 1825, No. 56. Sánchez Carrión, one of Bolivar's ministers, confirms this opinion in his *Memoria* of 1825. Further proof is to be found in the *Memorias* of Páez, p. 287.

As we have seen, in Chapter XX, the ideal of Bolivar was to be president of the federation which was to be formed at the congress of Panama.

At times early in 1825, Bolivar thought that the projected federation would include only Peru, Colombia, Mexico and Chile. It would exclude Buenos Aires, which was contradictory to the original idea of his Jamaican letter and to the spirit of the negotiations of the government of Colombia with the government of the Rio de La Plata. He thought also of excluding the United States: " confederation with Buenos Aires is harmful to us because it compromises us with Brazil and perhaps with the Holy Alliance. Federation with the United States will compromise us with England, for the Americans [of the United States] are the only rivals of the English in respect to America." In a letter of May 30 to Santander he clarifies his thought: " Haiti, Buenos Aires and the United States present many difficulties. Mexico, Guatemala, Colombia, Peru, Chile and Upper Peru can form a magnificent federation. Guatemala, Chile and Upper Peru will do what we shall ask, Peru and Colombia have but one mind, and Mexico would remain isolated in this confederation which has the advantage of being homogeneous, compact and solid. The North Americans and the Americans of Haiti, because of their foreign blood have an heterogeneous character for us." In a letter of July 21, Santander agrees on the inconvenience of inviting Buenos Aires since it might cause friction with Brazil; but he maintains his opinion in regard to the United States and England and believes that the United States will ask the permission of England " as I am certain President Monroe asked it when he announced, in his message, his opposition to the policy of the Holy Alliance in regard to the new American states ".[2]

Moreover, Santander had invited the United States to the congress from the very beginning " with the firm conviction ", as he said to Bolivar, " that our close allies cannot but regard with satisfaction the participation of our sincere and illustrious friends in our deliberations over a common interest ".[3]

Sucre was in favor of the presence of Brazil, if we may judge by the satisfaction with which he received news of the Emperor's having been invited to enter the confederation: " This is a great thing ", he said, " for now this congress of Panama will labor for an American continental cause ".[4]

Bolivar foresaw clearly the opposition of Buenos Aires to the formation of an American federation. This opposition was due to the fear that the congress of Panama would constitute a supreme or sublime authority on the continent, as Rivadavia expressed it.[5]

The Argentine could not accede to the erection of this authority or hegemony which it feared would be controlled by Colombia and, personally, by Bolivar. We must grant, seeing these things as we can today with the aid of the

[2] *Archivo de Santander,* XII, 306, 385; XIII, 82.

[3] *Ibid.,* XII, 242.

[4] Lecuna, *Creación de Bolivia,* II, 176.

[5] See the debates in the Argentine Congress on the Congress of Panama in the important speeches published in Carranza, *Oratoria Argentina,* I, 345. According to a Peruvian newspaper of the same period, *El Duende,* the fear of Colombian hegemony was lessened when it was learned that the United States had been invited.

testimony of private documents, that if Bolivar penetrated the thought of Rivadavia, the latter had a clear understanding of the innermost aspirations of Bolivar.

Bolivar also took into consideration the anarchical period through which Chile was passing, and which prevented her from adopting the plan of federation.

Concerning the composition of the congress, it is clear that Bolivar changed his idea of giving it a Spanish-American character, for he wished to exclude Buenos Aires and he never considered including Brazil. Nor did he wish to give it a continental character, for from the beginning he opposed inviting the United States. We have seen also that he thought Chile would be excluded. Moreover, whatever the composition of the congress, the important thing for Bolivar, in the year 1825, was the meeting of the congress with the acquiescence and presence of England.

Bolivar always had a very clear understanding of the identity of the interests of England and of Spanish America and of the decisive importance of English support. This phrase expresses his thought exactly: " if we bind ourselves to England, we shall exist, if we do not bind ourselves we shall be lost without fail ". In the year 1826 he made the following statement to Minister Revenga: " it seems to me that the alliance with Great Britain at the present moment would give us great importance and respectability, because in her shadow we would be able to grow and become men, educate ourselves and strengthen ourselves in order to be able to present ourselves before the nations with the kind of civilization and power which is becoming to a great people ".[6]

[6] Lecuna, *Cartas del Libertador*, V, 217.

Bolivar was not unaware of the danger " which is ever present when there is one very strong nation with other weak ones "; but in spite of this, he considered the English alliance to be fundamental. With romantic exaggeration and with no understanding of the practical psychology of the English people, Bolivar thought that England would be able to assume a kind of moral protectorate or cultural leadership of Spanish America.

It was contrary to the character of England to assume such a rôle. After a short time, Bolivar received official notice that England did not wish to give wider scope or greater emphasis to the relations which she had in Spanish America.

Minister Revenga discussed Bolivar's idea concerning the English protectorate. He agreed with Bolivar that England should form part of the alliance, either directly, or as guarantor or protector of the federation. Revenga rejected the idea of a protectorate like that which England exercised in the Ionian Islands, or that of Austria in the Germanic Confederation, and he inclined to interpret the idea of Bolivar as the immemorial alliance between England and Portugal.

Although it is certain that the congress of Panama was destined to be staff headquarters of the federation against the Holy Alliance, this policy did not prevent Bolivar from attempting to calm the uneasiness of the Holy Alliance, especially France, in regard to the form of government of the American countries. In regard to France, Bolivar's diplomacy had borne fruit. France had recalled her fleet from Havana and the French Minister assured the Colombian Minister, Hurtado, that France would not partici-

pate in the war of Spain against her rebellious colonies.
The important thing for France, as well as for the United
States, was simply that Cuba and Puerto Rico should remain in Spanish hands. This requirement is what determined first the postponement and then the abandoning of
the liberating expedition to the Antilles, which was one of
the dreams of Bolivar.

Bolivar was able to dissipate the fears of the Holy Alliance and of France by ordering the Colombian Minister,
Hurtado, to explain his political thought. Bolivar refers
to his discourse of Angostura which outlined a conservative
and even hereditary senate. As we shall see presently, in
the chapter concerned with the Federation of the Andes,
Bolivar indicated to the agents of England and France that
he was preparing conservative reforms in American institutions in order to conciliate the attitude of Europe now
fearful because of the spread of radicalism and of jacobinism in America.

We know that Bolivar, in 1825, alluded only to the conservative character of the parliament, without making any
reference to the life presidency and to the monarchic plan.
The events of this year, the happiest in Bolivar's career, did
not modify to any great extent his political and international
ideas. At the beginning of 1826 his orientation in foreign
policy was exactly like his internal politics to which we
have referred in Chapter XX. Bolivar hoped to set up a
national government in Peru like that which existed in
Colombia and at the same time to erect an American amphictyonic union under his direction and with the protection
of England.

The rough draft, discovered and published by Vicente
Lecuna, leaves no doubt on the matter. Bolivar approved

the invitation which Santander extended to the United States, and in principle, at least, he granted the right of all the countries of America to enter the Federation. It is quite worthwhile to quote the text of this document.

The congress of Panama will bring together representatives from all the governments of America and a diplomatic agent of the government of his Britannic Majesty. This congress seems destined to form the vastest league, the most extraordinary and the strongest which has ever appeared on earth. The Holy Alliance will be inferior in power to this league, if England consents to take part in it. The human race would give a thousand thanks for this league of salvation, and America and England would receive manifold benefits from it.

A code of law to regulate the relationship between political bodies would be one of its benefits.

1. The new world would take shape in the form of independent nations, all joined by a common law which would control their foreign relations and would offer them the stabilizing force of a general and permanent congress.

2. The existence of these new states would obtain new guarantees.

3. Spain would make peace because of the presence of England among her foes, and the Holy Alliance would grant recognition to these nascent countries.

4. Internal order would be preserved among these countries and within each of them.

5. No one of them will be weak in respect to any other; no one will be stronger.

6. A perfect equilibrium would be established in this truly new order of things.

7. The strength of all would come to the aid of any one which might suffer from the aggression of a foreign enemy or from anarchic factions within.

8. Differences in origin and in color would lose their meaning.

9. America would no longer fear this tremendous monster which has devoured the island of Santo Domingo, nor would it fear the numerical preponderance of the indigenous inhabitants.

10. Social reform, finally, would be achieved under the holy auspices of liberty and of peace—but England necessarily must hold in her hands *the balance of this scale.*

Without doubt Great Britain would derive considerable benefits from this arrangement.

1. Her influence in Europe would become greater, and her decisions would come to be those of destiny.

2. America would serve her as an opulent commercial dominion.

3. America would become the center of her relations between Asia and Europe.

4. The English would be considered equals to the citizens of America.

5. The mutual relations of the two countries would bring them in time to unity.

6. The Americans would adopt the British character and customs for the normal conduct of their future existence.

7. In the march of the centuries it may perhaps come about that only one nation will cover the universe—the federal.

Such ideas are to be found in the minds of some Americans of the highest quality; they wait with impatience for the congress of Panama to initiate this project which may be the occasion for the consolidation of the union of *the new states with the British Empire.*

BOLIVAR.

LIMA, February 1826.[7]

From an examination of this text we arrive at the following conclusions. The idea of the federation with the collaboration or direction of England is still held. The American amphictyony is based on equality, on a policy of true equilibrium. There will be an alliance against external danger and against the monarchic factions. All conflict between races will be avoided—a preoccupation which appears in the mind of Bolivar with an intense note of sincerity and is

[7] *Simón Bolívar, Un Pensamiento sobre el congreso de Panamá.* Washington, 1916.

revealed in his correspondence. The continental character of the arrangement and the basis of equality exclude every idea of hegemony, although the federation assumed a moral or political direction in which, evidently, Bolivar was to play a decisive rôle.

It has been said that Bolivar, as he is revealed in this document, is the true precursor of the League of Nations. In fact, the similarity of the principles of Bolivar and those which inspired the plan of Wilson is extremely striking.

The historian Carlos Pereyra has pointed out the identity and similarity between the rough draft discovered by Lecuna, which we have quoted, and the sheet of paper handed to the English Consul Rickets and which the historian Carlos Villanueva published.

The Congress of Panama was organized under the influence of these ideas. Only the delegates of Peru, of Colombia, of Guatemala and of Mexico were present. England named an observer. The delegates of the United States arrived late.

England's observer had the simple mission of being a witness to the conferences. The policy of Great Britain oriented itself toward these two practical propositions: to impede the formation of a general league directed by the United States, and to oppose any military enterprise on the part of Mexico and Colombia which might be directed at Cuba.

The instructions to the Peruvian delegates corresponded to the propositions or principles sketched out in the memorandum of Bolivar. The instructions of Colombia, with a greater sense of reality and of caution, had basically the same orientation. In contrast with the realism and measure

of the Colombian delegates, the Peruvian delegate Manuel
Lorenzo Vidaurre, departing from his instructions, as he
ingenuously said, expressed a concept of extreme idealism
in regard to the work of the congress. Vidaurre dreamed
of the constitution of a true federal state, enormous, formed
by all the countries of America: " once the credentials have
been exchanged ", he said, " there will be no representatives
of the different nations, only representatives of all America ".
Vidaurre, moreover, favored a frank interventionism in the
internal politics of each country in order to prevent monarchic reactions or demagogic disorders. His utopian and
exalted spirit brought him to the point of extending the
power of the congress to the ecclesiastical organization of
America, and he dreamed of a kind of gallican constitution.

The congress of Panama opened its sessions after the
change in ideas to which we have referred in Chapter XX
had taken place in the mind of the Liberator. By the middle
of 1826, Bolivar was no longer interested in an American
federation limited to Mexico, Guatemala, Peru, Colombia
and Chile. Pando leaves the Peruvian delegation at the
congress of Panama and is named Minister of Foreign
Affairs, and he, quite as much as General Heres, the intimate counsellor of Bolivar, considered it more practical to
set up a federal state—composed of Colombia, Peru and
Bolivia—instead of the imperfect alliance which was about
to be acclaimed in Panama following the instructions given
by Santander.

The change which had taken place in the mind of Bolivar
since March 1826 brought about an orientation quite different from that which had guided the congress of Panama.
This orientation transcended the work of that assembly.

Vidaurre was retired, having been named minister to Colombia. Bolivar insinuated to Revenga, Minister of Foreign Affairs of Colombia, that the prerogatives of the delegates should be limited to preliminaries which would be ratified only after the approbation of their respective governments.

When Bolivar learned of the project for a federal and military league which was agreed on at the congress, he expressed himself in the following manner in a letter to the plenipotentiaries of Colombia, Gual and Briceño, Aug. 11, 1826: " I think [he is referring to the Federal League] that the first will be no more than nominal, because a federal pact with an entire world will in reality amount to nothing; now that the Mexicans wish a military League, I am of the opinion that we should form one between Colombia, Guatemala and Mexico, which are the only states that fear attacks from the north. Peru and Bolivia can be counted on to assist Colombia because of the services which they owe her, although they will not be parties to the compact." [8]

This means, then, that in August 1826, Bolivar had already been won to the idea of the Federation of the Andes; in perfect agreement with the plans of Pando and of Heres, he considered the essential work of the congress of Panama, that is the Federal League of all the countries of America with its amphictyonic assembly, useless, and he limited the military alliance to Mexico, Guatemala and Colombia, believing that these countries, through the Federation of the Andes, would form a single political unity with Peru.

But there is something more, on September 14, 1826 Bolivar said to General Briceño Méndez: " the transfer

[8] Lecuna, *Cartas del Libertador,* VI, 54.

of the assembly to Mexico will put it under the immediate influence of that power, which is already unduly influential, and also under the influence of the United States of North America. These and many other reasons, which I shall communicate to you by word of mouth, oblige me to decide that you should not proceed to the ratification of the treaties before I arrive at Bogota and before I have examined them in great detail with you and with others ". He added these significant words: " The [treaty] of union, league and confederation contains articles whose admission might embarrass the execution of projects which I have conceived and which are in my opinion very useful and of great importance ".[9]

These projects were none other than those relative to the Federation of the Andes, that is to say the plan of a great Andean federal state with the life-term presidency which had come thus to replace in the mind of Bolivar the old ideal of the letter of Jamaica and a continental amphictyony on the basis of absolute equality.

[9] Lecuna, *Cartas del Libertador*, VI, 68.

Chapter XXIII

THE FEDERATION OF THE ANDES AND THE MONARCHIC PLANS

In the years 1825 and 1826, in letters which are documents of supreme importance, Bolivar and Santander discussed the constitutional problem. Independence was won, Spain conquered and powerless, the Holy Alliance held in check by England; but how were strong and stable governments to be established in America, convulsed by 15 years of warfare which had destroyed economic foundations, overturned the social structure, and almost annihilated a generation? The church had joined the movement late; property was half destroyed; and the fatal Iberian individualism had been intensified by military enterprises and an environment of continuous heroism. Bolivar thought that the constitution of Cucuta, and even more, the Peruvian constitution of 1823, providing for congresses elected by the conventional popular suffrage, carried the seed of the perpetuation of anarchy; he wished to replace this figment of constitutionality by the reality of a strong and stable government based upon personal influence and inspired by a lofty ideal of political morality. Bolivar trusted in men; Santander in institutions. Bolivar desired free creative action, Santander, continuity and reform within the existing structure. Bolivar believed that legalistic structure was an obstacle to well-considered personal action; Santander held that personal prestige and initiative could consolidate and bring efficiency to established institutions. It must be confessed that in this discussion between Bolivar with his flashes of genius and the unquestionably talented Colombian Vice President, it was the latter who was right.

Santander accepts the principle of gradual reforms accomplished within existing legality. Bolivar wished an integral and plebiscitary reform. This plan presupposed the extension of the constitution of Bolivia to all of Andean America.

The organization of Peru and Bolivia called for special institutions to conform with their organic structure. Neither the life-term presidency nor, much less, the semi-federalism of the plan of 1826 was suitable for these countries. On the other hand, a perpetual personal power presented itself as the most tangible bond of union for peoples separated by enormous distances, and the concessions to federalism were a clever means of political strategy by which this perpetual personal power was made acceptable to public opinion.

Bolivar, immediately on his arrival at Lima, after his triumphal tour in southern Peru, declared to the English Consul, Rickets, that he considered his plan essential for the government of Colombia, Peru, and Bolivia.[1] This plan was no other than the one Bolivar was preparing and which we have previously analyzed.

Following the idea of applying the Bolivian constitution to the grandiose scheme of uniting all Andean America, he outlined the bases, the details of which have been preserved for us in his letter to General La Fuente, which we shall study later. He also directed a circular to the departments of the North, in which he recommended the plan of 1826, saying: " I conceive that the project of constitution

[1] Villanueva, El Imperio de los Andes, 103.

which I presented to Bolivia can be the seal of union and strength for these governments." [2]

What had caused Bolivar to abandon the ideas expressed in the Jamaica letter regarding the over-large nations with many dependencies? We recall his wise words: "A state too extensive, either in itself, or on account of its dependencies, finally falls into decadence and converts its free form of government into tyranny, weakening the principles which should preserve it and finally relapsing into a despotism. . . . A large monarchy is hard to consolidate and a large republic is impossible." In this same letter, Bolivar traced, with a master hand, the characteristics of the diverse regions of America which would tend to lead them to form separate nations. Peru is shown to be different in nationality from Colombia, and it is even stated that New Granada could form a separate state by itself.

At the end of eleven years, Bolivar believes precisely the opposite. There were various reasons for this change; some due entirely to individual psychology, others to international political trends. In the study of the plan of 1826, we have alluded to the first and we have seen how Bolivar, victorious and acclaimed, could feel higher ambitions for power and glory. There is nothing more human than that the Liberator should wish to maintain his influence over the land that he had freed. His personality in the epic that he had lived was confused with the nations that he had founded. He was eager to maintain, under a single rule, the integrity of his nations with the same instinctive force that he might have exerted to defend his life or his glory. It could be said that a kind of *fatum* led Bolivar to the idea of a super-nation which would contain all the vast theatre

[2] *Ibid,.* 173.

of his military action. Nothing would be more unjust than to criticise this plan by the criterion that would be applied to mediocre political figures. The extraordinary and unique case of Bolivar cannot be compared with other historical cases, nor be evaluated by the normal and usual judgment which historians often make.

His project embodied an ambition in keeping with the mighty character of the hero. It was the natural culmination of his glorious career from Orinoco to Potosi; it came with the impulse of fifteen years of struggle and triumph. Its reappearance, in the historic period of which we speak, was in response to a decree of destiny, determined by conditions as much as by the mental reactions of Bolivar. Let us not forget, that at this time he was inclined to become the type of genius whose personality cannot be separated from his work; and in the political world, there are few cases in history where the leader does not identify himself with his ideal, unless he consciously and vigorously subordinates himself to it.

The disproportion between the plan and the situation in America, where geographical inequalities were accentuated by the individualism and particularism of the race, far from minimizing his greatness, lends him aspects of tragic grandeur. What gives real interest to human history are the sublime attempts which are frustrated by the hard exigencies of reality.

Only with this point of view, can we judge the deeds which we are studying, or examine them in their proper historical perspective. This criterion, however, does not prevent us from pointing out the errors and the variance from reality of the Bolivian project. At the same time, it permits us to appreciate its grandeur and its character of historic destiny.

Besides the psychologic factors which explain this project we have alluded to others of an international character.

The consolidation of the independence of America, in the face of the plans of the Holy Alliance, and the principles of hegemony which were beginning to be outlined by the United States, called for a permanent union of the young republics. To accomplish this end was the purpose of the congress of Panama.

Before the inauguration of this congress, Bolivar was convinced of the failure of the confederation that he had planned. In his letter to the Minister of Foreign Affairs, Revenga, on February 17, 1826, he said: " I have no hope that Chile and the United Provinces of the Rio de la Plata will enter the confederation in good faith, nor adopt the project which has been presented." [3] Bolivar also knew that he could not count on Brazil, which, according to the declarations made in 1825 was to observe strict neutrality in the war between Spain and her former colonies. Reflecting Bolivar's thought, Minister Pando said, " That the policy of Mexico and of Buenos Aires, in particular, gave just cause to suspect any cordial concurrence on their part in the assembly of Panama, in spite of the good faith with which Colombia, Bolivia and Peru had worked; and that, consequently, they should not neglect the natural bonds of their union and of their self-preservation, when they were in direct agreement with the true interests of America in general."

Before the evident failure of the idea of a general Ameri-

[3] Gil Fortoul, I, 383.

can union, Bolivar had thought to maintain it with respect to the nations which his sword had liberated. In this state of mind, and under the influence of the psychological reactions that we have indicated, Bolivar believed that the lesser amplitude of this union would be compensated for by its greater cohesion and efficiency. An agreement of confederation could be the uniting force for all America; a federal government, under a life-term presidency, presented itself as the most effective medium for the union of the smaller group of the Andean countries. The establishment of a powerful state, in his concept, was made necessary, not only by the policy of the Holy Alliance, but principally by the policy of Brazil, a nation bordering Colombia, Peru, and Bolivia, whose interest would conflict with their interests.

It is convenient to quote here the words with which Minister Pando commented on the project: " First, the power, the policy, and the parental bonds, upon which the Empire of Brazil is founded; these elements being in contact with us throughout nearly all the Andean Chain, menace the existence of every people, whose resources are inferior, and whose policy differs from this kingdom. Second, the plans of the Holy Alliance are directed towards obliging us to adopt monarchic forms, and thus to destroy the prestige of the revolutions, making people see that personal ambition is the goal of all the revolutionary leaders, and, at the same time, accrediting the fundamental principles of legitimacy.

" These purposes are made clear, first, with the declared protection which all the monarchs offer the Emperor of Brazil; second, with the aid that Austria and Portugal are lending him in the present war with Buenos Aires; third, by the similar measures which the crown of France is using with Spain, it being evident that the squadron and the army which the latter is commanding in the islands of Cuba and Puerto Rico has been equipped by means of French loans; fourth, because the French government has not hesitated to say that it is disposed to recognize the independence of these countries if their governments would take a more solid form, and that they would see with pleasure the coronation of our fortunate generals." [4]

Great Colombia, that is the union of the nations of Quito, Venezuela, and New Granada, was a necessity of the war and the basis for the success in the conflict with Spain. The Federation of the Andes was in Bolivar's opinion, indispensable for the consolidation of the peace and the preservation of the fruits of victory, in face of the dangers presented by European and Brazilian policy.

Naturally, with a freer and more impartial viewpoint— which Bolivar could not have at this time—we believe to-day that this purpose of establishing peace and defending the new nations against foreign complications, could have been answered more easily by, first, consolidating the organization of each country, and later uniting them in a defensive alliance. The project of fusing them immediately in a new political plan, far from uniting the young nations, came to create germs of discord among them and produced divisions and factions in the internal make-up of each one of them. Santander was right when he believed that, " The federation between Peru and Colombia was impractical, and that if the Empire from Potosi to Orinoco was strong and powerful, and could conciliate us with Europe, yet it would carry within it an eternal germ of wars between monarchists and democrats."

[4] O'Leary, *Memorias,* XXIV, 8.

Sucre was of the same opinion. He said to Bolivar: " I personally, do not know whether, with the interests of Bolivia and of Colombia well considered, it would be convenient to form this great mass, because I am becoming more and more convinced that Colombia will not enter into a project of federation with these three states under a single government." [5]

These difficulties were not foreseen by Bolivar, which suggests how he was carried away by the greatness of his ideal.

With the constitution of a single state out of the Andean countries resolved upon, there remained the problem of ascertaining the form in which it was to be organized. There were only two choices presented: first, a monarchy, under a European prince or Bolivar himself as the only candidates possible for the new throne; second, a life-term presidency within republican institutions.

The monarchic solution had many partisans, principally among the lieutenants of Bolivar. The idea of a monarchy had surged forth as a reaction against revolutionary anarchy. According to impartial observers, public opinion desired a strong government. The English Minister, Dawkins, wrote to Canning from Panama saying that he had found that the principles of the delegates were much less republican than he had expected.[6]

[5] *Cartas de Sucre al Libertador*, II, 85.

[6] Villanueva Papers, Ms. Through the courtesy of Señor Laureano Carlos Villanueva, son of the Venezuelan historian, Carlos Villanueva, distinguished author of the series *Monarquia en América*, I have been able to examine many documents copied by that Americanist in the archives of London and of Paris and which he had used in his unpublished books *Bolivar en Lima, La Guerra, Páez*.

The first one who proposed to Bolivar the establishment of a monarchy was Páez, who wished to cover with the name of the Liberator his plans against the oligarchy of the learned which was governing in Bogota. The most influential elements of the country figured in the monarchic conspiracy of Venezuela called the Cosiata conspiracy.[7]

In the old kingdom of Quito, General Juan José Flores said that the army under his command would support Bolivar unto death. Mosquera said that this army was in favor of a constitutional monarchy.[8]

The monarchic feeling was caused principally by the necessity of maintaining order in the face of the anarchy which was beginning, by establishing a stable and strong government; besides, the monarchic form would impede the extension of the plans of the Holy Alliance to South America.

[7] Concerning the monarchic conspiracy called " Cosiata " we read in the *Historia de la Revolución de Colombia* (Restrepo, III, 505): public opinion seemed so favorable to the partisans of this plan that in December of the previous year they decided to send two commissions: one to Bogota with the task of sounding out General Santander and the influential persons of the capital about the project, the other to Peru, with the object of persuading the Liberator that he set up a constitutional monarchy in Colombia. They believed that the clergy, the army, the proprietors and other citizens of influence and position in Venezuela would support them in this grave enterprise. The commissions went to their respective destinations accompanied by General Pedro Briceño Méndez who was in the conspiracy and who was going as commissioner to the congress of Panama. The commission which came to Bogota could accomplish nothing, for they found the vice-president, the members of the government and the public opinion of the capital against them. Thus it was that in the month of May the friends of the monarchy and their partisans did not know what the decision of the Liberator would be about such a dangerous business.

[8] Villanueva, *Imperio de los Andes,* 169.

In opposition to all monarchic plans were Bolivar's sister, Doña María Antonia, Bolivar's best and noblest friend, Sucre, and, by a curious coincidence, his ablest and most dangerous rival, Santander. Confronted by reports of a coronation, Doña María Antonia thus expressed herself in a letter to her brother: " I always tell everyone that it is a calumny; that you have never thought of it nor desired it; that you are greater with the title of Simon Bolivar than that of Emperor. . . . And men will see that, after having gained so many triumphs with your sword, you retire to your home to be only a meritorious citizen, leaving frustrated all those who believe you are ambitious for scepters and crowns; this I believe and hope from your enlightened and great soul, since it is not North America alone that can produce great men like Washington." [9]

Sucre directed this objection to the monarchic plan, assuming that Bolivar should become King of Colombia: " Since you have no sons who by their succession would insure this peace, it would only last while you live; and at your death, a most terrible and bloody war would be the result of this invention. If the King were a European prince, we would bewail the outcome of our revolution." [10]

Santander makes a similar observation to him: "And after your death, Who will succeed? Páez, Montilla, Padilla? I care for none of them as a supreme, life-time, and crowned leader." [11]

Bolivar decided frankly against a declaration of monarchy. He had said in his answer to the letter in which Páez offered the crown: " I am not Napoleon, . . . neither do I wish

[9] Vicente Lecuna, *Papeles de Bolívar,* 357.
[10] Villanueva, 80.
[11] *Ibid.,* 77.

to imitate Cæsar, much less Iturbide. Such examples appear to me to be unworthy of my glory. The title of Liberator is superior to all those which human pride has received. . . . They are republics which surround Colombia. . . . A throne would frighten as much by its height as by its glitter." [12] Bolivar then asked Páez to lend his support to the reform of the constitution on the basis of the project that he prepared for Bolivia.

Identical views were found in the letter he sent to Santander, in which he referred to the manner in which Iturbide suffered because of the excessive confidence of his partisans and to the fear of a horrible reaction on the part of the people because of their just suspicion of an aristocracy destructive of equality. In this letter Bolivar qualified the monarchic plan as fatal, absurd, and little glorious, affirming that " it would dishonor us before the world and in history; it would bring us the hate of the world of the liberals and the scorn of the tyrants; a plan which horrifies me by principles, prudence, and by pride." [13]

The tone of the answer to Páez and the letter to Santander and the publicity which was given them, lent them the character of a public manifesto rather than that of private letters; but this does not authorize us to suppose that they did not contain the sincere expression of Bolivar's thought. The ideas set forth in them are in complete accord with the speech that accompanied the Bolivian constitution, stating the lack of a basis for a monarchy in America and the difficulties of maintaining a new prince on his throne. There is absolutely no real reason to doubt the sincerity of his words. As we have already said, the difference between a

---

[12] O'Leary, *Memorias,* XXX, 183.
[13] *Ibid.,* 170.

monarchy and the life-term presidency was very great, in spite of apparent similarities. That the life-term presidency was a step towards the proclamation of an empire was impossible in the case of Bolivar, since, as Sucre pointed out, he had no family. Bolivar knew very well the difference between the monarchic and life-time rule, and if the first was considered feasible, he was convinced by the stern lesson of the case of Iturbide in Mexico and of Christophe in Haiti, that a transformation leading to an Empire, although it was more in the title than in the reality of power, was still pregnant with difficulties and dangers. To Bolivar the effectiveness of a perpetual power was sufficient. He had no interest in establishing a social hierarchy or an aristocracy, nor had he any interest in the principle of heredity, or the decorative part of a monarchy.

According to the testimony of Páez, Bolivar in the interview he had with Don Martín Tovar, declared: "that it was delirium to think of monarchies, when we ourselves have ridiculed crowns, and if the adpotion of such a system were necessary, we have the constitution of Bolivia, which is nothing other than a monarchy without a crown." [14]

The lack of a crown had a fundamental importance, not only in its effect on public opinion, but because of the different structure that it could give society. Bolivar was perfectly aware of this. At any rate, the previous declarations reveal to us that Bolivar, in keeping with his earlier sentiments and ideas, rejected completely a monarchy under a European prince, and made a frank proclamation regarding one with himself at the head. On the other hand, we do not have any document coming directly from Bolivar which would permit us to suppose that, during the years 1825-26, he

[14] Gil Fortoul, I, 454.

was won to the monarchic idea, which he had considered inapplicable to America. José Ricardo Bejarano rightly says: "The only thing which was written by him concerning monarchy was what he wrote in opposing it." [15]

The opposite viewpoint, which has inspired the copious and interesting volume of Villanueva on the *Imperio de los Andes* does not have any other basis than the interpretation given, by some foreign representatives in South America, to the declarations of Bolivar or some of his generals, concerning the form of government which the South American nations should adopt. This testimony lacks value as proof, because, (1) it does not represent the direct expression of Bolivar's thought, but a foreign interpretation and (2) the declarations which Bolivar made were of a diplomatic nature and could not reflect his intimate thought, but rather followed the plan of reconciling America with Europe, then in full monarchic reaction.

Captain Thomas Malling, in his report to the English government, March 20, 1825, attributes these declarations to Bolivar: "You may say that I have never been an enemy of monarchy, as far as general principles are concerned; on the contrary, I consider monarchies essential for the respectability and well-being of new nations; and if the British Cabinet should present some proposition for the establishment of a regular government, that is to say, a monarchy or monarchies in the New World, it would find in me a strong and certain collaborator in the project, entirely decided to support the sovereign that England should propose and sustain on the throne. I know that it has been said that I desire to be king, but it is by no means true. I would not

---

[15] *Simón Bolívar por los más grandes autores Americanos,* 483.

accept for myself the crown, because when I see this country happy under a firm and good government, I shall return to private life. I repeat to you that if I am able to second the desires and purposes of the British Government in order to realize this desired object, it may count on my services."

Gil Fortoul makes the following observations concerning this document. "At the time that Captain Malling wrote, the most likely thing is that Bolivar, able diplomat that he always was, took advantage of that mariner to sound out the British Cabinet, with the purpose of attracting its sympathy and support for the questions which were going to be discussed at Panama, and for his projected expedition to Cuba and Puerto Rico which ran counter to the wishes of the United States. And he thought of England before any other European power because there he found, during the most trying years of his career, the materials of war which were indispensable to him.[16] The celebrated historian is inclined to believe that Bolivar thought of one or several monarchies with British princes, but as a project which should not be realized until after his death, or in case he could not realize his aspiration for the life-term presidency.

The explanation that Gil Fortoul suggests is also given by José Ricardo Bejarano, when he says, referring to Bolivar: " It was, then, necessary not to compromise his anti-monarchic ideas and not to relinquish, on the other hand, the advantages arising from a good position, dismissing from all minds, once for always, his pretensions to a throne in America." [17]

It may be affirmed, in the most positive manner, that the monarchic declarations of Bolivar collected by Captain

[16] I, 455.
[17] *Op. cit.,* 293.

Malling, had no other purpose than to facilitate the recognition of the independence by the European powers, deter the Holy Alliance, and obtain England's good will.

We should not forget that Bolivar for some time had known that the recognition of independence by the European powers would call for a monarchic or semi-monarchic form of government. Zea, Minister in London, said to Bolivar: " Our independence will be recognized by all the powers on the day that a hereditary power is established in the new republics, under whatsoever denomination."

It is also true, however, that British policy was always to preserve for itself a free hand in the American problem, being able to recognize the new states without imposing monarchy as the price of this recognition. The French policy, however, was evidently to favor Spain in order to obtain the establishment of monarchies in South America. According to Chateaubriand, Canning agreed that it was desirable that England and France try to found aristocratic governments in these nations. In January of 1825, Bolivar stated to Sucre his fears: " that the Holy Alliance would try to assist the Emperor of Brazil with troops to subjugate Spanish America and to support the principle of legitimate government and destroy the revolution." [18] And in the month of March, 1825, in his letter to Santander, he refers to the news received from Venezuela concerning the approach of French naval forces.[19]

Such were the facts which would influence the spirit of Bolivar in the sense of making the European powers understand, principally the Holy Alliance, and France in particular, that monarchic governments could be established in

[18] O'Leary, *Memorias,* XXX, 34.
[19] *Ibid.,* 47.

America. This is clearly revealed in the following letters
which constitute full proof against the interpretation given
by some historians of the declarations made by Bolivar to
Captain Malling. Bolivar said to Santander in his letter
of the 11th of March: " I believe that France should be
made to understand that I am not opposed to combining
our ideas with those of the Holy Alliance, and that, by
means of my influence, the reform of our government can
be obtained without the sacrifice of a war which would decide the fate of the Universe." [20] In a letter to Hurtado,
Colombian Minister to Paris, he said: " You are authorized
by me to acquaint the Britannic government with my determination to use all my influence in America to obtain the reform which would gain for us European recognition and the
peace of the world." [21]

With this same plan in mind Bolivar had made similar
declarations to Vice-Admiral Rosamel. The latter in his
report to the French Minister of Marine, says: " He [Bol-
ivar] recognizes the fact that purely democratic governments are not suitable to these peoples, so long accustomed
to a despotic rule." [22]

Towards the middle of 1825, the situation, that had
caused Bolivar to follow the diplomatic plan of the letters
referred to, had changed. The victory of Ayacucho had
produced its effects; the Count de Villele stated to Minister Hurtado that he would take no part, direct or indirect,
in favor of Spain. In the face of this vanishing international
danger, Bolivar retracts his promises as to changing the
form of government in America, as he says in his letter to

[20] Lecuna, *Cartas del Libertador*, IV, 287.
[21] Lecuna, *Papeles de Bolívar*, 70.
[22] Villanueva Papers, Ms.

Santander of May 23, 1825.[23] Santander, on his part, says to Bolivar that it is not necessary to make the sacrifice of a change in internal politics.

The historian Carlos Villanueva, with the probity that was characteristic of him, having examined the documents transcribed above, recognizes that the declarations of Bolivar to Vice-Admiral Rosamel and to Captain Malling, and the letters to Santander, are parts of the same mechanism, and affirms that it was all a political manœuvre made in the face of rumors of French intervention, and the necessity of obtaining recognition of the independence.[24]

In 1826, with the international atmosphere entirely different, Bolivar took the occasion to speak to an English representative of higher authority than Captain Malling, Consul Rickets. He did not allude then to the famous project of monarchies under British princes; on the contrary, he explained the unusual circumstances under which he spoke to Captain Malling " fearful that a French squadron might present itself in these seas, and under the impression that the allied sovereigns, imbued with the false concept that a radical spirit had surged forth in South America, would be disposed to join Spain to combat and destroy it." And Bolivar said that if Captain Malling did not grasp his ideas, the notes he wrote for this purpose were enough.[25] Let us not forget either that Bolivar explained his plan of a life-term constitution to Consul Rickets, and this embodied his real intentions.

The other *dossier*, that has served as the basis for the opinion that Bolivar in 1826-27 desired the establishment

[23] *Archivo*, XII, 292.
[24] Villanueva, *La Guerra*, 167.
[25] Villanueva, *Imperio de los Andes*, 104.

of a monarchy, is the collection of notes of the English
Consul in Maracaibo, Sutherland, which were sent to Minister Canning and which contains declarations and news
relative to General Urdaneta, Governor of Zulia and a
person in Bolivar's confidence. From these it is inferred
that, according to Urdaneta, the idea of proclaiming a
monarchy occurred first to Bolivar himself and that Páez
had proceeded with great imprudence. According to Sutherland, the true intention of Bolivar was that the great convention called together by Colombia should not reassemble
and that the plan for his coronation should be matured
during the period of the dictatorship, for the purpose of
preserving the peace. Villanueva recognizes that this information of the English consul is due to a mistaken interpretation placed on the words of Urdaneta in respect to
the decision of Bolivar; and he transcribes a letter of
Urdaneta to Páez, in which the former denounces as absurd
the plan of crowning Bolivar. Consul Sutherland, nevertheless, said: "As is easily understood, Bolivar cannot recom-
mend that he be named Emperor or King of the united
Empire of Peru and Colombia; but he hopes that his friends
will do it and England not be opposed."

In new documents proceeding from the Sutherland *dossier,* which we have examined in an unpublished work of
Villanueva, entitled *Páez,* the ideas of the group of monarchic friends of Bolivar, are clearly presented, principally
those of Urdaneta. Sutherland entered frankly into the plan
of presenting to the British government the monarchy as
inevitable and absolutely necessary for the preservation of
peace and to make possible the retirement of Colombia's
foreign obligations. These new letters of Sutherland
strengthen the opinion which must be formed by any im-

partial reader that they lack any relation with the plans of Bolivar. They do not have any direct value as to the thought of the latter, they reflect the personal impressions and desires of a functionary, in accord, it is true, with one of the generals or lieutenants of Bolivar, whose desire for monarchy was well known. Villanueva, himself, who gave so much importance to the Sutherland reports in his book, *Imperio de los Andes* and in the unpublished book *Páez* recognizes " that Bolivar did not listen to the man of the monarchic plan, Urdaneta, and if manœuvered in diplomacy, he did it with great prudence."

The English representative of this period, the beginning of 1827, was Minister Cockburn. He was in direct contact with Bolivar and received from him not only the expression of his private feelings but also a special mission to the British government. In his reports, he refers only to the Bolivar plan of obtaining England's protection and obtaining by its intercession an armistice or pact of recognition from Spain. He also refers to the plan of the Bolivian constitution. Naturally, Cockburn interprets this plan as a hereditary monarchy.[26]

The result of all the foregoing foreign testimony, provided by people who spoke directly with the Liberator, tells us nothing of a definite monarchical plan or of the elevation of Bolivar to the throne. We hear only of the life-term presidency, as in the case of Consul Rickets and Minister Cockburn. The French agent in Bogota, Buchet de Martigny, although he believed that Bolivar was monarchic at heart, saw clearly that he was not able to take the radical step of proclaiming the Empire. Martigny said: " He will take

[26] Villanueva Papers, Ms.

a round-about course by moderate changes. The Bolivian constitution gives us an example of this, joining the most opposed principles of republics and of monarchies." [27]

This middle line of action of which Martigny spoke was not due to the influence of monarchic ideas in Bolivar, but simply to the necessity for conciliating the new régime established by the revolution with the need for a strong government, and also for the purpose of establishing the union of the new states upon the basis of the bond formed by a single, life-term presidency.

In what manner could the life-term presidency serve as an instrument in forming the Federation of the Andes? Bolivar, himself, explained it to General La Fuente, in the following terms:

"After having thought very much, persons of the best judgment and I have agreed that the only remedy that we can apply to such a tremendous evil is a general federation among Bolivia, Peru and Colombia, closer than that of the United States, and ruled by a president, and a vice-president under the Bolivian constitution, which could serve each state in particular and the federation in general, with some modifications made in it. The intention of this pact is to establish the most perfect union possible in a federal government. The government of the states, federal or special, would remain with the vice-president and his two chambers with power over all affairs relating to religion, justice, civil and economic administration, and, in short, all that did not pertain to foreign affairs or war. Each department would send a deputy to the federal congress and these would be divided into sections, a third of each section

[27] Villanueva *Imperio de los Andes*, 284.

being composed of the deputies of each republic. These three chambers with the vice-president and the secretaries of state, which were to be recognized in all the Republic, would govern the federation. The Liberator, as supreme chief, would go each year to visit the departments of each state. The capital was to be at a central point. Colombia would be divided into three states, Cundinamarca, Venezuela, and Quito. The federation would have whatever name was desired. There would be a single flag, army, and nation. Whether or not that be done, it is necessary to initiate this plan in Bolivia and Peru since because of their relations and situation they need each other most. Afterwards, it will be easy to make Colombia adopt its sole means of salvation." [28]

We gather from these words of Bolivar that the Federation of the Andes was going to be composed of five states, Cundinamarca, Venezuela, Quito, Peru, and Bolivia. Later it was thought that Colombia could be divided into four states, Venezuela, Cundinamarca, Cartagena, and Ecuador. The historian Restrepo tells us that the plan Bolivar communicated to Santander was to divide Colombia into three states only, and Peru into two. Villanueva interprets this to mean that these two states were Lima and Arequipa. The division of Lower Peru appears to have been suggested to Bolivar in a letter from Sucre, as a means of removing the fears of some who were opposed to the Peruvian-Bolivian Federation. In any case, the project of Andean Federation called for the division of Great Colombia, and the maintenance of Peru and Bolivia as separate states. If Colombia were divided into four states, and Peru and Bolivia should form three more, the federation would include seven great unities.

[28] O'Leary, XXX, 228.

According to Bolivar's letter, the federal states would have their own legislative chambers. The jurisdiction of these state governments would include everything but foreign relations and war.

The real federal government of the nation was vested in a congress, divided into three houses, in the vice-president and secretaries of state. Over this organization as supreme chief, was the life-term president. There was also a life-term president for each state. Villanueva supposes that Bolivar did not accept the life-term presidency of Bolivia, because he desired to be the protector of the entire federation. But, according to Restrepo, Bolivar, as chief of the federation " would also be the president of the state in which he resided, which would be governed by the vice-president in his absence." This explains the important rôle that is given to this official by the constitution.

The political plan explained to General La Fuente really called for serious modifications in the Bolivian constitution. As for the federal congress, although it retained three houses, the departments chose only one representative each, and these were distributed in sections, each house keeping a third of its members from each state, as Bolivar clearly explains to us. The project of Bolivar called for a *sui generis* federation with a life-term executive power and a legislative power in which not the states, but the simple departments, were represented. Pando, commenting on this project, affirmed that it would return to the people the losses they had suffered by the division of the continent into so many different nations.

Other letters of Bolivar in which he speaks of his project, do not make his thought in this respect any clearer. He said to Páez, August 8, 1828: [29] " I would like the Bolivian code, with some modifications, to be accommodated to the small states inside of a large confederation, applying the part which pertains to the executive to the governor-general and the electoral power of the several states." Nothing is said, however, concerning the form in which this division of functions could be realized. We know that the federation which Bolivar proposed was not of provinces but of states, since he affirmed the unity of the many existing nations which he wished to unite later into a vast organism. Bolivar always protested that it was desired that his projected federation of Colombia and Peru be formed under the Bolivian constitution with the old federal ideas. Precisely this same difference between federation of provinces and federation of states is found in the letter to General La Fuente in which he alludes to the confusion that had arisen many times concerning these two systems.[30]

That which most occupied Bolivar's attention in this historic moment was the problem of giving force and permanence to the executive power. This he stated in the letter to Páez cited elsewhere in this study: " Later the thing that is most convenient to do is to maintain the public power, employing force to calm the passions and redress abuses, now with the press, sometimes with the pulpit, and sometimes with the bayonet. The theory of principles is good in periods of calm, but when agitation is general, these theories would be pretending to rule our passions by the ordinances of Heaven, which, although perfect, sometimes do not have any connection with the problem in hand."

[29] O'Leary, XXX, 257.
[30] *Ibid.,* 376.

Months later he was to repeat to Páez, this same thought, in an even more radical form:

" Those who have been reared in slavery, as we have been, do not know how to live with simple laws and under the authority of liberal principles." [81]

[81] *Ibid.*, XXX, 368.

CHAPTER XXIV

THE COLLAPSE OF THE FEDERATION OF THE ANDES

The project of Bolivar would naturally arouse the resistance of the nationalistic elements in each one of the countries he was trying to unite. Moreover, rivalries between Colombians and Peruvians would arise. It is necessary to remember that the nationalistic feeling in the ancient kingdoms or major provinces of the Spanish Colonial Empire was an undisputed psychological reality, one of the few positive factors which can be pointed to in the history of the Revolution.

The government of a state as large as the federation of Bolivar naturally would bring out the predominance of one section over the others. Peru would resist the hegemony of Colombia, just as Venezuela resisted the hegemony of Bogota. And if this entity, Great Colombia, which was developed by the war, and which victory had appeared to consolidate, was difficult, if not impossible, to hold together, how much more difficult would the preservation of unity be if there were added to this area all the vast territory of the Incan Empire!

Faced with the impossibility of basing this union on popular feeling, the proposed Andean Federation had to rely for support on a strong Colombian army in the Peruvian and Bolivian provinces. Such a method would, of course, cause protest and, perhaps, be the source of disorder and even of wars. For many in Peru, the presence of Colombian troops could not be other than a disgrace and more hateful than the Spanish rule.

There was, also, the problem of locating the capital of this new empire. The English chargé d'affaires, Colonel Campbell, stated it well when he said that, to the rivalry existing between Bogota and Caracas would be added a new rivalry between Bogota and Lima.[1]

Even graver was the rivalry between different sections, which was the result of the plan for internal organization. Each country was strongly divided, as Santander had foreseen, into partisans of Bolivar and enemies of Bolivar. And as each party had to have a distinctive policy, the Bolivar party became conservative, while the opposing party became ultrademocratic and federalist. Due to political strategy, the nationalistic groups, which would have normally been conservative and unionist, became liberal and federalist. The Peruvian nationalistic group became provincialist and the Venezuelan nationalists accepted the principle of federation. Besides this lamentable deviation of the national feeling, the plan of Bolivar stimulated party rivalry, giving each party the added support which came from outside the country. It would be an exaggeration to attribute all the dissention that arose between Peru and Colombia, and later between Peru and Bolivia, to the Bolivar project, but it is evident that it had primary influence in these events. To the bad state of affairs arising from anarchy and lack of organization, the plan added a new factor. To bring about harmony among the various national unities liberated by Bolivar, and, above all, to develop their best internal organization, it was necessary to leave each

[1] Villanueva Papers, Ms.

one of them under the direction of its own elements, as inadequate as these were.

Bolivar was of this belief in 1825. In his communication to Vice-President Santander, on February 18 of that year, he spoke as follows concerning the extension of his dictatorial powers: " I have agreed through complacence, being very far from convinced. . . . A terror amounting to panic still dominates the Peruvians as they think of anarchy. To calm this regrettable feeling I felt obliged to offer my services here until the session of the coming congress, in 1826, provided that the representatives of the national sovereignty in Colombia permit my absence and the exercise of an authority which I realize is monstrous in itself, and too unseemly when vested in me." [2]

According to this letter, 1826 was to usher in a purely Peruvian rule in Peru; this idea is confirmed by other letters of Bolivar. In one addressed to Tomás de Heres (July 9, 1825) he said:

"At the end of December or January, I shall go there to terminate my Peruvian government and report on Lower Peru and the southern departments. I will be happy if I can leave the Peruvian government recognized, an American congress assembled, a constitutional government established, the country free, General LaMar at the head of affairs, anarchy destroyed, and the constitution reformed by the legitimate representatives of the nation." [3]

Even when exercising dictatorial powers, Bolivar, at first, believed that he should respect Peruvian nationalistic ideas and sentiments. In a letter to General LaMar we read these words: " My conscience tells me not to employ any Colom-

[2] O'Leary, XXX, 39.
[3] *Ibid.*, XXX, 84.

bian in Peru." ⁴ His idea was that the administration should remain in native hands. In another letter to Tomás de Heres (August 14, 1825), he says: " Tell Señor Unánue that I do not wish to interfere in the political or administrative affairs of Peru, so that I may avoid embarrassment, sometimes with the Peruvians, other times with the Argentinians. You will remember that when I came from Colombia I did not reserve to myself anything other than the military command of the South, and that will be my conduct here, when I cross the Desaguadero River. . . . Try to explain clearly to Unánue the meaning of my purpose and thought, so that we need have no conferences or delays in the matter." ⁵

Following these plans, he announced his resolve to return to his beloved Colombia, as soon as he could " disembarrass himself of the affairs of Upper Peru." ⁶

With this idea in view, he suggested to General Heres the reorganization of the government in this form:

" I would like Señor Unánue to be named vice-president, and Señor Larrea be sent to the Isthmus in place of Señor Pando, and that Señor Luna Pizarro be named secretary of internal affairs, and that the foreign relations be turned over to the ministry of Pando. Tell this to General LaMar when he comes. Then every one will be in his proper post, since the Ministry of the Government requires a man, like Luna Pizarro, of talent, credit, energy, a friend of LaMar, and an enemy of Torre Tagle; Pando would do the rest perfectly." ⁷

Nothing could be more significant than this letter. Luna Pizarro, whose good qualities were recognized by Bolivar, represented the nationalistic party. His participation in the

---

⁴ *Ibid.*, XXX, 72, May 8, 1825.
⁵ *Ibid.*, XXX, 115.
⁶ *Ibid.*, XXX, 127.
⁷ *Ibid.*, XXX, 144.

administration as the head of the most important secretariat was a pledge that this government was to be inaugurated and consolidated.

But, with the coming of 1826, Bolivar's ideas changed suddenly. Had the triumphal tour to Potosi caused this change? Surely new plans were incorporated in the advice given to the Liberator. Bolivar referred to them in his letter to Santander on February 21, 1826.

" Many gentlemen of the Congress intend to proclaim this bolivarian Republic, like that of Upper Peru, before a treaty has been made with that country. Their idea is to gain my support by this flattery, take Sucre as leader, and use the constitution I have written in place of the bad one they have. If this plan goes through, both of our nations will be needed to arrange their affairs." [8]

The adoption of the new constitution meant the exclusion of the elements with which Bolivar first intended to form a national government and the continuation of Colombian hegemony.

Bolivar had the idea that Peru lacked capable men for government,[9] but this lack which was not so grave, was going to be increased by the exclusion of the nationalistic element, which included men of positive value who could not be displaced by the foreign element without many inconveniences.

An impartial observer, like the American Consul, Tudor, believed that there was, in Peru, enough material for a capable and illustrious national government. In his note to Secretary Clay, he said:

---

[8] *Ibid.,* XXX, 167.

[9] *Cf.* the letter to Wilson, (O'Leary, XXX, 403) and to Santander, (*Archivo de Santander,* XII, 219).

" There were several individuals of fine talent & pure character & popular in the country, who would have been adequate to its administration. Marshall LaMar, the Canon Luna Pizarro, the Count de Vista Florida, Generals Necochea, Alvarado & others were of this class. These individuals are all of irreproachable character, & their probity is proved by their poverty." [10]

The foreign governing element was not very abundant. Colombia needed the services of its own sons. The élite fit for government were not very numerous in any American country and had become considerably smaller because of the war. For that reason the policy that was imposed was the utilization of all the elements of value in each one of the nations, a policy of conciliation and attraction, not of exclusiveness. Unfortunately, Bolivar's plan tended toward exclusiveness, and the men of the best intellectual preparation in Peru, such as Luna Pizarro and Vidaurre, would soon form the opposition to the government.

The nationalistic program, or the establishment of national unities, besides being the only possible and convenient plan, was also the only one to conform with the ideas of the revolution. Independence could not mean the replacement of the hegemony of Spain by the nearer and more effective rule of another American nation.

The idea of a super-nation also added serious difficulties to the permanent alliance of the new countries and their union by a plan of exterior policy. Strong national governments were the true basis for future alliances of confederations. Bolivar altered the terms of the problem. To secure peace and internal progress, he believed it convenient to create an exterior union; in reality, to secure this union, it was indispensable, first to stabilize the internal organization.

[10] Manning, *Diplomatic Correspondence*, III, 1808.

The progress of international policy in America should have been working outward from within, rather than proceeding from without. The different nations, organized spontaneously and solidly, could later seek alliances for their external defense.

The principal reason that Bolivar gave to support his project, was the probable failure of the attempt to unite the countries at the Congress of Panama.

Minister Pando, imbued with these ideas, believed that it was necessary to replace the treaties of alliance agreed upon, by the establishment of a new political organism. These were his words: " that to assure this, regarding the constitution, the treaties of alliance would not be sufficient, since experience has shown such treaties to be elusive after the moment in which the mutual need which dictated them ceased." [11]

In reality, the treaties to which Pando referred were not elusive, they had given important service. And in the face of future peril, they could be revived, as experience later proved. As for the expected failure of the Congress of Panama, it is necessary to admit that the obstacles which had become apparent in the American amphictyony, proved that Chile and Argentina feared Colombian hegemony. And, unfortunately, the project of Andean federation came to present these suspicions as justified. If the idea of alliance or union had encountered opposition in the South when Colombia and Bolivia were different states, although both were under the influence of the Liberator, how much greater would that opposition be once the Andean Empire was created. The American amphictyony was, by its very nature,

[11] O'Leary, XXIV, 9.

opposed to any project of partial integration or the absorption of one nation by another. The amphictyony implied respect for the various nations and the application of the principle of equality and equilibrium. The Andean Federation represented an element which would at once assume the primacy and the directive power. In short, the amphictyony partook of international equality; the plan of Bolivar involved the affirmation of a hegemony. The sincere ideal of the congress of Panama was in contradiction with the idea of of an Andean Federation.

Neutral observers of South American politics at this time held this same view. The chargé d'affaires, Campbell, said to Canning: " On another side, Colombia is confederated or united with Chile, Peru, and Mexico by the treaties of July 12, 1823, and July 30, 1824, which are conducive to the re-assembly of the Great American Convention to serve the federated nations with advice in great conflicts, as a point of contact in common dangers, and as a faithful interpreter of public treaties, in case of any doubt, and as a mediator of the differences which may arise. Those opposed to the new plan declare that the League of Panama is sufficient, as it has in addition, the advantage of being able to avoid any attempt to destroy the liberty of the confederated states. They also believe that the new confederation would give just cause for suspicion to Mexico and Buenos Aires." [12]

The project of Andean Federation was unpopular in Colombia. A vigorous war was waged against it by the writers of the Capital. " Such a project ", they said, " is a beautiful chimera, which could not endure, even if it were realized. The territory which is involved is immense and lacks means

[12] Villaneuva Papers, Ms.

of easy communication. For its permanence, it would need a man of great influence, like the Liberator, always at its head. This is impossible. With his death, the confederation would be dissolved, Colombia remaining divided into three very weak parts. The name that reminds us of so many glories would be lost, and with only three states it would be impossible to form a confederation similar to the United States. This is the system that is most convenient for us in order to preserve unharmed the integrity of the republic, since it is now supposed that the Liberator and a large proportion of the people of Colombia do not wish that the Constitution of Cucuta continue ".[13]

Turning to Peru, let us listen to the impartial testimony of the historian Restrepo who tells us how opposition to the life-term constitution was growing: " Some months ago, a rumor was heard in family groups and in private gatherings of many Peruvians. They repeated in them the promise of Bolivar, made in his proclamation of March 11, 1824, that ' he would put away the palm of dictatorship, after the triumph, and return to Colombia with his companions-in-arms, without taking a grain of sand from Peru, but leaving it in liberty '. How badly has he carried out this solemn promise, they said, when he tries to impose on us a charter and a life-term president; we find ourselves oppressed by the despotic authority of a foreign leader and four thousand Colombian bayonets, besides the two thousand which are garrisoned in Bolivia! The auxiliaries do not depart as they should, and Peru is obliged to suffer all sorts of hardships in sustaining them." [14]

[13] Restrepo, *Historia de la Revolución de la República de Colombia*, III, 578.
[14] *Ibid.*, III, 522.

If the federation was unpopular in Colombia and Peru, and made evident the serious dangers and inconveniences we have indicated, the form in which it was instituted was imprudent, and above all, illegal. It was not a question of gaining, by means of a free campaign, the good will of the public and bringing the reform about through existing legal channels. Resort was had to the violent recourse of establishing the fact of Bolivar's dictatorship by giving him unusual and extraordinary powers to modify the constitution. The new political plan, to establish the Andean Federation with the life-term constitution, involved the destruction of the existing legal organizations in Colombia and Peru. The first, created by the document of 1821, was in complete operation; and the second, by the document of 1823, which, although suspended by the temporary dictatorship of Bolivar, had not been repealed. The need for peace, the continuity which order implies, and the most elementary sort of prudence would council respect for established institutions, however imperfect they might have been, and proceeding through these institutions to bring about the desired reforms. Gual stated the situation well. In speaking of the defects of the constitution of 1821, which he was the first to recognize, he said: "After all, I believe that much would be gained by putting an end to all the conventions which are dangerous in every country of the world, and that the reforms which are to be made be brought in a regular manner and be well thought out. . . . Any plan of regular constitutional government would be convenient and the true principles are beginning to be advanced."

Bolivar did not follow this wise policy. Instead of affirming the existing constitutionality in order to bring about suitable reforms within it, he followed the unfortunate plan of a group of his admirers who advised him to bring about what we today call a " revolution from above ", violently to implant the life-term constitution in Peru and to work for popular pronouncements in favor of it in Colombia.

Concerning the sad process which followed the setting-up of the constitution in Peru, we also have the unquestionable testimony of Restrepo and that of the American Consul, Tudor, which has been published recently by Manning in the collection, *Diplomatic Correspondence of the United States Concerning the Independence of the Latin-American Nations*. Both agree on the fundamental facts: the opposition that arose against the government's council of deputies assembled in Lima, the conflict that was aroused between the latter and the government concerning powers; the menace of Bolivar's retirement, which produced much unrest; and, lastly, the petition of the governing party asking that Bolivar continue to exercise dictatorial power with adjournment of the Congress until the next year.

Consul Tudor affirmed that the congress lacked a little of having the quorum necessary for its definite installation when the decree was published which declared the powers of some deputies irregular.

Later, he tells of an important interview that he had with Luna Pizarro, leader of the opposition, which throws light on this decisive moment in the history of Peru and the life of Bolivar. By this it is seen that the Peruvian nationalist party did not oppose Bolivar's continuance as constitutional president, nor the reform necessary in the constitution of 1823, and that nothing could justify the attitude of Bolivar.

Tudor says of Luna Pizarro:

" He is a man of talents, of agreeable manners, very republican in his principles, & seems to have little more of the priest than the dress.

" I asked him what were the views of the opposition. He told me that they were most anxious that the Libertador should continue in the direction of affairs, that his talents, his experience & the influence of his name, were most important to them but that he should be the constitutional President of the Republic. . . . That they could not always be governed by bayonets, that General Bolivar might die, or be called home, & the longer a liberal constitutional administration was deferred, the greater would be the danger & difficulty of introducing it.

" In reply to what changes they wanted in the Constitution, he said: principally in the Senate, to change it from its present form (in which however it has never been organized) of a kind of Council, into a regular legislative body, so that there may be two houses for legislation. They wished also the Courts to be formed according to the principles & regulations of the Constitution; that the arbitrary power now exercised by the Prefects as delegates of the supreme authority should begin to exist under a legal & constitutional government."

The impression of an impartial observer, like Tudor, is that Bolivar had yielded to the urging of his friends, " Military habits, have perhaps too much influence with him." From Tudor's account we gather that Bolivar proceeded with an uncompromising attitude when he sustained the government council against the congress, and when he did not receive Luna Pizarro, and refused to receive him in the future, when Pizarro sought to reach him in Magdalena, on account of the conflict with the congress. O'Higgins had told the Liberator that there was no liberty or public spirit without opposition; but Bolivar could not endure the slightest opposition.

" The Libertador is a very ardent, impetuous character; he has achieved such great things, has had such a sole direction of affairs, that the jarring movements of civil government are regarded by him too much in the light of military insubordination, & to be resisted in the same summary way. . . . there is a tone of excessive adulation & absolute deference in those of this country who approach him, that has nothing of a republican complexion. . . .

". . . I think the situation of things to be regretted, & that it would have been better to attempt with his great influence, to conciliate the most able of the members of the Congress, & have endeavoured to concert measures to enable this feeble country to stand & go alone." [15]

Unfortunately, this was not the line of conduct that Bolivar followed. Restrepo states that the requests of the petition signed by fifty-two deputies, " probably suggested by the persons acquainted with the mysteries of the Peruvian Cabinet, were expressly approved by the Liberator and the government council, who stated that the questions submitted by the deputies were to be given to the electoral colleges ". The plan was to take advantage of this referendum to introduce the constitution that Bolivar had written for Bolivia and establish the life-term presidency.

In the circular of June 1, 1826, the government council offered the Bolivian constitution for the approval of the electoral colleges.

Restrepo says rightly: " Neither Bolivar nor his councillors, nor his blind admirers stopped long enough to think of the illegality of this means. The electoral colleges had been established only for the purpose of choosing the representatives and other government officials; it lacked; therefore, authorization to adopt fundamental laws. Moreover, a con-

[15] Manning, III, 1788-1791.

stitution which required extensive knowledge and understanding to be appreciated could not be sanctioned by the
provincial electoral colleges of Peru, which were composed
largely of farmers, miners, and other men who lacked governmental science. At that time the bad results that such a
constitution would have, could have been foreseen, since it
was based on such weak foundations." [16]

Naturally this Napoleonic plebiscite was to be held under
the influence of authorities who would exert their efforts to
have the electoral colleges approve the new political charter
without any changes. The letter of Bolivar to General
Gamarra contains instructions which show that he was trying to justify such a summary and novel procedure because
of the inconveniences of constitutional assemblies.

" The government council had ordered the project of the
Peruvian constitution republished, with the object of turning
it over to the prefects, the latter turning it over to the electoral colleges, accompanied by an authoritative explanation
circulated by the Minister of the Interior. This is, my dear
General, an operation which should be executed with the
greatest delicacy and ability, because its result is of immense
importance. It is the operation which can produce a lasting
good for the republic, and consequently should be managed
by you and Doctor Torres in perfect agreement in order to
obtain a good result. You should occupy yourself with the
electoral colleges of that department so that they will approve the project as a unit. In case that one article presents
objections to them, it may be reserved for discussion or reform in the coming constitutional congress. With the approbation of the colleges obtained, the fundamental law
will be sanctioned; it will free us of the conflict of a constituent congress, since now it is not necessary that one be
called, and the constituent congresses cannot alter the essential bases of the fundamental law already sanctioned by the

[16] Restrepo, III, 522.

people in the electoral assemblies. Look at all the evils that the assemblies have produced in the new republics, at the dangers to which they have exposed the nations, at the collision of uncontrolled passions irritated by strong feelings of hate, of interest, and of vengeance. You know for how many reasons I beg you to exert your efforts to cause the project of constitution to pass in the electoral colleges, which will have the question submitted to them. I am sure that if this is not obtained, and Peru has to pass through another terrible crisis of a constitutional assembly, the republic is going to disappear irrevocably and the efforts of so many years are going to be wasted and destroyed forever." [17]

The struggles and impassioned conflicts that Bolivar described were going to arise even more violently when the congress was not called together; the opposition which could have been legal had to be revolutionary. Bolivar himself knew this when he said to General La Fuente: " I am preparing to go to Colombia to untangle a labyrinth of passions and interests, while here another one is developing." [18]

Within the ideal orientation of the revolution it was not possible to put aside the assemblies. Bolivar understood this when he favored the convention of Ocaña in 1827 and called the congress together in 1830, after his dictatorship. The assemblies had fewer inconveniences surely than the normal congresses, such as the Colombian, which was functioning, and the Peruvian whose assembling he prevented. These congresses were the inevitable instrument of all ordered government, demanded by the political ethics of the time, and already incorporated in South American customs.

It was not proper to suppress them, but to direct them.

[17] Letter to General Gamarra, Prefect of Cuzco, June 30, 1826. O'Leary, XXX, 234.
[18] *Ibid.,* XXX, 240.

In Peru, nothing caused one to believe that the congress of 1826, after the bitter experience of 1822-23, would not have been docile before a sane conservative influence, without accepting, certainly, plans openly or indirectly imperialistic.

The plan to extend the new constitution to Colombia was even more radical than that employed in Peru. Popular pronouncements were to be made proclaiming acceptance of the new rule.

Bolivar sent two commissioners, one to the southern departments, the other to the northern. These were Dernarquet and Guzmán. Both brought about the act of Guayaquil, August 28, which proclaimed the dictatorship of Bolivar, to which Quito agreed September 16. The Guayaquil act authorized Bolivar to call a great convention and declared itself in favor of the Bolivian constitution.

Owing to the suggestions of Guzmán, Panama, on October 4, declared for the dictatorship. In spite of the orders of Santander, Guzmán also succeeded in causing Cartagena to declare for the dictatorship.

Restrepo says: " we should infer that the project of making himself dictator had occurred to Bolivar, and that his friends were to hear of it through Guzmán, since he did not trust it to the pen through fear of the effect it would have on the friends of the existing order in Colombia, and its effect on the zealous republicans."

Restrepo bases his statement on the communication of Bolivar to the *Intendente* of the Isthmus of Panama, which begins with these words: " The situation at present in Colombia has forced me to think profoundly of the means of avoiding the calamities which menace it. I have thought it convenient, while engaged in my journey there, to send citizen Antonio Leocadio Guzmán to communicate the ideas which have occurred to me. You will hear them from his mouth." [19]

The private letters of Bolivar confirm what he says in the notation taken from Restrepo. Consider this pertinent part of a letter addressed to General Briceño Méndez, August 8, 1826: "Among others it has occurred to me to send Guzmán to Venezuela with the object of communicating to General Páez and all other influential persons the project that I have conceived, and Guzmán will explain in detail. He brings letters for General Páez, General Toro, Carabaño, and others. I hope that you, being conversant with the matter, will write also to Venezuela and to all parts where you can address yourself with result. Guzmán will also speak in Cartagena to Generals Montilla, Padilla, and to others whom he may think necessary." [20]

Later, informed of the happenings in Guayaquil and Southern Colombia, he published his acceptance. In a letter to Larrea, September 14, 1826, he said: " In the South there is a complete uniformity; all the departments have named me Dictator. It is possible that Colombia will do the same. The road will then be greatly facilitated for a complete arrangement." [21]

The sincere friends of Bolivar did not wish to believe that Guzmán carried his authorization. On this point we have unimpeachable evidence. General Soublette said: "All that the Liberator wrote to Montilla, Padilla, and Amador is attributed to him. As for Guzmán he is the one to whom

[19] *Op. cit.,* III, 53, 655, n. 55.
[20] O'Leary, XXX, 252.
[21] *Ibid.,* 266.

they should communicate their feelings and desires. It seems that, in consequence, Guzmán said that the ideas of the Liberator are those of the pronouncement that has been made. I assure you that it does not bother me yet, because I shall never believe Guzmán even though the Liberator tells me to believe him." The attitude of Bolivar in regard to the Guayaquil pronouncement was soon to be stated officially. A note from the secretary, General Pérez, alluded to the fact that the Liberator had made his confession of political faith in the Bolivian constitution. Restrepo says: "this was a blow that stupefied all those who composed the Colombian administration, just as it did the defenders of the laws and institutions of the republic. They could scarcely believe what they saw and still suspected that someone had abused the name of the Liberator. Such was the high opinion they had of his talent and of his disinterestedness proved by a hundred acts and on solemn occasions. But it was soon necessary to believe that the first military genius of South America had become lost in the labyrinth of politics and, misled by servile and perhaps treacherous counsel, he had resolved to lend the prestige of his name to the destruction of his country's constitution." [22]

In contradiction to this policy in which his part was undeniable, Bolivar had written Vice-President Santander, saying that the Bolivian constitution could be used as a basis for reform when the time came to reform the constitution. He added that he would not like to be president in the period directly after the new ideas were incorporated, in 1831, the time of the real Colombian crisis, because in that year the institutions should be reformed.

[22] Restrepo, III, 532.

The plebiscite movement which had proclaimed the dictatorship of Bolivar spread to Puerto Cabello. In Zulia, he was authorized to call the convention. In short, the plan of Bolivar and Guzmán had won the South of Colombia and the littoral departments; but in the center, due to the influence of Santander, the municipalities asked that the constitution be maintained. In Caracas, Guzmán's mission failed miserably. Opinion was against even the continuance of Great Colombia, much less that of the Andean Federation. The town council, after long deliberations, and under the influence of Páez, voted that a constitutional assembly of all the people of old Venezuela be held. This was November 7. This measure was nothing but the last phase of a process that had begun in 1824 because of differences among the Bogota government, the town council of Caracas, and the superior head, Páez. Great Colombia was coming to an end. In another chapter we will particularly refer to this sectional movement. We record here only that it passed through its most acute phase at the time that Bolivar had fully embraced his idea of Andean federation. The alarming news from Venezuela brought Bolivar back to reality. In the middle of 1826, he took full cognizance of the gravity of the situation in these provinces and saw that only his presence there could prevent the outbreak of a civil war. Then he decided to leave Peruvian territory, but without abandoning his project of federation or his idea of returning to consolidate it. In his letter to General La Fuente, July 3, he said: " I shall soon return from my trip to Colombia, and be in Lima, at least for the month of September next year, with the purpose of installing the new congress which is called to decide on the new constitution, or to see the congress of the Federation of the Sister States. This will be the goal of all my steps, and if I do not achieve this I abandon my career." [23]

Still carried away by his persistent imperialistic dream, he committed the error of failing to leave a national government, but only a delegation of his own authority and the aggravating factor, the Colombian troops. Only the hope of realizing his project could lead him to such a serious error as keeping these troops in Peru. They were going to make it hard to preserve the unity of his country and would cause disorders in the country where they were staying. Villanueva says: "Although liberators of Peru, the Colombians were strangers and foreigners there, and their indefinite stay, with the abuses and exigencies proper to conquerors, was beginning to tire the people already trying to loosen the yoke of Bolivarian hegemony." [24]

Arriving at Guayaquil and Quito, Bolivar did not assume the dictatorship which, in conformity with his plan, the people had offered him. He maintained the constitutional system, and thus, as Restrepo says, left all those who had attacked the constitution compromised in the eyes of the people. This sage Colombian historian qualifies the conduct of Bolivar, now as illegal, again as vacillating. " In politics, as every one knows, no system may be set up without a display of firm and consistent will. It was unfortunate that Bolivar took some steps forward and then retraced them, astounded and terrified by the difficulties. He could never succeed in great enterprises, and will end by destroying his prestige and ruining his reputation. It was not thus that

[23] Lecuna, *Cartas del Libertador,* VI, 5.
[24] Villanueva, *Imperio de los Andes,* 247.

the Liberator worked as first chieftain of the War of Independence." [25]

But if Bolivar did not assume the dictatorship and maintained the constitution, he did not renounce his plans, as will be seen later, to approve the constitution of his invention by means of a convention, and he even continued working for the Andean Federation.

And to this persistence in working for the Bolivian constitution is due the rise of serious political opposition in Bogota and the development of nearly insuperable difficulties. Let us hear once more Colonel Campbell's opinion:

" If General Bolivar, on arriving at Guayaquil, had declared his purpose of supporting the constitution and only reforming it in some details of administration which were felt to be of undoubted value, it appears to me that he would not have encountered the least opposition and his presence would have immediately established tranquillity throughout the country." [26]

From Guayaquil and Quito, Bolivar continued his journey to Popayan where he received news concerning public opinion in Peru.

The first contact with reality in Colombia sufficed to convince Bolivar, that his dream of an Andean Federation was impossible and that if he wished to render any useful service, he would be obliged to accept even the division of Great Colombia. The vision was some time in vanishing. The situation was similar to that contemplated in his Jamaica letters when he thought factors of fatal influence determined the organization of different nations in America. The news

[25] *Op. cit.,* III, 550.
[26] Villanueva Papers, Ms.

regarding the pardon of Admiral Guise who had rebelled against his authority, was bitterly disillusioning to Bolivar, and he wrote General Santa Cruz the following letter in which is to be found an essentially nationalistic conception:

" You would be sacrificed if you undertook to sustain me against the national vote, and I will pass for an ambitious person, and even as an usurper, if I do my best to serve other countries outside of Venezuela. I, therefore, free you and my worthy friends the ministers to follow the plan of continuing to compromise and further the proposals which have already been formed by some generous minds. I advise you to abandon yourself to the torrent of national feeling, and in place of sacrificing yourself to it, place yourself at its head; and in place of American plans, adopt purely Peruvian ones, I say more, designs for the exclusive good of Peru. I can conceive of nothing that will fully carry out this thought. But it is my duty, and it is to my glory that I counsel it.

" Be convinced, General, of the intimate nature of these thoughts and of the force with which I prefer these feelings, true children of my conscience, my reason and of my glory. I am going to do all the good I can for Venezuela without attending to anything more. You do the same with respect to Peru. Now that I cannot lend aid from such a distance, I wish, at least to offer you my advice and a laudable example. Put the native soil before anything else, it has formed our being with its elements; our life is nothing else than the essence of our country, the creators of our existence and those who have given us a soul through our education, the sepulchres of our parents lie there, and they give us security and repose; all reminds us of a duty, all excite our tender sentiments and our delicious memories; there was the place of our innocence, our first loves, our first sensations and all the things that have molded us. What more serious claims could it have to our love and veneration? Yes, General, let us serve the native land, and after this duty we will decide the rest. You and I shall have no cause of repentance if we do thus." [27]

[27] Lecuna, *Cartas del Libertador*, VI, 92.

Sucre was to advise Bolivar to follow the same policy later, in respect to Peru. " That the Peruvians may agree as they can. . . but that you and I never mix in their affairs." Was the policy advocated by Bolivar in his letter to Santa Cruz sincere? Did he really have the definite purpose of abandoning Peru to the direction of the essentially nationalistic elements? According to Villanueva, Bolivar's policy in respect to Peru was not sincere. He wrote to Santa Cruz, convinced that Lara, chief of the Colombian troops, would not allow a change in any case. The disinterest shown towards Peru was nothing but a policy of delay while Bolivar made himself strong in Colombia.

In truth, the proof of the change in Bolivar would have been the recall of the troops left in Lima. According to Villanueva and Restrepo, General Lara asked Bolivar that the order for their return be given. He asked the same of Santa Cruz who opposed it because he hoped to utilize the Colombians to make himself president.

Whatever the true feeling of Bolivar, the letter to Santa Cruz is an eloquent profession of nationalistic faith. It was a very brusque change but easily explained by Bolivar's psychological make-up. He had done nothing but return to his old convictions, from which he had been turned for a while by the Napoleonic atmosphere that had surrounded him in Lima. Naturally the vision that inspired this letter was not one of definite repentance but simply an advanced position in the vacillations and changes with which Restrepo justly reproaches him. But they mark the beginning of a real tragedy which was to characterize the last four years of his life, which are also the years of agony for Great Colombia.

On arriving at Bogota, where he did not receive the enthusiastic reception he had expected in view of his former triumphs, this nationalistic feeling would naturally be reinforced. In this state of mind he wrote a letter to Páez which conformed in tone with the one he had written Santa Cruz: "At this time I have no other purpose than to serve Venezuela; I have served America too much, now it is time for me to dedicate all my endeavors and all my care to Caracas. I have served Peru for Caracas, for Caracas I have served Venezuela, for Caracas I have served Bolivia, for Caracas I have served Colombia, for Caracas I have served the New World and Liberty, since all its enemies should be destroyed to make it truly happy. . . . I was an American in Lima, I was a Colombian when I came to the South, but the terrible ingratitude of Bogota has made me renounce all except my citizenship of Caracas, and I can yet be a Venezuelan if Zulia and Oriente do not pay me as did Cundinamarca." [28]

In spite of the sentiments expressed in these letters, Bolivar did not fully abandon his project of federation, since, according to Restrepo, he explained it on this occasion to Santander, thinking he was facilitating the division of Colombia which was inevitable.

Months later, April 11, 1827, he said to General La Fuente: "Here let us arrange everything as soon as possible, so that I can put myself in readiness to go to the South and Peru, where I am called by interests that must be attended to." [29]

The trip to Caracas that Bolivar undertook had as its

[28] Lecuna, *Cartas del Libertador*, VI, 100.
[29] *Ibid.*, 265.

immediate objective the prevention of Great Colombia's dissolution. No one better than he could understand the obstacles which opposed its continuance. Endowed with a sense of reality, only obscured at times by his ambition, he saw the inevitableness of this division and sought to realize it in peace and to substitute for it a simple alliance or confederation. But his love of his task and the elements of his heroic nature prevented him from renouncing the struggle for his old ideal. His destiny forbade him rest. The task that he had before him was more difficult than the struggle for independence. His genius had triumphed over the Spanish armies, but it was to be shattered against the rocks of civil dissention, internal conflicts, petty ambitions, and the growth of newly formed factions led by the various chieftains. The gravest difficulty proceeded from the lack of any definite course or unchanging direction. When Bolivar fought the Spanish, his orientation remained constant. With his ideal of liberty realized, while he was yet middle-aged, his intelligence began to hesitate and he developed another viewpoint on affairs. We know the just observation of Restrepo in this respect. He is at times nationalist, at times a Colombian; he thinks of the federation of states to preserve the unity of Colombia, and later recognizes the dictatorship as the only means of maintaining this unity. These hesitating moments do not detract from the greatness of Bolivar, but rather give increased grandeur and a human aspect to his personality.

Gil Fortoul would have liked a change in the life of the Liberator. Assuming that Peru, Bolivia, and Quito could have liberated themselves, Bolivar, after the battle of Carabobo, should have dedicated his efforts to giving Venezuela as perfect an organization as he, with his incomparable political genius, could have given it. Such a change could not have been possible with the course that American history took. The expedition to Quito and the expulsion of the Spanish from the Peruvian *sierra* were necessary to the securing of independence. The errors of San Martín had made it impossible to drive the Spanish out of Peru without the aid of Colombia. If any change had taken place in the life of Bolivar, it should have been in 1825 after Ayacucho with the liberty of Upper and Lower Peru consolidated. If Bolivar, instead of remaining in this country, following his dream of Andean Federation, had left the new nations to establish themselves with purely local elements, and had returned to Colombia before the conflict between Páez and Santander had become so acrimonious, perhaps the history of America would have been different. The opportune presence of the Liberator in Bogota would have prevented the imprudence shown with respect to Venezuela; and the dissentions of 1826-27 would not have taken place during the reform of the Colombian constitution. The fortunes of Peru and Bolivia would also have been different, and if they had not formed a great nationality, they would, at least, have been able to maintain a treaty of alliance which would permit them to defend their common interests.

In this, as in other points, the vision of Restrepo has to be accepted by impartial history. "If Bolivar, by a deplorable fortune, had not forgotten all these promises and considerations [pertaining to his return to Colombia with his troops], if he had not remained so long in the Peruvian *sierra*, organizing the recently liberated country, enjoying the praises of those people, enthusiastic on account of his position as Liberator, and beguiled by the sweetness of power, and lastly, if he had not allowed himself to be led astray by the alluring counsels which were often treacherous, but which flattered his vanity and self-love, causing him to believe that he was the only man who, while he lived, should command South America, the splendor of his glory would not have lessened in his last years. . . . Colombia, also, would not have had to lament the immorality and weak discipline of its army which, introduced into Peru during warlike riots, became the scourge of the people and the assassin of Liberty." [30]

The destiny of Bolivar was changed at the moment of the fatal life-term constitution, the instant that he abandoned the wise thought of Jamaica and of the speech of Angostura.

The tragedy of Bolivar begins when the visionary and the dreamer are superimposed on the realist and the man of action, when the vital man takes predominance over the ethical man.

[30] *Op. cit.,* III, 477.

CHAPTER XXV

THE REBELLION OF VENEZUELA AND THE UPRISING IN PERU

The rebellion of Venezuela against the centralist régime of Bogota was not due solely, as many have believed, to the personal ambitions of Páez. It was rather a manifestation of the nationalist spirit which existed in Venezuela. This was the fundamental cause of the movement.

According to the historian, Gil Fortoul, not only the élite, but also public opinion was in favor of this movement, and although vacillating and divided in respect to political programs, there was a well determined objective: to obtain the autonomy of the ancient captaincy-general. The strength of this movement lay in the " conformity of opinion of the majority of influential men of Venezuela, both military and civil." The regionalist sentiment which before had been local or municipal, was concentrated in the capital of the ancient captaincy, " contributing to the end of substituting for municipal autonomy a vigorous and tenacious centralism " (within the unity of Venezuela, is to be understood).[1]

José de la Vega confirms the opinion of Gil Fortoul, attributing the separatism of Venezuela to the union of the two federalists with Páez. He points out as an important factor the reaction against the exaggerated centralism of the constitution of Cucuta. He alludes to the effective ex-

[1] Gil Fortoul, *op. cit.,* I, 394.

istence of three great sections in Great Colombia; north, south, and center, repeating the words of the historian Restrepo, who had said that the acts of the government were only effective in the center, and that in the equatorian provinces they called Venezuelans and natives of New Granada, " Colombians " as if these other countries did not exist.[2]

A close study of the problem of Venezuelan separatism requires us to add to the political reasons, interests and opinions which Fortoul and Vega point out, others which pertain more profoundly to the Venezuelan organism. They belong primarily to the geographic factor to which Restrepo has already referred, and second to the colonial tradition, which is the factor that has determined the formation of the diverse national spirit in America.

No one can doubt that between New Granada and the captaincy-general of Venezuela there did not exist the effective bond of a true geographical unity. Considerable distances and marked differences intervened between the plateau of Cundinamarca and the Venezuelan littoral, and between the valley of the Magdalena and the plains of the Orinoco. Moreover, Venezuela during the colonial epoch formed a political and judicial entity distinct from New Granada. Bolivar himself, as we have had occasion to point out, saw clearly from the time of the celebrated letter of Jamaica, that New Granada might form a state distinct from Venezuela. Great Colombia was more the fruit of the necessities of the war and of the genius of Bolivar than the result of a natural evolution; and it could only exist, if these causes disappeared, in a formula of superior

[2] *La Federación en Colombia*, 84.

integration giving complete autonomy to the great districts of which it was formed. Great Colombia, a community of absolute and exaggerated centralism, was not able to maintain itself in face of territorial inconveniences and the exigencies of the nationalist spirit in Venezuela, New Granada and Quito. In order to save her there was no other possible means other than to accept geographic reality, the historical tradition and the orientation of public opinion toward the formation of entities or distinct unities, establishing between them a bond of union for common interests.

Between the extremes of radical unitarianism and of particularist or provincialist federalism, there was a possible middle way: namely federation by integration or federation of the great districts, as Nariño had urged after 1821; a federation of states, as Bolivar desired, opposing the federation of provinces. Unfortunately, in the period which we are studying, the guiding spirits of Colombia adopted one or the other of the two extreme opinions, and the bitter struggle between them led to the absolute separation of New Granada and Venezuela and to the weakening of the organic forces in each of them. Only at rare moments did one or the other of these parties contemplate the possibility of the middle way to which we have referred. Passions and interest soon swept compromise aside. Such is the sad fate in the history of America of all solutions which have been inspired by prudence and by a sense of reality!

The immediate cause of the separatist movement in Venezuela was the judicial proceedings against General Páez who held military command in that department. Páez refused to appear before the senate, thus revealing himself as opposed to the government of Bogota. He was sustained in this attitude by the municipalities of Valencia and of Caracas. It is interesting to observe that the proceedings against Páez had been initiated by the municipality of Caracas because of the alleged abuses of the new recruiting.

The Constitution of Cucuta established the responsibility of functionaries to the senate, thus giving this body an opportunity to meddle in the administration. The conflict which the case of Páez aroused was a result of the application of this unfortunate constitutional provision.

On the other hand it is obvious that since the hegemony of Bogota was resisted in Venezuela, it was not prudent to conduct the affair of Páez in such a strictly legalistic manner. To what extent was this case utilized as an arm to destroy the influence which Páez enjoyed in Venezuela as head of the military and as a person whose prestige represented an obstacle to the policy of Bogota to affirm the influence of the central government? To the geographic, ethnic and historical causes for conflict, which are taken for granted, to the demand for unity of government and unconditional submission of Venezuela to the government at Bogota, was there also some feeling of rivalry between the Colombian vice-president and the military commander of Venezuela? We do not intend to consider these points of historical psychology. At the critical moment in the conflict created by the rebellion of Páez, Vice-President Santander addressed him an eloquent letter, which marked the highest expression of what we can call the sense of legality and of constitutionality in America. Santander, in this notable document, demonstrated how the formation of Great Colombia was the work of Venezuela, and he emphasized the anarchy to which the program of federation of the friends of Páez would lead: Finally, he sent a very

forceful exhortation to Páez, urging him by submitting to
the senate to give a sterling example of patriotism and as-
suring him that he would come out of the affair triumphant.[3]
This eloquent appeal had no effect. Páez was not alone.
Behind him Venezuelan nationalism played its part in many
hidden ways, while the absurd federalist program was agitated openly. An impartial observer, Ker Porter, said that
the great mass of citizens of that department wished to
change the form of government.

Today we can judge the rebellion of Páez in the light
of his own declarations. Páez says in his *Memorias:* " in a
fatal hour for me I reassumed the command from which
I had been so unjustly suspended, and having taken the
first step, it was necessary to be consistent with the error
already committed ".[4]

But at the same time Páez realizes the impossibility of
maintaining the unity of a single government for all of
Colombia: the vast extent of Colombian territory, the extreme difficulty of communications between the provinces
and the central government which was established at Bogota, the jealousies and rivalries between Venezuelans and
the people of New Granada, all of this indicated that the
Republic of Colombia would have an ephemeral existence
in the period covered by our study. Symptoms were already
appearing of the separation which was inevitable and which
sooner or later would come to a head; and no man might
prevent it.[5]

---

[3] Letter of June 12, 1826. *Archivo de Santander,* XIV, 377.

[4] *Op. cit.,* 336.

[5] *Ibid.,* 329. See also the following pamphlets of the rebellion
period in Venezuela; *Manifiesto que el P. E. de Colombia presenta
. . . sobre los acontecimientos de Venezuela,* Bogota, 1826; *Refuta-*

The secessionist movement, which had begun approximately in the year 1825, after the bickerings and strife between the partisans of the Constitution of Cucuta, the life-term constitution and the federation, now began to orient itself toward the last named position. The assembly of November 7 recommends the meeting of the electoral colleges of the ancient Venezuelan provinces, and Páez fixes the date of the election and of the meeting of the future congress (January 10, 1827).

What was the attitude of Bolivar toward these actions? With admirable realism he saw that he could not openly oppose the authority of Páez and follow the repressive policy of Santander. At first he writes letters full of energy and of tact, and he always stresses his position as president, the highest authority of the state. But at the same time he assured Páez of not imposing an already decided solution on the constitutional problem. " Believe me ", he said to him, " that I do not attempt, nor shall I ever attempt, to cause one party to triumph over the other in the convention or out of it ". (He refers to the convention that was soon to be called.) " I shall not oppose the federation. Neither do I wish that the Bolivian constitution be established." [6]

Bolivar is determined to follow a policy of conciliation, of tolerance. His decree of Puerto Cabello (January 1, 1827) proclaims complete amnesty for the insurrection which had broken out the year before; Páez is confirmed

---

ción de la Acta acordada por los diputados de Venezuela, Bogota, 1826; Páez y la Asamblea de 7 de Novembre, Representación del síndico, Discurso de Páez, 1826; Acusación contra el General Páez, 1826.

[6] Gil Fortoul, I, 411.

as supreme head, in Venezuela, of the civil and military authority. The solution of the political problem is put in the hands of a convention, and the summons for the meeting of the exclusively Venezuelan congress is cancelled.

This conciliatory attitude of Bolivar saved, at least in form, the unity of Colombia. In the bargain which was struck, Páez retained power in the district of Venezuela; Bolivar obtained the preservation of the union and the postponement of the political problem. He profited by his stay in Caracas to improve the university, to reorganize the collection of the taxes and to make effective the laws prohibiting slavery.

Bolivar could not have been unaware of the nationalist sentiment which was at the bottom of the attitude of Venezuela. We have seen with what sincere and eloquent words in the letters to Santa Cruz, and to Páez himself, he had pictured these nationalist sentiments. He repeated them in his program at the time of leaving Caracas, July 4, 1827. "All of my actions have been directed to serve the liberty and glory of Venezuela. I have served Colombia and America from Caracas because your fate was bound to that of the rest of the hemisphere of Columbus. Born a citizen of Caracas, my highest ambition will be to preserve this precious title." [7] Words of a politician, one will say, but words which reflected to what extent Bolivar had taken into account the nationalist spirit which animated that part of Colombia. The genius of Bolivar had prevented the crises to national unity which the rebellion of Venezuela represented; but it cannot be denied, as Restrepo observed, that his attitude in regard to constitutional reform had contributed to the heightening of this crisis. The historian of

[7] *Ibid.,* 417.

Colombia says: " if the Liberator had not adopted a policy
so irregular and so lacking in solidity, it might have meant
the end of his influence. . . . But Páez and the other dis-
sidents found support in the acts of the southern departments
and of some of those of the center who reanimated and
expanded the reformist party." [8]

Bolivar, moreover, realized that his work in Venezuela
was not going to be lasting and that a transcendental reform was indispensable. He said in his letter to General J. G.
Pérez: " Venezuela is tranquil and prosperous under the
reforms which have been made. Public spirit has been
sufficiently reconciled. The ideas which prevail are dependent on the combinations which I make and they [the
Venezuelans] desire to please me in this respect. Everyone desires reform and no one gives his opinion about
what must be done. What is most necessary is that a government be established in Venezuela in order to take care of
its needs and interests." [9]

On abandoning Peru to go to Caracas, Bolivar succeeded
in pacifying his native country; but anarchy and disorder
continued to appear in the territories which he left and
at the moment of his departure. In the month of January,
1827, when he began the pacification of Venezuela, there
occurred the mutiny of the troops stationed in Lima. It
had as object the plan attributed by the revolutionary leaders
to their superiors, of disavowing, in complicity with Venezuela, the constitution of Cucuta, and substituting the
Bolivian constitution for it. After arriving at Guayaquil,
the mutineers brought about another insurrection there, and
the municipality, which before had pronounced for the dic-

[8] Restrepo, *Historia de Colombia,* III, 578.
[9] Lecuna, *Cartas del Libertador,* VI, 299.

tatorship of Bolivar, now declared for the maintenance of
the Cucuta constitution. The situation of Colombia is
graphically described in these words of Gil Fortoul: " Dictatorship and anarchy are the terms which best characterize
the existence of the Republic; dictatorship where Bolivar
is to be found, anarchy far from him." [10]

But the rising of the Colombian troops in Peru was only
a symptom of the profound division between the two parties
which had come to exist in Colombia: one wished the
maintenance of a constitutional and liberal government to
be headed by Santander, and another desired, in one form
or another, the personal government of Bolivar, considering
this as the only guarantee of peace and order. Bolivar had
conciliated Páez; but on assuming command in Bogota and
retaining it on his journey to Venezuela, he had accentuated
the rift which had been produced between Santander and
himself.

Unfortunately, this division between the two men passed
the stage of being simply ideologic and political, and took
on a personal character. Newspapers which the Colombian
vice-president inspired or directed had attacked the policy
of the Liberator. Santander himself had applauded the
uprising of the Colombian troops in Peru. On the other
side Bolivar had let slip some phrases of bitter criticism in
regard to the vice-president, even in the affair of the English
loan. Santander attempted a reconciliation which was re-
buffed by Bolivar.

The ideologic struggles became of secondary importance.
Programs for gradual and legal reform or for plebiscitary
changes are no longer considered. In the personal strife

[10] *Op. cit.*, I, 422.

which began inconceivable mutations were brought about. The federated program and the unitarian program are no longer convictions but simply strategic positions; there were only two camps in all of Colombia, and unfortunately in Peru and in Bolivia: the friends of Bolivar and the enemies of Bolivar. One can say that the name of Bolivar is the symbol of controversy in the period of anarchy which develops in all the countries which he had liberated. This is the true criterion with which to contemplate, not only the internal political movements of the epoch, but even the international struggles which will derive from them.

Friends and enemies of Bolivar agreed at that moment on the necessity of reforming the constitution of Cucuta; the former because they believed that the executive established by it was weak and ineffective; and the latter because they desired the establishment of the federation as a means of opposing the omnipotence of Bolivar. Under these converging influences the Colombian congress met for its great convention. It agreed that there was urgent necessity for examining and reforming the constitution and it summoned the great convention. The congress thus anticipated the time which the constitution had provided for constitutional reform (as ten years was the period which the letter of 1821 provided, reform was to be taken up in 1831).

Before this same congress Bolivar presented his irrevocable renunciation of the presidency. He alluded in this document to the suspicion which hung over him, and he invoked the example of Washington. This allusion and the idea which he expresses that his presence was the pretext for anarchy and for political dissentions indicate that Bolivar had a clear understanding that the moment might come when the preservation of his work or the avoiding of greater evils would demand his absolute retirement. He says ingenuously: " I do not feel myself to be innocent of ambition and therefore, I wish to tear myself from the claws of this fury." Bolivar had outbursts of sincerity becoming to the strong in spirit. An ambition, yes, but high and noble, lay upon him, inexorably; and I consider it united in an inseparable manner with his work. He felt himself the victim of a kind of fate against which it was vain to struggle alone. He was profoundly sincere in the wish that a strong external force tear him from it. But this force did not exist; the friends of Bolivar were more interested than he that he not abandon the government. The congress did not accept the renunciation; but decreed in exchange a series of measures to limit his authority and to make his influence lacking in efficacy.

Santander openly assumed the rôle of chief of the opposition. Under his influence and that of his friends there took place the elections for the convention which was to meet in Ocaña; thus a majority of enemies of the Liberator might have been predicted. And without doubt, as often happens, the electoral results did not correspond to reality. The documents of the convention of Ocaña, examined by Joaquín de Herrera, reveal that opinion was unanimous for the unitarian system and the partisans of Bolivar were an overwhelming majority. The acts of all the people asked for the maintenance of the unity of Colombia, and the command of Bolivar.

According to the testimony of the historian Restrepo, Bolivar believed the division of Colombia to be inevitable as is proved by the project, which he had outlined to Santander the previous year, of uniting Colombia and Peru, and of forming three states of Colombia. But in the year

1827, Bolivar thought only of obtaining for Colombia an organization of a central power of immense influence. He said to Rafael Arboleda in his letter of August 24, 1827: " the republic must either confer immense authority on me or it is lost "; [11] and to Briceño Méndez that he believed only in a powerful and just government, "provisional or not provisional, since everything is provisional in a revolution and, therefore, the provisional is better for it quiets jealousies and fears ". This is an observation of great political wisdom which, unfortunately, Bolivar did not heed when the life-term constitution was proposed.

When the convention was about to meet, he reiterated his old ideas on the need of a strong government: " the destruction of Colombia seems inevitable to me if you do not give her a government of immense power, capable of struggling with anarchy which will raise its thousand heads ".[12]

[11] Lecuna, *Cartas del Libertador*, VII, 13.
[12] *Ibid.*, VII, 138. Letter to Páez, Jan. 29, 1828.

CHAPTER XXVI

THE FEDERALIST ANARCHY AND THE ARGENTINE CONSTITUTION OF 1826

Reacting against the jacobinism and disorder of the first years of independence, the assembly of the United Provinces of Rio de La Plata adopted the constitution of 1819, so exaggeratedly conservative and centralist that " provinces " were not even mentioned. Moreover, it must be pointed out that the reaction of 1819-20 was not only centralist, but also monarchic. The congress of 1819 accepted the conditions proposed by France for the establishment of a constitutional monarchy. The candidate to the throne of La Plata was the Duke of Luca.[1]

The provinces showed their opposition to the constitution of 1819 by the appearance of a movement of anarchic disintegration which culminated in 1820, the darkest year of Argentine history, according to all historians, when national unity seemed to perish. The national government in reality does disappear. The province of Buenos Aires— with the economic resources which the possession of the port gave it, and with the tradition of greater culture which came from the viceroyship—organizes a government under the presidency of General Manuel Rodríguez, whose prime-minister, Rivadavia, displays his exceptional abilities as organizer and as statesman in work that bears many similarities to that of Santander in Colombia. Like the latter,

[1] González Calderón, *op. cit.*, I, 73.

Rivadavia had a liberal and cultured orientation. He was preoccupied with the problems of cultivation and improvement of the land. The decrees of 1822 are the basis of the law that is adopted four years later on the subject of emphyteusis, upon which the prosperity of Argentine agriculture depended. With the object of facilitating his domestic efforts, Rivadavia sought peace with Spain by means of the pact of 1823 to which we have alluded.

It was natural that around the nucleus formed in Buenos Aires, national unity, which had been compromised by the anarchy of 1820, would then be restored. Nevertheless, two factors militated against this orientation: the interests of the *caudillos* and the rivalry between the provinces and Buenos Aires, which was to create the problem of the location of the capital not to be resolved until fifty years later.

There did not exist merely a struggle between unitarians and federalists, and between the inhabitants of Buenos Aires and the provincials. In Buenos Aires, as Ingenieros justly remarks, there was a federalist and autonomous tendency whenever the province held the customs house and the port. The provinces of the littoral were federalist, like Buenos Aires, but of a more marked democratic hue. Finally, the provinces of the interior did not want a central government, but an economic federalism, in order to share in the benefits of commerce by taking from Buenos Aires her exclusive rights in the port. The problem of Argentine unity presented, then, more serious problems than those of Colombian unity. There was an economic struggle between the provinces and Buenos Aires in addition to the political anarchy resulting from the appearance and increasing power of local *caudillos*. In the north of South America this struggle was limited in part by the personal influence of Bolivar at the apogee of his career. But as early as the year 1826, the federalist party of Venezuela will discover their chief in Páez, and this same federalist party will appear at the convention of Ocaña under the direction of Santander.

Due to the influence of Buenos Aires, a national assembly was called·into session, and to it there was submitted a plan of constitution destined to save Argentine unity.[2] At that assembly the two tendencies were clearly separated: the unitarian and the federal. Dorrego, who, exiled in 1815, had passed a long time in the United States, made an eloquent defense of federalism. The party of Rivadavia represented the unitarian tendency, and it was this tendency which triumphed in the constitution that was approved. The document shows the obvious influence of the constitution of 1819. The executive power was conferred upon a president chosen by the electoral colleges. He continued in office for five years and possessed important powers. The right of suffrage was limited to those who could read and write, and was denied to servants and day laborers. The constitution establishes a bicameral system, with a chamber of deputies which held office for four years and to which new members were elected biennially and a senate elected by the provincial *juntas*. It gives to the executive power a right of veto which may be overridden by a two-thirds vote of the legislative power. The judicial power is

[2] The ministers Rivadavia and García had initiated the movement for the calling of a general assembly. This movement culminated in the law of February 27, 1824, which authorized the convocation of the assembly. One must bear in mind that since the anarchy of 1820 and the failure of the constitution of 1819, only interprovincial pacts had existed.

named by the president, excepting the supreme court, which requires the approval of the senate. What differentiates the constitution of 1819 from that of 1826 are the councils of administration which are established in the provinces by the later charter. Elected like the deputies, these councils have the right to determine their own financial needs and to levy direct taxes accordingly, and to approve the budgets that will be submitted to the national legislative power. At first the constitutional convention had the idea of allowing the government to select provincial governors, but afterwards it agreed to give the provinces the right to submit a tern from which the gubernatorial choice would have to be made. There were no municipalities. The adoption of the principle of selecting a governor from a slate offered by the provinces was considered of the highest importance, as is gathered from the following words of the introduction to the constitution: " By reserving for each one of the provinces the right of electing its own officials, the constitution allows the provinces every means of taking care of their own welfare. . . . Provinces, towns, cities of the Argentine Republic! Here you see how easily is resolved the great problem about the form of government which has shaken the confidence of some and aroused the fears of others. Your representatives—like you, bound to the destiny of the country, by identical rights, by equal interests— have retained all the advantages of federal government, rejecting only the disadvantages; and they have adopted all the benefits of unified government, excluding merely what might be prejudicial to public and individual rights." [3]

But after so many years of federalist rule and autonomy

[3] *Constitución de la República Argentina, 1826.*

of the *caudillos,* it was difficult for the mean discovered by the constitution of 1826 to satisfy the elements that were predominant in the provinces.

The mistake was made of submitting the constitution to the approval of the provinces, which was equivalent to granting the *caudillos* an opportunity to reject it.[4] This is exactly what happened. It was useless to think of convincing them. The only possible method of imposing respect for the new constitution was resort to force, and this would require the use of the army which was fighting the Brazilians in Uruguay. Such was not the policy of Rivadavia, Avellaneda says: " At this famous moment of our history, Rivadavia declared: ' I represent reason and I do not want to represent force.' And with the solemnity of a pontiff, he descended from the dais of the presidency to go into exile. His intention was noble and righteous, for never under the Argentine heavens has there been a more honest patriotism than his. . . . It is necessary, nevertheless, to control our admiration for the genius and, what is more difficult, our pity for the unfortunate man in order to point out the incorrectness of Rivadavia's conception of his rôle. Government is authority, and authority consists equally of two inescapable elements: reason and force. . . . The resignation of Rivadavia did not advance the prosecution of the war, nor did it leave an improved situation for the negotiation of an advantageous peace. On the contrary, as a

[4] The approval of the constitution was preceded by measures which wounded the feelings and compromised the interests of the provinces. Such were the creation of a permanent national executive; the election of Rivadavia, chief of the unitarians, to the presidency; and finally, the nationalization of Buenos Aires, which had been set up as the national capital.

result of this action, the opponents of war and even the *caudillos* who had conspired to refuse their contingents to the army, became the predominant group. Rivadavia's withdrawal did not bring to the councils of state a new system of government, not even a change in policy; it prepared the way purely, simply, and exclusively for national disintegration." [5]

With the failure of the constitution, only the *caudillos* will continue to exercise effective authority, and after a period of anarchy, Rosas, who had been elected governor of Buenos Aires, became the strongest. The unity of Argentina, which the constitution of 1826 failed to realize, will be created painfully and tragically in the course of the long tyranny that will not be ended until Caseros. Combating those whom he called unitarian savages, the federalist Rosas will unwittingly fulfil the program of the unitarian Rivadavia.[6]

The historian must sadly remark the tragic parallelism of the political events of Spanish America, even though methods varied from place to place. The group of intellectuals led by Santander, Azuero, and Soto struggled to raise the federal banner against the unity of Great Colombia. In 1827-28 the *caudillos* of provincial feudalism worked against Argentine unity.

[5] Avellaneda, *Escritos literarios,* 57-58.

[6] It is not our task to enter into polemics in connection with this dramatic period of Argentine history. It has been considered that the extreme unitarian reaction, which established the predominance of Buenos Aires, aggravated the situation and that the practical thing would have been to rely on a government of provincial autonomy existing by a federal constitution such as the one which ultimately triumphed in 1853. Would the provinces have accepted it? Feudal *caudillismo* is incompatible with any form of efficient central authority.

Bolivar persists uselessly in the North in maintaining the union of Venezuela and New Granada, when he might have preserved order in large sections of Great Colombia by renouncing a single strong government and substituting separate unified régimes. In contrast, Rivadavia voluntarily withdraws from the scene and leaves it in the hands of the blind forces of the *caudillos*. Neither the persistence of the one nor the resignation of the other could interrupt the play of the forces of disintegration and anarchy. America required a long and difficult apprenticeship in republican institutions.

CHAPTER XXVII

THE CONVENTION OF OCAÑA

The calling of a great convention came to defer the crisis regarding the constitution, and awakened the hopes of all the liberals who dreamed of establishing a federation, of the followers of Bolivar who hoped to strengthen the central government. The only one who did not base great hopes on the results of the convention was Bolivar himself. In a letter to Sucre he said: " The great Convention of Colombia will be a literary contest, or to speak more clearly, an arena for athletes: the passions will be the guides, and evil for Colombia will be the result. In a word, this new world is an angry sea which for many years more will not be calmed. Some attribute to me part of the evil, others blame me for all of it, and I, in order to avoid more censure, do not wish to proceed any farther with it. I shall be contented with whatever part is adjudged me in this diabolic partition." [1]

Although, at times, he thought that the enemies of the federation would be stronger in the assembly and that the neutrals would join them, for the most part he maintained his pessimistic outlook, and with it doubt and hesitation. It is evident that after the failure of his life-term constitution in the face of the Peruvian revolution and the unfavorable reception given by Venezuela and New Granada, Bolivar seems to have lost his clear sense of political direction. The constitutional reform was a very inexpedient venture. Boli-

[1] Lecuna, *Cartas del Libertador,* VI, 307.

var would have preferred a provisional government in order to secure internal peace and independence. Reform could come later. This was his personal desire, revealed directly in confidential letters, and indirectly in the acts and votes of the people and institutions which sought the preservation of unity and the continuing in power of Bolivar. It is evident that such acts were inspired by the friends and subalterns of Bolivar.) In the letter to Joaquín Mosquera of February 29, he said: " From all parts they write me that the general opinion is opposed to the constitution and the reform, which they did not wish to be instituted until peace is made, and until the new governments of America should find out which is the best system. They wish a provisional government, authorized to save and organize the republic. As far as I am concerned, I don't know what I desire or what is most convenient, but I do know very well that Colombia is going to be lost sooner or later and that only a miracle will save her from the fate that menaces her."

And under the date of March 24, he explained his thought in even greater detail to Mosquera: " The only convenient thing, dear Doctor, is a provisional government as strong as that I exercised to save Colombia: with such a government the parties would be destroyed and, in 1831, the republic could be constituted with free and adequate forms. I beg that you place yourself in accord with all my friends in order to gain an advantageous result. Unity does everything, and for that reason we should preserve that precious principle." [2]

This provisional government was incompatible with the spirit of the convention, whose object it was to construct

[2] *Ibid.*, VII, 171, 180.

a definite constitution. Bolivar, in this decisive moment of Colombian history, is found to be opposed to the course followed by the convention of Ocaña. His cooperation would mean not only harmony with its purposes, but also faith in the result. Bolivar lacked both of these requirements. This explains his attitude: expectant, indecisive, at times indifferent, and at times condemning. Collaboration and political success called for compromise, for the obscure but fruitful sacrifice of give and take. This spirit was not Bolivar's at this time. The failure of the convention seemed better to him than the saving compromise. Only for short periods did he change this attitude.

On April 9, the convention was definitely begun. Bolivar sent the message, which in conformity with the ideas in the letters previously quoted, asked for a government of great power and influence in Colombia. This message, like the earlier pronouncements of Bolivar, contains vivid descriptions of the political condition of the epoch. Colombia, he says, is occupied with its rights, rather than with its duties. Our government is badly constituted. It leaves us uncertain, because of its aspirations which are incompatible with human nature. He criticizes the laws promulgated: " made by chance, and lacking in plan, in method, in proper classification of legal idiom; they are self-contradictory, confusing, at times unnecessary, and even contrary to its ends ". He censures the constitution in force for the way in which the executive was subordinated to the legislative, " the only sovereign body ", and its lack of initiative in the making of the laws. He considers this executive power as a weak arm of the supreme power, not equal to the legislative or the judicial. " Congress ", he says, " interferes in the natural functions of the executive, in the judicial administration, and in ecclesiastical and military affairs. . . . The government, which should be the mainspring of the state, must search for its task outside of its regular functions." He adds the following statement which confirms what we have said regarding the extraordinary powers given the government in the constitution of Cucuta: "The executive branch has in itself a superabundance of power coupled with extreme weakness; it has not been able to repel foreign invasion or seditious plots without assuming the powers of a dictatorship.

"The constitution itself recognizes its own lack by supplying in profusion (at certain times) those same powers which it had reserved so jealously, so that the government of Colombia is either a trickling fountain or a raging torrent." He later points out the small influence the executive authority has in the organization of the judicial. "Even the right to choose among eligible persons previously selected has been denied him", he says, referring to the president of the Republic. In saying this, he completely contradicts the ideas he had expressed regarding the division of powers in his explanation of the Bolivian Constitution. What had caused this radical change? His reference to the excessive extension of the judicial authority in the matter of setting up new tribunals in the cantons, which would be confusing although profitable to the judges, seems to indicate that the relatively independent judiciary established in Colombia had led to excessive curialistic development.

The organization of this department was now a question of whether it should be submitted to the executive, or whether it should be allowed to become a numerous bureaucracy.

Regarding the municipalities, Bolivar maintained the opinion that led him to suppress them in the constitution of 1826. He renewed his attack on them even more bitterly, saying that they had sought the sovereignty of the nation, fomenting conspiracies, and that they had made themselves odious by the taxes they had levied. His words are: " If I were to express all that is believed about them, there would be no decree more popular than the one by which they would be eliminated." These words explain Bolivar's attitude perfectly, and it is no doubt true that these organizations suffered from the defects he mentioned. More than in the seats of the Congress, the opposition to strong central government was found in these local organisms, the guardians of the tradition of direct autonomy. It was evident 'that a great reform was needed, which would confine their powers to strictly local matters and which would free them from demagogic influence. Bolivar preferred the radical measure of suppressing them completely, a course that was inconvenient if not impossible.

Bolivar later paints the deplorable state of the economic forces of Colombia, an inevitable result of the wars and political instability. The lack of security was the greatest cause of agricultural decline. The ruin of agriculture had caused that of the other industries. " The rural dwellers having been demoralized and their means of acquiring anything reduced, they have sunk into the most desolate misery. Foreign commerce has fallen to the same low scale as industry."

Vivid words describe the state of the army: " They are covered with their arms, because they do not have uniforms." Even those ancient virtues that made them invincible have been defiled by the regrettable influence of the civil tribunals in matters of insubordination and the clemency shown towards military crimes in this ominous epoch.

Concerning foreign relations he makes these statements which are equally true at the present time: " The progress of foreign relations has always depended on the wisdom of the government and the agreement of the people. No nation has ever made itself respected, save by the practise of these virtues. None has been respected unless Union made it strong."

He concludes thus: "A strong government, powerful and just, is the cry of the country. . . . Legislators, those living and those dead, tombs and ruins beseech you for guarantees. . . . Give us a government in which the law shall be obeyed, the courts respected, and the people free.

" Consider, Legislators, that the energy of the public force is the safeguard of individual weakness. . . . Consider that the corruption of the people is born of the indulgence of the tribunals and the impunity with which the laws are broken. Be aware that without strength there is no health, and without virtue the republic perishes. Realize that anarchy destroys liberty and that unity preserves order." He asks for the people, for the army, and for the magistracy, " inexorable laws."

The party that we may call the conservative or unitarian (*godo* or *servil* according to the epithets of the time) found its program well defined in Bolivar's message: to maintain the unity of the Colombian nation, to build up a strong government, to strengthen military discipline, to restore the exchequer, and to suppress or limit the powers of local organisms.

In opposition to this party and this program, the enemies

of Bolivar had to explain their stand. They called themselves liberals and their platform had to be federalism. The political discussion that was beginning had to revolve around one man. The partisans of Bolivar invoked the necessity of maintaining national unity: the enemies of Bolivar, as a means of limiting his influence, upheld the old federal idea. The political ideologies in conflict did not depend on the actual needs of the time or on the high ideals of the contestants, but on the interests of the two parties in conflict. It was another case in which the leader was the issue. Federation is an arm against Bolivar, the unitarians would say. The unifying constitution, answered the liberals, will be an instrument by which Bolivar will organize the most insupportable despotism. No more eloquent proof of what we have said can be found than the case of Santander, the chief of the liberals. He had always been the most outstanding enemy of federalism, both in theory and in practise. Yet, nevertheless, he made himself the standard bearer of this program in the convention of Ocaña. In his letter to Alejandro Vélez he has left us a frank and revealing explanation of this change of front. "I shall occupy myself with nothing but the interests of this country, to restrain the colossal power that Bolivar exercises, to assure the rights of the people and the citizens, to divide the executive power in order to curb it . . . and do not be astonished to see me a Federalist in 1828, because our Colombia has come to such a state that I would become a Mussulman if that were necessary to obtain a strictly liberal government." [3] In the Convention of Ocaña, both the party of the right and that of the left, as we would call them today, were guilty of going to the assembly with a closed mind, with

[3] O'Leary, Appendix, III, 230.

their ideas previously oriented in favor of certain special interests. The convention came to fulfill all the dire prophecy made by Bolivar in his letter to Sucre of June 8, 1827: The convention will be " an arena of athletes, the passions will be the guides, and evil for Colombia will be the result."

Not all of Santander's party upheld the radical policy of the old federalism. Vicente Azuero, whom O'Leary considered " the least violent and the most decent of the party ", proposed a reform policy inspired by an impartial and clear view of the situation. Azuero said that the insurrection had been general and popular in Venezuela; that Bolivar, convinced of the necessity of separating Venezuela and Quito from the center, left those sections under the authority of higher chiefs and a system of laws unused in New Granada. Founded partly on the strength of the nationalistic spirit and partly on Bolivar's own authority, he presented a project on this basis: first, the division of the republic into three districts, Venezuela, Cundinamarca, and Quito, each district to have two legislative chambers to enact its economic laws, a governor elected by its own electoral colleges, a superior court from which no appeal was possible in its own jurisdiction, and prefects for the provinces and committees for municipal police. Second, the establishment of a national government with a president, having about the same powers as formerly, a senate composed of ten senators from each district, and a chamber of deputies with representatives for every thirty-five or forty thousand inhabitants.[4]

---

[4] It is curious that we find that Azuero himself had expressed the inconveniences of the Federation of New Granada and Venezuela seven years before, in a letter to Santander (June 6, 1821. *Archivo de Santander*, VI, 232): 1. The rivalry which would exist if they were considered separate states. 2. The difference of adminis-

Azuero's projects harmonized the unity of Colombia with the nationalistic spirit. The first was maintained by the common president, senate, and house of representatives; the second was reflected in the separation of the republic into three separate districts. It was what we might call federation by nations, or federation by integration.

Venezuela, Cundinamarca, and Quito preserved a central and unified rule within their own territory. Contrary to the old federalistic idea, which would break the republic up into autonomous provinces, dividing what had been united, the project of Azuero accepted the reality of the existing national organisms, uniting that which had been separated or was about to be separated. Azuero was only applying to Colombia the idea of the large autonomous districts advocated by Bolivar in his project for the Federation of the Andes. With his habitual exactness, Gil Fortoul says of the plan, " if it had been calmly discussed, and perhaps altered in some details, it would probably have been the most opportune solution of the problem ".

Naturally the project of Azuero could not satisfy the partisans of the left, nor those of the right. O'Leary said to Bolivar that the project was bad in theory and unacceptable from any viewpoint. Unfortunately, at the time that it was presented, this was Bolivar's opinion also. His spirit vacillated between the two extreme solutions: a strong and

---

tration. 3. The lack of presidental authority, in case there were two vice-presidents. 4. The scarcity of men.

Azuero is of a different opinion in 1828; and probably he was right both times: in 1821, sustaining the Colombian unity which was indispensable for the success of the war; in 1828, the division of Colombia and Venezuela, inevitable in the face of late events and the growing spirit of nationalism.

overpowering government, or the absolute abandonment
of all political action. "All or nothing" was his motto
in these critical moments of the convention. Nevertheless,
with his profound awareness of the situation, before the
convention assembled, he had considered the possibility
of the peaceful separation of New Granada and Venezuela.
He told Páez in a letter of January 29, 1828, "We should
fortify the government so that this vast nation may not be
lost; that, if this cannot be done, Colombia should be divided before it should come under a federation destructive
of all the essential principles and all guarantees . . . I
shudder to behold the terrible scene of our future . . . all
is bad and all is worse . . . division is ruin itself, but federation is the sepulchre of Colombia." [5] On February 7 of
the same year he reiterated these ideas in a letter to Arboleda.
"The federal system will destroy the remains of Colombia
. . . to divide Colombia will not be quite so bad, but
it will be only a postponement of destruction. I see no other
means but strength in the central government." [6] From
the evidence of these letters we may be sure that Bolivar
saw that the convention could result only in a return to
the ancient federalism or in the peaceable separation of
Venezuela and Colombia. The second was bad, but the
first worse, in his opinion. But this opinion, instead of
leading him to accept the lesser of the evils, brought him
to such a sickened spiritual state that he considered only his
old ideal of a united Colombia with an all-powerful government, or else relapsed into indifference as far as other solutions were concerned. The latter was the state of mind re-

[5] Lecuna, *Cartas del Libertador*, VII, 138.
[6] *Ibid.*, 146.

vealed in his letter to Briceño Méndez on April 23: "You are going to compromise with the federalists . . . because virtue is modest and crime violent. . . . Every triumph of my enemies opens for me a great gate by which I may leave Colombia. . . . Little does it matter to me the means by which Colombia is going to be lost, because these gentlemen are only choosing between two things that will delay ruin, but not between two real remedies." [7] He evidently refers to the old federation and the federation of the great districts. He was at this time radical. On April 24, he tells O'Leary with stubbornness very easily explained in a character like his: "Absolute triumph or nothing is my device. If we lose a single article of our project, the republic is left tottering or ruined." [8]

But this state of indifference as to the bad and the worse—the federation of the great districts or the federation of the old type—could not long exist in Bolivar. The realist was to overcome the dreamer. He had to choose the lesser evil, he had to sacrifice the attractive effectiveness of an unlimited authority in order to preserve the unity of the country, however attenuated. It was the sacrifice of a legitimate ambition which was also a great ideal, and the possible elimination of his own person from the political scene. Such a course was indicated by the facts: Venezuela was practically under the rule of Páez, the South was in the hands of the other leader, Flores. This sacrifice, finally, was the only means by which a future union could be made possible for the national entities his sword had liberated. In the early part of May, Bolivar had decided on the middle

[7] *Ibid.*, 236.
[8] *Ibid.*, 240.

course, the peaceful separation of Venezuela and New Granada and the establishment of a federal tie between them. He wrote to this effect to his friends in the convention.

According to General Soublette the idea was exclusively Bolivar's. "When it was suggested to me, I had already considered it", he told the general. In Soublette's opinion the plan was good, but his views had not influenced Bolivar. It is evident that a spontaneous development of his own thought on the subject had determined Bolivar in his latest move. Soublette, who was a stranger to the political interests and passions that were rampant at Ocaña, gave Bolivar a disinterested and exact opinion.[9] (It was the same Soublette who could not believe that Bolivar would concur in the unfortunate error of a plebiscite campaign in favor of the Bolivian constitution.)

Unfortunately, the partisans of Bolivar at the convention were not of the same opinion. They were inflamed by the struggle, every compromise seemed to them to be a defeat. The new idea of Bolivar could be nothing else to them but the reproduction of the ideas of Azuero which they had fought with such fervor. Its acceptance would be the confession of their own defeat. On this occasion the followers of Bolivar out-Bolivared Bolivar. The matter concerned more than their *amour propre,* it cast aside the political interests of the party. What position would Bolivar have in this plan? He would have to leave politics entirely and be an ordinary citizen, as he said, or perhaps accept the presidency of the loose confederacy, without other powers than those relating to foreign affairs and war. The effective influence of the government would be in the hands of the

[9] O'Leary, Appendix, III, 272.

presidents of the three federated countries. In either case the Bolivar party would suffer *capitis diminutio maxima.* In Venezuela, the friends of Páez would dominate, not those of the Liberator; in New Granada, Santander and his circle would rule, instead of the group of friends who had remained faithful to Bolivar. These reasons amply explain the attitude taken by the Bolivar party in advising him to abandon his latest project. Knowing as they did the psychology and the weak points of Bolivar, they advanced arguments whose success could not be doubtful. They only had to invoke the glory of the Liberator, his love for his great work, and his heroic sense of sacrifice in the struggle. Briceño Méndez said to him: "Your name and your glory are so intimately linked with the name and the glory and welfare of Colombia, that it is impossible to separate them . . . I am persuaded that my reasons will authorize you to save the country and preserve your great work, by yourself, if all refuse to aid you." He adds later with unquestionable tact and sagacity, touching the crux of the question: " If a faction opposes you, the people sustain you; if fifteen or twenty criminals calumniate you, the people bless you and place themselves in your hands . . . to abandon the field to the enemy is to confess yourself beaten, and perhaps would cause the ones who calumniated you to be believed. It would not be said that you gave up the command because you believed it to be the last benefit you could confer, but that you lost it because you could not keep it, and because you had personal ambitions which you could not advance. San Martín left the command and no one has forgiven him." [10]

[10] *Ibid.,* 276.

Perhaps it is true that no one excused San Martín at this time, but posterity not only excuses, but applauds him. It is said that in some moments flight or abandonment requires more courage than struggle. This is perhaps the course which Bolivar should have taken in face of the inevitable problem created by the nationalistic spirit and interests in the various sections of Great Colombia.

Castillo Rada, another of the men in Bolivar's confidence at the convention, said to him: " The division of Colombia would be a calamity for America . . . I cannot understand how you can think of this plan. . . . You should not contribute to it, you should not permit that your work be wrecked." [11]

In the face of such open opposition, Bolivar desisted for the moment from his project. He wished to wait, without renouncing his plan. " I preserve them intact " he said, " because no intellectual power is capable of penetrating to the abysmal depths of my unhappy conjectures."

That wait was to be a definite giving up of his plan; the voice of his friends and courtesans was to predominate. Bolivar himself, in a letter to Páez, on the second of June, explains the abandonment: " I have had to give up, because my duty is to save the republic which is in such imminent danger; but my intention has never been to sacrifice it or lose my glory." [12] Bolivar accepted the opinion of Briceño Méndez concerning the union, the safety of Colombia, and his own glory.

On abandoning his last project, Bolivar returned to his radical attitude. "All or nothing " he repeats in his letter

[11] *Ibid.*, 282.
[12] *Ibid.*, 318.

to Urdaneta. " I entomb myself alive among the ruins of this country, because of docile compliance with the councils of fools and perverse men, and for that reason I should destroy the evil. The last would be tyranny, and the first cannot be called weakness, for I do not have it. I am convinced that I could fight, triumph, and save the country—and you know I do not fear combat, but why do I have to combat the will of the good people who call themselves liberal and moderate? They answer me that I did not consult these people before destroying the Spanish, so I should disregard the opinion of the people; but the Spanish were called tyrants, servile, slaves, but those I now face, bear proud names of republicans, liberals, citizens. This is what restrains me and makes me doubt." [13]

But in spite of these doubts he is decided to demand

---

[13] *Ibid.*, 277. In a letter to Arboleda of June 1, he gives us these details of his idea and of the opposition of his friends:

" Before now I had indicated to my friends of the Great Convention that, in the event that we could not hope to obtain a government adequate for our nation, we should divide the republic so that each section might govern itself according to its desires and needs. But my friends became alarmed and begged that we should not take up this project, asking me not to abandon them, offering to do anything other than accept a bad constitution. Thus they were resolved to try it if it were possible, and here I was in a compromise from which I could see no way to extricate myself; but since then I have counted on all my friends in Colombia, in case of having to proceed to extraordinary measures, and now, on my friend Arboleda and all my friends of Cauca, from whom I hope the most effective cooperation." (Lecuna, *Cartas del Libertador*, VII, 299.)

The terms of this letter are profoundly revealing. They prove our affirmation regarding Bolivar's doubts, the influence of his friends on his plan of " risking all " and principally his resolution to proceed to " extraordinary measures " in case the convention was a failure.

of his friends a constitution such as he had dreamed of. He told O'Leary, on May 8: " If these gentlemen do not make what I call a strong government, tell them that they need not count on me." He was more explicit in a letter to Briceño Méndez: " Tell the federals that they will have no country if they triumph, for the army and the people are resolved to oppose them openly. The national sanction is in reserve to prevent that which does not please the people. There is no exaggeration here, and I believe that the good members ought to retire rather than sign any act which is not in accord with their consciences." [14] Such a requirement was not necessary. The attitude of Bolivar's friends was even more radical than his, and the Liberator was encouraged by them. Their plan, following Bolivar's instructions, consisted in nothing else than obtaining the constitution they desired or else cause the convention to fail. Bolivar not only inspired this plan, as we have seen, but expressly approved it. He told Castillo Rada in a new letter of May 15: " What you have told me has caused me to hope again. A paragraph of your letter tells it all. . . . I shall repeat it so that it will not be forgotten: ' We will do nothing that does not advance our purpose, if we cannot, we will suspend the sessions and the reforms until another time, and if none of this is obtained, we will go, denouncing to the public the doers of evil.' This course is perfect and contains all that can be done. Therefore, I shall remain tranquil and await without impatience, the good that my friends will do." He concludes thus: " May all our friends be united in this feeling, and may there be removed from my tongue forever these unworthy words of danger and fear. May they order

[14] J. J. Guerra, *La convención de Ocaña*, 305.

me to save the republic, and save all America, that I may exile anarchy, so that even the memory shall not remain. When the law authorizes me, I know nothing impossible. These are not vain boasts or presumptions of my heart and of my patriotism; no, friends, he who has been able to preside at so many prodigies, has the right to hope for all things." [15] The triumph of Bolivar's strong and unitarian constitution was impossible in the face of the determined opposition of Santander's party and the hesitation of a large group of undecided delegates. This was clearly revealed by the decision of the convention regarding the motion to call Bolivar. The motion presented on the matter was not accepted by the assembly, a clear sign that the Bolivar party could not count on a majority for the approval of its plans.

In reality, neither the friends of Bolivar nor his enemies could muster a majority, since there existed a large camp of neutrals in whose hands rested the balance of power. The frank plan of federalism, proposed by the extremists, could be rejected, precisely because of the attitude of these neutrals. A contribution to the affirmation of the principle of national unity was the eloquent address of Mosquera which merited all the encomiums of Bolivar. The convention decided to preserve unity in the executive, legislative and judicial departments and, at the same time, to improve the administration by the establishment of assemblies or administrative committees in the territorial divisions. The program of the convention was to be decentralization within unity. But federalism, defeated in its frank presentation, tried to reappear in the defining of powers of these local assemblies and their relation with the executive author-

[15] O'Leary, Appendix, III, 293.

ity. A commission named to draw up the projected constitution, had to be reorganized on account of disagreement between the representatives of the two parties. Through the efforts of Azuero only the federalists retained their places.

Here are the principal features of the plan: The republic was divided into twenty departments with local assemblies, sovereign in many respects, as they completed the election of members to the national congress and presented appointments for prefects and vice-prefects. The national congress, with powers similar to those in the constitution of Cucuta, was to be renewed annually. Electoral colleges were created, not only in every province, but also in every canton, there being one elector for every five hundred citizens. The government was slowed up in its action by a council composed of the vice-president, four members named by the congress, and two secretaries of state. This body could initiate or veto laws.[16] Besides the great inconvenience of the local assemblies, Azuero's plan added an even greater limitation on the president's powers to an extent that the executive power was virtually vested in a committee.

As an answer to the above project, the Bolivar party presented a plan which Briceño Méndez sums up in these terms: "A congress composed of two houses, of which the house of representatives is reduced to sixty-two members, with the same powers as under the Cucuta constitution, with the change that the senate does not intervene in the nominations of the executive branch, save in the case of the councillors of state and plenipotentiaries. The executive's term is eight years with nothing said concerning re-

16 *Ibid.,* 306.

election. He can remove or suspend all employees except judges; he has the right of initiative and of a veto which suspends matters until the following legislative session. The council of state is composed of the president, six councillors and six secretaries. The executive authority has extraordinary powers in the case of invasion or internal disorder. This power he exercises under the direction of the council. The courts are to remain as they are, with the difference that a government commissioner is appointed to oversee their conduct. Departmental assemblies are set up, whose decisions must be approved by prefects." [17]

The convention, which had approved Azuero's project in the first debate and had already started to discuss it article by article, confronted with the Bolivarist plan, decided to admit it to discussion. Thus a chaotic process began, by which two projects were being discussed at the same time. The idea of considering the Bolivarist project as a modification of that of the commission further confused the issue, showing the impossibility of expecting all these different men and ideas to be fused into a common work. The obvious intention of some of the Santanderists was to accept the Bolivarist project in the debate, and transform it. making all the changes imaginable. Thus the discussion was a maelstrom of propositions, modifications, and submodifications. The Bolivarists, convinced that this futile discussion could not but result in defeat for their project, on account of the many radical changes made in it, and tired of the scheming, intrigues, and in some cases, disloyalty of the Santanderists, decided to retire from the convention, setting forth their reasons in their note of July 2. The Santander-

[17] *Ibid.*, 308.

ists, alarmed at this attitude, which was defeating the convention, proposed holding several friendly conferences to settle their differences. In these conferences, " The Santanderists were uncompromising while the Bolivarists showed themselves disposed to yield in some cardinal points regarding the new constitution, such as a reduction in the presidential term, the composition of the council of state, formalities for the reelection of the president, and regular and special powers of the executive, which were the principal questions upon which the controversy had turned." [18]

These conferences were interrupted by the Santanderists who censured the other faction for their non-attendance at the convention. They were not relieved of all responsibility by the argument of Santander that he was under no obligation to continue the conferences. On the other hand, the failure of the convention did not seem to alarm or displease the Bolivarists. Briceño Méndez had said: " I have no hope of the approval of the project. . . . We will finish by presenting your proposal of provisional government, which of course will not be admitted to consideration. Then after having touched on all possible means without success, we will retire to inform you and the nation of our conduct and that of our opponents." [19]

The Bolivarists did not have the opportunity of presenting their proposal of provisional government. On the contrary, the Santanderists, alarmed by the failure of the convention, decided to suspend the discussion simultaneously on all projects of constitutions, and commenced to discuss an additional act to the constitution of Cucuta of 1821,

[18] Guerra, 421.
[19] O'Leary, Appendix, III, 310.

designed to repeal Section 25 of Article 55, to modify Article 128 concerning unusual powers of the executive, giving him the right to initiate laws and to organize the provincial assemblies, giving him powers over taxes, public works, petitions, arraignments, etc. But this project, instead of calming the minority, increased its displeasure, since it limited the executive powers. The friends of Bolivar, following the plan already expressed by Castillo Rada, retired from the convention, leaving it without a quorum. They issued a manifesto from the town of La Cruz, in which they set forth the particulars and tried to make the full blame for the failure of the convention fall on Santander and his friends. The truth is that their long list of allegations is not convincing. Whoever studies that document with impartiality will find that the blame falls on one faction as much as it does on the other. The manifesto, throughout, reveals the uncompromising attitude taken by both sides. The Santanderists on the one side, were resolved at all cost to set up a weak and ineffective executive authority on account of their concessions to the federalistic spirit. The Bolivarists, on the other side, were blind and obstinate in not having accepted Azuero's first plan, which Bolivar made his in a certain sense, later. And finally, the latter from the beginning had adopted the plan of abandoning legal means and causing the convention to fail. Legality is, in many cases, a fiction; but it is a useful fiction, often necessary. To destroy it is to leap into the void, it is the open door to the realm of the unforeseen, to anarchy or to dictatorship.

Some historians have weighed Bolivar's responsibility for the failure of the convention caused by the withdrawal of his friends. General Posada Gutiérrez, on the testimony of Castillo Rada, chief of the Bolivarists, affirms that the Liberator did not play the slightest part in that withdrawal. The deputy Michilena, in the confidential letter cited by Guerra, affirms that the resolution of the deputies was absolutely spontaneous.[20]

The opinion of Posada Gutiérrez and of Michilena is contradicted by the correspondence of Bolivar which we have quoted at length. The opinion of Baralt and Díaz seems more authoritative: they attribute to Bolivar the plan followed at Ocaña. In the *Diario de Bucaramanga*, which reflects the story of the life of rest and diversion led by Bolivar during his residence there—games of cards, walks with aides, and conversations with the priest—we see no evidence of the inquietude which appears in his letters, and but few references to the convention at Ocaña. We should note, however, those relating to the convention's rejection of Bolivar's appeal, in which it is seen that Bolivar was unacquainted with the motion presented in the matter and was, in fact, opposed to it. As for the withdrawal from the convention, Perú de Lacroix attributes to Bolivar the following declarations: "I do not know what to say of this, but I find it preferable to the scandal which I feared might take place in that same convention hall, by means of which a struggle, perhaps bloody, would proceed, resulting in the dissolution of the convention. In short, whether I approve or not of this project of Señor Castillo Rada, there is no time now to take council and prevent it, because the day after tomorrow or the following day, it will be put into effect; but I have determined not to receive, in this villa, the deputies who should come with Castillo

20 Guerra, p. 490.

Rada if I cannot prevent his resolution, neither should I approve or disapprove of it publicly; it is not of my doing, and, therefore, I should not receive them here." [21]

Note: For the text of the message of Bolivar and the manifesto of his friends see *Memorias del General O'Leary,* Appendix, III, 218-329. For other documents pertinent to the Convention of Ocaña see *Documentos relativos a la vida pública del Libertador,* XIV and XV; Herrera, *Convención de Ocaña.* The point of view of the friends of Santander is presented in R. Botero Saldarriaga, *El Libertador Presidente.* The position of the Bolivar party is analyzed by C. Parra Pérez, *Bolívar-Contribución al estudio de sus Ideas Políticas.*

---

[21] Lacroix, *Diario de Bucaramanga,* 190.

Chapter XXVIII

THE FEDERALIST TENDENCIES IN CHILE AND THE DECENTRALIST PERUVIAN CONSTITUTION OF 1828

In the oscillating movement of political institutions in America, after the federalist anarchy of the early years there is a tendency toward centralism which is represented by the constitution of 1819 in Argentina, the constitution of Cucuta in Colombia, the Chilean constitutions of 1822, and 1823, and the Bolivarian rule in Peru. But beginning with the year 1826—and even earlier—there is foreshadowed a federalist tendency that appears in the constitution of Mexico of 1824, in the Central-American constitution of 1825. It gives its special coloring to the Venezuelan insurrection in 1826, and brings about the failure of the Argentine constitution of this same year; and it is reflected, finally, in the Chilean federalist movements of 1826-28 and even in the constitutional debate that arises in Peru immediately after the fall of the régime of Bolivar.

We must refer—in its broad outlines—to the political evolution of Chile in this period. Violent opposition arose to the Chilean constitution of 1823, manifested in the disorders of the following year. Director Freire reassumed the dictatorship and convoked a congress to be elected in conformity with more liberal provisions. This congress declared void the constitution of 1823, but it was powerless to prevent the anarchy that broke out in 1825. This parallels the situation in Rio de La Plata in 1820. There does not exist a real public opinion. The factions are stirred by passion. The provinces recall or withdraw their representatives to the congress and begin to organize local assemblies for the conduct of their affairs. The Director adjourns the assembly and there is established in fact federalist rule in the territory of Chile. A directorial council is charged with the government and decides to undertake a campaign for the conquest of Chiloe and provides for the administration of the provinces within a federalized system. At the return from Chiloe, General Freire called an assembly which met in 1826 and in which federalist ideas predominated. It was ordered that the republic of Chile be constituted according to the federal system. The organization of the provinces presented serious difficulties. The following year elections are called and the liberal constitution triumphs. The newly-elected congress approved the constitution of 1828, which established national sovereignty and individual security and which abolished the rights of primogeniture and slavery. Chaos in the provinces brought about strong opposition to the federal form of government. The constitution declares that Chile is a popular representative republic. It establishes a chamber of representatives that is renewed in its entirety every two years. The senate is elected by the provincial *juntas*. Initiative of laws is a right of the representatives and of the executive power. The latter has the right of veto, but the chambers can override this veto without the two-thirds vote required in the United States. The government of the provinces is intrusted, as under the federal system, to the *intendentes* and the autonomous assemblies, but the *intendentes* are named by the executive power from a tern proposed by the respective assemblies. The oligarchic unitarianism of Egaña was followed by the democratic federalism of Infante. One may say that the constitution of 1828 sought to follow a middle road: it was decentralizing, but not federalist. This orientation—in its form more perfect than the other constitutions—was due to the influence of the Spanish writer José Joaquín de Mora.

The application of the articles concerning presidential elections produced a new crisis. The assembly of Concepcion revolted against the resolutions of the congress, and in 1828-29 Chile returns to a state of anarchy. And this was not ended until the battle of Lircay, with the triumph of the conservative forces and the beginning of a period of order under the rule of the republican oligarchy presided over by Diego Portales.[1]

Of all the countries of America the one with the strongest unitarian and centralist tradition was Peru; the tradition of the Incan empire and the viceroyship of Lima had been most hospitable to Spanish bureaucracy. Peru did not pass through the federalist period of Venezuela and New Granada. The régime of San Martín and the dictatorship of Bolivar consolidated this unitarian predominance. Within the plan of the Federation of the Andes there developed in the South under the inspiration of General La Fuente—who, in turn, was inspired by Bolivar—the tendency to unite the departments of Arequipa, Puno, and Cuzco to form a state that would be joined federatively with Bolivia and with the north of Peru. But this tendency got no further than the mere suggestions or speculations of

[1] Consult the important work of the historian L. Galdames, *Evolución constitucional de Chile*, Chapters III and IV.

those who were planning the Andean Federation. With
the insurrection of the Colombian troops in 1827, the régime of Bolivar disappears. Santa Cruz continued in the
government, but with a new cabinet in which Manuel
Lorenzo Vidaurre was the leading figure. The reaction
against the rule of Bolivar assumed a definitely nationalist
direction and was tinged, at the same time, with provincial-
ism and federalism—in accordance with the tendencies of
the period. At this moment Luna Pizarro embodies the national sentiment. He was without doubt the great civilian
figure of the Peruvian revolution. His opposition to Bolivar and his banishment to Chile conferred upon him an
incomparable influence. Fortunately for Peru the orientation of Luna Pizarro sought only the recognition of the
independence of Peru from the old hegemony of Colombia
without falling into the error of adopting the banner of
federalism as the opponents of Bolivar in Great Colombia
had done.

A document of the highest importance in understanding
the ideology of the epoch is the speech delivered by Luna
Pizarro at the July 30 session of the Peruvian convention
which was charged with the creation of a new constitution.
Referring to England, he says: " She who can pride herself on being the first-born of liberty is ruled by a government as unitarian as it is monarchic. No subject of this
empire is afraid of his political and civil rights being taken
away; no one feels the unrighteous hand of the *caudillos*
held over him." Then Luna Pizarro alludes to the dangers
that federalism would hold for the security of independence.
" It may be said that to organize the state into a confederation, it would be necessary first to disorganize it, as, in

effect, it would be disorganized by such an inopportune transition." He points out the danger of foreign intervention which would justify itself on the grounds of subduing the anarchy that such a régime would produce. Finally, Luna Pizarro maintains the impossibility of discovering a mean between federal and unitarian rule.[2]

The plan of constitution originated in the federal idea, but following the evident influence of the constitution of Rivadavia, it established for the departments popularly elected *juntas* and gave them certain important powers. It was an attempt at decentralization. Before discussing this particular point, we must recall some of the features of the plan of constitution which, with slight modifications, was adopted. The Catholic religion is maintained, and other forms of public worship are forbidden. In order to grant it to the Spaniards, citizenship is extended to all foreigners, in spite of the opposition of Vidaurre who represents at this moment what we should call indigenous nationalism or racial demagogy. Colleges of parish and of province are set up, but the electors—the members of the electoral colleges—must be landholders or industrialists. To the chamber of deputies belong the matters of taxation, of loans, and the right of indictment. The senate is designated by the departmental *juntas* from a list of six candidates named by the electoral colleges. The vice-president is president of the senate. The right of veto is granted to the executive power, and a two-thirds majority in each house is necessary to override it. This latter was reduced by the assembly to a mere majority. Finally, there are the departmental *juntas*, to be elected in the same way as the

[2] *Mercurio Peruano,* August 7, 1827.

deputies. Among their important prerogatives is the presentation of terns for the prefects and sub-prefects. By granting the senate important powers, the constitution of 1828 departs from the project of 1823, which reduced it to a simple consultative body. On the subject of the departmental *juntas,* the letter of the constitutional commission said in presenting its draft: " The departmental *juntas* have been placed immediately after the legislative power as deliberative bodies to which are granted a considerable part in the writing of particular laws for their respective provinces. They are modeled after the legislatures of the federated states with all the powers that can possibly be given them, in order that the departments may be disposed to receive opportunely its independence in domestic affairs. The local assemblies may intervene in the department of internal revenue, in the allocation of men for the army, in the examination of municipal accounts, in the budgets of towns, and in all branches of charity, education, and police. Moreover, they prepare the provincial laws by discussing and proposing plans in the fields of agriculture, mining, and industry—the fountains of public wealth. The plans obtain the approval of the congress after a single discussion in each chamber. In this way, they are linked with the legislative power, and the nucleus of unity or consolidation of the system is strengthened. In nothing are the provinces so interested as in the naming of the immediate authorities with whom they are in close contact. This has been placed in their hands by granting to the departmental *juntas* the right to present candidates for the offices of prefects, sub-prefects, and judges of the primary court of claims. The *juntas* make up lists as well for the other civil offices. . . . Thus is precluded the danger inherent in the unitarian republics in which the arbiter of destinies, the executive, finds means to win followers for his personal interests and to satisfy his personal ambitions at the expense of the general welfare." [3]

The constitution of 1828 was able to discover this middle road which Luna Pizarro held impossible. The departmental *juntas* approached the model of the assemblies of the states in the federal system.

Such was the intellectual climate of the epoch; it was impossible to combat it. But one must recognize that the rights granted to the legislative power in the matter of sanctioning plans of the departmental *juntas* preserved the unity of legislation and of government.

It is worth noting, in the ideology of the years 1827 and 1828, the emphasis that was placed on the division of the land. The tendency was to intrust this matter to the *intendentes* and to the departmental *juntas.* In all this, one sees clearly the influence of the prerogatives conceded by the constitution of Cadiz to the provincial *diputaciones* which thus came to be the remote origin of the Peruvian departmental *juntas* and of the administrative councils established by the constitution of Rivadavia.

Since there did not exist in Peru the power of the *caudillos* that developed anarchy in La Plata, the constitution of 1828 was able to consolidate its position. The Peruvian régime that it created was overthrown not by domestic anarchy, but by foreign wars. The constitution of 1834 respected the decentralization and the organizations set up by the charter of 1828. The centralist reaction in Peru

[3] *Mercurio Peruano,* October 30, 31, 1827.

appears only in the year 1839, as a result of the fall of the Peruvian-Bolivian federation which was headed by Santa Cruz.

Note: To understand the ideology of the epoch, it is necessary to consult the periodicals: *El Peruano* of the years 1826-28, a journal which Vidaurre converted from an official magazine to a personal organ for the publication of his Panama speeches and of his many articles and plans; *El Mercurio Peruano,* which was the organ of Peruvian nationalism, directed by Pando; *El Telégrafo,* which represented an orientation more or less advanced and radical; *La Prensa,* of a somewhat similar hue. See as well *La Gaceta de Gobierno* of the year 1827.

CHAPTER XXIX

THE DICTATORSHIP OF BOLIVAR

After the failure of the convention, the only course open was the immediate declaration of the dictatorship of Bolivar. Everyone awaited it. Only the name and the genius of Bolivar could, for any length of time, preserve the unity of Great Colombia, then in its death throes due to the growing strength of the disintegrating forces.[1]

The new dictatorship had first to find a basis in the will of the people. The movement began in Bogota. A *cabildo abierto*, like those of the revolutionary period, decided not to be influenced by the convention but to give the supreme command, with full powers, to Bolivar. Other municipalities, including the Venezuelan cities, joined this movement. Bolivar, in his proclamation of August 27, 1828, accepted the responsibility conferred on him by the people in the full exercise of their sovereignty. He promised to protect the religion of the state, to administer the national income with economy, to pay the foreign debts, and, inside of a

[1] The historian Groot thus explains why it was impossible to return to the Cucuta régime after the failure of the convention: " But now [Bolivar] was not in the situation of 1826, when he could refuse the dictatorship and order the constitutional government to be observed, as he did in Guayaquil. The conditions were very different, because the revolution of Venezuela, which had died out with the hope of constitutional reform, would break out again, not only in Venezuela but also in other parts, which, having conceived false hopes, would break out in new revolts." (*Historia eclesiástica y civil de Nueva Granada,* III, 500.)

year, to call an assembly. He concludes by saying, with admirable frankness: "Colombians, I shall say nothing to you of liberty, because if I fulfill my promises, you will be more than free—you will be respected. Besides, who talks of liberty under a dictatorship? We pity equally the people who obey and the lone man who commands." [2]

The first step the dictatorship had to take was to reestablish military discipline. To effect this, Bolivar revived the rigorous Spanish ordinance of 1768. In order to maintain a dictatorship it was not only necessary to discipline the army, but also to enlarge it. It was decided to increase it from 9980 men to 40,000. Colombia could only exist as a gigantic military bureaucracy. Bolivar's idea was that the dictatorship should not be exercised entirely arbitrarily, but according to certain pre-determined rules. His inaugural decree organizing the state came to be a sort of provisional constitution. The territory was divided into departments, and the dictator could appoint and remove all employes. There was a council of state composed of the ministers and a representative for each department.

Bolivar sought the support of the clergy and the great mass of the population which remained strongly Catholic. His policy was frankly favorable to the church. He promised to protect the religion of the state; he gave a place in the council to the Archbishop of Bogota and issued various decrees in favor of the religious bodies then recruiting new members for the missions which had died out during the wars. A double reason led Bolivar to follow a new religious policy. It is evident that the experience of so many years would lead him to the conviction that religion constituted

[2] Gil Fortoul, I, 435.

the most solid base, not only for social virtues, but also for order and political stability. At the close of his life he must have been convinced of the state's inability to maintain a high and vital morality without which a wholesome political life is impossible. There was another reason purely political: the failure of the convention, the exclusion of the opposition elements, even the more moderate, from the government, led him to seek new support, and this he could find only in the most intense feeling of the masses, the religious feeling.

This second reason explains the attitude towards the church taken by so many dictatorships in Latin-American history. Political expediency leads them to respect and protect religion, which the jacobin *élite*, in other epochs had tried to destroy. From Bolivar to the present time, this policy in respect to religion has formed the only part of their program that could not be criticised.

The decrees in favor of religious recruiting were inspired not only by the desire of making a friend of the church, but also by an undeniable necessity. The long war of independence had caused the decadence, and in many cases, the extinction of the missionary establishments. These represented the grandest, most noble and heroic part of the Spanish contribution to America, the only irreproachable part of the colonial policy. Bolivar with his genius for forward-looking, perceived that the newly independent states should strengthen themselves not only by maintaining, but also by extending the civilizing work of the old Spanish missions.

The course of all dictatorships is fatal; either they dissolve into anarchy, or they become more arbitrary every day until they have become despotisms. Rare are the cases in general history, and rarer still in Latin America, in which a provisional dictatorship has become more limited all the time until it brings the restoration of legality. If the resistance to the dictator is strong, anarchy breaks out; if the resistance is overcome, despotism appears. Only the exceptional qualities of the man cast in the rôle of dictator could have produced a different result. It can be said that dictatorship, with increasing momentum, usually dominates the dictator. Even Bolivar is not, unfortunately, an exception to this law—at least, not in the years 1828 and 1829. At the end of the first of these years, Bolivar comes to exercise this great power without limits or hindrances. He excludes the study of Bentham from the curriculum of the university. All secret societies are prohibited. In line with his ideas expressed in 1826, and repeated to the convention, he suspends the municipalities; in this, copying the work of Páez, who had replaced the municipalities in Venezuela by *corregidores*, Bolivar gives their powers to the prefects.

To meet the financial crisis and the cost of sustaining this great military bureaucracy, he does not hesitate to restore the tribute. October 15, 1828, a personal assessment of three and a half pesos was placed on each native. This decree, coming scarcely four years after the independence was consummated, destroyed all that it had meant for the Indians. It made no difference to them whether they were exploited by a Spanish bureaucracy or a Creole one. Independence could only be reflected practically to them in a betterment of their condition. The abolition of the tribute had been the essential point in the program of all the uprisings and revolutionary declarations, from that of Hidalgo and Morelos in Mexico to that of the La Plata Assembly of

1813. What irony in the destiny of Bolivar! The Liberator restored the tribute, destroying the essential part of the revolutionary program!

In spite of these measures, the dictatorship was not successful in bringing about order or pacifying the country. Bolivar is conscious of his powerlessness, and his pessimistic state forms a contrast with the impulse that leads him to struggle on and put more force into his action. In his letter of October 8, 1828, he told Flores: " Neither in Colombia nor in Peru can anything good be done. Not even the prestige of my name has any value now. All has departed for ever. Yes, my dear Flores, it is sad to recognize this truth which is now beyond doubting. We can do nothing now but vegetate in a land of suffering and adversity. Renounce the chimeras of hope; instinct makes us live, but almost without object." [3]

His pessimism was not without foundation; in September, an infamous conspiracy had attempted to take his life (the conspirators had invaded the palace of the government, and Bolivar only saved himself by springing into the street). In December, there was an anarchical uprising. Lastly, in Popayan, Obando and López revolted. War with Peru broke out, as the result of the old hatred between Bolivarists and anti-Bolivarists. The war did not destroy the internal anarchy in either of the countries, but rather accentuated it. The spirit of revolt was in the air. Not even the peace signed with Peru could change the atmosphere in the affected countries. The spark of anarchy, extinguished here, broke out again elsewhere. It made itself felt like the dull subterranean rumble that precedes great cataclysms. Boli-

[3] O'Leary, XXXI, 224.

var, on account of his delicate sensibility and his ability to see beneath the outside appearances of things, was no doubt more aware of the unhappy situation than any one else. The dictatorship was really a failure. It had not been able to cure this general feeling of unrest, this absolute lack of moral unity, which, perhaps, brought the revolution inevitably. Bolivar saw that America was returning to original chaos, according to his picturesque phrase. The spectre of anarchy seemed to attach itself to the new nations. In this frightful dilemma, only two alternatives appeared to him: either a return to primitive barbarity, the fading of all civilization from the country, or the restoration of the colonial régime.

The unhappy condition of Colombia was not all that distressed Bolivar at this time; he extended his gaze over all Spanish America and found nowhere any reason for hopefulness. Although he had abandoned his plans for the congress of Panama and the Federation of the Andes, the Liberator still thought in continental terms. But his exultant Americanism of yesterday is now apocalyptical in its somberness. The famous pamphlet, *Una mirada sobre la América Española* attributed to Bolivar, and which appeared in Quito in 1829, contains the most harsh summary of revolutionary anarchy. It describes, in unusually realistic passages, the chaos in Argentina, the military barbarity in Mexico, the political assassinations in Bolivia, and the continuous disorders in Guatemala, Chile, and Peru. "There is no faith in America", it exclaims, "neither between men nor between nations. Treaties are only papers; constitutions, books; the elections, combats; liberty, anarchy, and life, a torment." [4] This crushing report of the revolution was

[4] José Felix Blanco, *Documentos para la historia de la vida pública del Libertador*, XIII, 493.

designed to create an atmosphere of unity, respect, and support for the congress which was about to convene. Its style, ideas, and finality did not leave its authorship in doubt. Letters of Bolivar to friends confirm it. In writing to Montilla and Urdaneta, friends then in his confidence, he refers to the situation in the other countries of America in exactly similar manner. The prolongation of the war with Peru contributed to his pessimism. Peru occupied Guayaquil and Bolivar got ready to attack it. The war was more than a struggle between Peru and Colombia, in Bolivar's opinion; it was a campaign against him, an episode of international intervention. In a letter of April 6, he told Urdaneta: " Everything makes me believe that this world of anarchy requires foreign intervention which will serve as mediator in our differences and follies. Would that the United States might do something for Peru who has named it guarantor in order to make a jest of it. And I would like our ministry to take some steps with friendly governments because through their mediation we might obtain peace." [5]

In April 1829 he wrote the Minister of Foreign Relations, advising him to speak with the diplomatic agents of the United States and England, in regard to the possible anarchy which would ravage the South American countries if some powerful state did not intervene in their differences. July 6, of the same year, Bolivar's secretary, Espinar, in a letter to the same minister, spoke of the dangers surrounding South America, anarchy on one side, and European colonization on the other. He alludes to the failure of the Panama amphictyony and the project for the Federation of the Andes, affirming the necessity of a regulating power. Lastly he

[5] *Memorias del General Urdaneta*, 414.

expresses the desires of Bolivar that America be placed under the custody and guardianship, mediation, or influence of the more powerful states which should preserve it from the destruction to which anarchy would lead it, or the colonial status with which it was menaced.[6]

With the international situation closely connected with internal policies in the South American countries, the foreign mediation and influence that Bolivar sought were not only reflected in foreign relations but also in internal affairs. With peace, anarchy began to abate. But it cannot be said that Bolivar sought a true protectorate, in spite of his efforts to secure mediation in internal affairs. Neither can this effort be interpreted as a desire to secure a radical change in existing institutions. Bolivar wished the moral and social influence of the great powers like England, but he did not wish to renounce national identity, sovereignty, or institutions. At this time, as on previous occasions, the idea of any monarchic plan to make foreign protection effective was repugnant to Bolivar.

His plan was entirely different: according to him, New Granada and Venezuela, whether separated or joined, should preserve their free and republican character. Exactly seven days after the writing of Espinar's famous note on the projected mediation, Bolivar wrote to the Minister of Foreign Relations, telling him that he foresaw a civil war between Venezuela and Colombia, and that it would be better to make the separation legally and with peace and harmony.

[6] Gil Fortoul, I, 459. See also the notes of Espinar, Bolivar's secretary, April 4, July 6. *Documentos para la vida pública del Libertador*, XVI, 93, 95.

" Only in the case that congress should not accept the division," he adds, " should the life-term government, as in Bolivia, be proposed, along with the hereditary senate that I proposed in Guiana." Referring to the division, he said: " The parties of Páez and Santander are at the moment in accord." In opposition to the monarchical plan, upheld by some of his partisans, he made the following irrefutable observations:

1. " No foreign prince would take for a domain an anarchic country without guarantees. 2. The national debts and the poverty of the country do not offer the means for maintaining a prince and a court. 3. The lower classes would become alarmed, fearing the effects of an aristocracy and inequality. 4. The generals and other ambitious persons of all sorts could not bear the idea of seeing themselves deprived of the supreme command." [7]

Bolivar wrote to the same effect to General Urdaneta: " There is no place for a monarchical project, because I do not desire, nor does any foreign prince desire to climb to a scaffold. If I were ever to forget what I said to Bolivia, I have at my side the example of Iturbide, which would remind me of it every day." [8]

The council of ministers was subject to the same unrest as Bolivar regarding the future of Colombia, especially regarding the not very remote eventuality of Bolivar's death. But, according to Restrepo, the members inclined to the monarchical solution " to cut short the dissolution of the state in the face of the antipathy existing on the part of Venezuelans and New Granada citizens, and the ambitions of local chiefs, each one soon to rise to the absolute con-

[7] Lecuna, *Cartas del Libertador*, IX, 21.
[8] *Memorias del General Urdaneta*, 418.

trol of his respective region." With this viewpoint they formulated a monarchic plan, the principal bases of which were: continuation of Bolivar in power until his death; establishment of a monarchy under a European prince, preferably French, for religious reasons; and the approbation of England and France, their protection to be gained to prevent the intervention of other countries, who might invade Colombia during the change of government. The council of ministers began negotiations with the French agent Bresson.

What was Bolivar's attitude in the face of this plan of the council? He could not ignore the budding of this project. A letter written to the chargé d'affaires of England, makes it evident that he knew of it. He says that he is not opposed, in principle, to the reorganization of Colombia to conform to European institutions, but he reserved a definite opinion until he learned the attitude of England and France.

These phrases cannot be considered the sincere expression of Bolivar's thought. We have seen that since 1825 Bolivar, with exquisite diplomatic tact, tried to convince England and France that there did not exist, on his part, any radical or unconditional opposition to the extension of monarchy to America. This attitude arose from two practical purposes: first, to gain the sympathy of the European countries which were dominated by the monarchic reaction and, second, not to close definitely the door to any solution, however inconvenient or improbable, which might be the only recourse to save order and independence.

In spite of his prudence and diplomatic reserve, he set forth to the English chargé d'affaires, Campbell, interesting objections to the monarchic plan. It is best to give his words:

" That which you have told me regarding the naming of a successor to my authority, a European prince, is not entirely new to me, because some of it has been communicated to me, not without some mystery and timidity, since they know my manner of thinking.

" I do not know what to say to you concerning this idea which involves in itself a thousand inconveniences. You know there is none on my part, determined as I am to resign the command in this coming congress; but who can appease the ambition of our chiefs and the fear of inequality on the part of the lower classes? Do you not believe that England will be jealous of the election of a Bourbon? Or that the new American states will be greatly opposed? And the United States, which appears destined by Providence to plague America with miseries in the name of liberty? It seems to me that I can see a general conspiracy against poor Colombia already envied by all the American Republics. All the presses will be put to work calling a new crusade against those guilty of treachery to liberty, advocacy of the Bourbons and violation of the American system. On the South the Peruvians would light the flame of discord; on the Isthmus, the people of Guatemala and Mexico; and in the Antilles, the Americans and the liberals of all parties. Santo Domingo would not remain inactive but would call its brothers to make common cause against a prince of France." [9]

England, as Bolivar had foreseen, was opposed to a French or English prince, preferring a Spanish Infante. It

[9] Lecuna, IX, 68. Definite testimony regarding Bolivar's lack of responsibility for the origin and development of the monarchical plan has been offered us by the publicist, Samper. Bolivar is freed of all responsibility by the words of the Minister of Foreign Relations Vergara, who told Samper " I affirm that the responsibility was all mine and my colleagues, Restrepo, Tanco, Urdaneta. The only blame due the Liberator, if blame there is, is in having delayed some months his disapprobation of the project which was repugnant to his sentiments." Samper, *Bolívar*, note 44.

was not probable that Spain, in this last case, would change the policy that had determined the failure of the Treaty of Cordova, and the bases of Punchauca. Moreover, as Lord Aberdeen said, no European prince could accept the crown after the death of Bolivar. On the other hand, the opinion of the people, especially in Venezuela, was against the plan. General Soublette said: " Every day I have more reason to believe that these departments would resist monarchy."

The monarchic plan in 1829 was as visionary as similar plans had been in previous years. The agreement of the principal countries of Europe could not be reached regarding the plan, and, on the other hand, popular opinion in Colombia and Venezuela was hostile to it.

In spite of the change caused by the peace with Peru and the new government set up in that country, Bolivar, in September 1829, had not changed his opinion of Colombia's situation. The letter which, he sent to O'Leary, the 13th of the same month, is a document of primary importance.[10] It is important, not only because it reveals to us the intimate thought of the Liberator, but also because it contains observations full of profound political wisdom. In this letter there appears the realistic vision of the situation, the serene and impartial manner of looking at things that distinguished the Bolivar of Angostura, but which seldom appeared after 1826. This letter also has the character of a political last testament. The idea of death gives it a certain stamp of gloomy majesty. Bolivar feels that his strength is beginning to fail him. He is conscious of the fact that his spiritual robustness had suffered a great decline. He felt his inca-

[10] Lecuna, IX, 120.

pacity for public service. He had triumphed in the foreign war, and at times had dominated domestic factions, but in spite of this, he could see that all the pillars of his edifice were not solid. A time would come when it would fall, and with it those supporting it. The union between Venezuela and New Granada had no other basis than the life of the Liberator. Bolivar studied the problem of what would happen to Colombia after his death. He analyzed the two solutions that presented themselves; the monarchic and the federal. He found arguments against both. He did not conceive it to be possible to establish a kingdom in a country democratically constituted. No one could be king in Columbia

" because no foreign prince would take a throne surrounded by dangers and misery, and the generals would not consider submitting to a companion and renouncing forever the supreme authority. . . .

" The poverty of the country will not permit the erection of a pompous government which would provide all the abuses of luxury and dissipation. The new nobility, indispensable in a monarchy, would come from the mass of the people, with all the envy of one part and all the haughtiness of the other. No one would patiently suffer this miserable aristocracy, covered with poverty and ignorance and animated by ridiculous pretensions. . . . Let us not talk any more, therefore, of this chimera.

" Yet I have less inclination towards the federal government; it is similar to a regulated anarchy, or rather it is a law which implicitly prescribes the dissolution and ruin of the state with all its members. I think that it would be better for South America to adopt the Koran rather than the government of the United States, although it is the best in the world. Here it is necessary to add nothing, but to view the sad states of Buenos Aires, Chile, Mexico, and Guatemala. . . . These examples alone tell us more than libraries."

Having discarded both monarchical and federal plans, Bolivar recognizes that there is no solution left to Colombia but to establish a central system competently designed according to the extent of the territory and the nature of the inhabitants. He returns to the viewpoint of the Jamaica letter, which view he held at times during the convention of Ocaña.

" The present government of Colombia is not sufficient to arrange and administer extensive provinces. The center is too far from the extremities. In the transit, force is lost and the central administration lacks means in proportion to the immensity of its remote domains. . . .

" The constitutional convention will have to choose one of the two possible resolutions that remain to it in the present state of affairs: 1, The division of New Granada and Venezuela. 2, The creation of a strong life-term government. In the first case the separation of these two countries should be complete, just, and pacific. Once consummated, each part should reorganize in its own manner and separately consider common interests and mutual relations. . . .

" I see no way of softening local antipathies or shortening enormous distances. In my opinion, these are the great obstacles in the way of the formation of a government and a single state. We always come against this barrier, and it is for our valor to find a way through.

" If two governments, united against common enemies, were set up, and an international pact concluded which would guarantee reciprocal relations, time would do the rest, for it has many recourses.

" While we had to continue the war, it seemed, and it can nearly be taken for granted, that the creation of the Republic of Colombia was convenient. Domestic peace having come, and with it new relations, we have become aware that this laudable project, or rather this attempt, does not promise to give us what we had hoped for. Men and conditions cry out for the separation, and every individual's unrest adds to the general inquietude."

Finally, he contemplates the solution offered by a strong, life-term government, and the advantages of such a government in international relations, but the analysis of the situation, principally in regard to the inconveniences of nationality and the civil and military status of the president, leads him invariably to the division of the country as the only solution.

Let us summarize Bolivar's thought here. In accordance with his old convictions, he entirely discards the monarchic plan. He even puts aside his old plan of a government under a life-term president and a hereditary senate. In absolute sacrifice of his dreams and old ideals, he proposes the pacific separation of the two countries New Granada and Venezuela. Precisely at this time, comes the unjust censure of General Harrison. Harrison, who had just retired as Minister from the United States, wrote Bolivar the famous letter of September 27, in which he imputes to him the monarchic and life-term plans, and recites the progress of the dictatorship which he had exercised since 1828. Diplomatic history does not record a more flagrant case of the violation of the duties of neutrality and diplomatic convention. Harrison's letter shows lack of information, and, at the same time, the definite purpose of intervening in the destinies of Colombia. Harrison, believing that he had come to a young republic to play the same rôle of political arbitrator as Poinsett had played in Mexico, showed from the very beginning, his sympathy for the opposition party, principally cultivating relations with the latter. It was not strange, therefore, that he had the same opinion of Bolivar as did the latter's enemies. His defense, printed in a pamphlet in Washington in 1830, contains his own condemnation.[11]

He did not wish to leave Colombia without giving the first man of America an impertinent and unjust lesson in political morals. If we subtract from it all his cheap philosophical principles, the only thing left is the tendency to interfere in political affairs and to exercise a decisive influence in the life of the new states.[12]

[11] *Remarks of General Harrison, Late envoy extraordinary and minister plenipotentiary of the United States to the Republic of Colombia, on certain charges made against him by that government. To which is added, an unofficial letter from General Harrison to General Bolivar on the affairs of Colombia; with notes, explanatory of his views of the present state of that country.* Washington, 1830.

[12] The instructions of Henry Clay to Harrison, which we know through the quotations of Professor Rippy in his book (*Rivalry of the United States and England in Spanish America,* 209) show that a tendency to constitutional imperialism existed even among the strongest partisans of democracy. Clay authorized Harrison to use his influence to awake Colombia's desire to preserve institutions analogous to those of the United States. In spite of these instructions, however, Harrison is not exempt of blame, because he could carry out this purpose without gaining Bolivar's opposition, and without directing towards the hero of Colombia the censures of his unfortunate letter.

Van Buren, with a more realistic viewpoint than Clay, and with the same purpose in view, contemplated the possibility that progress towards liberal institutions in Colombia might be retarded. He was thus better prepared to form a judgment of the Liberator.

Mrs. Goebel, in her life of General Harrison could not deny his tendencies to intervene: "From these dispatches, it may be concluded that Harrison held much the same position in Colombia as that occupied by Joel R. Poinsett in Mexico, at least as far as his sympathies were concerned. He himself took no hand in promoting the revolution, but his knowledge of the progress of the secret plans is amazing, and it is evident that he was anxious to

The revealing criticism of Harrison was not the only incident of the Bolivar dictatorship. In Europe it was the cause of an interesting debate between de Pradt and Benjamin Constant. The great liberal orator manifested his frank disapprobation of the Bolivar dictatorship in the *Courrier Français*. He said: Dictators are responsible, not only for the evils they cause, the crimes they commit during their life-time: they are also responsible for the evils they prepare, those that break out after their death." De Pradt quickly came to the defense of the Liberator, stating that Europe was different from America, where factions made the application of the laws impossible, and where at every instant the earth trembled, and it was necessary to create everything. He defended Bolivar, pointing out the luminous features of his career. Constant replied, analyzing Bolivar's political life during the later years. He blames him for having given Peru institutions which displeased a great part of the nation. He condemns the union of Páez and Bolivar to destroy the constitution of Colombia. He ridicules the promises to leave the high command, saying: " De Pradt has forgotten Cæsar and Cromwell. This affectation of respect for the people who are kept under the yoke is the artifice of all aspirants to tyranny. They always offer to give up their power, but this offer, humble in appearance, is accompanied by a show of force which intimidates the

---

check the growth of European influence at least," *William Henry Harrison*, 281.

The best study of the Bolivar-Harrison incident is that of the Venezuelan diplomat, Ángel Cesar Rivas, in which he examines the antecedents of the American minister, in order to explain his conduct. *Ensayos de historia política y diplomática*.

people who refuse it. The usurpers, condemned to power by their own will, wish, at the same time, to be obeyed and pitied as victims of their consecration." He concludes by asking: " Is there any instance where a despotism has given a nation, whatever its moral condition may have been, the education necessary for the enjoyment of liberty? "

Constant's criticism involved some very true obervations, but it is evident that his principles were too rigid for the situation in America, and that he did not take into account the fact that the dictatorship of Bolivar had, because of the decision of the latter, an essentially provisional character.

The Liberator could not long remain in ignorance of this debate. He said, July 22, 1829: " My name now belongs to history, it will do me justice. Thus you, my dear friend, need not bother yourself to vindicate me of the accusations by which Benjamin Constant has tried to stain my glory. He himself would judge me better if he knew more of the happenings of our history. I do not love my country's glory less than did Camillus, I am as great a lover of liberty as Washington, and no one can take away from me the honor of having humbled the Lion of Castille from the Orinoco to Potosi." [13]

In spite of the declarations in this letter, Bolivar occupied himself by putting his friends in charge of the drafting of his defense and the assembly of documents. They chose Abreu y Lima for this work. The defense of Abreu recalls that Bolivar did not impose the constitution on Colombia, and says that when the Liberator said good-bye to Peru it was a final farewell.

[13] Lecuna, IX, 33.

In spite of its deficiencies, Abreu's work contains this fundamental defense of Bolivar which is of undeniable value: " Bolivar has called together four constitutional conventions in Colombia; he sustained one in Peru and reconvened another; he convoked the first one in Bolivia and never suspended, even for a time, the sessions of any." [14]

[14] Abreu y Lima, *Resumen Histórico de la dictadura de Bolívar*, 286.

Chapter XXX

THE DISSOLUTION OF GREAT COLOMBIA AND THE DEATH OF BOLIVAR

Bolivar's idea about the peaceful separation of Venezuela and New Granada was good, but it came too late. The wise policy he outlined in his letter to O'Leary would have saved Colombia in 1827 or 1828; but, as a program for the year 1830, it was ineffective. In November of the same year, the canton of Valencia rebelled for the purpose of separating Venezuela from New Granada. The rebels gave as reasons for the separation the differences in climate, customs, resources and governmental antecedents.

Three days later, an assembly in Caracas voted for the separation from New Granada, for the calling of an exclusively Venezuelan convention, and for the annulment of Bolivar's government. In December, Caracas again, in the form of a statement to Bolivar and the government of Valencia, sought the separation on a *de facto* basis, under the leadership of Páez. The attitude was hostile, they even declared that Bolivar would not be permitted to return to Venezuela. In other parts of the Venezuelan territory, as in the eastern provinces, the idea of a federation of provinces predominated. In January, Páez called together a congress exclusively Venezuelan. Separation became inevitable.

Under these conditions, the congress of 1830 reconvened. It was a congress called " admirable " by its contemporaries. It was, in the quality of the men who com-

posed it, but not in the amount of work done. Preceding it
were interesting ideological debates between the partisans of
the old federalism and those favoring the centralistic rule
under one president. The true solution, the peaceable separation of Venezuela and Colombia, with a federal union to
be set up later, which was Bolivar's idea, was not considered
in this theoretical debate. Martín Tovar was the patron of
the federalists of the 1811 style. The basis of the state was
not merely the departments, but the small provinces. The
author of the pamphlet *Colombia en MDCCCXIII* rightly
said in 1828, that the federal idea could lead to an infinite
division of the central government.[1] In opposition to the
secessionist Utopia was the unitarian Utopia. García del
Río, in his celebrated *Meditaciones Colombianas* reproduces
arguments in favor of the strong and stable central authority.
He is a student of Bolivar who draws from his master correct principles but who tries to apply them to a sphere, in
Bolivar's own opinion, too vast. The stable and central government was doubtlessly the best plan for each national
unity, as it was in effect in Venezuela, Colombia, and Quito;
but it was not only inconvenient but impossible, when applied to the immense and disjoined territory of Great
Colombia.

Bolivar read his farewell message before the " admirable "
congress. In it he renounced the supreme command. This
document forms a marked contrast to previous messages. It
is principally retrospective. He alludes to the events of the
year 1826, to the meeting of the convention of Ocaña, in-
stalled in the midst of the exaltation of parties and dissolved in the same atmosphere, and to the state of anarchy

[1] Gil Fortoul, I, 469.

which followed. He defended the dictatorship, affirming that the republic wished to honor him with its confidence, a confidence he respected as a most sacred law. He exclaimed: "When the country was going to perish, could I hesitate?"

In his opinion, the calling of the Ocaña convention and the declarations made by it regarding the reform of the constitution was a verdict against the pact of Cucuta. "In the public opinion and in fact, the constitution of 1821 was no longer in force."

Bolivar summarizes the historical events, principally those of an international character, such as the war with Peru, congratulating the congress of the nation on the conclusion of the war and the attitude of the new Peruvian government. With pardonable complacency, he reminds them that domestic dissentions had been ended without the shedding of a single drop of blood.

Bolivar's message does not contain any plan of government. Everything led one to expect that in it would be found the wise counsel expressed in his letter to O'Leary. What motives caused the Liberator to neglect this opportunity to present the principles which, in his opinion, could save Colombia? He says: "Everyone can, and must, submit his opinions, fears, and desires to those we have authorized to cure this society, sick with weakness and unrest. I alone am deprived of the exercise of this civic function; because I have called you together and set forth your powers, I am not permitted to influence your decision in any way. Moreover, it will not be proper to repeat before the representatives of the people what Colombia proclaims in letters of blood."

Perhaps he was thinking of the peaceable division of Colombia and New Granada, and the need for a strong and stable government. Yet, he preferred to keep silent on these points, leaving the government in entire freedom. The clearest and most explicit necessity was that they should choose a leader to replace him.

This renunciation, though less emphatic than the others, has, nevertheless, a tone of the greatest sincerity. " Show yourselves worthy to represent a free people, banishing any idea that I may be necessary to the republic." He adds a great truth: " If one man were necessary to sustain the state, this state should not exist, and, finally, will not." He ends with these words: " I blush to say it, but our independence is the only good we have acquired at the cost of all the rest."

The work of the last 20 years could not be summarized in fewer words. The revolution had produced nothing more than mere independence. To others fell the burden of building political institutions, of economic development, and cultural extension. The genius of Bolivar was disappearing from the scene leaving these problems unsolved. But the rich treasure of Bolivar's political thinking remained, and to it the builders of the future were to come in search of inspiration and instruction.

The congress of 1830 had to make an effort to avoid the definite separation of Venezuela. It decided to invite the provisional government of that country to name commissioners to negotiate with those of the congress on the problem of unification. The conferences opened in April, in the historic town of Cucuta. The Venezuelan representatives first demanded the recognition of the provisional government they had set up. They proposed afterward that New

Granada, Quito, and Venezuela be allowed to organize as sovereign states, leaving to their congresses the nature of the bond which should unite the three; and that, meanwhile, the general congress should legislate regarding the maintenance of foreign relations and the credit of the country. Sucre then proposed that, for four years, the leaders who had held high positions in the republic between 1809 and 1830, be barred from the presidency or vice-presidency of the general organization or of the states. This idea of Sucre was accepted by three of the Venezuelan commissioners, but was rejected because of the disapproval of Marino, who represented the military caste there. The conferences ended without any definite result.

The congress continued to occupy itself with constitutional reform. Bolivar had retired definitely since the first of March. The government was in charge of General Caycedo. The opinion of the assembly inclined to administrative decentralization, federalistic ideas and the absolute centralistic solution having been discarded. Sucre presented a project for establishing assemblies in all the big districts. It was a kind of weakened model of the old project of Azuero and Bolivar. Sucre said: "With this plan, I have thought it possible to create an equilibrium which would preserve the unity of Colombia and leave the government sufficiently strong, and which would at the same time quiet complaints without plunging us into federalism." Sucre saw that the Republic was desirous of this, and that it was the explanation for Venezuela's separation and the discontent in the South. The chamber of districts, he added, could conciliate these desires. Unda recalls that the colonial régime permitted local ordinances, such as the ordinances of the *Llanos,* and believed, consequently, that the assemblies should be given the power to issue decrees and ordinances for their own districts. But García del Río accepted only the establishment of economico-administrative assemblies with local or municipal powers and without legislative functions. The constitution created district chambers without legislative powers, with the right to submit three names from which the magistrates were to be chosen and lists of eligibles for the positions of prefects and governors.[2]

Venezuela was offered the new document as a basis for union, but the Venezuelan Congress, assembled at Valencia, rejected this offer. Venezuela only wished to come to an understanding with New Granada after independent states had been established and Bolivar had left Colombian territory.

The Congress, with Bolivar's communication before it in which he forbade anyone to vote for his reelection, elected Joaquín Mosquera President, and General Domingo Caycedo, vice-president. Colombia was yet to enter its darkest period. The Venezuelan troops quartered in Bogota revolted. The department of Quito declared for separation. General Flores called a new constitutional assembly for May 31. Sucre, on returning from the Congress of Bogota, was assassinated in Berruecos. In him perished the only possible successor to Bolivar. The latter was in Cartagena, preparing for his voluntary exile, when he received this fatal news. Mosquera's government fell before the military uprising headed by Florencio Jiménez who took for his device the name of Bolivar. The Liberator, deceived, considered

2 Vega, *Federación en Colombia,* 113-114.

accepting the call, but later repented of it. " I do not expect well-being for the country ", he said in a letter to Vergara, September 25, 1830. " This feeling, or rather this inner conviction, quenches my desire and drags me to the most miserable depths of desperation. I believe all lost forever and the country and my friends submerged in a tempest of calamities. If there were only one more sacrifice that I could make, if it were of my life, my happiness, and my honor, be sure that I would not hesitate. But I am convinced that the sacrifice would be in vain, because one poor man can do nothing against a whole world, and because I am unable to bring about the happiness of my country, I deny myself its command. There is yet more, the tyrants of my country have deprived me of it and I am an exile; so that I do not even have a fatherland for which to make the sacrifice." [1]

It was Bolivar's fate to have these patriotic sorrows joined to the bitterness of his own people's ingratitude. In Venezuela they had pardoned and condoned the authors of the attempt of September 1828. In the Venezuelan congress, the expulsion of Bolivar had been proposed as the prerequisite to all negotiation with New Granada. After some hesitation and discussions as to the form, that body had definitely proclaimed the banishment of the Liberator.

Even before these ungrateful and monstrous resolutions, Bolivar had condemned himself to ostracism and waited only to embark with the remains of his ruined fortune. But it was not exile that awaited him, but the tomb. He left Cartagena for Santa Marta. The Greek tragedy which was the hero's life had ended, and in these moments

[1] Lecuna, *Cartas del Libertador,* IX, 326.

began the sublime Christian drama. Bolivar had offered to Colombia and America his youth, his fortune, his genius and his glory. And now he is about to offer it his death. In a scene which had the august solemnity of a sacrifice, he signed his last proclamation, pardoning his enemies and pleading for union. " My last prayers are for the happiness of the fatherland. If my death contributes to the cessation of parties and the consolidation of the union, I shall go tranquilly down to the sepulchre."

Vain prayer, fruitless oblation. The nations liberated by Bolivar have not realized, in the agitated history of the nineteenth century, that sublime wish, expressed at the door of death and glory.

Note: See the text of the Bolivar Message to the congress of 1830 in *Documentos para la historia de la vida pública del Libertador,* XIV, 119. In the same volume are the documents regarding the discussion with the commissioners of Venezuela, 151 ff. The last *Proclama* of Bolivar is also in this same volume, 460.

APPENDICES

APPENDIX TO CHAPTER X

Lista de los libros de S.E. el Libertador, que conduce el capitán Emigdio Briceño, remitidos por el coronel Tomás Cipriano Mosquera.[1]

Obras completas:
Dumeril.
Théorie des Révolutions.
Oeuvres de Hobbes.
Histoire d'Amérique.
Arrien: Expédition d'Alexandre y un Atlas.
Manuscrit de 1813.
Sismondi: littérature du midi de l'Europe.
Introduction à la politique.
Annales du règne de Georges III.
Contes de La Fontaine.
Simonde de Sismondi.
Description Générale de la Chine.
Réflexions Militaires.
Plutarque.
L'Odyssée d'Homère.
Fêtes et courtisanes de la Grèce.
Llorente.
Cours politique et diplomatique de Bonaparte.
Oeuvres de Napoléon.
Mémoires de Napoléon.
Histoire de Napoléon.
Histoire du Brésil.
Campagne de 1814 y un Atlas.
Goguet.
New Dictionary Spanish and English.
Gramática Italiana.
Science du Gouvernement.
Ensayo de la historia civil del Paraguay, Buenos Aires y Tucumán.
Oeuvres de Voltaire.

Républiques Italiennes du Moyen Age.
Histoire d'Angleterre.
Dictionnaire des Hommes Célèbres.
Analyse de la Philosophie Os Lusiadas.
Epoques de l'Histoire Universelle.
Espíritu de las Leyes.
Curso de política, por Constant.
Poésies d'Ossian.
La Eneida, de Virgilio.
Comentarios de César.
M. Mahon S. Gardeninos.
Montholon: Mémoires de Napoléon.
Jugement impartial sur Napoléon.
Influences des Gouvernements.
Code of law of the Republic of Colombia.
The Federalists.
Colon, Juzgados militares.
Principios de fortificación.
Ordenanza naval.
L'Iliade d'Homère.
Révolution Française.
Jérusalem délivrée.
Tasso.
Campagnes d'Italie.
Mémoires du Baron Fain.
Encyclopédie des enfants.
Beautés de l'Histoire de Turquie.
Beautés de Hollande.
Oeuvres du Roi de Prusse.
Bibliothèque Philosophique.

[1] Lecuna, *Cartas del Libertador*, VII, 155-156.

Dictionnaire Géographique.
Delius: Exploitation des Mines.
Grotius.
Mesure du Méridien.
Medias Anatas y Lanzas del
  Perú.
Voyage to the South Atlantic.
La colonne de la Grande Armée.
Colonne sur la Place Vendôme.
Histoire de Polibe.
Diccionario de la Academia.
Histoire de Prusse.
Viaje a la América Meridional.
Principes de Stratégie.
Congreso de Viena.
Richesse des Nations.
Guerres de la Révolution.
Beaujour, S., North America.
Life of Scipio.
Vie de Washington.
Espíritu del Derecho.
Tratado de Castramentación.
Les Cents Jours. Constant.

Mémoires du Géneral Rapp.
Biographies des Contemporains.
De Pradt.
Oeuvres de Madame de Staël.
Life of Washington.
Ramsay: Life of Washington.
Fables de La Fontaine.
Vertot: Histoire Romaine.
Découverte de l'Amérique.
Humboldt: Astronomie.
Viaje de Anacarsis.
Commentaires de César.
La Nouvelle Espagne.
Voyage au Nouveau Continent.
Exposición de Don José de la
  Riva Agüero.
Victoires complètes des Français.
Informe de la Ley Agraria.
Atlas de América.
Voyage de Humboldt.
La Nouvelle Espagnę, Atlas.
Colombia.
Viaje de La Cruz.

APPENDIX TO CHAPTER XII

BOLIVAR AND THE POPULAR WILL IN THE FORMATION OF NATIONALITIES [1]

NASCA, 26 DE ABRIL DE 1825

A. S. E. el Gran Mariscal de Ayacucho, Antonio José de Sucre.

. . . .

. . . . Usted supone que a mí me parecerá bien la convocatoria de la asamblea cuando llegue al Alto Perú. Tiene usted razón en suponerlo y diré más, que me gusta, y añadiré todavía más, que a mí me conviene sobre manera, porque me presenta un vasto campo para obrar con una política recta y con una noble liberalidad; pero lo dicho, dicho; y con la añadidura de que no siempre lo justo es lo conveniente, ni lo útil lo justo. Yo no debo obrar para mí, ni por mí. Mi posición pública es la conciencia de mis operaciones públicas. Por lo mismo, no sé todavía lo que me tocará hacer con ese Alto Perú, *porque la voluntad legal del pueblo es mi soberana y mi ley.* Cuando los cuerpos legales decidan de la suerte del Alto Perú, entonces yo sabré cual es mi deber, y cual es la marcha que yo seguiré. Usted me dice que si quiero entregar ese país a Buenos Aires, pida un ejército grande para que lo reciba. Esta observación me ha hecho pensar mucho sin hacerme cambiar de dictamen. También añade usted que las fracciones del Río de la Plata son soberanas y que la mitad del Río de la Plata reside en esas provincias altas; que, por lo tanto,

[1] Lecuna, *Cartas del Libertador,* IV, 318. The italics are mine.

un millón de habitantes bien podían constituir un gobierno pro-
visorio para evitar la anarquía. Todo esto es exacto y justo; pero
la ley del congreso no ha mandado esto. Así es que no sé como
haré para combinar la asamblea del Alto Perú con la determinación
del congreso. Cualquiera que sea mi determinación no será, sin
embargo, *capaz de violar la libertad del Alto Perú;* los derechos
del Río de la Plata, ni mi sumisión al poder legislativo de este
país. Usted sabe perfectamente que mi profesión ha sido siempre
el culto popular y la veneración a las leyes y a los derechos. Yo
no mandaré a buscar un ejército a Buenos Aires; tampoco dejaré
independiente, por ahora, el Alto Perú, y menos aun someteré ese
país a ninguna de las dos repúblicas pretendientes. Mi designio
es hablar con verdad y política a todo el mundo, convidándolos
a un congreso de los tres pueblos con apelación al gran congreso
americano. Entonces se verá que yo he respetado a todos y no
me he inclinado a nadie; mientras tanto el ejército unido ocupará
el país militarmente y estará sujeto al general en jefe que yo
nombre. Esta general en jefe es usted, debe ser usted, y no puede
ser otro sino usted.

APPENDIX TO CHAPTER XV

The Constitution of Angostura

It is worthwhile to give some details of the Constitution of
Angostura which has been interpreted equivocally.

O'Leary (XVI, 129) presents the bases for a project of constitution which is in harmony with the discourse of Bolívar. He
favors, in the matter of senatorial succession, a system whereby
on the death of a senator there be chosen among his male offspring
the most apt, the most virtuous and, in all respects, the most
worthy to assume the position in the senate previously held by
his father. The first senators are to be chosen from among the
generals of the Republic, the former members of the first congress
and from among those functionaries who have distinguished themselves in the service of the Republic.

The duration of the executive power is to be four years, but
reelection is not forbidden.

Concerning the powers of the provinces he has the following to
say: " no province can exercise any power reserved to the congress
or to the executive power as, for example, forming alliances,
concluding treaties, raising and maintaining troops, possessing
ships of war; nor can it pass laws concerning imports nor pass
any other kind of law, regulation or ordinance whenever the
general laws of the Republic regulate the matter."

From the book on the Constitution of Angostura published by the *Biblioteca de Historia Nacional* of Colombia we learn the difference between the bases proposed by O'Leary and the constitution which was adopted. There is a life-term senate. The chamber, in the event of a vacancy in the senate, presents a tern to that body from which the new senator is elected by majority vote. The president serves for four years and he may be reelected immediately on the expiration of his term.

Both the bases of O'Leary and the plan which was adopted gave to the senate the power to judge and sentence the president and all other public officials when they were indicted by the chamber for malfeasance in office. This power of the senate was included in the Constitution of Cucuta and created the conflict over the judgment passed on Páez.

APPENDIX TO CHAPTER XVI

THE PEOPLE, THE CONGRESS AND THE ARMY [1]

Carta de Bolívar al General F. de P. de Santander.
San Carlos, 13 de Junio de 1821.

. . . . Esos señores piensan que la voluntad del pueblo es la opinión de ellos, sin saber que en Colombia el pueblo está en el ejército, porque realmente está, y porque ha conquistado este pueblo de mano de los tiranos; porque además es el pueblo que quiere, el pueblo que obra, y el pueblo que puede; todo lo demás es gente que vegeta con más o menos malignidad, o con más o menos patriotismo, pero todos sin ningún derecho a ser otra cosa que ciudadanos pasivos. Esta política, que ciertamente no es la de Rousseau, al fin será necesario desenvolverla para que no nos vuelan a perder esos señores. Ellos pretenden con nosotros representar el segundo acto de Buenos Aires, cuando la segunda parte que van a dar la de Guarico. Piensan esos caballeros que Colombia está cubierta de lanudos, arropados en las chimeneas de Bogotá, Tunja y Pamplona. No han echado sus miradas sobre los Caribes del Orinoco, sobre los pastores del Apure, sobre los marineros de Maracaibo, sobre los bogas del Magdalena, sobre los bandidos de Patia, sobre los indómitos pastusos, sobre los guajibos de Casanare y sobre todas las hordas salvajes de Africa y de América que, como gamos, recorren las soledades de Colombia.

¿No le parece a usted, mi querido Santander, que esos legisladores más ignorantes que malos, y más presuntuosos que ambiciosos, nos van a conducir a la anarquía, y después a la tiranía, y siempre a la ruina? Yo lo creo así, y estoy cierto de ello. De suerte, que si no son los llaneros los que completan nuestro exter-

---

[1] Lecuna, *Cartas del Libertador*, II, 354.

minio, serán los suaves filósofos de la legitimada Colombia. Los que se creen Licurgos, Numas, Franklines, y Camilos Torres y Rosios, y Uztaris y Robiras, y otros númines que el cielo envió a la tierra para que acelerasen su marcha hacia la eternidad, no para darles repúblcas como las griegas, romana y americana, sino para amontonar escombros de fábricas monstruosas y para edificar sobre una base gótica un edificio griego al borde de un cráter.
. . . .

APPENDIX TO CHAPTER XIX

The Federal Constitution of Central America

Since I have referred to the Mexican constitution of 1824 in treating the fall of the empire of Iturbide, I must refer also to the Central-American constitution which was likewise based on federalist ideas. The project presented to the National Constitutional Assembly by the constitutional commission, October 25, 1823, appears in a pamphlet printed in Guatemala which opposes federal government: " Small republics . . . reflect the public will with great promptness. . . . The division of a great territory into small states assures these states liberty and freedom."

There is an allusion in this document to Bentham's theory on the equality of property and there is also a reference to Destutt de Tracy. The author is in favor of the direct vote. "A senate which share in the prerogatives of the three powers is both a moderating and conservative body."

The people are the base of national representation and the federal states of the senate. He is in favor, also, of the unity of the executive power, a system in favor among " the wise Anglo-Americans, the Colombians and the people of Lima ".

In 1825, the assembly sanctioned these bases for the general constitution of Central America.

APPENDIX TO CHAPTER XX

English Alliance or Protectorate: Letter of the Liberator to General Santander [1]

Cuzco, June 28, 1825.

. . . .
Mil veces he intentado escribir a usted sobre un negocio arduo, y es: nuestra federación americana no puede subsistir si no la toma bajo de su protección la Inglaterra; por lo mismo, no sé si sería muy conveniente si la convidásemos a una alianza defensiva y ofensiva. Esta alianza no tiene más que un inconveniente, y es el de los compromisos en que nos puede meter la política inglesa;

---

[1] Lecuna, *Cartas del Libertador*, V, 13-14.

pero este inconveniente es eventual y quizá remoto. Yo le opongo a este inconveniente esta reflexión: la exsitencia es el primer bien; y el segundo es el modo de existir: si nos ligamos a la Inglaterra existiremos, y si no nos ligamos nos perderemos infaliblemente. Luego es preferible el primer caso. Mientras tanto, creceremos, nos fortificaremos y seremos verdaderamente naciones para cuando podamos tener compromisos nocivos con nuestra aliada. Entonces, nuestra propia fortaleza y las relaciones que podamos formar con otras naciones europeas, nos pondrán fuera del alcance de nuestros tutores y aliados. Supongamos aun que suframos por la superioridad de la Inglaterra: este sufrimiento mismo será una prueba de que existimos, y existiendo tendremos la esperanza de librarnos del sufrimiento. . . .

Observe usted que yo propongo este plan; que yo soy el que me ofrezco como víctima de las oposiciones liberales y aun se dirán políticas; que yo soy el llamado a ser el jefe de esta federación americana, y que yo renuncio la esperanza de una autoridad tan eminente por darle la preferencia a la estabilidad de la América. La Inglaterra no me podrá jamás reconocer a mí por jefe de la federación, pues esta supremacía la corresponde virtualmente al gobierno inglés. Por consiguiente, nada es tan verdaderamente imparcial; nada es tan generoso como este dictamen, pues que ninguna mira personal puede lisonjearme ni seducirme con él. Así, mi querido general, si usted lo aprueba, consulte usted al congreso, o al consejo de gobierno que usted tiene en su ministerio para los casos arduos. Si esos señores apreuban mi pensamiento, sería importante tentar el ánimo del gobierno británico sobre el particular y consultar a la asamblea del Istmo. Por mi parte, no pienso abandonar la idea aunque nadie la apruebe. Desde luego los señores *americanos* serán sus mayores opositores, a título de la independencia y libertad; pero el verdadero título es por egoísmo y porque nada temen en su estado doméstico.

. . . .

APPENDIX TO CHAPTER XXI

THE BOLIVIAN CONSTITUTION

It is interesting to know the opinion which Bolivar held of the constitution of 1826. He said to Santander in a letter of December 27, 1825: "*à propos*, I am working on a very strong and very well organized constitution for this country, a constitution which will violate none of the three unities and which will destroy special privileges, beginning with slavery. . . . In general, the constitution is put together well, and the address which I shall give to prove its usefulness will be very strong. I have no doubt but that it will be better than the address I made at Angostura, for now I need not compromise with anyone. My constitution *will be more liberal than Colombia's* and it will also prove more durable." (Lecuna, *Cartas del Libertador*, V, 198.)

Bolivar took care that his project of constitution be given publicity when he thought of applying it to Peru and to Colombia.

Benito Laso wrote in favor of the life-term constitution (*Exposición*, Lima, 1826). This study of Laso contains interesting observations of sociological and political character about Peru and it cannot be overlooked in a history of American thought. Antonio Leocadio Guzmán wrote his famous *Ojeada* in favor of the life-term constitution. According to General Heres, Bolivar himself corrected Guzmán's *Ojeada* suppressing entire chapters.

The life-term constitution and the project of Andean federation also inspired unfavorable criticism and commentary. In the United States, judging by the evidence which Santander sent to Bolivar in his letter of May 23, 1826, there was an interest in the maintenance of constitutional order in Colombia.

In Europe, there was a good deal of comment on the views of the Liberator. Joaquín Acosta, in a letter to Santander of February 24, 1827, said: " M. Humboldt himself, who in public affects to have none of the fears widely held here about the views of the Liberator, has told me privately that the constitution of Bolivia is madness which he cannot explain." (*Archivo de Santander*, XVI, 241.)

The project of constitution underwent some modifications when it was submitted to the electoral colleges in Peru.

Instead of one elector for each ten citizens, one was named for each hundred (Art. XX) which to that extent lessened the inconvenience of an excessive number of electoral colleges. Article VI of the constitution which declared that the religion of Peru is Catholic, Apostolic and Roman was also modified. (See the pamphlet on the constitution published in Lima by the Masias press in 1826.)

The assembly of Bolivia also introduced some modifications when it approved the constitution. It declared that the religion of Bolivia was the Catholic, Apostolic and Roman and adding: " the government will protect it and make it respected, recognizing that there is no human power over the conscience."

About the reading and writing requirement for citizenship it decided that " this requirement will be enforced only after the year 1836." This change was doubtless due to the desire to save the vote for the natives.

It also established one elector for every hundred citizens. The discharge from office of the president was not possible without the assent of the executive power.

There were other minor modifications in the functions of the electoral colleges. According to Heres, General Sucre never approved the constitution of Bolivia and the congress changed the anarchic elements in it. Heres attributes the modifications to Olañeta and to Urcullu (Lecuna, *Creación de Bolivia*, I, 371).

APPENDIX BY CHAPTER XXIV

THE MISSION OF GUZMÁN: AN UNPUBLISHED LETTER OF BOLIVAR

We have seen that the Liberator sent Guzmán to Colombia with the object of working for the life-term constitution. The testimony about this affair which I have cited in Chapter XXIV is confirmed by the following portion of a letter of Bolivar to Francisco Rivas, August 2, 1826, which I discovered in the Bingham Collection at the Yale University Library:

"Por estas consideraciones me he determinado a enviar al Sr. Leocadio Guzmán quien comunicará a usted todas aquellas ideas que yo he alumbrado y que deben servir de base a las reformas que se quieren hacer en Colombia; él vá perfectamente instruido y desearía que le oyese y meditase profundamente el plan que yo me he propuesto . . . ella (la constitución del 26) es la arca que debe salvarnos de los terribles males que nos amenazan. A un tiempo se piden reformas en Guayaquil y en Venezuela sin considerar que en estas reformas se encuentran el peligro de la total destrucción de lo hecho y por hacer. . . . Así yo no encuentro otro remedio que el de la Constitución boliviana en ellos se encuentran reunidos como por encanto la libertad más completa del pueblo con la energía más fuerte en el Poder Ejecutivo. Esta Constitución tiene la ventaja de que con muy pocas manifestaciones se consigue reunir la libertad del Gobierno federal con la fuerza del central."

The words of this letter are similar to those of the rough draft of August 3, 1826 which Lecuna includes in Volume VI and which, according to Lecuna, is found among the papers preserved by J. de Francisco Martín. There was another rough draft of this same document in the Bolivian Museum which was labeled by O'Leary " Circular carried by Guzmán ".

Although this letter which I have here quoted contains no new fact, I thought it advisable, since it has never before been published to make it known at least in part.

SELECTIVE BIBLIOGRAPHY

Instead of the usual bibliography composed simply of a list of works, the author has preferred to present to students of American history a tentative classified bibliography of the source material. The following order of value may be established for the bibliographical sources in the field of Spanish-American independence:

A. Documents, the most authoritative and valuable sources;

B. Legislative Acts;

C. Autobiographies and *Memorias* of persons who took part in the struggle for independence or who were witnesses of it;

D. Contemporary Works, that is to say publications which without being autobiographical were written in the period of the independence movement and reflect the *ambience* of the epoch and present, moreover, the testimony of contemporaries;

E. Contemporary Pamphlets, which have the same character and value as the preceding group;

F. Periodicals of the Period, primarily those which were devoted in whole or in part to political and ideological discussion and controversy;

G. Travel Books, which present the testimony of foreigners who visited America in the independence period;

H. Colonial Organization; the essential books concerned with this problem are indispensable for a knowledge of the ideology of the revolution;

I. Law and Constitutional History, the works which pertain most directly to the subject of this book, that is the political thought of the revolution;

J. Works on Bolivar, which are necessary for the study not only of his biography and his military exploits, but also of his political ideology and work;

K. Historical Works, which, because of their general character, are not included in the preceding categories and which have to do either with the colonial period anterior to the independence or to the revolutionary process itself;

L. Miscellaneous Works, which are principally monographs or other studies of persons who took part in the revolution or of aspects of the revolution.

A. DOCUMENTS

Anales Históricos de la Revolución de la América Latina (Edited by Carlos Calvo). Paris, 1864-65. 4 vols.

Documentos literarios del Perú (Edited by Manuel Odriozola). Lima, 1875. Vol. II contains the discourses on the form of government given at the *Sociedad Patriótica.*

Documentos históricos del Perú (Edited by Manuel Odriozola). Lima, 1875. Vol. I contains material on the rebellion of Tupac Amaru, vol. III deals with the period of the first revolutionary movements in Peru, vols. IV, V and VI with the independence period in Peru.

Últimos días coloniales en el Alto Perú, Documentos inéditos, 1808-1809 (Edited by Gabriel René Moreno). Santiago de Chile, 1901.

Archivo de Miranda, Caracas, 1909-1933. 14 vols. Editorial Sud América.

Colección de documentos relativos a la vida pública del Libertador de Colombia y del Perú, Simón Bolívar. Caracas, 1826-1833. 22 vols.

Documentos para la historia de la vida pública del Libertador de Colombia, Perú y Bolivia (Edited by José Felix Blanco). Caracas, 1875-1877. This collection was finished by Ramón Azpurúa and is cited as " Blanco y Azpurúa ".

Memorias del General O'Leary (Edited by Simón O'Leary). Caracas, 1879-1888. This collection contains 26 volumes of documents, 3 volumes of narrative and 3 volumes of letters. The third volume of narrative was at first eliminated. There exist today two editions of this volume, one published by the son of O'Leary (Caracas, 1883) the other by Guillermo Comacho (Bogota, 1914).

Cartas de Bolívar, 1799-1822 (Published by Blanco Fombona). Paris, 1922. Editorial América.

Cartas de Bolívar, 1825-1827 (Published by Blanco Fombona). Paris, 1922. Editorial América.

Papeles de Bolívar (Published by Vicente Lecuna). Caracas, 1917. Republished by Blanco Fombona. Biblioteca Ayacucho. 2 vols.

Cartas del Libertador (Published by Vicente Lecuna). Caracas, 1929-1930. 10 vols. The best collection of the letters of the Liberator.

Proceso de Nariño (Edited by José Manuel Pérez Sarmiento).
Cadiz, 1914. Vol. I.

Archivo de Santander (Published by a commission of the Academy
of History). Bogota, 1913-1933. 24 vols.

Documentos referentes a la creación de Bolivia (Edited by Vicente
Lecuna). Caracas, 1929.

Documentos del Archivo de San Martín, Buenos Aires, 1910-1911.
12 vols.

Documentos del Archivo de Belgrano (Museo Mitre). Buenos
Aires, 1913. 6 vols.

Documentos para los anales de Venezuela (Edited by the National
Academy of History). 1889-1891. 7 vols.

*Colección de documentos para la historia de la guerra de inde-
pendencia de México,* 1808-1821. Mexico, 1877. 6 vols.

Oratoria Argentina (Edited by Neptalí Carranza). Buenos Aires,
1905. Vol. I contains the material of the independence period.

Documentos para la historia de la revolución de Colombia. Paris,
1827. Contained in vols. 8, 9 and 10 of Restrepo, *Historia
de la Revolución de la República de Colombia.* Paris, 1827.

Documentos Justificativos of vol. IV of the *Historia constitucional
Argentina* of Luis V. Varela. La Plata, 1910.

*Diplomatic Correspondence of the United States Agents Concerning
the Independence of the Latin-American Nations.* Oxford
University Press, 1925.

La Monarquía en América, Carlos Villanueva. 4 vols. as follows:
*Fernando VII y los estados, El General Bolívar y San Martín,
la Santa Alianza, El Imperio de los Andes.* Paris. Colección
Ollendorf. The works of Villanueva are placed among the
documents because of the large number of items they contain
transcribed from the correspondence of European agents in
America in the revolutionary period.

*Catálogo de los documentos relativos a la independencia de
América existente en el archivo de Indias* (Torres Lanzas).
First series Madrid, 1912. 6 vols. Second series Seville, 1924.

Tratados del Perú (Edited by Ricardo Aranda). Lima, 1890-1911.
The volumes relating to Bolivia, Colombia and Chile contain
the first treaties and diplomatic documents of the period of
the independence.

Congresos y Conferencias internacionales (Edited by Ricardo
Aranda). Lima, 1909. Vol. I contains some documents relating to the Congress of Panama.

Tratados de Chile (Published by Javier Vial Solar). Barcelona, 1903. 2 vols. Vol. I contains the transcription of the first documents relating to the Spanish Revolution.

Congreso de Panamá (Edited by Raúl Porras Barrenechea). Lima, 1930. An extremely valuable collection of documents about the assembly of Panama preceded by a brilliant study of the subject.

British and Foreign State Papers. The first volumes of this series were published in London in 1841. Vols. 1-18 cover the years 1812-1831 and contain the most important documents in regard to the independence of America.

MANUSCRIPTS

Archivo de Sucre. The author used the archives of Marshall Sucre which are in the possession of the Bingham Collection at the Yale University Library. These letters contain very important material for the study of military history. The author found a letter of Bolivar to Francisco Rivas, August 3, 1826, whose important paragraphs are reprinted in the appendix to Chapter XXIV. This letter has not been previously published.

Papeles de Villanueva. Through the courtesy of Señor Laureano Carlos Villanueva the author was able to consult the material which had been copied by Carlos Villanueva from the archives of London and Paris. The son was also kind enough to permit the author to examine and use the unpublished works of his father in the series *Monarquía en América: Bolívar en el Perú, La Guerra, Páez.*

B. LEGISLATIVE ACTS

Colección de los decretos y órdenes que han expedido las Cortes generales y extraordinarias desde su instalación, 21-24 de setiembre de 1810 hasta igual fecha en 1811, 2 vols., Madrid, 1813.

Diario de los discusiones y actas de las Cortes de Cádiz, 1812.

Colección de los Decretos leyes de las Cortes de España, Mexico, 1829.

La Constitución de 1812 en la Nueva España, Mexico, 1912.

Congreso Constituyente 1811, Caracas, 1911.

Congreso de Angostura; Libro de Actas, Biblioteca de historia nacional, Bogota, 1921.

Congreso de Cúcuta; Libro de Actas, Biblioteca de historia nacional,
Bogota, 1923.
Diario de las discusiones y actas de la Asamblea Constituyente,
3 vols., Lima, 1822.
Actas del Congreso Constituyente mexicano, 2 vols., Mexico, 1822.
Congreso de 1823; Actas, Biblioteca de historia nacional, Bogota,
1926.
Centenario de la constitución del año 24, Mexico, 1824.
Colección de leyes de la república de Colombia, Bogota, 1826.
*Colección de leyes y Decretos dados por el Poder Ejecutivo de
Colombia de los años de 1821 a 1826,* Bogota, 1833.
Colección de Decretos expedidos por el Libertador, Caracas, 1828.
*Colección oficial de Leyes, Decretos, órdenes y resoluciones Re-
pública de Bolivia,* 2 vols., Paz de Ayacucho, 1834. These
volumes include the material for 1827-1828.
Colección de leyes del Perú, 15 vols., Oviedo and Lima, 1861-72.
Leyes constitucionales de México (Edited by J. M. Gamboa),
Mexico, 1912.
Digesto constitucional de Honduras, Tegucigalpa, 1923.

C. AUTOBIOGRAPHIES AND *MEMORIAS*

Arenales, L. A. Álvarez de, *Memorias del General Arenales,*
Buenos Aires, 1821 and 1832.
Cochrane, Lord Thomas, *Memorias,* Madrid, 1917. Editorial
América.
Decoudray-Holstein, H. Lafayette Villaume, *Memoirs of Simón
Bolívar,* Boston, 1829.
García Camba, Andrés, *Memorias,* 2 vols., Madrid, 1846.
MacGregor, Gregor, *Memorias,* London, 1820.
Miller, John, *Memoires of General Miller,* 2 vols., London, 1829.
Miranda, Francisco, *The Diary. Tour of the United States 1783-
1784,* New York, 1928.
Morillo, Pablo, *Mémoire du Général Morillo,* Paris, 1826.
Mosquera, General Tomás C., *Memorias sobre la vida del Liber-
tador,* New York, 1853.
Paéz, José Antonio, *Memorias del General José Antonio Páez,*
Biblioteca Ayacucho, Madrid. Editorial América.
Perú de Lacroix, L., *Diario de Bucaramanga,* Paris, 1912.
Navarro, Monseñor Nicolás E., *Diario de Bucaramanga, estudio
crítico,* Caracas, 1935.

O'Conner, Burdett, *Independencia americana*, Biblioteca Ayacucho, Madrid. Editorial América.

Posada, Gutiérrez Joaquín, *Memorias histórico-políticas*, 2 vols., Bogota, 1865.

Pruvonena, P., *Memorias y documentos*, 2 vols., Paris, 1858.

Stevenson, W. Bennet, *Memorias de William Bennet Stevenson*, Madrid, 1917.

Torata, Conde de, *Exposición que dirige al Rey Don Fernando VII, Don Jerónimo Valdez*, 4 vols., Madrid, 1894.

Urdaneta, Rafael, *Memorias del General Rafael Urdaneta*, Madrid, 1916.

Urquinaona, Pedro, *Relación documentada del origen y progresos del trastorno de las provincias de Venezuela*, Madrid, 1820.

D. CONTEMPORARY WORKS

Antepara, José Maria, *South American Emancipation. Documents Historical and Explanatory*, London, 1810.

Florez Estrada, Alvaro, *Examen imparcial de las disensiones de la América con la España*, Cadiz, 1812.

Funes, Gregorio, *Ensayo de la historia, civil del Paraguay, Buenos Aires y Tucumán*, 3 vols., Buenos Aires, 1816.

Guerra, José (José Servando Teresa Mier), *Carta de un americano*, 2 vols., London, 1811-1812.

———, *Historia de la revolución de la Nueva España*, 2 vols., London, 1813.

Lallement, M., *Histoire de la Colombie*, Paris, 1827.

Pradt, M. de, *La Europa y la América en 1821*, 2 vols., Paris, 1822.

———, *Des colonies et de la révolution actuelle de l'Amérique*, 2 vols., Paris, 1817.

———, *Examen du Plan presenté aux Cortes pour la reconnaisance de l'Indépendance de l'Amérique meridional*, Paris, 1822.

———, *Congres de Panama*, Paris, 1825.

Presas, José, *Juicio imparcial sobre las principales causas de la revolución de la América española*, Bordeaux, 1828.

Restrepo, José Manuel, *Historia de la revolución de la República de Colombia*. Paris, 1827. (Citations are from the edition of 1858).

Riva Agüero, José de la, *Exposición*, London, 1824.

———, *Manifestación histórico-política de la Revolución de la América. Obra escrita en Lima, centro de la opresión y del despotismo en el año 1816*, Buenos Aires, 1818.

Rocafuerte, Vicente, *Ideas necesarias a todo pueblo americano independiente que quiera ser libre*, Philadelphia, 1821.

———, *El sistema colombiano*, New York, 1823.

Vidaurre, Manuel Lorenzo, *Cartas americanas, políticas y morales que contienen muchas reflexiones sobre la guerra civil de las Américas*, Philadelphia, 1823.

———, *Efectos de las facciones en los gobiernos nacientes. Principios fundamentales del gobierno democrático constitucional representativo*, Boston, 1828.

———, *Proyecto del Código Eclesiástico*, Paris, 1830.

Walton, William, *An Exposé on the Dissention of Spanish America*, London, 1814.

———, *Outline of the Revolution in Spanish America*, New York, 1817.

———, *An Appeal to the British Nation on the Affairs of South America*, London, 1819.

E. PAMPHLETS OF THE PERIOD

CHAPTER I.

Álvarez, Mariano Alejo, *Discurso sobre la preferencia que deben darse a los americanos en los empleos*, Lima, 1820.

Colección de los discursos que pronunciaron los señores diputados de América contra el artículo 22 del proyecto de constitución illustrado con algunas notas interesantes por los españoles de esta capital, Lima, 1812.

CHAPTER II.

Manual de un republicano para el uso de un pueblo libre, Philadelphia, 1812. *Manual del colombiano*, 1825 (in *Folletos de Colombia, 1825-1836*).

CHAPTER VI.

La Abdicación de Carlos y Fernando. Juicio crítico de los documentos publicados, Cadiz, 1808.

Expresión leal y afectuosa del Ayuntamiento de Lima con motivo de la solemne proclamación de nuestro católico monarca don Fernando VII, 15 de Octubre de 1808, Lima, 1808.

Manifiesto de la Junta de Sevilla, Cadiz, June 17, 1808.

La Junta Suprema del Reyno a la Nación Española, October 28, 1809. Reprinted in Lima, 1810.

414 BOLIVAR AND SPANISH-AMERICAN THOUGHT

CHAPTER VIII.

Bermúdez, Canónigo J. M., *Oración fúnebre del señor Vicente Morales Duárez*, Lima, 1812.

Montoya, J. González, *Rasgos sueltos para la constitución americana*, Cadiz, 1811.

Elección de diputados por América. Discurso escrito por un español americano, London, 1813.

Consideraciones filosóficas-políticas sobre el artículo 22, cap. 4° título 3 del Proyecto de la constitución, Cadiz, 1811.

Anonymous, *Ideas de una constitución*, Cadiz, 1811.

Dictamen del Dr. Antonio José Ruiz de Padrón (On the Inquisition), Cadiz, 1813.

Informe dirigido a su Majestad por el Consulado y comercio de Cádiz, Cadiz, 1811.

La Nación. Restablecimiento de sus principios sociales, Cadiz, 1811.

Representación del Cabildo de Santa Fe, 1810. Reprinted in Lima, 1820.

Consideraciones político-filosóficas por un español del Perú, Cadiz, 1811.

Exposición del Ayuntamiento de Caracas, Cadiz, 1813.

Discurso del Dr. José Moreno (Published by the Royal University of Lima), Lima, 1813.

Discursos pronunciados en la Real Universidad de San Marcos (In honor of the Defenders of the Callao), 1819.

Manifiesto del Ayuntamiento sobre elección de Alcaldes, Lima, 1820.

Villalta, M., *Breves reflexiones sobre la censura de los oficios*, Lima, 1811.

Demostración política del verdadero origen de los males que oprimen a España, Lima, 1811.

CHAPTER XV.

Manifiesto del soberano congreso federal de las provincias unidas en sud-América, Buenos Aires, 1819.

Examen y juicio crítico del folleto titulado Manifiesto que hace a las naciones el congreso de Buenos Aires, Lima, 1819.

Manifiesto. Congreso constituyente de las provincias unidas de sud-América, Lima, 1820.

El General Bolívar en la campaña de la Nueva Granada (Written by a citizen of New Granada), Lima, 1822.

Representación de Rafael Mérida al congreso de Venezuela, Bordeaux, 1819.

Chapter XVI.

Lima justificada, Lima, 1822.

Justificación de la conducta pública seguida por J. García del Río y D. Parroisien, London, 1825.

Manifiesto y documentos de las negociaciones de Punchauca, Lima, 1821.

Manifiesto de las acusaciones, Lima, 1823.

Biografía del General San Martín, London, 1823.

Chapter XIX.

Estatuto Provisional dado por el Protector del Perú, Lima, 1821.

Oración pronunciada el día 8 de Octubre por M. J. de Arce, Lima, 1821.

Proyecto de constitución presentado al Congreso Constituyente por su comisión de constitución, Lima, 1823.

Proyecto de decreto que contiene las bases o principios fundamentales de la constitución política del Perú, Lima, 1822.

Explicación del discurso de Moreno, Sociedad patriótica, Lima, 1822.

Cuadro histórico político de la capital del Perú, Lima, 1822.

Manifiesto al mundo de la justicia y necesidad de la independencia de la nueva España, Panama, 1821.

Proyecto de bases constitucionales para las provincias unidas de Centro-América presentado a la asamblea nacional constituyente por la comisión de constitución, 25 de Octubre de 1825, Guatemala.

Manifiesto de los acontecimientos de la Capital del Perú, Lima, 1823.

Chapter XX.

H. G., *Fastos de la dictadura,* Arequipa, 1826.

Manifiesto del Marqués de Torre-Tagle, Lima, 1824.

Vidaurre, Manuel Lorenzo, *Discurso del ciudadano . . . a los habitantes del Perú,* Trujillo, 1824.

———, *Discurso tercero del ciudadano . . . a los americanos,* Trujillo, 1824.

———, *Discurso quinto del ciudadano . . . ,* Trujillo, 1824.

Brandsen, Francisco de, *Apelación a la Nación peruana,* Santiago, 1825.

Memoria de Sánchez Carrión, Lima, 1825.

Villarán, Manuel Vicente, *Narración biográfica del gran Mariscal J. de la Mar,* Lima, 1847.

Carta pastoral sobre el nuevo estado del Perú del Obispo Orihuela, Cuzco, 1825.

CHAPTER XXI.

Ensayo sobre la conducta de General Bolívar, Lima, 1827.

Exposición de Benito Laso, Lima, 1826.

Guzmán, Antonio Leocadio, Ojeada del proyecto de Constitución que el Libertador ha presentado a la República de Bolívar, Lima, 1826.

Pedemonte, Carlos, Discurso, Trujillo, 1824.

——, Discurso con motivo de la jura de la Constitución vitálica, Lima, 1826.

Proyecto de Constitución para el Perú, Lima, 1826.

CHAPTER XXIII.

Pando, José María, Epístola a Próspero, Lima, 1826.

——, A sus conciudadanos, Lima, 1826.

Manifiesto de Pando, Lima, February 6, 1827.

Reflexiones sobre la renuncia del señor Pando, Lima, 1827.

Contestación al manifiesto que hace a la nación de su conducta pública, don José María Pando, Lima, 1827.

(Rodríguez, Simón), El Libertador del medio día de América, por un amigo de la causa social, Arequipa, 1830.

Promesas de Bolívar sobre el Perú, Lima, 1827.

CHAPTER XXV.

Manifiesto que el Poder Ejecutivo de Colombia presenta sobre los acontecimientos de Venezuela, Bogota, 1826.

Refutación del acta acordada por los diputados de Venezuela, Bogota, 1826.

CHAPTER XXVIII.

Representacion del síndico, Bogota, 1826.

Discurso de Páez, Bogota, 1826.

Acusación contra el General Páez, Bogota, 1826.

Vidaurre, Manuel Lorenzo, Discurso sobre elecciones, Lima, 1827.

——, Discurso sobre Impuestos y libelos: libertad de imprenta, Lima, 1827.

Manifiesto del Gobierno del Perú en contestación al de Bolívar, Lima, 1828.

Llosa, M. C., Proyecto de Constitución política, Lima, 1827.

Manifiesto de don José de la Riva Agüero al Congreso, Antwerp, 1827.

Nunavilca, Ignacio, Justo Juicio, Lima, 1828.

CHAPTER XXX.

García del Río, Juan, *Meditaciones colombianas,* Caracas, 1830.

Carta o reflexiones sobre las meditaciones colombianas, Caracas, 1830.

Remarks of General Harrison, Late envoy extraordinary and minister plenipotentiary of the United States to the Republic of Colombia, on certain charges made against him by that government. To which is added, an unofficial letter from General Harrison to General Bolivar on the affairs of Colombia; with notes, explanatory of his views of the present state of that country. Washington, 1830.

F. PERIODICALS OF THE PERIOD

Semanario crítico, Lima, 1791.

Mercurio peruano, Lima, 1791-1795 (The edition edited by M. A. Fuentes, Lima, 1861, was used by the author).

Gaceta de Buenos Aires. Facsimile edition edited by the *Junta de historia y numismática americana,* Buenos Aires, Vols. 2, 3, 6, 1910, 1911, 1915.

El español, 8 vols., London, 1812.

El Peruano, Lima, 1812.

El Repertorio americano, 4 vols., 1826-27.

El Peruano liberal, Lima, 1813.

Verdadero peruano, Lima, 1812.

Argos constitucional, Lima, 1813.

Anti-Argos, Lima, 1813.

El Consolador, Lima, 1821.

El Republicano, Lima, 1822.

El Investigador, Lima, 1814.

La Abeja republicana, Lima, 1822.

El Imparcial, 1822.

Diario de Lima, 1822.

El Católico, Lima, 1822.

El Loquero, Lima, 1822.

La Cotorra, Lima, 1822.

El Duende, Lima, 1821.

El Cometa, Lima, 1822.

Correo Mercantil, Lima, 1822.

El Pacificador del Perú, Lima, 1831.

El Hombre libre en el Perú, Lima, 1823.
El Triunfo de la Nación, Lima, 1821.
Gaceta de Gobierno, Lima, 1822.
El Sol del Perú, Lima, 1822.
La Gaceta del Gobierno, Lima, 1821.
El Tribuno de la República peruana, Lima, 1822.
El Pueblo, Lima, 1822.
El Nuevo Depositario, Lima, 1821.
El Censor Económico, Lima, 1821.
El Censor, Lima, 1821.
Nuevo Día del Perú, Trujillo, 1824.
El Observador, Lima, 1825, 1826.
El Peruano, Lima, 1826-1827.
El Mercurio Peruano, Lima, 1827-1829.
El Telégrafo, Lima, 1827-1829.
El Peruano, Lima, 1827-1828.
La Gaceta de Gobierno, Lima, 1827.
El Soldado de la Patria, Lima, 1827-1828.
La Prensa Peruana, Lima, 1828.
Atalaya Contra Vitalicios, Lima, 1828.

G. TRAVEL BOOKS

Adams, W. J., *Journal of voyages 1819-1820,* Dublin, 1824.

Brackenridge, Henry M., *Voyages to South America Performed by Order of the American Government in the years 1817 and 1818,* 2 vols., Baltimore, 1819.

Brown, C., *Narrative of the Expedition to South America,* London, 1819.

Cochrane, Charles Stuart, *Journal of a residence and travels in Colombia during the years 1823 and 1824,* 2 vols., London, 1825.

Chesterton, George Laval, *A Narrative of Proceedings in Venezuela . . . in the years 1819 and 1820,* London, 1820.

Duane, Colonel Wm., *A visit to Colombia 1822-1823.* Philadelphia, 1826.

Hall, Basil, *Extracts from a journal written on the coasts of Chile, Peru and Mexico,* 2 vols., Edinburgh, 1824.

Hall, Colonel Francis, *Colombia, its Present State.* Philadelphia, 1825.

Hamilton, Colonel J. P., *Travels through the interior provinces of Colombia,* 2 vols., London, 1827.

Mollien, G., *Voyage dans la République de Colombie en 1823,* Paris, 1824.

Proctor, R., *Narrative of a journey. Years 1823 and 1824,* London, 1825.

Pons, F. R. J. de, *Travels in South America,* 2 vols., London, 1807.

Rodney, C. A. and Graham, John, *The Reports on the present state of the United Provinces of South America,* London, 1819.

Ségur, Comte de, *Mémoires ou souvenirs et anecdotes,* 2 vols., Paris, 1844.

Thompson, J., *Letter on the moral and religious state of South America,* 1822.

Walker, A., *Colombia.* London, 1822.

————, *The present state of Colombia, by an officer late in the Colombian service,* London, 1827.

————, *Reflexions on the State of the late Spanish Americans,* London, 1823.

H. COLONIAL ORGANIZATION

André, Marius, *La fin de l'Empire espagnol d'Amérique,* Nouvelle Librairie nationale, Paris, 1922.

Ayarragaray, L., *La iglesia en América y la dominación española,* Buenos Aires, 1920.

Bareda y Laos, Felipe, *Vida intelectual de la colonia,* Lima, 1909.

Basadre, Jorge, *La ciudad, la multitud y el campo en la historia del Perú,* Lima, 1929.

Castañeda, C. E., "The *Corregidor* in Spanish colonial administration," *Hispanic Historical Review,* IX, 446-470, November, 1929.

García, J. A., *La ciudad indiana,* Buenos Aires, 1909.

García Icazbalceta, D. J., *Obras,* 10 vols., México, 1896-1899. Vol. IX.

Humboldt, Alexandre de, *Voyages aux régions équinoxiales,* Vienna, 1830.

————, *Essai politique sur le royaume de la Nouvelle Espagne,* 2 vols., Paris, 1811.

Jovellanos, G. M., *Obras publicadas e inéditas,* 2 vols., Madrid, 1858-1859.

Lavalle, J. A., *Pablo Olavide,* Lima, 1859.

Levillier, Roberto, *Organización de la Iglesia y órdenes religiosas en el Virreinato del Perú,* Madrid, 1919.

——, *La Audiencia de Charcas*, 3 vols., Madrid, 1918.

——, *Correspondencia del Presidente y de los Oidores de la Audiencia de Lima*, Prologue by José de la Riva Agüero, Madrid, 1922.

Llanos Zapata, José Eusebio, *Memorias histórico-físicas-apologéticas de la América meridional*, Lima, 1904.

Matienzo, Juan de, *Gobierno del Perú*, Buenos Aires, 1910.

Montes de Oca, M., *Los Cabildos coloniales*, Buenos Aires, 1899.

Moreno, Gabriel René, *Últimos días coloniales en el Alto Perú, Narración 1807-1808*, Santiago de Chile, 1896.

Moses, Bernard, *South America on the Eve of the Emancipation.* New York, 1908.

——, *The Spanish Dependencies in South America*, 2 vols., New York and London, 1914.

——, *Spain's Declining Power in South America, 1730-1806*, Berkeley, Calif., 1919.

Oliveira Martins, P., *Civilización Ibérica*, (English edition, London, 1930).

Parras, Pedro Joseph, *Gobierno de los regulares de la América*, Madrid, 1783.

Parra Perez, C., *El régimen español en Venezuela*, Madrid, 1932.

Prado, Javier, *Estado social del Perú durante la dominación española*, Lima, 1894.

Quesada, Vicente G., *Virreinato de La Plata*, Buenos Aires, 1881.

——, *La vida intelectual de la América española*, Buenos Aires, 1917.

Ruiz Guinazu, Enrique, *La magistratura indiana*, Buenos Aires, 1916.

Sody, Demetrio, *Revista jurídica de la escuela libre de derecho.* N° 14. December, 1916.

Solórzano Perreyra, Juan, *Política indiana*, 6 vols., Madrid, 1648.

Vidaurre, Manuel Lorenzo, *Plan del Perú. Defectos del gobierno español antiguo. Necesarias reformas*, Philadelphia, 1823.

Zavala, Silvio A., *La encomienda indiana*, Madrid, 1935.

——, *Las instituciones jurídicas en la conquista de América*, Madrid, 1935.

——, *Juicio de límites entre el Perú y Bolivia, Prueba peruana:*
    Vol.   I, *Virreinato peruano,*
    Vol.   II, *Organización audiencial sud-americana,*
    Vol.   III, *Audiencia de Charcas,*
    Vol.   IV, *Virreinato de Buenos Aires,*

Vol. XI, *Obispados y audiencias del Cuzco,*
Vol. XV, *Ovando. Antecedentes de la Recopilación de
Indias,* Barcelona-Madrid, 1906.

I. LAW AND CONSTITUTIONAL HISTORY

Alberdi, J. B., *Obras selectas,* Buenos Aires, 1920. Vol. XVIII.

Arcaya, Pedro, *Estudios de sociología venezolana,* Madrid, 1917.

Arosemena, Justo, *Estudios constitucionales sobre los gobiernos de la América Latina,* Paris, 1888.

Aulard, François Victor A., *Histoire politique de la révolution française,* Paris, 1901.

Ayarragaray, Lucas, *La anarquía argentina y el caudillismo,* Buenos Aires, 1925. Second edition.

Barthélemy, Joseph, *Traité élémentaire de Droit Constitutionnel,* Paris, 1926.

Blanco Fombona, Rufino, *Evolución política y social de Hispano-América,* Madrid, 1911.

Bryce, James, *South American Observation and Impression,* New York, 1912.

Duguit, Léon, *Les constitutions et les principales lois politiques de la France depuis 1789,* Paris, 1915.

Fernández Almagro, Melchor, *Orígenes del régimen constitucional en España,* Barcelona, Buenos Aires, 1928. Editorial Labor.

Galdames, Luis, *La evolución constitucional de Chile,* Santiago de Chile, 1925.

García Calderón, Francisco, *La démocratie de l'Amérique latine,* Paris. English translation, New York, 1913.

———, *La création d'un Continente,* Paris, 1913.

Gil Fortoul, José, *Historia de Venezuela,* 2 vols., Berlin, 1907.

González Calderón, Juan A., *Derecho constitucional argentino,* 3 vols., Buenos Aires, 1923-1926. Second edition.

Gómez de Baquero, Eduardo, *Nacionalismo e Hispanismo,* Madrid, 1928.

Gorriti, Juan Ignacio, *Reflexiones,* Buenos Aires, 1916.

Groussac, Paul, *Estudios de Historia argentina,* Buenos Aires, 1918.

Guerra, José Joaquín, *La convención de Ocaña. Biblioteca de Historia nacional,* Bogota, 1908. Vol. VI.

Herrera, Luis Alberto, *La revolución francesa y Sud América,* Paris, 1910.

Ingenieros, José, *La evolución de las ideas argentinas,* 2 vols., Buenos Aires, 1918.

————, *Sociología argentina*, Buenos Aires, 1918.

Lastarria, José Victorino, *Historia constitucional de medio siglo*. ————, *La América*, 2 vols., Madrid. Editorial América.

Lockey, Joseph Byrne, *Pan-Americanism*, New York, 1920.

Levene, Ricardo, *La revolución de Mayo y Mariano Moreno*, 2 vols., Buenos Aires, 1920.

Levillier, Roberto, *Orígenes argentinos*, Paris, 1912.

Matienzo, J. M., *El gobierno representativo federal en la República argentina*, Buenos Aires, 1910.

Monteagudo, Bernardo, *Obras públicas*, Buenos Aires, 1916. Biblioteca argentina.

Montiel y Duarte, Isidoro, *Derecho público mejicano*, Mexico, 1871.

Moreno, Mariano, *Doctrina democrática*, Buenos Aires, 1915. Biblioteca argentina.

Moses, Bernard, *The Intellectual Background of the revolution in South America, 1810-1824*, New York, 1926.

Piaggo, Monseñor Agustín, *Influencia del clero en la independencia argentina*, 2 vols., Barcelona, 1912.

Pombo, Manuel Antonio, *Constituciones de Colombia*. Bogota, 1911.

Posada, Adolfo, *Instituciones políticas de los pueblos hispano americanos, Madrid*, 1900.

Ramos, Juan P., *El derecho público en las provincias argentinas*, Buenos Aires, 1914.

Rodríguez, Licenciado Ramón, *Derecho constitucional*, Mexico, 1875.

Saldias, Adolfo, *La evolución republicana durante la revolución argentina*, Buenos Aires, 1906.

Samper, José María, *Apuntamientos para la historia política y social de la Nueva Granada*, 1853.

————, *Curso elemental de ciencia y de legislación*, Bogota, 1873.

————, *Derecho público interno de Colombia*, 2 vols., Bogota, 1886.

————, *Ensayo sobre las revoluciones políticas y la condición social de las repúblicas colombianas*, Paris, 1861.

Valle, A. del, *Derecho constitucional*, Buenos Aires, 1911.

Vallenilla Lanz, Laureano, *Disgregación e integración*, Caracas, 1830.

————, *Críticas de sinceridad y exactitud*, Caracas, 1921.

————, *Cesarismo democrático*, Caracas, 1919.

Varela, Luis V., *Historia constitucional de la república argentina*, 3 vols., La Plata, 1910.

——, *Revista jurídica*, Nos. 13 y 14. Mexico, 1916.

——, *Revista de jurisprudencia*, Vol. 14, Mexico (contiene un estudio de Rodolfo Reyes; "contribución al estudio de la evolución del derecho constitucional en México").

J. WORKS ON BOLIVAR

Abreu y Lima, José Ignacio de, *Resumen histórico de la última dictadura del Libertador Simón Bolívar*, Rio de Janeiro, 1922.

André, Marius, *Bolívar et la démocratie*, Paris, 1924.

Angell, Hildegarde, *Simon Bolívar, South American Liberator*, New York, 1930.

Arocha Moreno, Jesús, *Bolívar juzgado por el general San Martín*, Caracas, 1930.

Arrocha Graell, C., *El Libertador en Guayaquil*, Panama, 1926(?).

Carbonell, Diego, *Influencias que se ejercieron en Bolívar*, Caracas, 1920.

Cruz, E. de la; Goenaga, J. M.; Mitre, B.; Villanueva, C. A., *La entrevista de Guayaquil*, Madrid. Editorial América.

Espejo, Jerónimo, *San Martín y Bolívar; entrevista de Guayaquil (1822)*, Buenos Aires, 1873.

Finot, Enrique, *Bolívar pacifista*, New York, 1936.

González, Eloy G., *Bolívar en la Argentina*, Caracas, 1924.

González, Fernando, *Mi Simón Bolívar*, Manizales. Edición Cervantes.

Hispano, Cornelio, *Los cantores de Bolívar*, Bogota, 1930.

——, *Historia secreta de Bolívar*, Paris, 1924.

——, *El libro de oro de Bolívar*, Paris, 1925.

Ibarra, T. R., *Bolívar, the Passionate Warrior*, New York, 1929.

Julio, Sylvio, *Cerebro e la coracao de Bolívar*, Rio de Janeiro, 1931.

Lafond, Georges and Gabriel, Tersane, *Bolívar et la libération de l'Amérique du Sud*, Paris, 1931.

Larrazábal, Felipe, *Vida del Libertador Simón Bolívar*, 2 vols., Madrid, 1918.

Lecuna, Vicente, *Un pensamiento sobre el Congreso de Panamá*, Washington, 1916.

Lemly, Henry Rowan, *Bolívar*, Boston, 1923.

Carvajal, Ángel L., *Bolívar desde los puntos de vista sociológico, político y jurídico*, Quito, 1932.

Leturia, Pedro S. J., *La acción diplomática de Bolívar ante Pío VII*, Madrid, 1925.

——, *Bolívar y León XII*, Caracas, 1931.

Mancini, Jules, *Bolivar et l'émancipation des colonies espagnoles des origines à 1815*, Paris, 1912.

Monsalve, José D., *El ideal político del Libertador Simón Bolívar*, Bogota, 1916.

Parra Pérez, C., *Bolívar, contribución al estudio de sus ideas políticas*, Paris, 1928.

Pereyra, Carlos, *Bolívar y Washington; un paralelo imposible*, Madrid, 1915.

Pérez y Soto, Juan B., *Defensa de Bolívar*, Lima, 1878.

Petre, F. Loraine, *Simón Bolívar "El Libertador"*, New York, 1910.

Porras Troconis, G., *Gesta bolivariana*, Caracas, 1935.

Rojas, José M., *Simón Bolívar*, Paris, 1883.

Salaverría, José M., *Bolívar el Libertador*, Madrid, 1930.

Samper, José María, *El Libertador Simón Bolívar*, Buenos Aires, 1884.

Santovenia, E., *Simón, Bolívar y las Antillas Hispanas*, Madrid, 1935.

Schryver, Simon de, *Esquisse de la vie de Bolívar*, Bruxelles, 1899.

Sherwell, Guillermo, *Simón Bolívar*, Washington, 1921.

Silva, J. Francisco, *El libertador Bolívar y el dean Funes en la política argentina*, Madrid, 1918. Biblioteca Ayacucho.

Vaucaire, Michel, *Bolivar, the Liberator*, Boston, 1929.

Villarán, Manuel Vicente, *Ideas políticas de Bolívar*, Lima, 1921.

K. HISTORICAL WORKS

Altamira, Rafael, *Historio de España y de la civilización española*, Barcelona, 1900. Vol. IV.

——, *Resumen histórico de la Independencia de la América española*, Buenos Aires, 1910.

Amunátegui, Luis Miguel, *Los precursores de la Independencia de Chile*, Santiago de Chile, 1910. Vol. III.

——, *Crónicas de 1810*, 2 vols., Santiago de Chile, 1876.

Arguedas, Alcides, *La fundación de la República*, La Paz, 1920.

——, *Historia general de Bolivia, 1809-1921*, La Paz, 1922.

Ballesteros y Beretta, Antonio, *Historia de España y su influencia en la historia universal*, Barcelona, 1934. Vol. VII.

Baralt, Rafael María and Díaz, Ramón, *Resumen de la historia de Venezuela*, 3 vols., Curaçao, 1887.

Barros Arana, Diego, *Historia general de Chile*, Santiago de Chile, 1887. Vols. VIII to XIII.

Basadre, Jorge, *La iniciación de la República*, 2 vols., Lima, 1929-1930.

Belaunde, Víctor Andrés, *Hispanic-American Culture*, Rice Institute, Houston, Texas, 1923.

Bulnes, Gonzalo, *Últimas campañas de la Independencia del Perú, 1822-1826*, Santiago de Chile, 1877.

———, *La expedición libertadora del Perú, 1817-1822*, 2 vols., Santiago de Chile, 1887.

———, *Nacimiento de las repúblicas americanas*. 2 vols., Buenos Aires, 1927.

———, *Bolívar en el Perú*, Madrid, 1919. Biblioteca Ayacucho.

Bustamante, Carlos María, *Cuadro histórico de la revolución mejicana*, Mexico, 1854.

Duarte Level, Lino, *Cuadros de la historia militar y civil de Venezuela*, Madrid. Biblioteca Ayacucho.

Gonzales Guinán, Francisco, *Historia contemporánea de Venezuela*, Caracas, 1909.

Groot, José Manuel, *Historia eclesiástica y civil de Nueva Granada*, 3 vols., Bogota, 1869.

Groussac, Paul de, *Santiago de Liniers*, Buenos Aires, 1907.

Haring, C. H., *South American Progress*, Harvard University Press, 1934.

Henríquez Urena, Max, *Literatura cubana*, (Articles published in *El Archipiélago*), Cuba, 1928.

Mariátegui, Javier, *Anotaciones a la historia de Paz-Soldán*, Lima.

Mendiburu, Manuel, *Diccionario histórico-biográfico del Perú*, 8 vols., Lima, 1874-90.

Mitre, Bartolomé, *Historia de San Martín*, 4 vols., Buenos Aires, 1889-1890.

———, *Historia de Belgrano*, 4 vols., Buenos Aires, 1858.

Navarro Lamarca, Carlos, *Compendio de la historia general de América*, 2 vols., Buenos Aires, 1910-1913.

Otero, José Pacífico, *La révolution argentine*, Paris, 1917.

———, *Historia del Libertador don José de San Martín*, 4 vols., Buenos Aires, 1932.

Parra Pérez, C., *Miranda et la revolution française*, Paris, 1925.

Paxson, Frederic Logan. *The Independence of the South American Republics*, Philadelphia, 1903.

Paz-Soldán, Mariano Felipe, *Historia del Peru Independiente*, (second period 1822-1827), Lima, 1870-1874. Vols. I and II.

Pereyra, Carlos, *Historia de la América española*, 8 vols., Madrid, 1920-1926.

Posada e Ibáñez, E., *Los comuneros, Biblioteca de historia nacional*. Vol. IV. Bogota, 1903.

Riva Agüero, José de la, *La Historia en el Perú*, Lima, 1910.

Restrepo, José Manuel, *Historia de la revolución de la República de Colombia*, 4 vols., Besançon, 1858.

Robertson, William Spencer, *Rise of the Spanish American Republic*, New York and London, 1928.

Rojas, Ricardo, *La literatura argentina*, 3 vols., Buenos Aires, 1917-1922.

Sierra, Justo, *México y su evolución*, 3 vols., Mexico, 1910.

Suárez, José León, *Carácter de la revolución americana*, Buenos Aires, 1917.

Torrente, Mariano, *Historia de la revolución hispano-americana*, Madrid, 1829.

Vargas, Nemesio, *Historia del Perú Independiente*, 8 vols., Lima, 1903-1917.

Vicuña Mackenna, Benjamín, *La revolución de la Independencia del Perú*, Lima, 1860.

Villanueva, Carlos, *Napoleón y la independencia de América*, Paris, 1912.

Wiesse, Carlos, *Historia del Perú Independiente*, Lima, 1925. Vol. III.

L. MISCELLANEOUS WORKS

Alayza y Paz-Soldán, Luis, *Unánue, San Martín y Bolívar*, Lima, 1934.

Aldao, Carlos A., *Miranda y los orígenes de la Independencia americana*, Buenos Aires, 1928.

Amunátegui, Miguel Luis, *Don Manuel de Salas*, 3 vols., Santiago de Chile, 1895.

————, *Camilo Henríquez*, Santiago de Chile, 1889.

Avellaneda, Nicolás, *Escritos literarios*, Buenos Aires, 1915.

Benvenuto, Neptalí, *Sánchez Carrión*, Lima, 1930.

Biggs, James, *The History of don Francisco Miranda,* London, 1809.

Becerra, Ricardo, *Vida de don Francisco Miranda,* 2 vols., Madrid.

Caldas, Francisco José de, *Obras,* Bogota, 1912. Biblioteca de historia. Vol. IX.

Fregeiro, G. L., *Don Bernardo Monteagudo,* Buenos Aires, 1880.

Gálvez, Anibal, *Zela,* 2 vols., Lima, 1911.

Goebel, Dorothy B., *William Henry Harrison a Political Biography,* Indianapolis, 1926.

Lamas, Andrés, *Rivadavia. Cultura argentina,* Buenos Aires, 1915.

Leguía, Jorge Guillermo, *El Precursor,* Lima, 1922.

———, *Manuel Lorenzo Vidaurre,* Lima, 1935.

Means, Phillip A., *Ciertos aspectos de la rebelión de Tupac Amaru,* Lima, 1920.

Parra Pérez, C., *Miranda y la revolución francesa,* Paris, 1925.

Pereyra, Carlos, *Humboldt en América,* Madrid, 1917.

Porras, Raúl, *Mariano José de Arce,* Lima.

Rippy, J. Fred, *Rivalry of the United States and Great Britain over Latin America (1808-1830),* Baltimore, 1929.

Rivas, Ángel Cesar, *Ensayos de historia política y diplomática. Biblioteca de ciencias políticas y sociales,* Madrid. Editorial América.

Robertson, William Spencer, *The Life of Miranda,* 2 vols., Chapel Hill, N. C., 1929.

———, *Hispanic-American Relations with the United States,* New York, 1923.

Rojas, José María, *El General Miranda,* Paris, 1884.

Salas, Manuel de, *Escritos,* 3 vols., Santiago de Chile, 1910.

Solar, Emilio del, *Insurrección de Tupac Amaru,* Lima, 1926.

Suárez, Marcos Fidel, *Escritos,* Bogota, 1914.

Teran, Juan B., *El nacimiento de la América española,* Tucuman, 1927.

Unánue, José Hipólito, *Obras científicas y literarias,* 3 vols., Barcelona, 1914.

Valle, José Cecilio del, *Obras,* Tegucigalpa, 1906.

INDEX

Abad y Queipo, Manuel, cites Montesquieu, 25; real author of *Informe*, proposes reforms, 51; mentioned, 52, 108, 109, 125, 154.

Abeja Republicana, 212.

Aberdeen, Lord, says no European prince could accept crown after death of Bolivar, 383.

Abreu y Lima, chosen to draft defense of Bolivar, 389.

Absolute Sovereignty, concept of, develops slowly, 113-117.

Academy of Drawing, founded, 48.

Acosta, 20.

Act of the Provinces of New Granada, 150.

Adams, John Quincy, speech translated, 29.

Adams, Samuel, meets Miranda, 75; correspondence with Miranda, 78.

Adelantados, first appointed *regidores*, 5; mentioned, 8.

Agia, Father Miguel de, 17, 18.

Alberdi, Juan Bautista, praises *cabildos*, 4; mentioned, 97, 141.

Alcabala, cause of rebellion in New Granada, 64; mentioned, 69.

Alcaldes, elected by *cabildos*, 3; replaced by *corregidores* in certain cases, 3; chosen by *regidores*, 4.

Alcedo, dictionary of, 27.

Almagro, Melchor Fernández, 63, 87.

Altuna, 63.

Alvarado, 193.

Álvarez, Mariano Alejo, quoted, 12; pleads for rights of natives, 20; educated at Charcas, 20.

Alvear, Director, mentioned, 138; confronted with Spanish expedition to La Plata and other difficulties proposes monarchy in La Plata, Peru and Chile, 157; deprived of power by army, 158.

American Letters, 110.

Amunátegui, Luis Miguel, cites repressive measures, 16; deplores Spanish monopoly of positions, 19.

André, Marius, mentioned, 136; suspects Bolivar of political chicanery at Angostura, 175; believes Bolivar lost democratic faith, 209; mentioned, 236; notes similarity in thought of Bolivar and Comte, 249.

Andujar, Padre, 44, 125.

Angostura, speech of Bolivar, fullest development of ideas of Jamaica and Cartagena, 171; Congress of, adopts life-term senate, favors formation of Great Colombia, 195.

Apatzingan, first Mexican constitution signed, 155.

Aranda, Campillo, 22.

Aranda, Count of, project for Spanish-American kingdoms, 13, 202; progressive minister of Charles III, 40; mentioned, 102, 125.

Arango y Parreño, initiates economic studies in Cuba, 47; mentioned, 125.

Aranjuez, *Junta* of, establishes hegemony, 88; appeals to other *juntas*, 88; succeeded by Supreme *Junta* of Seville, 88.

Arboleda, 350.

Arcaya, Pedro, cited on rebellion of Coro, 71.

Arce, Mariano de, in oration on sovereignty treats "rights of man", 213.

Areche, 67.

Arenales, signs demand of Feb. 18, 1823, that Riva Agüero be made president of Peru, 215.

Argentina, Constitution of 1826, provisions, 336-339; introduction cited, 337.

429